STOIC PHILOSOPHY

STOIC
PHILOSOPHY

J. M. RIST

Professor of Greek, University of Toronto

CAMBRIDGE

AT THE UNIVERSITY PRESS

1969

Published by the Syndics of the Cambridge University Press
Bentley House, 200 Euston Road, London N.W.1
American Branch: 32 East 57th Street, New York, N.Y.10022

© Cambridge University Press 1969

Library of Congress Catalogue Card Number: 79-85736
Standard Book Number: 521 07620 x

Printed in Great Britain
at the University Printing House, Cambridge
(Brooke Crutchley, University Printer)

CONTENTS

PREFACE

Although there now exist excellent studies of areas of Stoic thought, such as Mates' *Stoic Logic* and Sambursky's *Physics of the Stoics*, the scope of these studies is limited, and those who read them will form a one-sided picture even of the Old Stoa if they are not supplemented by more rounded accounts. But these more rounded accounts are not readily accessible, particularly in English. The English-speaking reader is driven back to works written fifty years ago; and these works, though helpful, are full of errors. Readers of French or German are better placed, but it is disturbing that the work which is most helpful was done by Bonhoeffer at the end of the last century. Since then the labours of Reinhardt, Bréhier, Pohlenz and many others have added enormously to our knowledge of the details of Stoic thought, but purely philosophical considerations have often disappeared from sight in a concentration on Stoicism as a historical movement. In the present book, therefore, no attempt has been made to provide biographical details about individual Stoics; and the effects of Stoicism on the social life of antiquity have taken second place. What I have attempted is to present a series of Stoic philosophical ideas in some detail. I hope that reflection on these ideas may both give a clearer picture of what Stoic philosophy is about and encourage the view that the Stoics were serious philosophers.

The once voluminous work of the Old Stoics is now represented only by fragments. The problem facing the interpreter is to breathe life into these drying bones. I have found that this task is made considerably easier if two basic truths are constantly remembered: that Stoic philosophy began at a time when Aristotle's work dominated the philosophical scene; and that the divergent psychological theories of Chrysippus and Posidonius are symptomatic of a fundamental difference of outlook. Posidonius, though still a Stoic, failed to understand many of the more interesting philosophical theories of Chrysippus. The loss of so much of Chrysippus' work is the loss of philosophical work of the highest calibre, representing a view of the world and of man sharply opposed to the theories of Plato and Aristotle, but only the more interesting for that. For Stoicism is a curious mixture of the crude and the highly sophisticated. If it be objected that in these studies there is more concentration on the sophisticated, my defence is that any philosopher is best understood if his most mature work is taken as typical.

I have attempted to evaluate all work done on the Stoics that is relevant to the problems I have discussed. I have not, however, listed in footnotes every study of each particular problem and every supporter of each particular hypothesis; I have limited my references to studies which provide new information or insight. It is to be hoped that this procedure, designed to make the book more palatable to the less advanced student, will not offend the professional.

ACKNOWLEDGMENTS

I am very grateful to Dr A. A. Long and Professor F. H. Sandbach for reading *Stoic Philosophy* in manuscript. As a result of their comments I have managed to eliminate many errors. Naturally I have not always accepted their judgment, but where I have dissented it has been with hesitation and after a full reconsideration of the problem.

Cambridge, July 1968

ABBREVIATIONS

AJP	*American Journal of Philology*
BICS	*Bulletin of the Institute of Classical Studies of the University of London*
CN	Plutarch, *De Communibus Notitiis*
CP	*Classical Philology*
CQ	*Classical Quarterly*
CR	*Classical Review*
CW	*Classical World*
DG	*Doxographi Graeci*, ed. H. Diels
GCS	*Die Griechischen Christlichen Schriftsteller der Ersten Drei Jahrhunderte*
GR	*Greece and Rome*
HSCP	*Harvard Studies in Classical Philology*
JHS	*Journal of Hellenic Studies*
JRS	*Journal of Roman Studies*
NAG (NGG)	*Nachrichten der Akademie (Gesellschaft) der Wissenschaften in Göttingen*
PP	*La Parola del Passato*
PQ	*Philosophical Quarterly*
PR	*Philosophical Review*
RE	*Paulys Real-Encyclopädie der classischen Altertumswissenschaft*
REA	*Revue des Etudes Anciennes*
Rh. Mus.	*Rheinisches Museum*
SR	Plutarch, *De Stoicorum Repugnantiis*
SVF	*Stoicorum Veterum Fragmenta*, ed. J. von Arnim
TAPA	*Transactions and Proceedings of the American Philological Association*

ARISTOTLE AND THE STOIC GOOD

Carneades was in the habit of claiming that the Stoics and Peripatetics taught substantially the same ethical doctrines, varying only in their terminology.[1] Cicero, who gives this information, seems to find the idea ridiculous, and doubtless was in agreement on the point with both Stoics and Peripatetics themselves. And there is obviously much that could be said, for example about the correct attitude to πάθη, which might make us believe too readily that Carneades was either joking or talking nonsense. But what we know of Carneades does not allow us to think he was a fool; and if he was joking, good jokes often represent exaggerations of facts as facts themselves. Now that the phrase 'post-Aristotelian philosophy' is gradually being taken to refer to philosophy largely governed by Aristotle rather than to philosophy posterior to Aristotle but largely unrelated to him, we are more ready to accept that the thought of the post-Aristotelian schools is frequently grounded on philosophical problems bequeathed to them not by the Presocratics or even by Plato but by Aristotle and his followers.[2] And the Aristotelian school was in its early days much concerned with problems of ethics, the most important of all philosophical problems for Zeno and his associates. It would *a priori* be rather strange if the Stoics did not take notice of what had been said in the Lyceum. It is the purpose of this chapter to suggest some of the ways in which the Stoics reacted, both favourably and unfavourably, to certain key positions of Aristotelian ethics.

According to Aristotle in the *Nicomachean Ethics* the end of life is happiness.[3] Both philosophers and the general public are in agreement so far, and both talk of happiness in terms of 'living well' and 'prospering'. But, continues Aristotle, it is what happiness is that causes the trouble; here there is no kind of

---

[1] Carneades in Cicero, *N.D.* 3.41. Cf. *Tusc. Disp.* 5.120.
[2] This point has recently been emphasized in connection with the Stoics by Edelstein, *The Meaning of Stoicism* 19–22.
[3] *N.E.* 1095a 18 ff.

agreement. All this, including the assumption that happiness is the end, the Stoics, and the other post-Aristotelians as well, could accept as traditional. The problem is at the next stage, and Aristotle's solution, with which the Stoics were familiar, is that happiness is to be defined as an activity of the soul in accordance with perfect virtue.[1] Now in view of the fact that Aristotle has already said that happiness consists in 'living well', and since he regularly maintains that the activity of the mind is life *par excellence*,[2] it is reasonable to assert that for Aristotle virtue is the name given to the living of one's life in a certain way. One's activities and one's way of life depend on motives and intentions, and hence it is only to be expected that Aristotle will hold that it is not only what a man does that matters but the state of mind he is in when he does it.[3] Moral virtue, as Aristotle goes on to argue, is a disposition (ἕξις) by which one chooses what is good and rejects what is evil. And this choice must be a rational choice. Hence children cannot be virtuous, because, although they may perform an act which if performed by an adult would be virtuous, yet, since they have not developed their powers of deliberation, they cannot have the right attitude towards their behaviour; they cannot have the proper intentions.

Happiness is also the end of life for Zeno; and happiness is to be equated with a smoothly flowing life.[4] This smoothly flowing life is a reasoned life lived in accordance with nature.[5] In other words the end, the source of happiness, is a certain way of living. In fact, as Zeno says, it is living in accordance with virtue (ζῆν κατ' ἀρετήν).[6] This latter definition is, as we can now

---

[1] *N.E.* 1102a 5–6.

[2] Cf. *Met.* Λ, 1072b 26–7, ἡ γὰρ νοῦ ἐνέργεια ζωή.

[3] *N.E.* 1105a 30, ἐὰν ὁ πράττων πως ἔχων πράττῃ. See Long, 'Aristotle's Legacy', 78.

[4] Stob., *Ecl.* 2, p. 77, 21 W. (*SVF* 1 184) etc.

[5] *SVF* 1 179. Whether Zeno added the words τῇ φύσει to his definition of the end as τὸ ὁμολογουμένως ζῆν, or whether this was due to Cleanthes, is not of great importance, since no good reasons have been offered for regarding the addition as other than explanatory. On balance it is perhaps more likely that the addition was due to Cleanthes. For Cleanthes see Stob., *Ecl.* 2, p. 75, 11 W.; Pohlenz, *Die Stoa* 2.67, and 'Zeno und Chrysipp', 199 ff. For the meaning of ὁμολογουμένως, Pohlenz, *Die Stoa* 1.116.

[6] D.L. 7.87 (*SVF* 1 179); Clem. Alex., *Strom.* 2.21.129 (*SVF* 1 180).

see, still very much what was offered by Aristotle, though the explanation of virtue, that it is harmony with nature, is non-Aristotelian. We shall have to enquire later exactly where the divergencies appear and what their significance is, but for the moment we may proceed a little further with the Stoic account of virtue, leaving the problem of the harmony with nature aside. According to Plutarch Zeno and Chrysippus were agreed that virtue is a fixed disposition (διάθεσις) of the ruling part of the soul, a power (δύναμις) produced by reason.[1] For Aristotle we found virtue to be a ἕξις προαιρετική. Aristotle uses the word ἕξις, but this should not mislead us on the content of the two theories. Both Aristotle and Zeno chose the words they prefer for the disposition of the wise man with the intention of selecting whatever would suggest the most stability of character. In the *Categories* Aristotle distinguishes ἕξις from διάθεσις on precisely this ground,[2] whereas the Stoics (oddly) prefer διάθεσις, but intending the sense of the Aristotelian ἕξις. For them, apparently, διάθεσις suggests rigidity, fixity of purpose.[3] However, in late antiquity the fact that the difference between Aristotle and the Stoics is, on this point, as Carneades would have said, merely one of terminology is recognized in a passage of Porphyry. Obviously thinking of the Stoics, Porphyry observes that there are two kinds of ἕξις, one of which suggests fixity while the other does not.[4]

Virtue then is for both Aristotle and the Stoics a fixed disposition. Again looking for points of agreement, we can proceed further. Virtue is also, by common agreement of Zeno and Chrysippus, a δύναμις which arises from reason.[5] Again we should be aware of confusions in terminology. Aristotle does not call a virtue a δύναμις because he takes δύναμις to mean potentiality or capability, and, as he rightly points out, we are not praised or blamed because we are able to act well but rather when we actually do so.[6] But, when Zeno and Chrysippus call virtue a δύναμις, they do not mean that the virtuous man

[1] *De Virt. Mor.* 441 C (*SVF* I 202).
[2] Arist., *Cat.* 8b 27.
[3] Simp. *In Cat.* p. 237, 30 ff. Kalbfleisch (*SVF* II 393).
[4] Porphyry, *In Cat.* p. 137, 29 Busse (*SVF* III 525).
[5] *SVF* I 202.   [6] *N.E.* 1106a 6 ff.

may (or may not) act virtuously, but that he has the power and will always use the power to act virtuously, for all the acts of the virtuous man are virtuous.[1] Hence for the Stoics the word δύναμις is very closely connected with ἕξις; in fact the word δύναμις is used to describe the use or operation of the ἕξις. We have a somewhat similar usage in English in the phrase 'He is capable of anything'. This does not simply mean that he may or may not perform a criminal act on a particular occasion, but that he is by disposition a criminal. The phrase is used, in a Stoic way, to describe moral character.

Aristotle insists that a man cannot be called happy until he is dead, and that his happiness, his activity of the soul in accordance with virtue, must endure throughout his whole life.[2] His attitude on this matter, however, is complicated by the problem of what external goods are necessary for happiness, and, indirectly arising out of this, by the difficulty about whether it can be said 'Once happy, always happy'. Both these problems arise in the Stoic context, as we shall see. Nevertheless, in the first instance the Stoics agree with Aristotle. Happiness and virtue must be life-long if they are to be significant. Virtue is a consistent disposition of the soul lasting throughout the whole of one's life.[3]

Before concluding this brief summary of the areas of agreement between Aristotle and the Stoics on the ends of life, and turning to the problems with which the Aristotelian formulations present the Stoics, we come to the most important point of all, the distinction between what is good in itself and what is good for the sake of other things. As we shall see, both here and in some of the other cases which we have touched upon, the Stoics start off in agreement with Aristotle, but by taking up problems which are blurred over in the *Nicomachean Ethics* they are forced into opposition. In the first chapter of the *Ethics* Aristotle argues that there must be a first good or end which is chosen for itself. If there is no such end, he holds, a vicious regress would ensue. This end, which of course turns out to be happiness, we choose for its own sake (καὶ ⟨εἰ⟩ μὴ πάντα δι' ἕτερον αἱρούμεθα). There must therefore be a radical differ-

---

[1] *SVF* III 557–66.   [2] *N.E.* 1101a 16ff.   [3] *SVF* III 39, 262.

4

ence between this end and everything else, for everything else, however 'good', can be treated as a means towards another end, as good for obtaining this other end. And this is precisely the Stoic position. Virtue is to be chosen entirely for itself; indeed it is not possible to choose it for any other reason. A supposed choice of virtue for any other reason would not be a choice of virtue at all.[1]

Aristotle and the Stoics are therefore in general agreement that moral virtue is to be measured by the state of mind of the doer, that it is dispositional, that it is intrinsically good, that it leads to happiness, and that this happiness is illusory unless it lasts a lifetime. But the student of Aristotle will be well aware that a number of problems in the *Ethics* have been passed over, and these problems gave the Stoics no little trouble. Some of them are as follows: If the end is radically different from the other so-called goods, what right have we to use the same word (good) in both cases? What is the role of these other 'goods' (assuming there are any) in the 'good' life? That is, do we *need* external goods for the moral life? Although the good is to be chosen for itself, is there any philosophical problem involved in the fact that the Stoics do not talk about virtue as a διάθεσις προαιρετική, indeed that they hardly ever use the word προαίρεσις before the first century A.D.? And, more generally, how can the concept of the immoral man's coming to act morally or the moral man's coming to act immorally be intelligible? Why should the moral man suddenly act immorally? If the moral man always (dispositionally) acts morally, how can 'choice' be included in the account of his disposition? Some at least of these questions will become less puzzling as we proceed.

According to Aristotle's account the happy man needs to be adequately supplied with external goods.[2] This statement is not as clear as it may sound, for the word 'adequately' could mean almost anything. There is, of course, a certain sense in which some external goods are necessary if a virtuous life is to be lived rather than a virtuous death died. Food and drink, in small portions, are obvious necessities of this kind; but Aristotle does not seem to have this kind of external good in mind; nor do the

---

[1] *SVF* III 39–48.   [2] *N.E.* 1101 a 15.

Stoics when the subject comes up. Aristotle gives examples of the kind of thing he is referring to when he suggests that, unless the 'really good' man has certain tools of his trade available and meets with tolerable conditions, he could not be called 'blessed' (μακάριος, 1101 A 7). The good man needs something to work on, just as the general needs an army and the shoemaker needs leather. Similarly in the description of the 'great-souled' man in book four, it is suggested that his virtue will somehow be diminished if he has not, for example, the opportunity to display his powers of generosity. But this is a dangerous way of proceeding, as much later Plotinus was able to point out, for the next step is to wish to have the means of plying one's trade. And would the doctor wish to have patients, that is, would he wish that people were ill?[1]

As is well known, the Stoics are brought up against this problem by their attitude to 'natural things' (τὰ κατὰ φύσιν). What is the attitude of the good man towards these to be? The classic Stoic answer is given by Chrysippus, who holds that they are the material on which virtuous action is based.[2] And it was doubtless on the basis of such a theory that Diogenes of Babylon was led to define the end of life in terms of selecting what is natural (τὰ κατὰ φύσιν) and rejecting what is unnatural.[3] What Diogenes meant by this was that the good man will select what is conducive to virtue and reject what is of no use. But the way in which this is expressed is misleading, to say the least, for the unwary could easily form the impression that the search for these natural things is itself the end. This misunderstanding is deepened if we use the term 'choosing' in relation to what is natural.[4] The Stoics themselves were careful to avoid this,

[1] Plot., *Enn.* 6.8.5.
[2] Plut., *CN* 1069 c 8 ff.; cf. Cic., *De Fin.* 3.23. The importance of these passages is well discussed by Kidd, 'The Relation of Stoic Intermediates to the *Summum Bonum* with reference to Change in the Stoa', 186. See also Long, 'Carneades and the Stoic *Telos*', 65.
[3] For Diogenes see Bonhoeffer, 'Die Telosformel...', 582–605, and *SVF* III 44. The term ἐκλογή 'selecting' may, as Pohlenz suggests (*Die Stoa* 2.95), be original with Diogenes. A passage of Epictetus (*SVF* III 191) where ἐκλεκτικός occurs and is put in the mouth of Chrysippus may, as Pohlenz thinks, not be a literal quotation. But Pohlenz is probably too arbitrary.
[4] As is done, for example, by Long, *op. cit.* 73.

speaking of selecting or taking what is natural but only 'choosing' the end itself, that is, virtue. However, the ambiguity becomes still more marked with Antipater of Tarsus, who was in the habit of speaking of the end of life as 'doing all in one's power to obtain (τυγχάνειν) the prime natural things'.[1] The situation here is probably that he was bemused by the criticism of the Stoic τέλος by Carneades, and in his difficult position tended towards untraditional formulations; he seems to have admitted both that virtue is forwarded, however slightly, by external goods,[2] and at the same time that the end is to exert oneself for certain of these externals.[3]

But although Antipater's position is not entirely clear, it brings our present problem very clearly into the open. If 'natural things' are the material on which virtuous life is built, in what sense can one say that virtue is self-sufficient? At least for Antipater it seems that it would not be possible actually to live a virtuous life unless the 'natural goods' were available; indeed we should strive to get them, for the possibility seems open that some of them are not invariably present to every man in so far as he is human. It appears from a very troublesome passage of Diogenes Laertius that some of these natural goods which are most important in this context are health, property (χορηγία) and strength. According to Diogenes it was the view of Panaetius and Posidonius, presumably developing that of Antipater, that virtue is not sufficient for happiness, but that these externals are also required. And it may even be that these three are only the most obvious of a much wider group needed to buttress the happiness of the wise man.[4]

There has been much discussion about how to take this passage of Diogenes, a passage which stands alone. Most interpreters have held that Panaetius introduced a major change in Stoic doctrine, while Kidd has argued powerfully against this.[5]

---

[1] Plut., *CN* 1071 A 6. Cf. Long, *op. cit.* 75–84.

[2] *SVF* III 56–7 Antipater; Sen., *Ep.* 92.5.

[3] The problem of Antipater is well discussed by Long, *op. cit.*

[4] D.L. 7.128. This is the view of van Straaten, *Panétius* 154 ff.

[5] Kidd, *op. cit.*, summarizes the views of Pohlenz, van Straaten and Miss Reesor, 'The "Indifferents"...', 106, 110. Laffranque (*Poseidonios d'Apamée* 364) also believes in a major innovation.

The passage is unique in attributing the unorthodox view to Panaetius, and Diogenes Laertius might seem unreliable about the ethics of Posidonius.[1] Perhaps Diogenes' statement in 7.128 should be dismissed as a distortion of Panaetius' position. Kidd suggests that Diogenes' view could arise either because the Stoics were sometimes prepared to be lax in their use of terminology—a matter to which we shall return—and hence willing to call some of the indifferents 'goods', or from the fact that, when the wise man is faced with the question Will you choose virtue or virtue plus preferred indifferents (προηγμένα)?, he would have to vote for the latter alternative. Hence the mistaken opinion could have arisen that the wise man actually *needs* external goods.[2]

However, Kidd's argument to set the testimony of Diogenes aside is not entirely successful or convincing,[3] and perhaps a little progress can be made if we consider the background of the problem. The standard position in Stoicism before Panaetius (or rather before Antipater if we do not treat him as merely confused) is that the wise man makes use of externals, employs them as the material on which he builds his virtue. It seems that at no time was the possibility considered that virtue could be built without these externals to provide a context. That would be building bricks without straw, in the style of the Cynics. Now we also observed that the problem of the material of the good life was one bequeathed to Stoicism by Aristotle, who thought that the good man would require to be adequately provided with external goods. Aristotle's word here is κεχορηγημένον, and we may ask whether it is entirely an accident that Diogenes speaks of the need for χορηγία.

Be that as it may, however, the Stoics from the beginning

---

[1] D.L. 7.103 says that Posidonius regarded wealth and health as goods. This is apparently contradicted by Seneca (*Ep.* 87.35) and Cicero (*Tusc. Disp.* 2.61). In these passages Posidonius will not call indifferents goods; only virtue is good. But we should be cautious about this. Even Chrysippus was prepared to talk loosely at times about 'goods'. See below, p. 12.

[2] Some plausibility is given to this suggestion by the appearance of the word χρεία both in Diogenes and in the passage cited by Kidd (Alex. Aphr., *De Anima Mantissa*, p. 163, 4 ff. Bruns (*SVF* III 192).

[3] It has recently convinced Long (*op. cit.* 90, note 75).

seem to have taught that virtue uses external 'goods', but is still self-sufficient. What then is the difference between the view attributed to Panaetius and Posidonius and the older position? The difference perhaps lies in the word χρεία, which is ambiguous. The normal sense of this word is 'need', and that is the sense which Diogenes attributes to Panaetius. But Diogenes does not seem to mean only that according to Panaetius and Posidonius health and the rest are essential for achieving virtue while for the early Stoics they are not necessary; what he seems to imply is that Panaetius and Posidonius called them goods, as he specifically says of Posidonius in chapter 103. As Kidd has pointed out, this might mean only that Panaetius and Posidonius were on occasions imprecise in their terminology. What they would actually have said, on this interpretation, is that to live the virtuous life the good man needs the wherewithal to work. They loosely called this wherewithal good rather than preferred. But what would this imply? Did Panaetius and Posidonius say that the good man *needs* these externals; and did they say, as Diogenes makes them say, that virtue is *not* self-sufficient (αὐτάρκης)? The word χρεία, which Diogenes attributes to them, normally means 'need', but can mean 'use'. So perhaps what was said was that the good man 'uses' externals.[1] But if that is all that Panaetius meant, he was merely repeating his orthodox predecessors and Diogenes is distorting when he claims that he held a new and unorthodox view. But if Panaetius and Posidonius meant to emphasize that the good man *must* use these externals and hence that virtue is not self-sufficient, they have said something much more interesting; and it looks as though this was the path along which Antipater had already been forced to move.

Kidd's thesis that the testimony of Diogenes should be disregarded gains its strongest support from the fact that there is no evidence that any Stoic could still be thought of as a Stoic unless he regarded virtue alone as the end of life; and there is no doubt that he is right to point out, against Miss Reesor, that there is no evidence that Panaetius or Posidonius regarded

---

[1] For the distinction between need and use in Chrysippus see Seneca, *Ep.* 9.14, and Arnold, *Roman Stoicism* 293.

external 'goods' as good in the strict Stoic sense. It seems, however, that this point can still be maintained without the harsh move of rejecting the evidence of Diogenes. What could Panaetius mean by saying that virtue is not αὐτάρκης but 'needs' certain external goods? Perhaps only that unless we have these external goods we cannot be virtuous. If this were the answer, it would mean that Panaetius had accepted the implications of the fact that the 'natural things' are not merely material for virtue but necessary material; that the wise man not only uses them but, because of his human situation, needs to use them if he intends to do anything whatsoever. This would involve no change in Panaetius' view of the end of life, but a clear recognition of what the earlier Stoics had blurred over, namely that although virtue is sufficient for happiness, we can only be virtuous through the achievement of specific acts and attitudes. If Panaetius took this step, he was clarifying the situation as it had been bequeathed to the Stoics by Aristotle. He is still, however, within the Stoic framework that the end, the life of virtue, is good in a sense wholly other than can be attributed to anything else in the world.[1] The statement that the wise man needs externals is orthodox in what it says, but heretical in saying it out loud. It clearly admits what Zeno and Chrysippus had kept somewhat veiled, namely that Stoicism and Cynicism are radically different on this issue.

Having sketched the problem of 'natural things' down to Panaetius and Posidonius and considered it against its proper Aristotelian background, we can pass on to further investigation of a problem to which we have alluded more than once, and which is inextricably involved with the difficulties about external goods: the problem of the terminology of ethics. Here again the Aristotelian positions immediately underlie those of the Stoics, and to a considerable extent govern the Stoic teachings. In this instance, however, a good case can be made that

---

[1] The *telos* formula of Posidonius (τὸ ʒῆν θεωροῦντα etc.) might be adduced in support of the view that virtue is in some sense not αὐτάρκης. Θεωρία requires leisure. Panaetius also talked about θεωρητικὴ ἀρετή (D.L. 7.92 = fr. 108 van Straaten). This point has been made by Professor Sandbach in an unpublished paper.

the Stoics advanced considerably in their understanding of the complexity and importance of the question.

In chapter 6 of the first book of the *Nicomachean Ethics* Aristotle argues at length that the word 'good' is meaningful in a large number of areas of discourse, and that it is philosophically misleading to propose that it has one basic underlying sense, as Plato supposed.[1] In Aristotle's view 'good' can be predicated in all the categories; it has as many senses as 'being' (τὸ ὄν). It is therefore not surprising that, as we have seen, Aristotle is able to distinguish the final end for man, happiness, from lesser ends which are not sought for their own sake. He might have said, but he did not in fact say, that 'good' has one sense when it is predicated of the end, that is, of happiness, and other senses when it is predicated of other goods, as in propositions like 'Health is good'. But although Aristotle sharply distinguishes the moral end from means to that end—the one is wished for, the others deliberated about, for example—he does not refuse to use the word 'good' of both the end and the means (or subordinate objects) of desire.

This distinction, however, is precisely the distinction which the Stoics make—and much misunderstood they have been for doing so. Their proposition 'The only good is virtue', when seen in this context, is very far from the absurd paradox it is usually supposed to be. It means that to confuse the goodness of the moral life with any other of those things which are commonly called good is to make a category mistake of dangerous proportions. To avoid doing this, the Stoics were prepared to exclude the word 'good' from technical discussion on everything except virtue. One might ask how else they could insist on their distinction. It was not open to them to use subscript or superscript numbers in the way a modern philosopher might if he wished to make the same point. The Stoics could not write that 'Virtue is good' while 'Health is good$_1$'.

The Stoics had good reason to emphasize their view that virtue is the only good and to state it in a striking form, hoping it would sink in; in fact they were not strict enough, and, as Kidd has pointed out, it only needed a slight concession by Chrysippus

---

[1] *N.E.* 1096a 11 ff.

to give Plutarch the chance to distort the whole theory.[1] Chrysippus said, according to Plutarch, that it is permissible to make a concession to ordinary Greek to the extent of calling preferred things 'good' when we are aware of what we are doing. Plutarch claims that this implies that the Stoics, including Chrysippus, were in fact unclear as to the status of things 'preferred'.[2] A recent commentator has remarked that a problem arises as to when the Stoics are talking technically and when they are making concessions to ordinary language,[3] but the technical distinctions are so emphasized in the general teaching of the school that it is hard to see how those who purport to be baffled, like Plutarch, are not guilty of wilful misunderstanding.

Let us look at some of the distinctions made. Stobaeus gives us the basic distinction: it is between what is to be chosen (αἱρετόν) and what is to be taken (ληπτόν).[4] Only the end, virtue, is to be chosen, and it is to be chosen for its own sake.[5] Things preferred, that is, external goods, are to be taken, for use in the procuring of virtue. Just occasionally a distinction will be made in things to be taken between those which have some intrinsic value and those which are to be taken purely for the sake of other things,[6] but even those which have some intrinsic value are not to be called 'chosen'. Even in these cases, furthermore, the intrinsic value (which is not moral value) only makes them 'preferred' for their own sake rather than preferred for the sake of something else.[7] Everything preferred, including things preferred for their own sake, is still only preferred in so far as it provides the material for the moral life. We can now see why Stoics like Diogenes of Babylon scrupulously avoided using the word 'chosen' (αἱρετόν) in relation to their definition of the end as living on a basis of *selecting* (ἐκλέγειν and its cognates) what is primarily natural.

What then does this strict thesis amount to philosophically?

---

[1] Kidd, *op. cit.* 188. [2] *SR* 1048 A (*SVF* III 137).

[3] Long, *op. cit.* 67, note 20.

[4] Stob., *Ecl.* 2, p. 75, 1 W. (*SVF* III 131).

[5] Plut., *SR* 1039 C (*SVF* III 29).

[6] Stob., *Ecl.* 2, p. 82, 21 W. (*SVF* III 142).

[7] D.L. 7.107 (*SVF* III 135), ἔτι τῶν προηγμένων τὰ μὲν δι' αὑτὰ προῆκται... Examples given are εὐφυΐα and προκοπή.

Diogenes sums it up well. Virtue is to be chosen for its own sake.[1] Virtue is good; everything else is 'good' for virtue. The Aristotelian distinction between the end and the means or subordinate ends is given precise linguistic formulation. In the Stoic world there is only one thing which can be called good without any qualification whatsoever. This end, which is the providentially ordered life in accordance with reason, is in a category by itself. Moral terms only have their sense in the moral sphere. Once we try to use them outside that sphere, only intellectual confusion and moral vacillation will ensue. Better than that is the paradox: Only virtue is good.

If there is a single good, virtue, and everything else has at best no positive moral value, there would seem to be a problem about how it is possible to become virtuous. How can the performance of non-moral actions (non-moral because not done with the moral intention) be transformed into morality? Before considering this, we must clear up a common misconception. It has been suggested by Edelstein that 'Posidonius, in opposition to the general Stoic dogma, assumes that there are not only immoral men and wise men but also men who make progress'.[2] There is no statement to this effect in the texts cited by Edelstein; the true position is that the Stoics often did not distinguish between amoral and immoral. There are simply moral men and others. Nevertheless, that some of the others make progress towards virtue while others do not is well attested for Chrysippus by the remark that the most successful aspirant to virtue, who does everything he should do (ἀποδίδωσι τὰ καθήκοντα), cannot yet be called happy—that is, he is not yet achieving the good life—because his motives are not yet entirely moral; if he continues as he is, however, he may become moral, because his actions may in time arise from the right kind of disposition.[3] There are many similar passages which suggest that for Chrysippus—and in all probability for all the early Stoics—the man who performs a large number of

---

[1] D.L. 7.89 (*SVF* III 39); cf. D.L. 7.127 etc.
[2] Edelstein, 'The Philosophical System of Posidonius', 311. Edelstein cites Diogenes Laertius 7.91 and 7.127 in support of this strange suggestion.
[3] Stob., *Flor.* 103.22, vol. 3, p. 906, 18H. (*SVF* III 510).

appropriate acts (καθήκοντα) for inadequate reasons can be called evil (φαῦλος), and was in fact so called; yet he is still on the road to virtue.[1]

It seems to be the case that, at least as early as Chrysippus, the Stoics held that the repetition of right actions tends towards the performance of right actions from the right motives; and this has often been recognized to resemble the theories of Aristotle.[2] By doing good deeds we become good;[3] or, as the Stoics would prefer to say, it is by acting appropriately from non-moral motives that one comes to perform the same actions from moral motives. This view, already apparent in Chrysippus, is clearly spelled out in a passage of Cicero.[4] It can only be understood on the basis of Stoic psychology. Repetition of right action will forward the development of a right concept (ἔννοια) in the soul. This concept will be confirmed and assented to because it will harmonize with the other rational concepts of the wise man.

At first sight there seems something strange here. If only the wise man is capable of acting morally, why will anyone else do 'good' deeds at all, except perhaps accidentally? To answer this, general considerations have to be invoked. Virtue, life according to reason, is not unnatural for man. Rather the healthy-minded individual will be virtuous; but there are so few healthy-minded individuals. But although we are almost all sick, some of us are less sick than others. What this means psychologically is that the less sick do 'good' deeds very often from mixed motives, as we should prefer to put it. And anyone who is capable of doing a 'good' deed from a mixed motive is obviously able to do a bad deed. Yet for the Stoics, since reason is present in every man to some degree, every man is capable of doing (and presumably will do) some 'good' deed at some time. And every 'good' deed in a particular sphere will do something (by forming or modifying the character of the doer) to make it possible for that 'good' deed to be repeated. Like Aristotle, the Stoics believe that every man has the possibility of virtue and vice within him, but the way they look on this possibility is con-

[1] E.g. Philo, *Leg. Alleg.* 210 (*SVF* III 512).
[2] Recently by Miss Reesor, 'The "Indifferents"...', 105.
[3] *N.E.* 1106b 36.　　　　　[4] *De Fin.* 3.20.

siderably different. Aristotle thinks of his moral man as possessed of a disposition to make the right decisions and choices. He will apparently evaluate the particular situation and then choose what is best. No metaphysics of this power of choice is offered, and indeed it is hard to see how it could be offered, for, according to Aristotle, the power is developed as the result of habit, but the power itself is a given in man, and in man alone. And the word 'choice' itself is ambiguous, for it is difficult to see why Aristotle did not say, as the Stoics did, that *all* the good man's choices will be good, that he cannot in fact choose the bad, that 'choice' in the good man is the conforming of the mind to a reality in the external world in so far as that reality is good. In fact Aristotle's theory of 'choice' evades this problem. We think of moral man as making choices and our moral language has words for choice for us to use; hence, Aristotle seems to say, we do in fact make choices. Indeed even the good man makes choices.

There is reason to believe that this is the light in which the Stoics, at any rate, saw the Aristotelian theory. And the language they use about the wise man in this connection indicates their criticism, for, whereas for Aristotle virtue is defined as a disposition to make choices, the Stoics define it as a fixed disposition that is consistent (ὁμολογουμένην).[1] The further definition of virtue as reason that is consistent (λόγος ὁμολογούμενος) is attributed to Zeno himself.[2] If the reason of the virtuous man is wholly 'consistent', then all his acts will be morally good, as the Stoics held, and he will not make any real choice between good and evil. It is probably not accidental that the early Stoics avoid the Aristotelian word for choice (προαίρεσις), both when talking about external goods and when observing that virtue is to be chosen for its own sake. For in any ordinary sense of choice the good man does not *choose* virtue; he simply is virtuous. And although the good is to be chosen for its own sake, the good man does not so choose it. It is only the aspirant to virtue who has need to calculate what is really good and what is not and then try to act accordingly. It should also be

---

[1] E.g. D.L. 7.89 (*SVF* III 39).
[2] Plut., *De Virt. Mor.* 441 c (*SVF* I 202).

evident that this explanation of the Stoic attitude to choice would not be affected if it were true (which is unlikely) that the word 'consistent' (ὁμολογουμένην) varies in meaning according to different Stoics, for example between Zeno and Chrysippus. For the Stoics there is no valid distinction to be drawn between self-consistency and consistency with nature, for the microcosm represents the macrocosm and *vice versa*. For the Stoics, then, it is not the special mark of the moral man to be able to select what will be conducive to virtue (though he will, of course, do that); rather he is to be defined in terms of the fixity of his disposition, which is itself measured in relation to a standard, namely reason. As we saw at the beginning of this chapter, Aristotle may have meant to say this, for he certainly emphasized that it is not what one does but why one does it that matters. But the Stoics have apparently good grounds for agreeing with this much, while rejecting the definition of virtue as concerned with choice (προαίρεσις), which tends to be in contradiction to it. Nevertheless, once again it is the lack of clarity in the Aristotelian starting-point which affords an opportunity for the further Stoic investigation.

From what we have said, it would seem to follow not only that all the wise man's acts will be good, but that the wise man will always be a wise man; in other words that virtue cannot be lost. This was in fact the original view of the school; but for some reason or other it was significantly modified by Chrysippus. Our evidence for the controversy is not at all good, but we are told by Diogenes that, whereas Cleanthes believed that virtue cannot be lost (ἀναπόβλητον), because it is the result of a secure hold on reality, Chrysippus thought that it can be lost as a result of drunkenness and melancholy, that is, black bile.[1] Simplicius also knows of both doctrines. In his version, which does not mention particular Stoic teachers by name, one passage says that according to the Stoics virtue cannot be lost, while another says that it can be lost in 'melancholy', heavy drowsiness, lethargy and as a result of taking drugs.[2] All these latter states were regarded by the ancients as physical illnesses;

[1] D.L. 7.127 (*SVF* III 237); cf. D.L. 7.128 (*SVF* I 569).
[2] Simp., *In Cat.* p. 401, 35 and p. 402, 25 ff. Kalbfleisch (*SVF* III 238).

and illnesses are obviously outside the wise man's control. They can therefore damage his mind and weaken his will without conscious decision on his part. Actions under their influence, therefore, may well not be rational actions. There is an illuminating story in Porphyry's life of Plotinus which demonstrates the point. Porphyry, under the influence of 'melancholy', decided to commit suicide. Now Plotinus agrees with the Stoics that whether or not to commit suicide is a matter for the wise man to decide rationally for himself.[1] His advice to Porphyry on this occasion, however, was that his decision to take his own life had arisen not as the result of a rational judgment but from a kind of melancholy sickness (ἐκ μελαγχολικῆς τινος νόσου). Here the matter is plain; 'melancholy' is outside human control and therefore it can adversely affect the action of the wisest of men.

It seems very likely that this was the kind of situation Chrysippus had in mind when he said that virtue can be lost. The reference to this loss being possible as the result of drugs is additional confirmation of this point of view, for Chrysippus could not have had in mind the taking, for example, of aphrodisiacs, since that would be regarded as a vicious act for which the taker would be responsible. Presumably he was thinking rather of the (unforeseen?) after-effects of drugs taken for purely medicinal purposes, where the intention of the taker is impeccable.

The passage in Simplicius, however, continues in a rather curious way. After melancholy or torpor or drugs virtue is lost because the 'whole rational disposition' is lost; but vice does not ensue. Rather, one's steadiness is weakened and what they (the Stoics?) call an intermediate disposition is present to the soul. This intermediate disposition seems to be analogous to that state of the *aspirant* to virtue who has not yet quite made the grade.[2] Surely to any orthodox Stoic it is technically vice. The suggestion that it is not vice is either made by Simplicius himself or by some late Stoic who has forgotten the implications of the original doctrine.

---

[1] Cf. Rist, *Plotinus* 174–7; Porphyry, *V.P.* 11.
[2] Cf. the phrase αἱ μέσαι πράξεις in Stob., *Flor.* 103.22, vol. 3, p. 907, 3 H. (*SVF* III 510).

Since, therefore, Chrysippus was not so foolish as to think
that the wise man is never physically ill, we can understand
why he held that virtue can be lost. There are circumstances
when the most moral man imaginable is not master of his intentions. If he can foresee such a circumstance arising, he
would be right, in Chrysippus' view, to commit suicide, but he
cannot always foresee what is in store for himself. So far, so
good; but one of the causes of the loss of virtue seems different
from the others given. The apparent odd man out is drunkenness. We can readily understand that drunkenness could lead
to the loss of virtue; but why should the virtuous man get
drunk? Aristotle does not seem to think there is any reason why
he should, for he alludes several times to a law of Pittacus of
Mytilene that those who commit crimes under the influence of
drink should have their sentence doubled.[1] Presumably Chrysippus has in mind occasions when it is incumbent on the wise
man to drink even to the point of drunkenness. Although it
seems to have been the general Stoic view—perhaps after
Chrysippus the universal view—that the wise man will not get
drunk,[2] the matter was apparently still a moot point with the
disciples of Zeno, and we have a reference to statements made
by Persaeus in his *Memoirs of Drinking Parties* that gentlemen do
get drunk.[3] The defence would presumably be that getting
drunk is in itself a matter of indifference; hence it can be in-
dulged on social occasions. The Cynic aspect of early Stoicism
is apparent here.

If this account of early Stoic views is correct, we can see the
attitude of Chrysippus in a different light. His statement that
virtue can be lost through drunkenness could serve as a warning
that, although drunkenness is an indifferent, it is not 'preferred',
since it is not the material on which virtue is built. That would
be true for the obvious reason that virtue depends on intention,
and intention is blurred by drunkenness. Hence Chrysippus
would appear to have argued that drunkenness is in the same
class as torpor and 'melancholy'. However, there had obvi-

[1] *N.E.* 1113b 31, and references given by Gauthier and Jolif (*L'Ethique à
Nicomaque* 2¹.214).
[2] S.v. μεθύω, *SVF* IV, p. 95.   [3] Athen., 13, 607A (*SVF* I 451).

ously been no dispute about whether one should become melancholy, since this was viewed as a physical illness. Chrysippus' argument is that allowing oneself to become drunk is virtually the equivalent of deliberately contracting a physical illness. Since the question whether the wise man should be drunk does not seem to occur again in later Stoics, it appears that he made his point.

There is a corollary to the problem about the doctrine that all the acts of the wise man will be good which should be briefly mentioned. It does not follow from this doctrine itself (in isolation from other Stoic positions) that the acts of the wise man are determined, that he cannot act in any other way than that in which he does in fact act. All that is required is that whatever action he undertakes is undertaken in accordance with virtue. There may be several equally good courses of action open to him, and he will be free to take any one of them.

Before concluding, we should notice one or two further areas where it seems clear that the Stoic account of virtue took its starting-point from Aristotle's definition in the *Ethics*. Aristotle, we recall, says that the disposition which is virtue is in a mean in relation to us, that this mean is determined by reason, and that it therefore takes a wise man (φρόνιμος) to determine it. Naturally enough, the Stoics will have nothing to do with virtue defined as a mean of any kind. Aristotle defines virtue as a mean in essence and by definition, but in relation to excellence it is an extreme. The Stoics have no room for such a dichotomy. Virtue is either an extreme or it is not. Its excellence and its definition and nature must coincide. However, the idea that virtue has some relation to reason (λόγος) is much more to their taste, although once again differences should be noticed. For whereas Aristotle says that virtue is a mean which is *defined* by reason, the Stoics, as we have seen, identify the two. Virtue is reason. Nevertheless, in practice this difference may be more apparent than real, for ultimately it is human beings, those who are wise, who are capable of deciding about what is virtuous and what is not—and it is their duty to lay down laws for the rest. The role of the Aristotelian man of practical wisdom (φρόνιμος) is not very different from that of the Stoic φρόνιμος

or σπουδαῖος. We saw how, from Diogenes of Babylon on-
wards, the Stoics were in the habit of saying that the good life
involves the correct selection of what is conducive to virtue
from among external goods. Here the role of the wise man is
clear. As Fronto puts it in a letter to Marcus Aurelius, it is the
peculiar task of the wise man to make his selections with the
proper moral motivation.[1] And the Aristotelian term itself occurs in a similar passage of Plutarch, where the Stoic end of life
is spoken of as requiring the selection and taking of external
goods in a prudent manner (φρονίμως).[2] And the parallel goes
further still if a valuable suggestion made by Kidd is applied
here. According to Kidd, the actions of the aspirant to virtue
are, in the opinion of the Old Stoa, governed by rules: do this;
don't do that.[3] These rules will be laid down by the man who
knows, the wise man, the φρόνιμος or σπουδαῖος. Perhaps it is
not fanciful to notice that, although both the Stoics and Aristotle were exercised over the question of the relation of the best
life to the life of politics, both of them tended in general to support political life as a valid activity for man. The wise man will
be involved in public life, wrote Chrysippus, unless there is
something specific to prevent him.[4] And in Imperial Roman
times this theme became dominant. If the aspirant to wisdom
is the aspirant to the forwarding of the universal rule of reason,
then the wiser he becomes, the more he will regard it as his duty
to attempt to regulate the world for the best by law. If this tradition goes back through Aristotle to Plato and even behind Plato,
it is likely that the Stoics took it in the first instance from Aristotelian ideas.

It has not been the purpose of this chapter to suggest that the
Stoic definition of virtue and related areas of Stoic thought are
unoriginal, or that they are mere glosses on the *Nicomachean
Ethics*. Despite Carneades' jibe that in ethics the differences between the Stoics and the Peripatetics are merely terminological,
the ancient world in general, and doubtless Carneades himself,
recognized the clash of the two schools. What we have tried to

[1] Fronto, p. 143 Naber (*SVF* III 196).   [2] Plut., *CN* 1071A (*SVF* III 195).
[3] Kidd, *op. cit.* 185; Seneca, *Ep.* 94.50, *hoc vitabis, hoc facies.*
[4] D.L. 7.121 (*SVF* III 697).

show is rather that the very originality of the Stoics is best understood in terms of an attempt to resolve certain (in their view) half-truths and confused truths in the Aristotelian account. Their attitude to Aristotle was not that of the commentator but that of the critic. We have tried to show that many of their positions arise from an attempt to pursue the logical consequences of Aristotelian theories. Often Aristotle would not have recognized, let alone accepted, these 'logical' consequences. Finally we have attempted to show that many of the modifications and changes offered by the Stoics were not the product of over-simplification or of fascination with ethical paradoxes, as they have often been represented, but were the result of philosophical puzzlement over significant philosophical problems.

ZENO AND CHRYSIPPUS ON HUMAN ACTION AND EMOTION

It is fashionable to regard the Stoic doctrine that all fools are mad with a wry smile. This attitude arises for two reasons. It is supposed that the Stoics confused moral and psychological categories, and that madness is an absolute term which was used by the Stoics to give sanction to their equally strange view that all sins are equal. The suggestion that all deviations from perfect behaviour are equally culpable will not be discussed directly here, though what follows may shed some indirect light upon it. The view that it is impossible to distinguish between folly and madness, however, needs immediate consideration, not least because, although it runs contrary to many traditional theories about the nature of moral activity, it bears some relation to views propounded by contemporary psychologists. The Stoic position, however, did not carry with it the corollary often added in contemporary discussions that folly, which is madness, is therefore not intelligibly blamed, or, in a cruder version, that we are not responsible for our actions.

The thesis, widely current in the Middle Ages and at the time of the Renaissance, that certain types of behaviour, for example, the behaviour of heretics, which the contemporary believer might explain in terms of mistaken judgments, are in fact motivated by a (diabolical) corruption of the whole personality, bears a much stronger resemblance to the Stoic view—and is perhaps one of the principal contributory factors in the common misunderstanding of it. For it is perfectly possible to argue that mistaken judgments are themselves aberrations of the personality (the view of Chrysippus), or that they are the direct cause of such aberrations (the apparent view of Zeno), without claiming that one is oneself free from such aberrations, or that they can be rooted out by the infliction of pain or by any other external means—or even that an outsider can determine precisely how and why the aberration arises. It is significant, and in the circumstances somewhat surprising, that none of the Stoic leaders thought of themselves as wise men, that is, as men who could properly diagnose the false judgment in individual cases; indeed they supposed such wise men to be as rare as the phoenix. This shows them in the light of a humility which is not commonly recognized.

When we think of someone committing a crime, our usual reaction is to imagine that he has done it either because he was 'carried away' or because he calculated that it was to his advantage. Even in the second case, the case of the calculating criminal, we usually hold that the criminal is not completely devoid of moral sense, but that he calculates that the rewards of crime, the satisfaction of one or other of his desires, make it worth while committing a crime, even if vestigial feelings of conscience have to be suppressed. In other words we operate with a quasi-Platonic model of a battle between two parts of the personality, a moral sense of what is right and a 'desiring faculty'. We think of these two faculties in conflict, and in the case of the criminal we imagine the 'desire' coming out on top. We may then go on to ask why in some men such 'desires' always seem to predominate, while in others they do not; and we tend to answer in terms of hereditary or environmental factors. Those of us who want to preserve some vestige of moral responsibility in the traditional sense, however, often argue that these factors are great suasions to action but do not ultimately determine any fixed course of moral behaviour. Men, we say, are different from animals, for animals cannot be said to act morally; there is in them no possibility of a sense of what is right restraining the animal from acting in accordance with its desires or instincts, whereas, in the human being, whatever factors, hereditary or environmental, have been operative on the nature of our desires and propensities, there is always the reason to counterbalance them. We can choose not to follow our desire for profit if the urge to steal comes upon us.

A common moral assumption, whether correct or not, is, therefore, that in human beings the will need not be corrupted. It can operate for moral ends whatever pressures are brought to bear upon it. This assumption is usually bolstered by the idea that the moral will is a will to rationality, that the human reason, properly used, will support the moral sense, the will, by enabling it to recognize that moral action is in the long run rational action. Hence we tend, on very good authorities from antiquity on, to view many moral problems as arising from the combination of knowing what is right with an inability to bring it about through our own deliberate actions. We assume that, even when we are being corrupted in our moral sense and in our will, we know the better course. Once again we view moral problems as a struggle between elements in the personality; and in general we make the assumption that either our reason or our will or the two together, or some other mental faculty, remains unsullied, presenting us with a possible alternative course of action to that to which our 'desires' impel us when we commit a crime.

This thesis, that moral action is the result of a struggle between various elements inside the personality itself, is what Zeno and Chrysippus deny. It will be argued here that on the more substantial points relating to this problem, as in most other cases, the two greatest of the early Stoics are in agreement. In place of the model of a struggle in the personality, they wish to set the model of the health or sickness of a unitary individual. Using for the time being the language which can definitely be attributed to Chrysippus, we can say that they argued that all moral activity (and indeed for Chrysippus all activity) must be viewed as different states of the 'personality' of man, for personality is in many ways the most convincing modern equivalent for the Stoic term ἡγεμονικόν.[1]

Before continuing, however, we should pause a moment on this question of the sense of ἡγεμονικόν. It has often been argued or assumed[2] that discussions about whether or not Zeno would have subscribed to Chrysippus' definition of πάθη as states of the ἡγεμονικόν are arguments about whether Chrysippus 'rationalized' the original Stoic theory. This misconcep-

---

[1] For walking as a state of the ἡγεμονικόν according to Chrysippus (and his disagreement with Cleanthes) see Sen., *Ep.* 113.18 (*SVF* I 525).

[2] E.g. recently by De Vogel, *Greek Philosophy* III 92–5 etc. This usage is common to Zeller, Pohlenz, Philippson and others.

tion of the problem arises from the fact that the Stoics tend to identify the ἡγεμονικόν in us with the divine Reason in the universe. The assumption is that the Stoic Reason, and therefore the ἡγεμονικόν, is rational in the sense of the word 'rational' with which we are familiar in everyday speech. Hence it is often said that according to Chrysippus πάθη are mistaken judgments (*simpliciter*). But it should be obvious, if from nothing else than the fact that for the Stoics Reason is identified with some kind of fire, that our own notions of what is rational need not tally exactly with those of the Stoics. It is in fact an interpretation, not a description, of Stoic doctrine to suggest that, if πάθη are judgments (κρίσεις), Chrysippus must be a rationalist in the normal sense of the word. We shall have to consider more precisely what sort of judgments Chrysippus is dealing with and how he analyses them.

If judgments are states of the ἡγεμονικόν, it is not obvious that the ἡγεμονικόν must be called rational in the normal sense of the word.[1] Indeed, for the Stoics, both rationality and irrationality would themselves be states of the ἡγεμονικόν. The ἡγεμονικόν is rational in what we may call a divine sense of the word, but it is best understood as the root of the personality, at least in Zeno and Chrysippus. The ἡγεμονικόν is something of what we might call the 'true self' or personality of each individual human being. It will therefore more aptly be rendered by words referring to personality than by words referring to rationality.

The unitary conception of personality which we have been considering is best understood in relation to the Stoic ideal of ἀπάθεια. This word, in contexts of orthodox Stoicism, does not point to states of total impassivity, nor were the Stoics foolish enough to imagine that such states are either possible or desirable for man. The wise man, in their view, so far from being emotionless, is possessed of the three basic and stable emotional —and at the same time rational—dispositions of joy, wishfulness and a sense of precaution (χαρά, βούλησις, εὐλάβεια).[2] In

[1] According to Cicero, *N.D.* 2.34, man differs from God in not being purely rational.
[2] Cf. D.L. 7.115 (*SVF* III 431), Lact., *Div. Instit.* 6.15 (*SVF* III 437), Cic., *Tusc. Disp.* 4.12 (*SVF* III 438) etc. That the theory of εὐπάθεια was in some form part of the original Stoicism of Zeno is suggested below, pp. 31-2.

the Stoic view, for a man in a healthy condition there is no contrast between reason and the emotions; hence these 'emotions' can be described as rational states. These rational states then are present in the wise man; they are called by the Stoics εὐπάθειαι. Obviously there is a difference between a πάθος and a εὐπάθεια; and the ἀπαθής, the wise man, is to be viewed as a man without πάθη. As for the sense of πάθος here, whatever it may mean in the writings of other philosophers, there is no doubt that Cicero's Cato has the matter in almost the right perspective in a passage of the *De Finibus* where he observes that the literal translation of the term πάθος in its technical sense would be *morbus* (disease).[1] He shrinks from this translation, however, and prefers the more colourless *perturbatio* on the ground that people do not call pity or anger diseases. This shrinking is not well suited to the originally radical Stoic conception, which is precisely that all πάθη *are* diseases, and that the victim is mentally deranged. It is probably no accident that Zeno himself defined πάθος as a πτοία (violent fluttering) of the soul,[2] for the most common πτοία is sexual excitement (Eros), and this was widely regarded from early Greek times as like a disease or as a disease itself (νόσος). In his refusal to admit the word *morbus* Cicero's Cato shows himself to shrink from the original conception of the πάθη. Lactantius, though confessing himself outraged at the idea, is nearer to the view of Chrysippus and Zeno when he observes that Zeno puts mercy among the vices and diseases (*inter vitia et morbos*).[3]

Πάθη then are not emotions but excessive and irrational impulses.[4] For Chrysippus they are not the product of an impulsive or desiring faculty of the human soul; that is generally agreed. Hence the Stoic language about the total elimination of πάθη becomes intelligible,[5] and the conflict between the Peripatetics and Platonists, who both advocated moderation of the emotions (μετριοπάθεια), and the Stoics, who advocated ἀπάθεια, is revealed as a battle in which both sides might have

---

[1] *De Finibus* 3.35 (cf. *SVF* III 381). Cf. *Acad. Post.* 1.39.
[2] Stob., *Ecl.* 2, p. 39, 8 W. (*SVF* I 206).
[3] Lact., *Div. Instit.* 3.23 (*SVF* I 213).   [4] *SVF* I 206.
[5] Sen., *Ep.* 116.1 (*SVF* III 443), Lact., *Div. Instit.* 6.14 (*SVF* III 444).

found themselves in agreement if they had been able to agree on what a πάθος is. For if the πάθη are viewed as diseases, as pathological disturbances of the personality, it is easy to see why the Stoics advocated their complete suppression. It would be rather stupid to argue that the effects of a disease should be moderated when it would seem to be possible to banish the disease altogether with much more desirable results. The Stoics, many of whom regarded their school as a kind of hospital, would have been very peculiar doctors if they had not fought for the total suppression of what they held to be serious mental illnesses (νοσήματα).[1] After all, who wants to be a partial neurotic?

It is agreed that from the time of Chrysippus there was a doctrine widely held among the Stoics that πάθη are states of the ἡγεμονικόν. There has been considerable argument about whether this formulation is due to Chrysippus or whether it was also offered by Zeno; and the debate has ranged beyond the question of the formal expression of the theory in terms of the Stoic categories, to the wider issue of whether Chrysippus' theory differs in substance from that of Zeno.

The problem of the formulation of the theory is the less important and can be readily disposed of. It is sometimes assumed, or even argued, that the Stoic categories, including of course the category of state or disposition (τὸ πῶς ἔχον), were introduced by Chrysippus.[2] There is no good evidence for this; it is assumed on the basis of the undoubted fact that Chrysippus had a great deal more interest in logic than Zeno or Cleanthes. Against it, however, are the statements of Diogenes Laertius that Cleanthes wrote a book entitled *Categories*,[3] and of Clement of Alexandria that Cleanthes referred to the categories as λεκτά.[4] If these statements are to be relied on, and Cleanthes did in fact talk

---

[1] Cf. (for example), for Chrysippus, Galen, *De Hipp. et Plat.* 5.437, p. 413, 12 Mü. (*SVF* III 471), but the language is a commonplace throughout the whole history of Stoicism. See Pohlenz, *Die Stoa* 2.82 for references.

[2] Pohlenz ('Zenon und Chrysipp', 181–5) writes ambiguously on this. Miss Reesor ('The Stoic Concept of Quality', 44–5) seems to believe that the categories of disposition and relative disposition were introduced by Chrysippus.

[3] D.L. 7.174 (*SVF* I 481).   [4] Clem. Alex., *Strom.* 8.9.26 (*SVF* I 488).

about categories, it is almost certain that some kind of doctrine of categories was part of the original teaching of Zeno, for modern scholarship has failed to modify the view of the ancients to any substantial extent that Cleanthes made only minor changes in the doctrine which he had learned from his master. It was possible for Posidonius to argue that a doctrine held by Cleanthes, even if apparently different from the positions of Chrysippus, must represent genuine Stoic opinion, that is, the opinion of Zeno.[1] Finally it should be recalled that Plutarch uses language which, if accurate, suggests that Zeno employed the category of relative disposition.[2]

Whether or not Zeno himself held the doctrine of categories, or what doctrine of categories he held, is, however, much less important for our present enquiry than whether he would have accepted a theory which was certainly explained by Chrysippus in terms of categories, the theory that πάθη are simply states of the ἡγεμονικόν.[3] Since we have no texts of Zeno which deal with this problem directly, we must approach it in a slightly circuitous way. It has been argued, particularly by Pohlenz in 'Zenon und Chrysipp', that Chrysippus' theory is very considerably different from that of Zeno, and that this difference is part of a wider difference between the two which affects their theory of knowledge as well as their psychology and ethics. According to Pohlenz an important area in which the differences between the two can be seen is their account of πάθη, for, whereas Chrysippus holds them to be 'judgments' (κρίσεις), Zeno thinks they are disturbances which arise in the soul after judgments.[4] A text of Galen to this effect has been generally taken, since Pohlenz, to suggest that, whereas Zeno held that the πάθη are essentially irrational, Chrysippus rationalized them. We must examine this text and certain other related material in detail.

---

[1] Galen, *De Hipp.* 5.475–6, p. 456 Mü. (*SVF* I 570). Other evidence that Zeno at least talked about quality is offered by Miss Reesor, 'The Stoic Categories', 63–5, and 'The Stoic Concept of Quality'. Cf. Rieth (*Grundbegriffe* 84–5) on Ariston.　　　　[2] Plut., *SR* 1034 C (*SVF* I 200).

[3] For Chrysippus see Alex. Aphr., *De An. Mant.* p. 118.6 Bruns (*SVF* II 823).

[4] Galen, *De Hipp.* 5.429, p. 405 Mü. (*SVF* III 461). Cf. Pohlenz, 'Zenon und Chrysipp', 188–9.

The first thing to be clear about is where Chrysippus does not diverge from Zeno. Pohlenz seems to have established that there are some significant differences between Zeno and Chrysippus in their accounts of πάθη,[1] that there is a real difference between saying that a πάθος is a kind of judgment and saying that it supervenes upon a judgment. But let us not be too ready to follow Pohlenz in his Posidonian interpretation of this difference.[2] There are some surviving verses of Cleanthes in which Reason is imagined debating with Passion (θυμός).[3] According to Galen Posidonius used these verses to 'prove' that Cleanthes (and therefore Zeno) held a quasi-Platonic doctrine of parts of the soul in opposition to or alliance with one another. It is easy to see why Posidonius wanted to father this doctrine on Cleanthes. He himself accepted a version of the Platonic tripartition of the soul, and wished to believe himself in agreement with the earliest Stoics and in opposition to the innovations of Chrysippus. But, as Zeller already recognized, the poem of Cleanthes need not be read in the way in which Posidonius read it. Clearly even for Chrysippus both λογισμός (reason) and θυμός can arise in the soul; in other words, we are able both to reason and to desire. And clearly these two powers of the human psyche can be dramatized. But Chrysippus could readily observe that, if a poet dramatizes true and false judgments as debates about a course of action, it does not follow that he subscribes to a philosophical theory of parts or faculties of the soul, each separate from the others and each forming a self-asserting principle of motivation. We must remember that apparently for all the Stoics, including Zeno himself, θυμός is a variety of πάθος, and that a πάθος is defined by Zeno as an unnatural movement of the soul, a once natural impulse which is now out of hand.[4] In the wise man, therefore, θυμός, like the other πάθη, will be eliminated. That being so, there is no reason to believe that Cleanthes (or Zeno himself) held the opinion that θυμός is a basic element in the soul in any quasi-Platonic fashion such as

[1] 'Zenon und Chrysipp', against Philippson, 'Zur Psychologie der Stoa'.
[2] Pohlenz, *Die Stoa* 1.90–1.
[3] Galen, *De Hipp.* 5.476, p. 456 Mü. (*SVF* 1 570).
[4] D.L. 7.110 (cf. *SVF* 1 205).

Posidonius wished to propose. The poem of Cleanthes must be read as a dramatic rendering of the chaos, the mental illness, in the unitary personality of the individual man when he is evil. If for Cleanthes θυμός is an unwholesome state, it is obviously not present in the healthy personality.

We should now turn from what Posidonius supposed Cleanthes to have believed to the key statement about the difference between the theories of Chrysippus and Zeno. Perhaps the truth will be easier to discern when the perpetually confused views of Posidonius have been cleared away. According to the relevant section of Galen, Chrysippus held that πάθη are some kind of judgment while Zeno said they arise as a result of judgments.[1] From this it is clear that Zeno and Chrysippus agree that the soul has no faculty independent of the ἡγεμονικόν in which πάθη can arise. The difference between Zeno and Chrysippus is rather in their account of a judgment (κρίσις) itself. Zeno must have held that judgments *qua* judgments are to be viewed as free from any irrational 'colouring', that the colouring is the inevitable result of misguided judgments which thus damage the ἡγεμονικόν. Chrysippus, on the other hand, held that there is no such thing as a merely mental act and that all judgments must have some kind of emotional colouring, correct judgments —made only by the wise—presumably involving εὐπάθειαι, false judgments involving some degree of πάθος. He certainly held that both impulsive and rational activity must be activity of the ἡγεμονικόν, the personality itself.[2]

Pohlenz has properly argued that late authors such as Themistius provide no basis for the belief that Zeno as well as Chrysippus thought of the πάθη simply as κρίσεις.[3] Zeno's account of πάθη as arising as a result of judgments must be taken seriously. We must also, however, take seriously the fact that these πάθη which arise from judgments are said by Zeno himself to be irrational, to be disobedient to reason.[4] So far then we

---

[1] *De Hipp.* 5.429, p. 405 Mü. (*SVF* III 461).
[2] D.L. 7.159 (*SVF* II 837).
[3] Them., *De Anima*, p. 107, 17 Heinze (*SVF* I 208). See Pohlenz ('Zenon und Chrysipp', 196–7) against Philippson, *op. cit.* 154.
[4] Clem. Alex., *Strom.* 2.13.59 (*SVF* III 377); D.L. 7.110 (*SVF* I 205); Stob., *Ecl.* 2, p. 88, 8 W. (*SVF* I 205).

must agree with the view of Zeller and Philippson that for Zeno the πάθη are essentially irrational. If Zeno maintained a doctrine of εὐπάθειαι, as there is every reason to believe, although the word is not attested in his extant remains, then these εὐπάθειαι would be rational. For Zeno, then, as the result of judgments, the ἡγεμονικόν is disposed rationally or irrationally; yet if he worked with the category πὼς ἔχον or something like it, he could still have accepted Chrysippus' account of all emotions, rational and irrational, as states of mind.

In the light of this attitude of Zeno we can understand a little more about the position of Chrysippus. First of all, just as the πάθη are irrational for Zeno, so they are for Chrysippus; the theory that Chrysippus rationalized the πάθη when he called them states of mind or mistaken judgments is quite absurd. There never was any dispute between Zeno and Chrysippus about whether a πάθος is rational or irrational; of course it is irrational. The dispute rather is about the nature of what they call judgments (κρίσεις); that is, it is about whether or not it is possible to perform a purely mental act. Zeno seems to have held that an immoral decision is taken impassively, but that various pathological states will inevitably follow; Chrysippus, on the other hand, thought that the decision and its emotional counterpart are totally inseparable. Even a conceptual separation would be misleading.

There are a number of reasons for believing that what Chrysippus assumed to be the theory of Zeno was in fact Zeno's theory, and that he was right in supposing that Zeno's intention was the same as his own. Chrysippus' attitude can be explained on the supposition that he thought that Zeno had the same intention as himself, but had been unable to get the logical form of his theory correct, and had thus been led to say some rather misleading things. As we have already observed, although there is no direct evidence that Zeno formulated the doctrine of proper emotional states (εὐπάθειαι), it is highly likely that he did so. Had he regarded the ἀπάθεια of the wise man as total indifference to everything whatsoever other than virtue and vice, his insensitivity would have been a good deal nearer to the deviationist Stoicism of his pupil Ariston than it was known to have been. It is true that Zeno was a pupil of the Cynic Crates, but his break with Crates was over substantial issues and the problem of the correct attitudes towards what is indifferent was almost certainly one of them. If this is so, then Zeno, like Chrysippus, believed that the unitary personality can be either well or ill affected, but that neither of these states depends upon an emotional 'root' in the soul apart from the ἡγεμονικόν. Once again we should emphasize that the question of how a judgment arises must be separated from the question of what a judgment is. It seems certain that Chrysippus modified Zeno's theory on the occurrence of judgments, but this modification has nothing to do with the question of the faculty or part of the soul in which judgments and emotional states arise.

It is Zeno's view that a πάθος is to be defined as a ὁρμὴ πλεονάζουσα, and although again we have no direct evidence as to the precise relationship in his philosophy between the ὁρμαί and the ἡγεμονικόν, there is a further indirect source of evidence to help the enquiry along. It seems to have been a Stoic doctrine from the beginning that the difference between 'rational' and 'irrational' creatures, that is, the difference between human beings and animals, cannot be overemphasized.[1] It might be supposed that those Stoics least likely to accept the validity of this distinction would be those closest to Cynicism. Yet Ariston, the pupil of Zeno who was the most attracted to the early Cynicism of his master, and who for this reason was repudiated by later Stoics, himself holds this doctrine firmly.[2] There can be no doubt that Zeno held it also.

We know, then, that for Zeno a πάθος, which is an impulse (ὁρμή) which has got out of hand, is the result of a wrong judgment. This would seem to mean that human πάθη are essentially different from those of animals in that they involve or are the result of some kind of intellectual activity. But what about the ὁρμή itself, before it has been translated as the result of a judgment into a healthy or pathological phenomenon? What is its status for Zeno? For Chrysippus we know that it too is a state

[1] D.L. 7.129 (*SVF* III 367) and many other sources listed as *SVF* III 368–76.
[2] Cf. Porphyry in Stob., *Ecl.* I, p. 347, 21 ff. W. (*SVF* I 377).

of the ἡγεμονικόν.[1] Again, unfortunately, there is no direct evidence. But it should be noticed that ὁρμαί in themselves are of value for Zeno; it is only when they become uncontrolled that they are pathological. And if they are healthy they must be rational, so that we can assume that in the case of a human being, as distinct from an animal, Zeno would agree with Chrysippus at least to the point of regarding the ὁρμή as an ἐπιγιγνόμενον of the reason of a unitary self.

If the foregoing arguments are correct and we are to conclude that a unitary soul is the desideratum of both Zeno and Chrysippus, where does the difference between them lie? What did Chrysippus intend when he replaced Zeno's definition of a πάθος as something supervenient upon a judgment with the theory that it is a judgment itself, though a mistaken one? It should again be emphasized that this has nothing to do with the question of the way in which (according to Pohlenz) Chrysippus reformed Zeno's theory of how knowledge is acquired. We are not concerned with theory of knowledge as applied to moral knowledge; we are not concerned with the problem of how we acquire the knowledge that cruelty is wrong, but with the state of mind in which one makes the (correct) judgment that cruelty is wrong and the (incorrect) judgment that it is right.[2]

Zeno's view is that first the judgment is made and then, according to the moral worth of the judgment, an appropriate state of mind follows. Chrysippus at least seems to have supposed that Zeno envisaged an actual temporal sequence; first the judgment, then the state of mind. There is no reason to think that this is incorrect. In the dispute between Chrysippus and Cleanthes about the nature of walking a similar problem arises. According to Cleanthes walking can be described as the movement of an air current from the *principale* (ἡγεμονικόν) to the legs. Chrysippus can hardly have denied this, but he thought it more informative to describe walking simply as a state of the

---

[1] D.L. 7.159 (*SVF* II 837).
[2] For alleged epistemological differences between Zeno and Chrysippus see especially Pohlenz, 'Zenon und Chrysipp', 176–7, on τύπωσις and ἑτεροίωσις.

ἡγεμονικόν.[1] It is not clear whether Cleanthes envisaged the transmission of the air current as instantaneous, but this seems unlikely, and even if he did so understand it, his formulation could easily suggest a temporal sequence of events to the unwary. What seems to have happened is that Cleanthes had in mind a concept of beginning to walk similar to that worked out by Aristotle, who envisages a sequence of events taking place in the potential walker. 'For this reason', he observes, 'a man sees that he must walk, and *virtually* simultaneously (ἅμα ὡς εἰπεῖν) he walks unless anything prevents him from doing so.'[2] The Aristotelian passage is echoed by Seneca, who remarks:[3] 'I must walk. I then immediately walk (*tunc demum ambulo*) when I have said to myself, "I must walk", and have assented to this opinion of mine.' To avoid this idea of a sequence,[4] which in fact explains beginning to walk but not walking, Chrysippus prefers to speak of walking as an act of the personality itself. And this has something to be said for it, for when we are walking, we do not keep on going through a process in which at one moment we decide to walk and the next moment we begin to do so. Rather, once we have decided to walk, we carry on walking, unless, as the Stoics might phrase it, anything stands in our way. Walking is in fact a showing forth or state of our continuing decision; or, we might say conversely, our continuing decision is the conceptual image of our action. At any rate it is often difficult to separate the two; and that is probably why Chrysippus refused to do so.

Essentially, according to Chrysippus, the problem about πάθη is similar to the problem of any bodily activity. In his view, it seems, we do not make judgments and then feel emotional effects. The emotional effects are a part—and indeed an in-

---

[1] Sen. *Ep.* 113.23 (*SVF* I 525). Cf. Aëtius, 4.21.4 (*SVF* I 150) on voice; and in general *SVF* II 836. For the medical background of Cleanthes' position see Solmsen, 'Greek Philosophy and the Discovery of the Nerves', 180–1; and in general Jaeger, *Diokles von Karystos*.

[2] *De Motu An.* 702 a. For the use of this passage by the Epicureans see Furley, *Two Studies in the Greek Atomists* 217–18.

[3] Sen., *Ep.* 113.18 (*SVF* III 169).

[4] Doubtless the ambiguity in words like ἀκολουθεῖν caused trouble here. This word can be used for both logical and temporal 'following'. Cf. Sext. Emp., *Adv. Math.* 8.12; Schuhl, *Le Dominateur et les Possibles* 72.

separable part—of the judgment itself. In other words, for Chrysippus there is no such thing as a purely rational act, if by rational we mean 'performed by an emotionless intellect alone'. All mental acts are coloured by being at the same time emotional acts. Thus all judgments are changes in the personality or new states of the personality. This is why the wise man is not totally passionless, why εὐπάθεια, a proper health of the soul, and not mere impassivity, is the Stoic ideal. Total impassivity is in Chrysippus' view a senseless and indeed unintelligible aim, since mental acts themselves are not impassive. Anyone who seeks ἀπάθεια, in the sense of total elimination of all feeling and emotion, is asking for a state when all activities, even mental activities, are suspended. Such a state would in fact be equivalent to death.

If our interpretation is right, therefore, the relation between the views of Zeno and Chrysippus about πάθη is that Chrysippus was led to correct Zeno's formulation because of his clearer grasp of the nature of human activity as totally psychosomatic activity, almost as personal activity. It is not entirely clear whether he was aware in his own mind of this relationship. He may have thought of himself as not so much correcting Zeno as clarifying him and working out the consequences of his insights in more detail. But if his dispute with Cleanthes about walking gives us any clues about the nature of his relationship to his predecessors in general, it may be that he was in fact aware that the concept of a corresponding and preceding mental act for each bodily movement or emotional response could not be sustained.

Zeno had at least moved in the direction of the concept of a unitary self. He had given up the idea of conflicting faculties in the human psyche and dropped the Platonic or quasi-Platonic talk about divergent parts of the soul. He was already suggesting, as were all the earlier Stoics, that it is changes in the self that matter when we are trying to explain moral behaviour, not civil wars in the soul. But he was still under the old rationalist sway in so far as he supposed that, although judgments inevitably lead to emotions, yet they themselves are 'pure acts of thought'. Doubtless the much misunderstood Stoic materialism had something to do with this, for it is obvious that it takes time for one material object to affect another. To avoid this difficulty, a difficulty akin to that of the now notorious 'ghost in the machine' theory of the soul, Chrysippus thought that there was only one way out: he must define emotions themselves as kinds of judgment. For Chrysippus all judgments involve emotion; some of them are good, others are bad. But this step proved too radical for a less tough-minded generation of Stoics, and under the guidance of Posidonius they reverted to the concept of warring faculties as the only possible explanation of moral struggle and consequent moral behaviour.

Seeing the radical theory of Chrysippus now in a clearer light, we can finally return briefly to the question with which we began, the question of the sickness and health of the soul and the necessity to extirpate the πάθη. This view, already outlined by Zeno in opposition to the Platonists and Peripatetics, was given renewed emphasis by Chrysippus. If πάθη are illnesses of the ἡγεμονικόν, it is natural to wish to be rid of them altogether. As soon as these πάθη become elements of something like a tripartite soul, the medical metaphors have to change their role also. From Chrysippus' doctrine that health is freedom from πάθη we have to return to something more like the Platonic view that health is a balance or harmony between different elements of the soul. And the problem of the nature of the unity of the self arises all over again.[1]

[1] Cf. Rist, 'Integration'.

3

PROBLEMS OF PLEASURE AND PAIN

There is a widely held belief, much fostered by the work of Pohlenz, that the Stoic philosophy should be viewed primarily in terms of a reaction to the Epicurean. The thesis is exaggerated, but has certain elements of truth. Clearly the radical antithesis between Stoic and Epicurean views on the role of pleasure in the life of the good man gives it a certain substance. But the fact that Epicurus regarded pleasure (of some kind) as the most important thing in life,[1] while the Stoics bestowed the accolade on virtue, has led to various misconceptions as to the treatment accorded by the Stoics to pleasure. These misconceptions have been partially corrected by Haynes in a recent article; but some still remain, and Haynes has introduced a few further sources of confusion.[2] In the discussion that is to follow, it should be assumed that the evidence offered relates to the views of Chrysippus, unless specifically attributed to others. However, there are no good reasons for denying that similar, though sometimes less sophisticated, positions are maintained by Zeno.

Only a fool would maintain that any human being could be totally insensible to pleasures and pains. Zeno accordingly held that, while the wise man does not feel πάθη, which arise from mistaken judgments,[3] he nevertheless feels 'certain suspicions and shadows' of these πάθη. These shadows are the scars remaining after a wound has healed up.[4] Working along similar lines, Chrysippus holds that the wise man will feel pain,[5] and it is the standard opinion in the school that, although 'pleasure' (in the sense of a mistaken judgment) will be eradicated from the wise man, yet he will enjoy a rational state of exhilaration

---

[1] Merlan, in *Studies in Epicurus and Aristotle*, thinks 'joy' is a better translation of Epicurean ἡδονή. This is a half-truth, but cannot be discussed in detail here.

[2] Haynes, 'The Theory of Pleasure in the Old Stoa'.

[3] See pp. 22–36 above.   [4] Seneca, *De Ira* 1.16.7 (*SVF* I 215).

[5] Stob., *Flor.* 7.20, vol. I, p. 314, 14 H. (*SVF* III 574).

(χαρά).¹ One thing that the term ἀπάθεια, which denotes the aim of the Stoic sage, does not mean, is insensibility. The wise man feels both pleasure and pain.

In order to understand the significance of this, we must consider in more detail the Stoic explanation of the phenomenon of pleasure. It is clear that they distinguished, implicitly if not explicitly, between two types of pleasure, which can roughly be described as the simple feeling of 'physical' satisfaction and the more positive open enjoyment of that satisfaction which must be in some way associated with a recognition that it is satisfying, and with an accompanying recognition that it ought (or ought not) to be satisfying. To give an example of how this distinction can be applied, we can say that eating a good meal affords simple 'physical' pleasure, whereas enjoying the meal in full knowledge that the food has been stolen is, as the Stoics would put it, an assent of the moral personality by which the eater agrees to enjoy delicious food in full knowledge of the fact that he should not be eating it at all. During the course of this chapter it will be convenient to call the 'physical' pleasure a first-order pleasure and the more psychologically complex pleasure a second-order pleasure. The use of these terms is not intended to suggest that either of the types of pleasure is more pleasurable, or more genuine in any other sense. What we should avoid is the use of terms like 'physical', which have had to be used up to this point, because they suggest a theory of the nature of man and of his capacities or faculties which, it will be argued, would be unacceptable to Chrysippus. Haynes, when discussing similar problems, is prepared, however, to call first-order pleasures bodily pleasures; second-order pleasures he refers to as 'mental attributes'.²

Haynes apparently seeks to justify this sort of language by reference to a passage of Aulus Gellius.³ Gellius is trying to explain how a Stoic sage, in present pain, struggles against being

¹ For the various εὐπάθειαι see *SVF* III 431–42.
² Haynes, *op. cit.* 417. Haynes' attitude is appropriate to a rather more dualistic Stoic like Epictetus. Cf. ἥδεσθαι τῇ σαρκί and ἥδεσθαι κατὰ ψυχήν in *Disc.* 3.7.4. We should also notice the assimilation of ἡδονὴ ψυχική to χαρά at 3.7.7. Cf. Bonhoeffer, *Epictet und die Stoa* 293.
³ Haynes, *op. cit.* 418.

deluded into the belief that pain is evil. He is, however, compelled to admit that the Stoic, though denying pain to be evil, will still feel it and be forced to groan. How can this be? To answer this question, Gellius, who is quoting a discourse of a philosopher named Taurus, gives some kind of Stoic explanation of the gradual growth of reason in the human being from his birth up to the time of his full maturity. Haynes points out that, according to Gellius, the Stoics hold that the sensations of pain and pleasure are given by nature before the appearance of judgment and reason. By this Gellius seems to mean that there are some pleasures and pains in the human being which are not judgments or, as Chrysippus would put it, states of the ἡγεμονικόν. But this would be a strange position for Chrysippus. In the first place the passage of Gellius is concerned not only with the development of the infant, for whom it might reasonably be argued that, overwhelmingly at first and decreasingly as time goes on and the child begins to develop into a rational creature, pains and pleasures precede judgments. But Gellius reports, as Haynes says, that even in the grown and developed man pleasure and pain precede and are separate from judgment in a number of cases, particularly in what we are calling first-order pleasures.

In order to understand this a little more clearly, we must outline Chrysippus' explanation of the psychological mechanisms of pleasure; and it should be emphasized that there is no reason to believe that there is any basic difference in kind, but only a difference in degree, between first- and second-order pleasures. When the word ἡδονή means a bad pleasure, it is regarded by the Stoics as denoting a πάθος or unhealthy state of the personality.[1] All πάθη are themselves to be defined as impulses (ὁρμαί) which have got out of hand, or as irrational movements of the soul. Similarly the proper emotional states should also be regarded as ὁρμαί, this time, however, of a rational nature. In other words all pleasures, whether acceptable or not, are ὁρμαί of some kind or other. Hence, if we want to know what a pleasure is, we shall have to know what an impulse (ὁρμή) is.

[1] Cf. (for example) SVF III 378, 391.

We are already aware that impulses are movements of the soul.[1] And what are these movements? Chrysippus at least teaches that they are acts of assent. There is no evidence that he thought that some impulses are assents while others are followed (temporally) by acts of assent.[2] It follows, therefore, that both first- and second-order pleasures are, for Chrysippus, assents of the reason and acts of judgment. Hence it cannot be true, as Haynes would have it, that the sensations of pain and pleasure are present to the adult without some kind of judgment and some kind of assent. Haynes has made his mistake because in the case of the child he, and perhaps Gellius or his source, believes that at a very early age, when the human is certainly not rational, he has no kind of rational faculty at all. In fact, what Gellius says is that the child has seeds (*semina*) of reason. On Haynes' theory these seeds would simply be 'potentialities'; there would be no actual reasoning power, and therefore no assenting power, however weak, present in the new-born infant. Perhaps a passage of Seneca makes this interpretation less likely, even for Gellius.[3] For, according to Seneca, nature produces us with a capacity for learning and gives us an imperfect reason (*ratio imperfecta*). In terms of the Stoic vitalism this 'imperfect reason' cannot be identified with merely the potentiality or possibility of reasoning. An imperfect reason must be an actual state of the personality according to which the individual is capable of the weakest possible acts of assent which still remain acts of assent. Now the very first act of the new-born animal, whether human or not, is an impulse towards self-preservation.[4] This is the first disposition (σχέσις) it adopts which is governed by its physical constitution as an animal.[5] In the case of the human being this disposition must, therefore, be a disposition of the *ratio imperfecta*. It is the first state of the per-

---

[1] Stob., *Ecl.* 2, p. 86, 17 W. (*SVF* iii 169).
[2] Stob., *Ecl.* 2, p. 88, 1 W. (*SVF* iii 171); Plut., *SR* 1037F (*SVF* iii 175). Stoics of the post-Posidonian period may have held that there is a temporal sequence: first impulse, then assent; cf. Seneca, *Ep.* 113.18 (*SVF* iii 169); but this is certainly not Chrysippus' view.
[3] Cf. Seneca, *Ep.* 94.29; 107.8; 120.4.
[4] D.L. 7.85 (*SVF* iii 178); Plut., *SR* 1038B (*SVF* iii 179).
[5] Stob., *Ecl.* 2, p. 82, 13 W. (*SVF* iii 141).

sonality or ἡγεμονικόν. It is obvious, of course, that all acts of any human being other than the wise man are inadequate acts of assent. This first childish sense of self-preservation, with which will immediately be associated feelings of pleasure and pain, will be the weakest possible act of assent. The important thing, however, is that the impulse (ὁρμή) will nevertheless involve assent. The Stoics apparently emphasized the distinction between human beings and animals in relation to their attitudes to the basic urge to self-preservation. In the case of rational beings, says Diogenes, reason is the craftsman (τεχνίτης) of the impulse.[1] It is true that Diogenes uses the word ἐπιγίνεται here, a word which could indicate a temporal sequence. It need not do so, however, and that it should not be so taken is shown by Seneca,[2] who observes that, while it is true that every animal has a natural sense of the value of itself, man naturally values himself not merely as an animal but as a rational animal. It is impossible even for the first glimmerings of man's self-awareness to be other than the glimmerings of a rational self-awareness. We may conclude, therefore, that every act of every human being, young or old, mature or immature, is both a rational and a physical act.[3] Hence there can be no such thing as a purely 'bodily' or 'physical' pleasure.

What then are we to make of the passage of Gellius? Obviously that it does not represent the views of the Old Stoa at all. The psychology in fact is that of Posidonius. The whole flavour of the passage is one of a conflict of parts of the soul, reason struggling against the passions. However, let us look at a part of the narrative to see if we can understand what Chrysippus' reaction to it would have been. The problem, we recall, is that the Stoic is groaning. And the question is: Why is the Stoic philosopher compelled to utter groans against his will? Gellius' answer to this is that it is only true that the wise man cannot be compelled on occasions when he has the opportunity to use his reason.[4] There are many actions, such as sweating in hot

---

[1] D.L. 7.86 (*SVF* III 178).
[2] Seneca, *Ep.* 121.14 ff. (*SVF* III 184).
[3] This problem has been discussed on pp. 22–36.
[4] Gellius, 12.5.11.

weather,[1] over which the wise man has no kind of control whatsoever. Here the will, the judgment and the reason do not operate. Man is under the sway of nature and necessity.

It would be very easy for Chrysippus to argue that the involuntary actions mentioned by Gellius are not at all analogous to groaning involuntarily when in pain. The difference is that Gellius pictures the sage struggling against his urge to groan, but no one struggles against the process of sweating in hot weather. Chrysippus would presumably say that sweating in hot weather is part of the nature of man *qua* man. Sweating is natural in the same way that self-preservation is natural. By this he would mean that all men sweat just as all men have the instinct for self-preservation. He would, however, deny that groaning when in pain comes under this same head. Some men might have sufficient fortitude to bear the most excruciating pain in silence. It is a matter of degrees of assent.

Chrysippus would insist that sweating is a psychosomatic activity just as much as anything else. All human activities, without any exceptions whatever, involve some degree of assent. A totally non-voluntary action is an impossibility. This is the only conclusion to be drawn from the large body of evidence which shows that for Chrysippus every action and reaction of the human being is in some sense 'in the ἡγεμονικόν'.[2] It is the consistent opinion of Chrysippus that the soul has eight 'parts', the five senses, speech, sex and reason (ἡγεμονικόν).[3] Since the ἡγεμονικόν is involved in every activity, every activity must be rational at least in an imperfect way. There are, therefore, no entirely involuntary actions.

If this assessment of Chrysippus' position is correct, it should be noticed that he rejects the distinction between voluntary and involuntary movements and behavioural symptoms like sweating which is drawn by Aristotle. In an important passage of the *De Motu Animalium*, to which attention has recently been drawn by Furley,[4] Aristotle speaks of movements such as the

---

[1] Some of the other 'necessary' actions mentioned, such as being terrified at thunder, are rather strange in the wise man!
[2] Cf. D.L. 7.159 (*SVF* II 837). [3] *SVF* II 823–911.
[4] Furley, *Two Studies* 220–1; Aristotle, *De Motu Animalium* 703 b 5 ff.

beating of the heart or the erection of the penis as involuntary because the bodily activity takes place without the command of the mind (οὐ μέντοι κελεύσαντος τοῦ νοῦ). Chrysippus' view would be that, although the mind may not command, it must assent (in the case of the heart or the penis) because such movements are natural and thus themselves manifestations of the *logos*. For Chrysippus the rejection of the Aristotelian theory of involuntary motion is the only alternative to breaking up the personality into actually, not merely conceptually, separate parts or faculties. And then, he would hold, how could these parts be joined together? If there were no ἡγεμονικόν, it would be necessary to invent one.

Furley has pointed out, however, that Aristotle's account of the involuntary is not completed in the *De Motu*. There is a passage in the *De Anima* which must have delighted Chrysippus.[1] 'The mind', says Aristotle, 'often thinks of something that arouses fear or pleasure, but it does not give the order to be afraid, but the heart moves, and if the object is pleasurable, some other part' (that is, in view of the *De Motu* passage, the penis). This text is clearly much to the Stoic taste. We have the moral imperative (οὐ κελεύει δὲ φοβεῖσθαι), which would be involved in second-order pains and pleasures, and the Chrysippean view that, although the mind does not command, it thinks of something painful or pleasurable. Perhaps the difference between the Stoics and Aristotle here is terminological. Aristotle seems to be calling reactions in which the mind thinks but does not command 'involuntary', while Chrysippus' view is that, if the mind is involved in any way (however 'imperfectly'), there is a degree of assent.

There is a passage of Diogenes Laertius, who quotes from Chrysippus, which bears out our interpretation of Chrysippus' view with almost paradoxical emphasis.[2] The first thing that is appropriate (οἰκεῖον) to every animal is its own nature and the awareness of this nature. The word used for awareness is striking; it is συνείδησις. Cicero, in a parallel passage, translates this as *sensus sui*,[3] which is almost inevitably going to

[1] *De Anima* 432 b 30–2.   [2] D.L. 7.85 (*SVF* iii 182).
[3] Cic., *De Fin.* 3.16 (*SVF* iii 182).

43

appear in English as consciousness or awareness of self. A similar phrase (*constitutionis suae sensus*) is given by Seneca with reference not only to man but to all animals.[1] Although animals and new-born infants are not conscious of themselves in the obvious sense of the phrase, Chrysippus was apparently prepared to argue that they have some rudiments (*semina*) of this consciousness. Consciousness, therefore, is in some degree essential for animal life and *a fortiori* for human life. There could hardly be a stronger affirmation that in some sense all human acts are partially mental acts, even the most primitive. Thus there can be no non-voluntary act in the sense of an act performed without the operation of the ἡγεμονικόν. It must follow, as we have argued before, that despite the Posidonian Stoicism of Gellius, for the Old Stoa all pleasures and pains, even first-order pleasures and pains, are acts of assent.

Before leaving this matter, however, we should observe that some scholars have tried to evade this solution by emending the text of Diogenes. Pohlenz was apparently the first to argue that instead of συνείδησις we should read συναίσθησις.[2] There is no manuscript evidence for this change, and it is not noticed (or perhaps is unnoticed) by the recent Oxford editor. Pohlenz' best ground for the change is that, as we have seen, Cicero uses the phrase *sensus sui* as an equivalent; and this usage is paralleled elsewhere. However, even if the reading συναίσθησις were correct, there is no reason to believe that our view of Chrysippus' theory is affected. Plutarch, in a most illuminating passage, defines οἰκείωσις as a perception and grasp of what is akin (αἴσθησις καὶ ἀντίληψις).[3] Even if it is claimed that the word αἴσθησις does not imply an act of assent, no such claim is possible about ἀντίληψις. The word is admittedly used both for perception and for thought, but it represents an activity (perception) which is specifically contrasted with bare passive sensation.[4] If then Chrysippus, in the passage quoted by Diogenes, actually wrote συναίσθησις and not συνείδησις, the

[1] Cf. *Ep.* 121.5 (*SVF* III 184).
[2] Pohlenz, *Grundfragen* 7, *Die Stoa* 2.65. Pohlenz' view is accepted by Schwyzer, 'Bewusst und Unbewusst', 354–5, 357–8.
[3] Plut., *SR* 1038B (*SVF* II 724).   [4] By Ariston, *SVF* I 377.

apprehension, the mental act, must still have been in his mind. Plutarch's version would be the fuller formulation. However, considering the lack of manuscript evidence, there is little reason to change Diogenes' text; versions of Stoicism offered by Cicero or Hierocles or Musonius or Seneca or others produced by Pohlenz must not be regarded as providing evidence for the exact *words* Chrysippus may have used in works other than those with which these other writers are themselves concerned.

We are now in a position to determine the relation of the wise man to what we have called first-order pleasures. He will experience such pleasures provided they are not called forth by immoral objects. This is the true sense of ἀπάθεια. The sage is insensible to immoral (and therefore irrational) emotions. A modern analogy may help to make this clearer. It is apparently possible to cure various kinds of sexual pervert by putting them in front of a screen and flashing on to the screen pictures of those objects which arouse their sexual appetites. If they respond physically to the object on the screen, they experience an electric shock. Gradually, as this 'treatment' continues, they associate the particular sexual object with the pain of the electric shock. Hence the appetite is inhibited and eventually disappears. The Stoic wise man is in a similar position. Chrysippus regarded adultery as unnatural;[1] hence, while the sight of someone else's wife in the nude might have an erotic effect on the ordinary man, it would have no such effect on the sage. What this means in effect is that in the wise man the distinction between first- and second-order pleasures, with which we have been working up to this point, will be diminished almost to vanishing point. The wise man is far more in control of his pleasures than the ordinary mortal; and in so far as none of them will be pleasures over immoral objects, he will be entirely in control. He will not be in conscious control of all his feelings of pleasure, but will have a kind of veto power over them, so that he will automatically reject those that are bad. The pleasures which he will actually feel will be rational states of the emotions, or χαραί. This is the word which the Stoics prefer for the pleasures of the sage, but there are certain passages, some of them

[1] Stob., *Ecl.* 2, p. 93, 5 W. (*SVF* III 421).

discussed by Haynes, which suggest that at some times at least they are prepared to use ἡδονή as a virtual equivalent, provided, of course, that it bears its general and neutral sense of 'pleasure', not its technical Stoic sense of 'irrational impulse'.

This brings us to the problem of the metaphysics and status of pleasure in general. According to Diogenes Laertius pleasure (ἡδονή) is an experience which supervenes on a natural activity (ἐπιγέννημα).[1] Elsewhere Diogenes records the Stoic view that joy (χαρά), the rational pleasure of the good, supervenes on virtue, while conversely misery and the like supervene on vice.[2] The Aristotelian influence on this position has often been observed.[3] Now, in his dispute with the Epicureans and other hedonistic philosophers, Chrysippus was apparently prepared to argue that pleasure cannot be a good, and that some pleasures are disgraceful (αἰσχραί).[4] If Diogenes reports Chrysippus' words precisely, he actually said, 'There are *also* disgraceful pleasures'. And the words entail that some pleasures are not disgraceful—a view which, as we have seen, Chrysippus in fact held. Whether Diogenes reports the actual words of Chrysippus or not, our previous argument suggests that Chrysippus distinguished at least between acceptable and unacceptable pleasures.

Haynes thinks that Zeno and Cleanthes place pleasure in the class of what is indifferent in respect of good and evil.[5] This is a little misleading; what they must have placed in this class are good pleasures. Pleasures of the kind which Chrysippus calls 'disgraceful' arise from vicious and inappropriate activities, and are, as we have seen, supervenient upon vice. The details of Zeno's view are difficult to ascertain, but he must have spoken of certain pleasures as indifferent morally.[6] He probably thought of those which accompany good or appropriate actions as indifferents possessed of only slight value,[7] though it is just

---

[1] D.L. 7.85 (*SVF* III 178). [2] D.L. 7.94 (*SVF* III 76).
[3] E.g. by Haynes, *op. cit.* 414, and by Long, 'Aristotle's Legacy', 80.
[4] D.L. 7.103 (*SVF* III 156). [5] Haynes, *op. cit.* 413.
[6] Gellius, 9.5.5 (*SVF* I 195); Stob., *Ecl.* 2, p. 57, 18 W. (*SVF* I 190).
[7] Sextus says that it is the orthodox view of οἱ ἀπὸ τῆς Στοᾶς (*Adv. Math.* 11.73 = *SVF* III 155) that pleasure is ἀδιάφορον and οὐ προηγμένον. This might mean that it had slight value or no value. D.L. 7.102 (*SVF* III 117)

possible that he regarded them as 'preferred'. He must have regarded the pleasures supervenient on inappropriate actions as vicious.

Cleanthes' position is clearer, and apparently caused comment. In his view pleasures (again presumably those which are innocuous) are not only indifferent in respect of good and evil; they have no value whatever and are non-natural (μήτε κατὰ φύσιν αὐτὴν εἶναι μήτε ἀξίαν ἔχειν ἐν τῷ βίῳ).[1] This is certainly more than an explanation of Zeno's position. Cleanthes holds that the threefold division of what is neither good nor evil is also threefold in relation to nature. Things may be natural, non-natural or unnatural. Pleasure, which as an ἐπιγέννημα is, according to Cleanthes, like a cosmetic, falls under the heading of non-natural. That would seem to imply that it has no relation to what the ordinary man will want to do or not to do—a most extraordinary proposal.

Cleanthes' description of pleasure as a cosmetic probably helps to explain his odd position. He obviously wished to emphasize the fact that pleasure always accompanies human activity; that it cannot, therefore, be called a human activity itself; that only direct activities can properly be called natural or unnatural; above all, that 'natural' things are in some sense to be preferred and sought out, whereas it is too dangerous to seek out pleasure. Chrysippus is specifically quoted as saying that the citizens of the best state will not act 'for the sake of pleasure'.[2] It is certain that Cleanthes would have subscribed to that.

Chrysippus' general position, however, is much more realistic. While agreeing with his predecessors that pleasure is indifferent in respect of good and evil, he certainly thought of it as natural and may have put it in the class of things to be preferred.[3] How he could have maintained this while still arguing that it is not a proper motive for action is made clear by Stobaeus, who records

would suggest the former, and this is confirmed by the fact that Sextus seems to attribute a stricter position to Cleanthes than to οἱ ἀπὸ τῆς Στοᾶς (possibly including Zeno). For problems about things preferred, things of slight value, natural things and non-natural things see below, pp. 102–7.

[1] *SVF* iii 155. [2] Plut., *SR* 1044 B (*SVF* iii 706).

[3] D.L. 7.102 (*SVF* iii 117). Contrary evidence, however, is perhaps provided for Chrysippus by *SVF* iii 136, 154, 155.

the Stoic view that of things which are natural (and therefore possibly preferred) some are preferred for their own sakes and others for the sake of other things.[1] Pleasure would fall into the latter class. Chrysippus may have been unwilling to neglect the obvious fact that pleasure is an incentive to the achievement of both what has value and what has not. Hence good pleasures are to be sought because they encourage us to seek the valuable (or preferred) things which bring them about. At any rate, by removing pleasure from the class of the non-natural and putting it into the class of the natural, Chrysippus is able to admit the obvious fact that 'nature' (in this case living things) aims at pleasure,[2] while still denying the Epicurean view that pleasure is the first natural aim of man.[3]

Chrysippus seems to have settled the matter of whether some pleasures are natural, but there was apparently still a certain hankering after the more extreme view of Cleanthes. Hence we find Archedemus admitting that pleasures are natural, but saying that they have no value, that they supervene like hair under the armpits.[4] This is a suggestion which could have led to great difficulties within the general framework of Stoic theory; and our evidence does not give any indication as to how (or if) Archedemus would have met them. The burden of what he says is that 'good' pleasures, and hair under the armpits, though natural, have no importance for man. It would seem that this is an attempt to assimilate such ἐπιγεννήματα to the status of necessary consequences, things that exist κατὰ παρ-ακολούθησιν, like Aristotelian 'accidentals'.[5] But although some

---

[1] Stob., *Ecl.* 2, p. 82, 21 W. (*SVF* III 142). Cf. D.L. 7.107 (*SVF* III 135).

[2] D.L. 7.148 (*SVF* II 1132).

[3] D.L. 7.85 (*SVF* III 179); Cic., *De Fin.* 3.17 (*SVF* III 154).

[4] Sext. Emp., *Adv. Math.* 11.73 (*SVF* III 155).

[5] The equation between ἐπιγεννήματα and τὰ κατ' ἐπακολούθησιν (= τὰ κατὰ παρακολούθησιν) is explicitly made by Marcus Aurelius, 6.36 (cf. 3.3; 7.75; 9.1; 9.28). It is possible that ἐπακολούθησις is a term of later Stoicism, replacing παρακολούθησις. (Cf. *SVF* II 318 from Origen's *De Oratione* for ἐπακολουθητική and Aulus Gellius, 7.1.10 (*SVF* II 1170) for παρακολούθησις (*sequella quaedam necessaria*).) For natural things without purpose cf. Cic., *De Natura Deorum* 2.167 (*Magna di curant, parva neglegunt*); Seneca, *De Prov.* 3.1 and *Ep.* 74.20. According to Chrysippus God does not know everything (*SVF* II 1183, cf. 1178).

of the Stoic 'absolute indifferents' might be so assimilated, it is possible that Chrysippus would have thought that both pleasure and hair under the armpits have a purpose. At any rate the purpose of pleasure would be to encourage the performance of καθήκοντα.

According to Diogenes Laertius, as we have seen, pleasure seems to be classed with things preferred (7.102). The word used is ἡδονή. We do not find the word χαρά in any similar class list, but that is unimportant. Clearly the ἡδονή which is to be preferred, or at the least is natural, is the pleasure which accompanies either καθήκοντα or moral action (κατορθώματα). Ἡδονή is being used in a general sense; and doubtless χαρά is to be understood in this context as one of its species. Pleasures then are of various kinds, depending on the activities which they accompany. They range from the 'joys' of the wise man to the disgraceful pleasures of the vicious. They provide an index of moral character; for a man will show himself in his true colours when he feels various kinds of pleasures. Let us now turn to the opposite pole and consider the question of pain. We have already seen that pains are felt by the wise man, though, of course, he does not admit that they are bad. But an immediate difference between pleasures and pains should be noticed. Although there are rational states of pleasure (χαραί), and these are an attribute of the sage, there is no corresponding state of pain.[1] This must be considered further.

Some kinds of pain, like some pleasures, are mistaken judgments or the results of mistaken judgments. Pain in this sense is defined as an irrational contraction (συστολή) of the soul,[2] just as pleasures are called irrational buoyancies (ἐπάρσεις) of the soul. But while it makes sense to oppose a rational buoyancy of the soul to an irrational, it is understandable that the Stoics could not treat a 'rational contraction' of the soul as a εὐπάθεια. It would have been unnecessarily paradoxical, not to say foolish, of the Stoics to argue that any pain is *per se* even a preferred state. It may be preferred if it leads to specific advantages, but not *per se*. Nor, obviously, can pain be any kind of natural

---

[1] Cic., *Tusc.* 4.14 (*SVF* III 438).
[2] *SVF* III 391. Cf. μείωσις, *SVF* III 463.

accompaniment of virtuous activity, as are the proper kinds of pleasure. But while it is easy to see why there is no εὐπάθεια which is pain, it is not so easy to see what explanation the Stoics would give of the pain which they admit the wise man feels. Clearly this pain is not irrational in the sense that it can overcome the reason. But is it parallel to pleasure in that it is an act of assent? In a certain sense this must be the case, for the wise man admits that the pain he feels really is painful. The difference from pleasure, however, is that, whereas in the case of pleasure assent can be withheld to such an extent that the wise man will not necessarily experience even bodily pleasures under the same circumstances as the fool, he will still experience many of the same pains. Clearly all the same things will not necessarily pain him. He could not be pained, as the vicious man would be, by being thwarted in his intention to commit a crime, but he will feel a weight which is dropped on his toe in exactly the same way as his vicious counterpart. But if this pain itself, though understood and accepted by the wise man, is nevertheless a 'contraction' of the soul, are the Stoics not still in trouble? Why does the wise man assent to the contraction of his soul?

There is no answer to this specific question in the texts available to us, but the general lines of the Stoic reply are clear enough. The problem is one aspect of the general problem of the suffering of the good man; and the Stoic answer to it is a part of their general answer to questions about the origin of evil. They would say that things go by contraries;[1] that there cannot be pleasure without pain; that the existence of local pain, even to the good, is justified by the 'economy' or necessary arrangement of the world.[2] Evil happenings cannot be entirely erased; that is a matter of brute fact.[3] Presumably, therefore, we must conclude on the rather unsatisfactory note that the sage will accept 'contractions' of the soul, provided they do not become irrational, when he has to. Indeed the experience of pain itself must be regarded as an assent to such a contraction.

[1] Cf. Gellius, 7.1 (*SVF* II 1169).
[2] Cf. Plut., *SR* 1050E (*SVF* II 1176); cf. *SVF* II 1181.
[3] Plut., *SR* 1051A (*SVF* II 1182).

This does not mean that we should accept the picture given by Aulus Gellius of the Stoic sage engaged in a struggle against groaning as an authentic representation of the views of the Old Stoa. That picture is painted by an adherent of the theory of a struggle in the soul; he is a Panaetian (or Posidonian) Stoic. In the view of the founders of Stoicism there will be no moral struggle in the soul of the wise man. All his reactions to external stimuli will be rational. Only the postulant, the would-be virtuous man, will be in trouble of spirit. He will have to overcome the temptation to misvalue the pains he feels. Plutarch, apparently quoting from Chrysippus' work *On Justice*, presents the orthodox picture.[1] From what he says we can see what kind of 'contraction of soul' the wise man's pain must be. Chrysippus admits, says Plutarch, that there are some fears and pains and deceits which harm us but do not make us worse. This means that the contraction of the soul of the wise man is not a moral contraction. Naturally the Stoics did not think that all assents are assents with a moral flavour. Assent to pain, provided that it is only the mental awareness of pain and not an assent to the proposition that pain is either good or bad, is a non-moral assent.

At first sight there seems to be a further problem and a further variation in the Stoic attitudes to pain and pleasure respectively. We have suggested that the wise man can shut off certain pleasures altogether. He will not feel pleasure, even first-order pleasure, in many cases where the ordinary man will. Surely, however, he will always feel pain like anyone else. But in fact this misses the point. There are some pains, 'physical' pains particularly, which he will feel like anyone else; but many things which pain the ordinary man will not pain the wise.

How far do these conclusions about pain modify the interpretation we offered of the Stoic view of all human activity as psychosomatic activity? They do not modify it at all. Let us take the case of the wise man feeling the pain of the weight dropped on his toe. Is this pain to be regarded as totally non-voluntary? Apparently the Stoics did not think so. Pain cannot be felt without the activity of the ἡγεμονικόν. The ἡγεμονικόν

---

[1] Plut., *CN* 1070E (*SVF* III 455).

assents that it is painful. But what of the fact that no human being could not feel the pain? It is similar to the fact that all human beings sweat in hot sunshine. It is an act of man *qua* man. Being men, we cannot help assenting to the pain, that is, admitting that it is painful; but that assent is a matter of in-difference.[1] What we are not compelled to do is assent to more than that it is painful. Such assent, which involves a moral de-cision, is up to us. Whether Chrysippus really used the word 'semi-slavery', which is attributed to him, we do not know.[2] But the word conveys the point he wants to make very well. It is often natural to assent to what is morally irrelevant; and, since it is natural, it is, in Stoic terminology, in our power. It would be unnatural to assent to moral evil. Hence we cannot be forced to do it. Hence such assents are in our power.

The conclusions of this discussion of the Stoic attitude to pleasure and pain are important for a proper understanding of the 'feel' of Stoicism as a system. We have in English the word 'stoical', and it tends to vary in meaning from 'being able to put up with anything' to something akin to insensibility. The Stoics never proposed insensibility, or anything like it, as an ideal, but they were thought to have proposed it even in an-tiquity, when the original meaning of ἀπάθεια had become ob-scured. According to Taurus, in Aulus Gellius, 'not only in my opinion, but in the opinion of some of the wise men among the Stoics, such as Panaetius, insensibility (ἀναλγησία) and ἀπάθεια are disapproved and rejected'.[3] This is a curious state-ment, since it seems to equate ἀναλγησία and ἀπάθεια. Whether such an equation was made by Panaetius is impossible to say, but if it was, it was nonetheless mistaken. For the Old Stoa, the wise man feels pleasures and pains; what he does not feel are those pleasures and pains which are (the result of) mistaken judgments. In relation to these only he is ἀπαθής. If Panaetius misunderstood the original Stoic sense of the word it was prob-ably because, like Posidonius, though to a lesser degree, he had

---

[1] Assent—presumably non-moral assent—is listed among the totally in-differents by Stobaeus (*SVF* III 136).
[2] Cf. *SVF* II 978.
[3] Aulus Gellius, 12.5.10.

not grasped the implications of early Stoic psychology, with its insistence on the psychosomatic nature of man.[1]

In modern times the problem has been further obscured, as we have seen. On top of the long established and misinformative use of the word 'stoical', we have Pohlenz' too frequently accepted thesis that Zeno's system was formulated in conscious opposition to the views of Epicurus. Hence, it is argued, while Epicurus is some kind of hedonist, Zeno reacted strongly, even grotesquely, against hedonism. But there were hedonists and anti-hedonists before either Epicurus or Zeno, and far more sense will emerge if, instead of looking at Zeno as the opponent of Epicurus, we rather see them both forming their own views against a common background in which the thought of Aristotle is the dominant factor. In view of the fact that the doctrine of pleasure as an ἐπιγέννημα is so close to Aristotelian positions expressed in the tenth book of the *Nicomachean Ethics*, it is most unlikely that it was worked out in conscious opposition to anybody. It is in their doctrine of πρῶτα κατὰ φύσιν that the Stoics set about contradicting Epicurus specifically. Since for the Stoics pleasure is already defined as 'supervenient' or parasitic on activity, it would have cost them little time and trouble to relate it to their theories on what is natural. For them pleasure must be, at best, a concomitant of what is primarily in accordance with nature. Zeno probably thought that Aristotle had invalidated the Epicurean solution in advance.

[1] Panaetius certainly seems to have held the un-Chrysippean view that some ὁρμαί do not involve assent. Cf. the chapter on Panaetius, below, pp. 182-4.

4

CYNICISM AND STOICISM

It was well known in antiquity that there were close connections between Cynicism and Stoicism. In the Roman period of the Stoic movement we find a teacher like Epictetus tending to equate the life of the good man with that of the Cynic. In this, as in much else, Epictetus was going behind the Stoicism of Panaetius and Posidonius and returning, in part, to the origins of the school. It will be the purpose of this chapter to consider those aspects of Cynicism which influenced the Stoics and to suggest that the Cynics were raising serious problems even where giving unsatisfactory answers, as well as to show where the Stoics, particularly Zeno and Chrysippus, modified Cynic teaching to fit it in with their own much more sophisticated theories. There is a considerable problem about our evidence for Cynicism, most of which comes from collections of stories selected by Diogenes Laertius about Antisthenes, Diogenes, Crates and the rest. Though we shall, therefore, suggest that certain views are to be attributed to one or other of the Cynic leaders, our primary task is to show that there was a specifically Cynic attitude towards the world, and that Zeno knew what it was. We shall then be better able to estimate his reaction to it.[1]

Diogenes Laertius claims that both the Cynic and Stoic schools were influenced by Antisthenes.[2] Antisthenes himself had been a pupil of Socrates much impressed by his determination of moral character. If Diogenes' account is to be relied on in general—and there is still no good reason for not relying on it, for it tallies in essentials with the portrait in Xenophon's *Symposium*—Antisthenes developed a kind of Sophistic antithesis between the life of virtue and life according to the laws of the city into which one has been born.[3] It is a man's behaviour that

---

[1] For Cynicism in general see the sometimes inaccurate work of Dudley, *A History of Cynicism*; cf. von Fritz, 'Quellenuntersuchungen'.
[2] D.L. 6.15 and 19.   [3] D.L. 6.11.

matters, not what he says or what he knows. The attitude to the city is partially Socratic—Socrates refused to obey what he thought of as unjust commands of the Athenian government—but seems to differ in that Socrates, as the *Crito* makes plain, held that, although it may be right for a man to break the laws if he thinks them unjust, it is one of the consequences of citizenship that he must accept the penalties prescribed by the laws if he chooses to break them. There may be only a shade of difference between this position and what seems to underlie the attitude of Antisthenes, but that shade represented the thin end of the wedge which was driven in further so that a position was reached that the established laws and the law of virtue are enemies. That is the Cynic position. We are not clear how far Antisthenes advanced towards it, but the view of the ancients, who bracketed him with Diogenes, suggests that he progressed a fair distance in that direction.

If it is city life and its conventions which are most dangerous to the life of virtue, we should expect to find Antisthenes attacking various of the established habits and norms of that life. Accordingly we find in the tradition the statement that, when he was looking for examples of hardihood, he cited Heracles and Cyrus, disregarding the fact that one was a Greek and the other a 'barbarian'.[1] Among the writings attributed to him is one on freedom and slavery, a theme beloved of Diogenes, as we shall see.[2] Whether this was a genuine work of Antisthenes matters little: there is no reason to think that it was not the kind of subject with which he was concerned. Finally there is the social problem with which all the Cynics were much engaged and which also engaged the attention of Zeno, the problem that had already been mooted by Plato in his *Republic* and mocked by Aristophanes in his *Ecclesiazusae*, the problem of the relation between men and women in an ideal society.

Like the majority of Greek philosophers, Antisthenes was suspicious of physical pleasure. The remark 'I would rather be mad than feel physical pleasure' is attributed to him;[3] and he probably held that pleasure is the principal obstacle to that

---

[1] D.L. 6.2. [2] D.L. 6.16.
[3] D.L. 6.3.

absence of feeling (τὸ ἀπαθές) which was his ideal.[1] Yet he was not opposed to sexual intercourse and said that men should make love to women who would thank them for it.[2] It is not clear how far this is the origin of the much clearer and more obviously radical position of Diogenes, but, in so far as it seems to mean that women's preferences are important, it tallies well enough with the view, reported elsewhere,[3] that the virtue of women is the same as that of men. In one matter, however, he did not offer the full-blown Cynic position; for Antisthenes marriage is desirable for the sake of children.[4] If Antisthenes actually favoured marriage (γάμος) for the sake of having children, it probably means that he had not reached the stage of regarding city law and the law of virtue as radically opposed; for what made a γάμος a full marriage, as distinct from a union between two parties, was precisely that its major function was to provide legitimate children to be citizens of the state. Marriage was the fundamental example of an institution directed towards the life of the *polis* rather than the life of the parties, particularly the women. Sexual intercourse could not by itself constitute a marriage, even though the word γάμος is occasionally used to refer to intercourse only. Marriage was an institution designed for childbearing, and as such it was a civic institution. Diogenes probably attacked it as such; it looks as though Antisthenes was more conventional.[5] However, although his attitude to marriage looks conventional, of more relevance from our present standpoint is the attitude towards women, presumably women other than wives, which we mentioned above. Intercourse is with those who will be gratified; and in

---

[1] D.L. 6.2. The origin of the concept of ἀπάθεια as the end of life is unknown. It is alluded to by Aristotle, and the commentators have made various guesses as to which thinkers he has in mind. Speusippus has been mentioned (on the basis of a reference in Clement of Alexandria), and Antisthenes also. Doubtless the concept was already a commonplace in the middle and late fourth century. Cf. *E.E.* 1222a 3 and Gauthier and Jolif's note to *N.E.* 1104b 24, as well as *Phys.* 246b 19–20, *Top.* 4.125b 22–3; Ruether, *Die sittliche Forderung der Apatheia.*

[2] D.L. 6.3.　　　　　　　　　　　　[3] D.L. 6.12.

[4] D.L. 6.11.

[5] On Athenian marriage see Jones, *The Law and Legal Theory of the Greeks* 176, 186–7.

the case of homosexual affairs the wise man will love those whom he alone will recognize as worthy of love.[1]

While reflecting on the idea that we should love those who are worthy and those who will be grateful, we become involved with what was probably the basic principle of Antisthenes' ethics, the principle of the independence of the wise man. Virtue is adequate by itself for happiness; all we need is the strength of character required for the good life. If we have this, we are not ruled by external demands. But Antisthenes does not seem to cut the wise man off completely; he recognizes value in the objects of life and thinks that the wise man's actions should be governed by that recognition; he even thinks that the gratitude of women is worth having! So although his wise man may be rather like an isolated island, he is not absolutely cut off from his fellows. Eros is a bond between the good—a bond which will be considered by Zeno. Already in Antisthenes there seem to be the seeds of the concept of the kingdom of the wise, who are linked together by a mutual respect.

It should now be re-emphasized that what has been said about Antisthenes is not as reliable as could be wished. We are entirely dependent on the doxographical tradition, much of which cannot be given great credence. But we can allow a likelihood to the general picture. With Diogenes, the first Cynic properly so-called, we are still involved with doxographical problems, but the general impression left by Diogenes' words, and still more by his actions, is remarkably well attested throughout antiquity. When we come to Crates, the pupil of Diogenes and teacher of Zeno, some of whose writings survive in fragmentary form, we find that the portrait of a Cynic remains substantially unchanged.

The aim of the Cynics is to live 'according to virtue'.[2] Like the Stoics after them they classed all activities as virtuous, vicious or indifferent.[3] Differing from Zeno, however, as we shall see, they regarded everything indifferent as totally indifferent. Only virtue should be aimed at, only vice rejected. As for the

---

[1] D.L. 6.11 (the last sentence presumably refers to relations between men) and 6.12.

[2] D.L. 6.104.   [3] D.L. 6.105.

rest, it does not matter what the wise man does. However, to say that the good is life according to virtue does not get us much (if at all) beyond a circular proposition. And the principal difficulty in our understanding of Cynicism is to know what virtuous acts are. Again and again we find accounts of what the wise man will not be concerned with, the sham values of everyday life; but it is very difficult to find any account of a course of action which is positively good. Doubtless the Cynics claimed that it is good to be completely independent of one's society (αὐτάρκης), but what are the acts of a completely independent man? This is the problem of what the Stoics called the material of virtue.[1]

Diogenes himself claimed that freedom of speech and freedom of action are the most important things in life.[2] This freedom has been interpreted by a recent scholar as freedom from all restraint whatsoever; that is an understandable, but slightly misleading, explanation.[3] It is probably true that Diogenes thought that the wise man could say almost anything, and that he could (and would) do all kinds of things which the conventional public (the fools) would feel inhibited about. But clearly, however much he exaggerated his utterances about freedom, Diogenes would not have the wise man say that vice is good, even though he is perfectly free to say that public masturbation, for example, is totally indifferent morally. Diogenes is not an amoralist, as Baldry comes near to describing him. The freedom of his wise man is a freedom to act in accordance with what is right and to say what is right, regardless of any other considerations than his own judgment. Yet it is easy to see why Diogenes looks like an amoralist, indeed why for the same reasons he was called a 'dog' in antiquity. It is because he continually explained what is not vicious, because natural, while never giving details about what is virtuous. It might be argued that his real opinion was that virtue is simply the complete independence of the self; but even that would probably not be a full description of what Diogenes intended, for he seems to have thought that the completely independent man would act *qua* independent man in

---

[1] See pp. 5–10 above.   [2] D.L. 6.69 and 71.
[3] Baldry, *Unity of Mankind* 106.

certain specific ways in particular situations. But we do not know whether he worked this out very seriously, or, for that matter, whether Crates did either. What we do know is that this weakness in Cynicism found a ready critic in Zeno. Diogenes tells us that all our actions must be governed by virtue, by a recognition of what is good, but he does not tell us what virtue is.

The insistence on the importance of freedom and free choices in word and deed comes out very strikingly in Diogenes' apparent obsession with the contrast between free men (whom he seems to have called simply 'men') and slaves.[1] It comes out also in his rejection of city life. The wise man does not inhabit an ordinary city or respect ordinary laws.[2] He has no use for the trappings of civilization like weapons or currency.[3] He is a citizen only of the universe, not of any of the cities of men.[4] It is certain that, when Diogenes called himself a 'cosmopolitan', he meant it negatively; he did not belong to any particular city.[5] Crates later claimed to share common citizenship with Diogenes, though he was from Thebes and Diogenes from Sinope, on the grounds that they both belonged to the kingdom of the wise.[6]

It is the mark of the wise man to reject the conventions of the city. We have seen this trait in Antisthenes; it was developed further by Diogenes, who was prepared to practice what he preached to a much greater extent. Cities were ridden with taboos, particularly in the sphere of sexual morality. Diogenes

---

[1] D.L. 6.33, 43, 60.
[2] Philodemus, Περὶ Στωικῶν (in Crönert, *Kolotes und Menedemos*), col. 10. Cf. D.L. 6.38.
[3] Philodemus, *op. cit.* col. 14; Athen., 4.159 c.
[4] D.L. 6.63 and 72.
[5] There has been much dispute about whether Diogenes' social theories were incorporated in an authentic work called *Politeia*. Chrysippus certainly thought such a work existed, but in antiquity there was already considerable doubt (D.L. 6.80). The best discussion is that of von Fritz (*op. cit.* 55–7), who is in favour of authenticity. See also Baldry, *Unity of Mankind* 102–3. Whether such a work existed or not need have no bearing on the question of the thought of Diogenes itself, though I am inclined to agree with von Fritz that Diogenes did in fact write a *Politeia* and that later 'friends' of Diogenes wished to reject it because of its 'scandalous' contents. Late Stoics often wished to reject Zeno's *Politeia* also.
[6] D.L. 6.93.

set a Cynic fashion for public masturbation,[1] and regarded incest as a matter of indifference.[2] The eating of human flesh, he also argued, is not in any way objectionable *per se*.[3]

The wise man is totally independent of his fellows; that is why masturbation is permissible, since it relieves the sage of the need for outside help in satisfying the demands of nature. *Fiat amica manus*, as Martial put it. But Diogenes also held that sexual intercourse should be a matter of agreement between the parties concerned. If the man can persuade the woman, that is all that is required.[4] Presumably here he is talking about the activities of the wise, for the point is that there is no such thing for Diogenes as a civic marriage. The only marriage he recognizes is that by mutual consent to intercourse. Men should be allowed to have intercourse with many women—women should be 'in common'—and presumably with just as many, and as few, as they wish. Diogenes naturally also permits homosexual relations, though the suggestion of Philodemus, that the Cynics (admittedly he does not say Diogenes specifically) held that boys who do not agree to homosexual relations should be compelled to do so,[5] is probably a distortion of what can be called the Cynic ideal of free will. The Cynics argued that women should be 'in common', which their opponents may have distorted into the view that any man can have intercourse with anyone he likes (regardless of the wishes of others);[6] but this is contrary to the evidence of Diogenes Laertius, who tells us that the Cynic view is that, at least among the wise, free choice of the parties is the basis of every action and every relationship.

Diogenes' view is not merely that men should have intercourse with anyone they can persuade; he clearly holds that the same rights are possessed by women, a far more revolutionary position. Doubtless, like Antisthenes, he held that virtue is the same for men and for women, and therefore their choices of action must be similarly identical. This choice, the distinguishing mark of the free man—or rather of the man, since without it

---

[1] Cf. the evidence listed by Zeller, *Phil. der Gr.* 2¹.322–3.

[2] Cf. Philodemus, *op. cit.* col. 11.   [3] D.L. 6.73.

[4] D.L. 6.72.   [5] Philodemus, *op. cit.* col. 11.

[6] Philodemus, *op. cit.* col. 9.

we are subhuman slaves—is to be governed by reason. If a man cannot live by reason, he had better hang himself.[1]

Diogenes' teachings about sexual relations are the key to various apparent inconsistencies which have been detected in his outlook. Baldry thinks that the 'philanthropy', the concern for mankind, attributed to Crates and to some extent to Diogenes himself, conflicts with the barren doctrine of complete self-sufficiency.[2] But a distinction, of which Diogenes was probably aware, must be drawn. The wise man has dealings with other wise men, who are his fellow citizens, but he does not *depend* on them. Plutarch rightly remarks that Diogenes, like Zeno, recognizes concord as a factor in the ideal society.[3] Cynic self-sufficiency does not make the wise man an isolated individual;[4] what it makes him is an independent individual, able to enter upon relationships based on mutual freedom with other individuals. And clearly the Cynics believe that the basic human urge to sexuality provides an opportunity for such free relationships. Naturally the Cynic is to be master of this urge, as of all others.

Scholars have sometimes attempted to contrast Diogenes with his principal successor Crates.[5] The contrast seems to be much overdrawn, certainly in the matters with which we are presently concerned. The famous Cynic marriage of Crates and Hipparchia is an excellent example of the precepts of Diogenes being applied in the area of personal relationships.[6] For that reason it is worth detailed consideration. The account given by Diogenes Laertius is that Hipparchia fell in love with Crates and insisted on being 'given to him'. When her parents failed to dissuade her and she threatened to commit suicide if she was thwarted, they asked Crates to dissuade her himself. He tried to do so and failed. He told her that, if she was to be his partner, she would have to share the Cynic life. She chose to do so, and, as Diogenes puts it, 'travelled around with her husband and had intercourse publicly and went out to dinners'.[7] It is clear

---

[1] D.L. 6.24.   [2] Baldry, *Unity of Mankind* 111.
[3] Plut., *Lycurgus* 31–2.
[4] As Baldry wrongly remarks, *Unity of Mankind* 108.
[5] E.g. Dudley, *op. cit.* 43.   [6] D.L. 6.96–7.
[7] Diogenes' phrase ἐν τῷ φανερῷ συνεγίνετο certainly refers to sexual intercourse. Apuleius (*Florida* 14) has a story that after Hipparchia had accepted

from this story that the essence of the Cynic partnership is the free choice of the partners, exactly as Diogenes had proposed. City conventions and civic marriage are irrelevant. Nor is there any question of the 'marriage' being undertaken, as in Antisthenes, for the sake of childbearing. It is a matter of one free individual recognizing another; it is what we may call a marriage between citizens of the cosmos.

Before turning to Zeno and the Stoics, therefore, we can summarize some of the important characteristics of the Cynic movement as it existed when Zeno came into contact with it. First of all comes the distinction between the wise and the fools; and the fools, as Diogenes apparently held, are to all intents and purposes mad.[1] What distinguishes the two classes is that the wise attribute no value whatever to anything except virtue, while regarding vicious acts as the only acts which should not be performed. Everything else is totally insignificant to the wise man. Whatever customs, institutions and convention may suggest, the wise man will be governed solely by reason.[2] He will accept not what is conventional but what is natural.[3] Apparently Diogenes and Crates believed that to act virtuously is natural, to be unconcerned with what is neither virtuous nor vicious is natural, and to avoid vice is natural. If a man is free, they held, he will behave 'naturally'; hence Diogenes can speak almost as though freedom is the good for man. The difficulty is that he gives no justification for his use of the words 'nature' and 'natural'; nor does he attempt to explain why it is good to behave naturally. Certainly he does not attempt to justify his talk about nature by introducing physical theories. For all his remarks about the cosmos, he despises learning about the nature of that cosmos.[4] It almost (but not quite) seems that it is the will

a Cynic life, Crates led her off to a portico and would have consummated the union in full view had not Zeno covered them with a cloak. The story bears the marks of allegory in that it distinguishes Zeno as not 'assimilating the Cynic shamelessness' (D.L. 7.3); but apart from the role played by Zeno, there is no reason why the account should not be correct. Dudley (*op. cit.* 50) is unjustified in rejecting it as a scabrous invention of Apuleius; it chimes in with the remark of Crates, when taking his son to a brothel, that that was how he had married (γάμον, D.L. 6.88). Cf. also Sextus Emp., *Hyp. Pyr.* 3.200.

[1] D.L. 6.35.   [2] D.L. 6.73.   [3] τὰ κατὰ φύσιν, D.L. 6.71.   [4] D.L. 6.73.

of the free man that determines what is natural. Diogenes probably did not intend to say that the man who could will to be free sets up his own standard of virtue and vice; he seems to have held that virtue and vice have some kind of objective reality about them which the wise man will recognize; but in the absence of any clear expression of what that reality is, we can be pardoned if we conclude that in practice, for the Cynic, the man who makes his own decisions about his own life is the wise man. As we have said, that does not mean that the wise man must be an isolated man, though obviously the wise are few. The wise can choose to enter into relations with other people. But if the others do not accept the relationship, the wise man will be no less happy, for he is his own master. That is the full implication of the word ἀπαθής; it cannot be separated from the word αὐτάρκης. The wise man is as free from spiritual dependence as he is from physical needs above the bare minimum required for survival.[1] And even survival is a matter for his own decision.

There is a further point to be raised. Clearly Diogenes and Crates believed that it is possible to become wise, since wisdom is in some undefined sense natural; and once wisdom has been attained, it cannot be lost[2]—a position which caused the Stoics certain difficulties. Why the Cynics held this view is not entirely clear; perhaps they would have argued that, whereas the fool is unstable and thus can change, even for the better, the wise man is stable by nature. He would not be wise if there was even the possibility of his becoming a fool. But lack of a Cynic logic or physics ensured that no attempt was made to give this thesis any basis outside dogmatic assertion.

We can now turn to Zeno and his pupils and immediate successors to see what they made of their Cynic heritage. Zeno was a pupil of the Cynic Crates,[3] and although he was unable or

[1] The origins of the Cynic concept of independence are outside our present scope. A sketchy introduction to the subject is provided by Miss Rich, 'The Cynic Concept of ΑΥΤΑΡΚΕΙΑ'.

[2] D.L. 6.105.

[3] D.L. 7.2–3 (*SVF* I 1). According to Numenius (*SVF* I 11) Zeno 'heard' Crates after Polemo. That this order is less likely will be clear from our discussion.

unwilling to assimilate some of the more extreme Cynic modes of behaviour, he was nevertheless greatly influenced by his teacher. The series of stories recounted about him in Diogenes Laertius are often similar to those told about the Cynics themselves; and it is noteworthy that on one occasion, when a Cynic begged oil from him, he accompanied his refusal with the words: 'Which of us is the more shameless?'[1] Doubtless it was because of the original attitudes of Zeno that later Stoics were in the habit of calling Cynicism a short cut to virtue, and of holding that the wise man will play the Cynic.[2]

The tradition of Cynic influence on Stoicism was given a firm basis by Zeno's work called the *Ideal State* or *Politeia*.[3] There is no doubt that this was an early book, written, according to Diogenes Laertius, when Zeno was still a pupil of Crates.[4] Some of the more conventional later Stoics tried to expurgate it or even to deny its authenticity, but Chrysippus knew that it was genuine, and similar ideas were apparently expressed in other authentic writings of Zeno.[5] In this work Zeno set out to describe what the society of the wise would be like,[6] while at the same time trying to indicate the attitude of the wise towards one another and towards the outside world in any ordinary political situation.[7]

Before considering the kind of life the inhabitants of the ideal state will live, however, we must clear up a problem about membership of the state. In a passage of Plutarch,[8] unreasonably alleged by some to depend on Eratosthenes,[9] it is said that according to Zeno we are to consider all men as our fellow demesmen and fellow citizens. It has been suggested that Zeno

[1] D.L. 7.17 (*SVF* 1 296). [2] D.L. 6.104; 7.121.

[3] Evidence for this has recently been conveniently collected and well analysed by Baldry, 'Zeno's Ideal State'. See also Baldry's *Unity of Mankind* 153–63, and the review by Murray, *CR* 80 (1966) 368–71.

[4] D.L. 7.4 (*SVF* 1 2); Philodemus, *op. cit.* col. 15.

[5] D.L. 7.34.

[6] That the state is only for the wise has been generally admitted since the time of Zeller. Cf. Baldry, 'Zeno's Ideal State', 6–7.

[7] Murray, *art. cit.* 369. Cf. Philodemus, *op. cit.* col. 18.

[8] Plut., *De Alex. Magni Fort. aut Virt.* 329 A (*SVF* 1 262).

[9] This is the view of Schwartz, 'Hekataeos von Teos', 252–4. See Baldry, 'Zeno's Ideal State', 13.

is thinking of something approaching a world-state, but there is no evidence for that. Baldry tends to find the passage inconsistent with Zeno's normal view that only the wise are citizens, and thinks that Zeno may in this section of his work at least have had a remote future time in mind.[1] But he knows objections to this view as being the explanation of the *Politeia* in general.[2] What then is the explanation? Murray has rightly reasserted that the 'all men' who are to be our fellow citizens are only all wise men.[3] But why does Plutarch say 'all men', when he is apparently referring not to some remote future time when all will be wise, but to the present world where most are fools? Perhaps the answer is that Zeno was using the word 'man' in the Cynic sense we have already noticed. All *men* are to be our brothers; but 'men' means 'free men', and the majority of the population of the world are slaves.

We have to remember, when discussing Zeno's *Politeia*, that only very small amounts of it survive, and those who talked about it in antiquity were most concerned with its more unconventional features. In our evidence for it, we have no passages which deal with things neither virtuous nor vicious in terms of the Stoic theory that certain types of behaviour are conducive to virtue while others are conducive to vice. On the other hand we have no evidence that this theory, Zeno's major contribution to the ethical problems of the day, was not mentioned. What we know about the *Politeia* is that in accordance with Cynic views Zeno argued that many of the conventions of city society have no moral significance. Again, as with the Cynics, this has most interesting consequences in the sphere of sexual relations. Again we hear that women are to be 'in common' and that relations between the sexes shall be on a carnal basis.[4] But again this seems to be based on mutual consent.

[1] Baldry, *Unity of Mankind* 160.
[2] Most commentators have thought that Zeno was concerned with an ideal future. See Baldry, 'Zeno's Ideal State', 7. Pohlenz thought that the state was in the past (*Die Stoa* 1.137–8).
[3] Murray, *art. cit.* 369.
[4] D.L. 7.131 (*SVF* I 269). Dyroff (*Ethik der alten Stoa* 208) thinks this is a more extreme view than that of the Cynics, but in fact it seems identical. See below.

Diogenes Laertius recalls Thrasonides, the hero of Menander's *Misumenos*, who gained control over his beloved, but refrained from intercourse because she had come to dislike him. The moral which the Stoics drew from this was that friendship is essential for love, and that sexual relations between the wise will depend on the free choice of the partners, as in the case of Crates and Hipparchia. Although this interpretation of the story is attributed to the Stoics in general, there is no reason why it should not represent the view of Zeno in particular.[1]

Apparently Zeno argued that, if sexual relations are free, the children of the wise will be beloved by all and the problems of adultery will be eliminated.[2] However, there is no reason to believe that his argument was that, since free love will lead to various goods, it is therefore desirable, nor that he held, as Baldry suggests in connection with the proposal elsewhere in the *Politeia* that men and women are to wear the same clothes, that this should be done to ensure harmony and concord (ὁμόνοια) among the citizens. After all, the wise, as we shall see, are naturally in harmony with one another; harmony does not have to be promoted by law. Rather, the natural result of being a wise man or woman is that one determines one's own sexual relations entirely on a basis of a personal and reasoned decision. According to Zeno no part of the body should be entirely concealed.[3] This was doubtless because, if parts of the body are concealed, a limitation is imposed on the freedom of an individual to evaluate his prospective partner—apart from being the cause of unnecessary inhibitions. Again the thought is Cynic: Crates took off his clothes before asking Hipparchia

[1] D.L. 7.130.

[2] D.L. 7.131 (*SVF* III 728). This was also the Cynic view (Philodemus, *op. cit.* col. 9).

[3] D.L. 7.33 (*SVF* I 257). Pohlenz (*Die Stoa* 2.75), following Zeller, thought that this referred only to dress at the gymnasia; but, as Baldry notices ('Zeno's Ideal State', 10), there are to be no gymnasia in the Ideal State (D.L. 7.33 = *SVF* I 267). The Old Stoic view of this matter is to be contrasted with the 'decorous' view of Panaetius: '*Quae enim natura occultavit, eadem omnes, qui sana mente sunt, removent ab oculis ipsique necessitati dant operam ut quam occultissime pareant; quarum partium corporis usus sunt necessarii, eas neque partes neque earum usus suis nominibus appellant*' etc. (*De Off.* 1.127). A polemic against Cynics and Cynicizing Stoics follows.

whether she wished to be his partner,[1] and later gave his daughter to a suitor on the basis of a trial marriage.[2] The same idea recurs in More's *Utopia*, where the Utopians think it absurd that two persons should enter upon a marriage without first seeing one another naked.

Diogenes Laertius attributes to Zeno in the *Politeia* the view that the wise man will marry and have children.[3] Some scholars have regarded this as inconsistent with the doctrine of free love; Pohlenz, Baldry and others think it is simply an expression of the wise man's duty in any ordinary city, not in the ideal state.[4] Baldry argues that this view is 'confirmed' by the fact that the previous sentence in Diogenes Laertius is concerned with the bourgeois city, but in view of Diogenes' methods of compilation that proves nothing. His other argument is that in a passage of Cicero the idea of marriage and family is contrasted with the Cynic ideal.[5] This is a misreading of Cicero, who writes that marriage and having children are natural happenings, that pure love is compatible with the life of the wise, and that the Stoics are divided about their attitude towards the principles and way of life adopted by the Cynics. Some argue that Cynic behaviour can be justified by particular circumstances (this was probably Zeno's view); others reject the Cynic habits outright. In fact Zeno is not mentioned in this passage, and there is no suggestion that marriage of some kind, and having children, is in contradiction with Cynic ideals. After all even some Cynics married and had children. The question rather is: What is a marriage and how is it to be fitted into the conventions of society? For the wise man it is a freely chosen, permanent, though not necessarily exclusive, relationship.

We have already argued that in the ideal state concord is the relationship which will subsist between the inhabitants. It does not need to be produced by legislation. It will arise out of the nature of the wise, and, as Zeno particularly stresses, from the erotic side of their personality. Eros, he argued, is the god of

---

[1] D.L. 6.96.   [2] D.L. 6.93.
[3] D.L. 7.121 (*SVF* I 270).
[4] Pohlenz, *Die Stoa* I.139; Baldry, 'Zeno's Ideal State', 9–10.
[5] Cic., *De Fin.* 3.68 (*SVF* III 616).

friendship and freedom is the preparer of concord.[1] The wise man will love those with an aptitude for the good life,[2] and love is directed not to physical satisfaction—though this will certainly be enjoyed—but to friendship.[3]

In the course of our discussion of the *Politeia*, and particularly of Zeno's attitude to personal relations among the wise, we have found many points of contact with Cynicism. More could easily be added: Zeno wanted to abolish coinage, for example, as well as gymnasia, law courts and temples.[4] But, as has often been noticed, there is something of a divergence from the Cynics at the root of his thought. Although Zeno's precepts are both to be observed by the wise at all times and to be the 'ground rules' for a city of wise men whenever it may exist, he is talking about a community which is recognizable as such. The difference between the Stoics and the Cynics can be exaggerated at this point, but it did exist. According to Baldry Zeno differed from Crates in his emphasis on the *kinship* of the wise (his italics).[5] But this should not be taken to mean that there is no kinship of the wise for the Cynics, or that the Cynics did not believe that philosophical wisdom is a bond among those who possess it. The difference is a difference of emphasis, perhaps of optimism. Zeno seems to have thought that it was still worth while talking about communities of men, however much existing cities might need the most radical reform; the Cynics, on the other hand, thought rather in terms of one wise man per generation. The view of Zeno is the less extreme, but it is probably a matter of degree rather than of kind.

However close many of Zeno's theories in the *Politeia* and in others of his works are to those of the Cynics, he did not practise what he preached in the same way. He was not notorious for his behaviour as were Diogenes and Crates. As the doxo-

---

[1] Athen., 8.561 c (*SVF* 1 263).   [2] D.L. 7.129 (*SVF* 1 248).

[3] D.L. 7.130. Both homosexual and heterosexual love are permissible under the proper circumstances (*SVF* 1 249–52). Incest is not ruled out automatically (*SVF* 1 256).

[4] D.L. 7.33 (*SVF* 1 267). Cf. Dyroff, *op. cit.* 210. On Zeno's attitude to Cynic αἰσχρουργία see *SVF* 1 253–6; on public intercourse Sext. Emp., *Hyp. Pyr.* 3.200.

[5] Baldry, 'Zeno's Ideal State', 14.

graphers say, he did not practise Cynic shamelessness. Our immediate problem is why he did not. A number of easy answers
spring to mind. It might be said that he was not an exhibition-
ist; but Diogenes and Crates, even if exhibitionists, were not
merely exhibitionists. Their behaviour was designed to shock,
but there was a pedagogical intent to it. The aim, in part at
least, was to force people to realize that conventions have
nothing to do with morality. If Zeno agreed with much of this,
if he could argue, for instance, that it is not immoral to eat
human flesh, why did he not actually eat it? The answer to this
brings us close to the point where we can see why Zeno parted
company with the Cynics; it is that he introduced the doctrine
that many actions not themselves moral can promote morality,
while many others can promote immorality, the doctrine of
'appropriate things',[1] of things to be preferred and rejected. It
is stated twice by Diogenes Laertius that Zeno was the first to
make common use of the term 'appropriate things'—and there
is no reason to doubt the evidence.[2] And clearly if some things
are to be preferred, even if they cannot be justified as in themselves moral, and therefore good, there must be another justification for this preference. That justification is provided for
Zeno by the theory that everything preferred is natural, while
whatever is to be rejected is contrary to nature. And by appeal-
ing to nature, he has not appealed only to a moral law but to a
law of the physical universe. Some things are natural in that
they lead to physical survival; our first impulses, before we are
corrupted, are concerned with this. Thus the introduction of a
class of things preferred compels the philosopher to break with
the Cynics and re-introduce the study of physics into the activities of the wise man. Brink is right in detecting the influence of
Polemo, whose pupil Zeno became some time after leaving
Crates, behind this development.[3]

There is a difficulty here, though one which has often been
overestimated. The earliest reports of the doctrine of natural

---

[1] See especially Grumach, *Physis und Agathon in der alten Stoa*; Nebel, 'Der
Begriff des ΚΑΘΗΚΟΝ in der alten Stoa'; Pohlenz, *Die Stoa* 1.129–31; Dyroff,
op. cit. 126–150.   [2] *SVF* 1 230.
[3] D.L. 7.2 (*SVF* 1 1); Cicero, *De Fin.* 4.45 (*SVF* 1 198). Cf. Brink, 'Οἰκείωσις
and Οἰκειότης...', 142–4.

impulses towards, for example, physical survival, and then to various other non-moral achievements, do not specifically credit it to Zeno but to Chrysippus.[1] The attempt to trace it back to Peripatetic sources behind Zeno must certainly be accounted a failure;[2] it has even been doubted whether it originated with Zeno himself. Pohlenz argued in 'Zenon und Chrysipp' that the whole moral theory of the Stoics depends upon it, and that therefore it must have already been formulated by Zeno.[3] Our surviving evidence, which refers either to Chrysippus or to no particular individual, is, he thinks, comment and elaboration on the original Zenonian theory. Brink finds the matter still open to doubt,[4] and hesitatingly seems to settle for the view that Zeno's theory, which he learned from disputes with Polemo and the Academy, was only 'a theory of οἰκείωσις in embryo'. He supports this non-committal approach by arguing that the theory of οἰκείωσις is not, as Pohlenz held, a fundamental principle of Stoic ethics. This seems to be a mistake of the same kind as that which leads him to say later that 'Zeno maintained that nature was the same all the way, from the "first goods", which are natural, to the "Intermediates", also κατὰ φύσιν, and thence to truly moral action, eminently κατὰ φύσιν'. The mistake is in the understanding of the importance of Zeno's break with Cynicism and consequent reformulation of the concept of nature.

Pohlenz is certainly correct in believing that οἰκείωσις is fundamental to Stoicism from the beginning, for only on the basis of this theory could Zeno have defended himself against the Cynics, his former teachers. Zeno's problem is how it is possible to justify 'preferring' certain of the intermediates to the others, and how it is possible to reject a course of action on grounds other than that it is in itself vicious. The defence he

---

[1] D.L. 7.85 (*SVF* III 178).

[2] There has been much dispute about the origin of the theory of οἰκείωσις, according to which we have 'perception and apprehension of what is akin to ourselves' (Plut., *SR* 1038 c (*SVF* II 724)). Von Arnim ('Arius Didymus' Abriss') and Dirlmeier ('Die Oikeiosis-Lehre Theophrasts') argued for Peripatetic origins. This has been refuted several times (e.g. by Philippson, 'Die erste Naturgemässe', Pohlenz, *Grundfragen*, and Brink, *op. cit.*).

[3] *NGG* 1938.   [4] Brink, *op. cit.* 142.

offers, namely that certain actions are in accordance with 'nature', where nature is understood as having ramifications in the realm of physics and biology as well as in the realm of morals, necessitates the theory of οἰκείωσις. If we 'naturally' do what is 'akin' to us, we then call such actions 'preferred' actions, for they are aids towards the acquisition of a moral frame of mind. Brink was doubtless right, as we have argued, to associate the move with Zeno's studies in the Academy of Xenocrates and Polemo.

We might well expect, therefore, that the introduction of the doctrine that some of the intermediates are to be preferred and others to be rejected, would coincide with the introduction of physics into the old Cynic way of life. Would Zeno have had any alternative to this? The alternative, as we shall later argue, realized both by Zeno and by his pupil Ariston, was to fall back on the will of the wise man as in itself able to determine what course of action to follow. This in practice was what Diogenes and Crates had done; Diogenes' almost exaggerated praise of the self-determination and freedom of the wise is evidence of it. But, at least theoretically, even Diogenes would probably have admitted that the sage does not decide as he sees fit but, somehow, as virtue dictates. What he did not believe was that the dictates of virtue can be formulated as rules; nor did he think that they bear any relation to the physical and biological constitution of man and the world. What Zeno was probably afraid of was that what might be dignified with the name of acts of will might in fact be acts of whim and caprice. Since virtue itself seemed so difficult to understand or describe, the danger of this was very real indeed. That is why so many of the Cynics give the impression of being merely irresponsible exhibitionists.

It is possible, though not certain, that the development of Zeno's thought on this matter is visible to us. In our fragments of his *Politeia* and in the available discussion of it, we hear practically nothing about the sort of studies with which the wise man will concern himself. There is one reference to the fact that ordinary Greek education is worthless, a typically Cynic attitude, but nothing about what to put in its place.[1] It is possible

[1] D.L. 7.32 (*SVF* I 259).

that no suggestions were made in the *Politeia*, but that it was only later, when Zeno came to realize the importance of nature in the physical and biological sense, that he introduced what was to become the standard Stoic view that physics is a necessary partner for ethics.[1]

We have argued that the introduction of the classes of the preferred and rejected among the intermediates marks Zeno's major break with Cynicism, and that it leads to considerable further breaks, including the abandonment of the Cynic contempt for certain kinds of traditional learning. We have also argued that Zeno's attitudes to Eros and Concord are such that, contrary to the Cynics, he is more optimistic about a genuine community of the wise. There is one further point to be considered, before we go on to discuss the Cynic reaction within the Stoic school itself. According to the Cynics the wise man is ἀπαθής—and the word seems to mean 'totally detached', and, in some of the Cynics at least, 'unemotional' in the fullest sense. We recall Antisthenes' remark that he would rather be mad than feel physical pleasure. Now we know that the Stoics, certainly from the time of Chrysippus, offered a theory very different from that of the Cynics, the theory that, although πάθη, which are irrational movements of the soul, must be extirpated, yet there are rational states of emotion which will be characteristic of the wise man; these are called states of εὐπάθεια.[2] It has often been observed that there is no evidence which unmistakably points to this doctrine existing before the time of Chrysippus, and some have thought that it was introduced by Chrysippus as a reply to charges brought against the Stoics that they were teaching a senseless doctrine of complete impassivity.[3] But the Stoic doctrine of ἀπάθεια never was a doctrine of impassivity. For Zeno himself, we are told, although the wise man will not feel πάθη, he will feel certain traces of them, certain shadows. The scars of πάθη remain in his soul.[4] Nor does the wise man give up feelings of physical pleasure; it is true

[1] *SVF* I 45–6; cf. II 41–4.
[2] *SVF* III 431–42. See pp. 25–6 above.
[3] This is the view of Arnold (*Roman Stoicism* 324), tentatively approved by Haynes, 'The Theory of Pleasure', 413, note 4.
[4] Seneca, *De Ira* 1.16.7 (*SVF* I 215).

that such pleasures are 'indifferent', but they are none the less felt.[1] And if the wise man feels pleasure, he must adopt a proper attitude towards it. In other words, if πάθη are irrational movements of the soul,[2] the pleasures felt by the wise man must be rational movements of the soul, or at least the necessary accompaniments of such rational movements. It is true that Cleanthes, the usually orthodox successor of Zeno, holds that 'pleasure' is not only indifferent, but non-natural and possessed of no value whatsoever, and perhaps Zeno's view of its value was not greatly different from this.[3] But there are two points to be made: the first is that even Cleanthes was probably thinking only about physical pleasure;[4] the second that, if the wise man feels pleasure, whatever value this pleasure may have, it must itself be associated with reason. In other words, even if pleasure is totally indifferent, the wise man may or may not assent to it. If he assents, the pleasure will be rational pleasure. That is probably what Chrysippus had in mind when he employed the term εὐπάθεια. Hence, even if Zeno did not use this *term*—and we have no evidence that he did not—nevertheless the concept is already there in his attitude to the wise man. Again it looks like a moderation of the original Cynic theory.[5]

We are now in a position to understand rather more clearly the nature of Zeno's break with Cynicism. We can understand too how he would have justified his refusal to take over some of the more unconventional Cynic modes of behaviour. While still agreeing with the Cynics that all that is neither virtuous nor vicious has no *moral* worth, Zeno now justifies his view that it has worth of some other kind. Hence, while it may be theoretically a matter of indifference whether the wise man will commit incest, incest will normally be rejected as a course of action. Yet, while admitting this, we must also remember that Zeno can still maintain the 'Cynic' utterances of his *Politeia* and other

---

[1] Gellius, 9.5.5 (*SVF* I 195).   [2] D.L. 7.110 (*SVF* I 205).

[3] Sext. Emp., *Adv. Math.* 11.74 (*SVF* I 574). See p. 47 above.

[4] Cf. Haynes, *op. cit.* 417.

[5] According to Edelstein (*The Meaning of Stoicism* 4) Zeno himself used the term εὐπάθεια, defining it as an easy flow of life. I can find no evidence for this, and Edelstein gives none. I suspect that in Edelstein's text εὐδαιμονία should be read for εὐπάθεια. Cf. *SVF* I 184, 554.

works. Incest is still indifferent, and the wise man may still sometimes choose it. But whereas for the Cynics it seems to have been almost a matter of spinning a coin whether one commits incest or not, and it is impossible to make a general statement to the effect that the wise man will not normally commit incest, such a rule will be, for the Stoics, both morally desirable and physically justifiable.

That our interpretation of the attitude of Zeno to his Cynic teachers is basically correct is confirmed by our knowledge of the Cynic reply, or perhaps we should say the neo-Cynic reply, since Zeno's opponent, at least for a time, was one of his own pupils, Ariston of Chios. This man, who gained a degree of notoriety in antiquity, is consistently associated with the Cynics by the doxographical tradition represented by Diogenes Laertius.[1] The opening of Diogenes' account of him may be quoted in full, since it sums up his position admirably:[2]

Ariston of Chios, the Bald, nicknamed the Siren, said that the end is to live a life of indifference to what is between virtue and vice and not to admit any distinction whatever in things of this kind, but to behave identically to all of them. For he said that the wise man is like the good actor who can play the part of both Thersites and Agamemnon, acting appropriately in either case. He wanted to discard the logical and physical branches of philosophy, saying that the one is beyond us and the other irrelevant. The only relevant subject is ethics.

And a little later Diogenes quotes a passage from Diocles Magnes to the effect that at a time when Zeno was ill, Ariston met up with Polemo and retracted his views.[3] This may or may not be true, but the alleged connection of the thought of Ariston with that of Polemo is certainly of interest, since we have argued that Polemo exerted some influence on Zeno's original attitude to the Cynics.

It is clear that Ariston's fame in antiquity depended on his rejection of the doctrine of naturally preferable courses of action. He is described, as we have already seen, as advocating that we should be completely indifferent to what is neither vir-

---

[1] D.L. 6.103 (*SVF* I 354).   [2] D.L. 7.160 (*SVF* I 351).
[3] D.L. 7.162 (*SVF* I 333).

tuous nor vicious; and elsewhere Diogenes makes the curious remark that he 'introduced the doctrine of indifference' (ὁ τὴν ἀδιαφορίαν εἰσηγησάμενος).[1] It is not immediately obvious what this means. It clearly does not mean that Ariston was the first to posit a class of intermediates between virtue and vice. It has sometimes been held, perhaps rightly, that he was the first to use the term 'indifferent' for the members of this class. Others may have called them simply intermediates; but this is not certain and in any case it is comparatively unimportant. What the phrase means is that Ariston introduced the theory that within this class there are no *a priori* or natural reasons why any member of the class is to be preferred to any other. This attitude was widely misunderstood in antiquity. Cicero frequently takes the view that the whole doctrine of things to be preferred and rejected was a rather unsubtle proposal of Zeno to avoid the 'absurd' consequences of the original theory that the only good is virtue and the only evil is vice.[2] But, as Moreau has shown, Cicero is quite mistaken in his attitude to both Zeno and Ariston.[3] For Cicero Ariston was right to reject Zeno's crude subterfuge; but the result of doing so was that he himself was driven into a Sceptic position like that of Pyrrho. Cicero often mentions the two in the same breath.[4] In fact, however, there is little similarity between the views of Ariston and Pyrrho, apart from their common use of the term 'indifference'. Pyrrho is indifferent to everything because he has no criterion of judgment; Ariston is only indifferent to what is neither virtue nor vice, precisely because he knows this is neither virtue nor vice.

The correct interpretation of Ariston's doctrine is provided by Sextus Empiricus. There is nothing preferred by nature, he tells us; what is to be preferred must be determined by the wise man, who will have to make a series of *ad hoc* judgments according to the particular circumstances in which action is required.[5]

---

[1] D.L. 7.37. Cf. Clem. Alex., *Strom.* 2.21.129 (*SVF* I 360).

[2] *De Fin.* 4.56 (*SVF* I 232); 3.50 (*SVF* I 365). Cf. Moreau, 'Ariston...', 31.

[3] Moreau, *op. cit.* 30–1.

[4] *De Fin.* 2.43; 3.11; 3.12 (*SVF* I 364); 4.43 (*SVF* I 369); Moreau, *op. cit.* 30.

[5] Sext. Emp., *Adv. Math.* 11.63 (*SVF* I 361). Cf. Plut., *De Exilio* 600 E (*SVF* I 371), where Ariston says that we have no fatherland by nature. Ariston's doctrine should be compared with the orthodox view that under special

The wise man will make the relevant decisions with nothing in his mind except his knowledge of what is virtue and what is vice. From this we can see why Ariston is (misleadingly and understandably) coupled by Cicero not only with Pyrrho but also with another heretical Stoic, Herillus,[1] for the heresy of Herillus was to propose that the end is life governed by knowledge, or perhaps simply knowledge. He doubtless meant knowledge of virtue and vice.[2]

Ariston has certainly reverted to a position like that of the Cynics in his rejection of the thesis of Zeno that the study of the physical and biological world has some relation to man's progress towards virtue. Hence Ariston not only joins with the Zeno of the *Politeia* in condemning ordinary Greek education— those who pursue it are like the suitors who enjoy the servant-girls instead of Penelope[3]—but he condemns Zeno's introduction of physics and logic into the Stoic curriculum,[4] though without actually mentioning Zeno's name in the fragments available to us. We recall that according to Zeno the end of life is defined as 'living in harmony' (τὸ ὁμολογουμένως ζῆν);[5] and there has been much discussion as to whether this formula is equivalent to 'living in harmony with nature' (τὸ ὁμολογουμένως τῇ φύσει ζῆν). There is little reason to doubt that Zeno, who introduced the study of φύσις into Stoic thought from the beginning, would have regarded the two formulae as identical —and he probably used both himself. For in his view Reason and Nature are ultimately to be identified. But Ariston could

circumstances (ἄνευ περιστάσεως) some acts which are normally καθήκοντα are to be rejected, and again in special cases (κατὰ περίστασιν) that what is normally παρὰ τὸ καθῆκον should be done (D.L. 7.109 = *SVF* III 496). Ariston has made *all* καθήκοντα dependent on individual circumstances and abolished the possibility of the formulation of rules of conduct for normal circumstances. There is no need to suppose with Wiersma ('Τέλος und καθῆκον...') that the orthodox position was first developed by Chrysippus in opposition to Ariston. Zeno himself is known to have opposed his pupil's wilder ideas. For orthodox Stoics some προηγμένα, e.g. προκοπή, must always be the object of appropriate actions (καθήκοντα). Cf. D.L. 7.109 (*SVF* III 496).

[1] *SVF* I 363. [2] *SVF* I 411, 417, 419.
[3] Stob., *Flor.* 4.109, vol. I, p. 246 H. (*SVF* I 350).
[4] Moreau, *op. cit.* 33, 42. For references see Moreau, 43.
[5] *SVF* I 179.

have accepted the formula τὸ ὁμολογουμένως ζῆν without explaining it in this way. In his view a life according to reason has nothing to do with any study of φύσις; it is simply the equivalent of a life according to virtue, *and no more need be said*. Virtue is the only 'natural' thing of interest to him—a genuinely Cynic standpoint. This enables us to understand a further position of Ariston's, that it is idle to hand on moral precepts.[1] Virtue is solely a matter of choosing the proper course.

It is clear that the view of Ariston was much further from that of Herillus than Cicero supposed. The good life should not be *defined* as a matter of knowing what is virtuous, but of choosing the virtuous path in all circumstances. The only guide the wise man has, or needs, is virtue. Hence the Cynic tendency to overestimate the importance of freedom recurs,[2] and with it, as Moreau points out, the problem of whether the wise man's decision is in practice, if not in theory, the real criterion of virtue; of whether the wise man actually creates his own values.[3] Like the Cynics Ariston certainly holds that he does not; but, also like them, he speaks almost as though he does, since he gives no clear idea of how the concept of virtue can be related to one's day-by-day behaviour in any positive sense. Ariston is compelled to dogmatize about the wise man's right choices, based on his knowledge of virtue alone. It is not surprising that this dogmatism was received somewhat sceptically. Arcesilaus of the Academy also criticized Zeno for relating courses of action to knowledge of the apparently non-moral facts of nature. The conclusion of Arcesilaus, diametrically opposed to that of Ariston, was that since the wise man has nothing on which to base his judgments, he had better suspend them.[4]

Our knowledge of Ariston is comparatively limited. Part of

---

[1] Sext. Emp., *Adv. Math.* 7.12 (*SVF* I 356); cf. *SVF* I 357–9.

[2] Cf. *De Fin.* 4.79 (*SVF* I 368).

[3] Moreau, *op. cit.* 47–8; *De Fin.* 4.43 (*SVF* I 369); cf. 3.50 (*SVF* I 365). In 4.43 Ariston says that the wise man is aroused by *quodcumque in mentem incideret et quodcumque tamquam occurreret*. But what occurs to the wise man's mind cannot be vicious. Thus even here the wise man does not create his own values. Rather he accepts them. Ariston may be one of the opponents of Chrysippus mentioned by Plutarch (*SR* 1045 B = *SVF* II 973), but this is not certain.

[4] See Couissin, 'Le stoïcisme de la Nouvelle Académie', Moreau, *op. cit.* 41.

the reason for this is that his views were not accepted. Neither Cleanthes nor Chrysippus approved any of his major deviations from the thought of Zeno; according to the doxographical tradition Chrysippus expressed himself unfavourably on his popular following.[1] We have little evidence for Cleanthes' attitude towards the Cynic origins of Stoicism, but there is every reason to suppose it coincided with that of Zeno.[2] For Chrysippus there is more evidence. Zeno is defended and in one or two instances even more marked deviation from the Cynic path is proposed. Zeno's most important move against the Cynics, the introduction of the class of preferred things, is energetically supported,[3] as is his tendency to progress from the Cynic attitude to ἀπάθεια. Rational states of emotion are given more weight and probably classified in detail for the first time.[4] Above all, Zeno's emphasis on φύσις, on the study of the natural world as a necessary basis for the understanding and the performing of moral actions, is given the fullest possible weight; and Chrysippus rejects Ariston's contempt for moral instruction in favour of almost lyrical enthusiasm for the importance of laws, both physical and moral.[5] Furthermore Chrysippus goes beyond Zeno in at least one particular, perhaps in several. Contrary to the view of both Zeno and Ariston, Chrysippus is prepared to admit that ordinary Greek education is not without a certain value.[6] Contrary to the view of Cleanthes, and doubtless of Ariston as of the Cynics, virtue can, in certain circumstances, be lost.[7] We have no direct evidence for the view of Zeno on this. It is likely, however, that his opinion was not that of Chrysippus. In this instance the view of Chrysippus was not universally accepted among the later Stoics; those who rejected it probably had Zeno's position in mind.

[1] D.L. 7.182 (*SVF* II 10).
[2] Cf. *SVF* I 249, 254.
[3] *SVF* III 127–39. In this and the next two notes it is not necessary to assume that all the passages given by von Arnim refer to the view of Chrysippus; but that in general they are representative of it is to be denied only by the pathologically sceptical.
[4] *SVF* III 431–42.   [5] *SVF* III 140–6, 314.
[6] D.L. 7.129 (*SVF* III 738).
[7] For detailed discussion of this see pp. 16–19 above.

Yet Chrysippus was still close enough to the original Stoic spirit and to Stoic origins to be offensive to many. He retained and indeed re-emphasized many of the Cynic theories of Zeno's *Politeia*, when they were not incompatible with Stoic philosophy in general. Thus we find the same arguments that incest is not necessarily to be rejected, that women are to be 'in common' in the kingdom of the wise, and that there is nothing *per se* immoral about eating human flesh.[1] Similarly Chrysippus is concerned to advocate a city as wide as the cosmos with the stars as the fellow citizens of the wise;[2] similarly again, he combines his doctrine of women 'in common' with the teaching that the wise man will marry, presumably, again, advocating a marriage by consent of the parties and a contempt for the mere conventions of city life; similarly again, both homosexual love and heterosexual love are to be preferred in certain circumstances. The purpose of love is friendship and concord between the free and worthy. It arises from a recognition of the beauty of youth, and beauty is not the beauty of body but of a virtuous life. Love, as for Zeno, is the expression of the freely chosen partnerships of the wise. Whether it is physical is *per se* unimportant; that it should arise from nothing other than a recognition of the kinship of the wise is vital.[3]

After Chrysippus the possibility of a Stoic return to the Cynicism of Crates, Diogenes or Antisthenes was finally past. In fact the school moved so far towards respectability that the 'outrageous' teachings of Zeno and Chrysippus were forgotten, or remained only as a source of embarrassment. Attempts were made, as we have seen, to expurgate Zeno's writings,[4] and as for the Cynic freedom of speech, still valued by Chrysippus, we read in Diogenes Laertius as follows:

There are people who run Chrysippus down as having written much in a tone that is gross and indecent. For in his work *On the Ancient Natural Philosophers*, round about line 600, he interprets the story of Hera and Zeus coarsely, saying what no one would soil his lips by

---

[1] *SVF* III 728–31, 743–56.
[2] Plut., *CN* 1076 F (*SVF* II 645).
[3] For the views of Chrysippus and later Stoics on love matters see *SVF* III 650–3, 716–31.
[4] D.L. 7.34.

repeating. For, they say, he interprets the story in a most shameful way, even if he is commending it as physical doctrine, speaking in language more suited to prostitutes than to gods.[1]

Certainly the authorities on whom Diogenes relies did not regard such language as a matter of indifference. And later Stoics quietly dropped it.

Nevertheless, there is no Stoic more conscious of the gulf between the wise and the foolish than Chrysippus. And later Stoics may not have grasped the importance for their predecessors of understanding the doctrine of what is indifferent correctly. If the wise man becomes too squeamish, he may cease to realize the width of the gulf between the moral end and various other subordinate ends in life. Stoics later than Chrysippus did not always bear in mind the fundamental nature of this distinction.

In the Imperial period, although at times the word 'Cynic' meant little more than perfected Stoic, many of the original doctrines of the Cynics, even those which Zeno and Chrysippus had approved, were conveniently neglected, or, particularly in the sphere of sexual morality, rejected.[2] From the point of view of the philosopher, however, the neglect was not all pure gain; and even in the Imperial period there were still some Cynics who managed to steer a firm course between Stoicism on the one hand and mere exhibitionism on the other. Their most notorious role was that of opponents of monarchical rule.[3]

[1] D.L. 7.187 (*SVF* II 1071); cf. *SVF* II 1072–4.
[2] On the development of sexual morality, not to say asceticism, among the Stoics, particularly of the later period, see Arnold, *Roman Stoicism* 347–9. Babut's contention ('Les Stoïciens et l'Amour') that there is little variation in the Stoic attitude to sex and marriage from Zeno to Musonius entirely ignores the Cynicism of the Old Stoa.
[3] See the illuminating paper of J. M. C. Toynbee, 'Dictators and Philosophers in the First Century A.D.'

5

ALL SINS ARE EQUAL

Of all the Stoic paradoxes perhaps the most notorious was the bald assertion that all sins (ἁμαρτήματα, *peccata*) are equal. It is the reverse side of the coin to 'All moral acts (κατορθώματα) are equal', but proved much more infuriating. Evidence of the contempt, amused or otherwise, which the proposition aroused in antiquity is amply provided, not only by those professionally interested in philosophy like Cicero,[1] but by educated laymen like Horace.[2] A similar attitude has appeared among modern scholars and been perpetuated by them. In view of all this, in considering the thesis, which is fundamental to Stoicism from its beginnings, we should be clear in our minds what the Stoics meant when they persisted in their view in the teeth of the opposition. We also want to know not only what they meant but what could have led them to express themselves as they did.

We shall perhaps get to the heart of the doctrine most easily if we look at one of its most extreme formulations. According to Cicero, and his evidence is indubitably reliable on this matter, the Stoics were prepared to say that the man who unnecessarily kills a cockerel is no less guilty than the man who kills his father; for every fault is a wicked crime.[3] Obviously the word 'unnecessarily' is relevant here; for in the Stoic view guilt is determined by nothing other than motive. What matters is the reason for performing a particular action (*causa igitur haec non natura distinguit*),[4] and this reason is most commonly associated with the concept of an appropriate time. The wise man will know when each action is most appropriately performed.[5]

The Stoic position—at any rate in the time of Zeno and Chrysippus—presumably was that there might be circumstances in which the wise man would kill his father. If anyone

---

[1] *Par. St.* 3; *Pro Mur.* 61 etc.   [2] Hor., *Sat.* 1.3.120 ff.
[3] *Pro Mur.* 61 (*SVF* I 227); cf. *Par. St.* 3.24.   [4] *Par. St.* 3.24.
[5] For the connection with the right time see *De Fin.* 3.45 (*SVF* III 524), 3.61, 3.68; Stob., *Flor.* 6.3, vol. I, p. 281 H.

kills his father at the wrong time, however, he is guilty. If he kills a cockerel at the wrong time, he is also guilty. How can they possibly justify placing the two wrong actions on the same level? Their first move is to argue that the results of any activity have nothing to do with the question of guilt.[1] In modern terms, they reject consequentialism, thus ridding themselves of the enormous difficulties inherent in it. This helps us to understand rather more of their view that the man whose character is changing in the direction of virtue is in exactly the same unfortunate state (miseria) as the hardened villain wallowing delightedly in his crimes.[2] It makes no difference to the question of guilt qua guilt whether one guilty action is more or less likely to lead to another.

The situation becomes a little clearer when we turn to their attitude towards the punishment of 'sins'. If a man kills his slave for a good, though still inadequate, reason, he has committed a single crime; if he kills his father in similar circumstances, he has by one and the same action committed more than one crime. As Cicero puts it,[3] he does violence to the man who begot him, nourished him, educated him, and so on. Since he has thus by a single action committed more crimes, he deserves a heavier penalty. Punishment, therefore, is to be meted out not in proportion to guilt, for all criminals are equally guilty, but in proportion to the number of crimes they have committed. A passage from the De Finibus,[4] attributed to Zeno himself, explains this theory further. Some sins (peccata) are pardonable (tolerabilia), while others are not. The reason for this is that some (those which are unpardonable) transgress more aspects of 'duty' (numeri offici) or aspects of virtue (numeri virtutis). The explanation of this is that the moral act (κατόρθωμα) is envisaged as a piece of entirely consistent behaviour which will involve a correct relationship between the wise man and various other individuals or groups of individuals.[5] Hence every

---

[1] Par. St. 3.20. [2] De Fin. 3.48 (SVF III 530), 4.63.
[3] Par. St. 3.25. [4] De Fin. 4.56 (SVF I 232).
[5] De Fin. 3.24 (SVF III 11). For numeri (ἀριθμοί) of appropriateness cf. De Off. 3.14, D.L. 7.100 (SVF III 83), Sen., Ep. 75.16, Marcus Aur. 3.1, 6.26. The term seems to be used to convey the note of right or wrong proportion (D.L. 7.100).

wrong action will involve wrong relationships with greater or smaller numbers of individuals, or in more or less ways with the same individual. When considering punishments, therefore, the Stoics seem to have held that these should be meted out in relation to the number of offences, on a *quid pro quo* basis. Punishments are therefore not tied to guilt—if they were, they would all be equally heavy; and the Old Stoics seem to have thought that they have two functions, as retribution and as a warning to other people.[1]

From first to last what interests the Stoics is the question: Is it a moral act or not? If it is non-moral, it is, strictly speaking, immoral; and the Stoics were fond of drawing homely analogies to indicate how they viewed the matter. When a man is under water, he cannot breathe just below the surface of the water any more than if he is lying on the bottom. Similarly a puppy which is just about to open its eyes is no less blind than one which has just been born.[2] Either it sees or it does not. Either one can breathe or one cannot; either one is guilty or one is not.

Cicero thinks that the Stoics are quibbling and being pedantic. The separation of 'numbers' of offences from the question of guilt as such is certainly rather strange. It is worth enquiring why the Stoics tolerated it and even preached it wholeheartedly. Various comparisons they make are illuminating. A piece of wood is either straight or it is not; there are no degrees of straightness any more than degrees of justice.[3] The wise man differs from everybody else not in degree but in kind.[4] Just as a proposition is either true or not-true, so men are either moral or not-moral. One thing cannot be 'more' true or 'more' false than another; and morality is similar.[5] If, therefore, we can see why the Stoics did not wish to posit degrees of truth, we may be helped in our enquiry. And the reason for their unwillingness

---

[1] Plut., *SR* 1040 C (*SVF* II 1175), 1050 E (*SVF* II 1176), and, for what it is worth, Lact., *Inst. Div.* 7.20 (*SVF* I 147). Seneca emphasizes that punishment is reformatory in this life (*De Clem.* 2.22.1), and apparently in the afterlife (*Ad Marc.* 25.1).

[2] Cic., *De Fin.* 3.48 (*SVF* III 530), 4.75 (*SVF* III 531); Plut., *CN* 1063 A (*SVF* III 539).

[3] D.L. 7.227 (*SVF* III 536).   [4] *De Fin.* 3.34.

[5] D.L. 7.120 (*SVF* III 527); Stob., *Ecl.* 2, p. 106, 21 W. (*SVF* III 528).

is fairly obvious: if truth admits of degrees, how can there be something absolutely true? Rightly or wrongly this is probably what worried them. If *a* is truer than *b*, can there be an *x* than which nothing else could be truer? But, the Stoics argue, some things are manifestly true (such as that it is not always daytime), therefore truth cannot be one of those things which admit of degrees.

If we apply this kind of reasoning to the problem of the words 'good', 'better', 'bad', 'worse', we can easily see what the Stoics were afraid of. If the concept of moral goodness admits of degrees, who can say that it could reach a term? If Smith is better than Jones, who is better than Thomas, how can any man be said to be perfect? Could not some moral improvement be imagined? In other words, how could there be a sage or wise man? The Stoics in fact reject a form of the ontological argument in advance. For them, if there are degrees of moral goodness, there cannot be a good, only a relative good. Their dilemma is a Platonic one. They want to say that the perfectly good man is of a different kind from people trying to be good. A Platonist would remove the perfect example to another world. The Stoics have no other world in which to put him, so, faced with their fixed belief in his existence in this world, they determine that only wholly imperfect examples must exist alongside him in the only world that there is.

'Guilty', therefore, is an absolute, not a relative term, just as, for the Stoics, 'false' is an absolute term.[1] Does this mean that the Stoics hold that the man who kills the cockerel might equally well kill his father? The doctrine of *numeri* seems to tell against that interpretation; and there is no evidence that any Stoic said that the man capable of sin is at any time equally capable of every sin. What they say is that all sins are equal. A passage of Stobaeus may clarify this somewhat. All sins are equal, quotes Stobaeus, but they are not alike (ὅμοια).[2] This means that, al-

---

[1] Cf. Luschnat, 'Das Problem...', 192; Sext. Emp., *Adv. Math.* 7.422. Luschnat's article has much other helpful information for our present topic, though in places the author seems to want to water down the extreme nature of the Stoic position.

[2] Stob., *Ecl.* 2, p. 106, 21 W. (*SVF* III 528). Similarly all κατορθώματα do not deserve praise (Plut., *SR* 1038E ff. = *SVF* III 211).

though they involve equal guilt, they are not comparable in other respects. Some, for example, may spring from a more incurably perverted character.[1] As the Stoics would put it, sins are qualitatively different. And this means that the physical state of the ἡγεμονικόν will differ from criminal to criminal, since qualities are physically describable as currents of air. The state of mind of the parricide will be different in terms of *pneuma* and in terms of quality from that of the deliberate chicken-killer, but they will be 'equal', that is, indistinguishable, in so far as they are both guilty men. Clearly the Stoics hold that the chicken-killer *could* become a parricide and in that sense is capable of parricide, whereas the wise man (barring exceptional circumstances) could not; but that is not the same as saying that he is to all intents and purposes a parricide already. This at least was the opinion of the Old Stoa, and, if we discount rhetorical exaggerations, it was probably also the view of later writers like Seneca. Seneca in fact alludes to the matter in the *De Beneficiis*.[2] The foolish man has all the vices, he says, but he is not prone to all of them by nature. One man inclines to avarice, another to extravagance, another to brutality. That does not mean, he continues, that we say that Achilles is cowardly. What we say is that all the vices are present in all ordinary men, but that they are not all equally prominent. Rather it is true to say that the bad man is not free from any of them. What this seems to mean is that, since the bad man's character is unstable, even someone like Achilles might at some future time behave in a cowardly way, not that he is actually and presently a coward. If this is so, we have no reason to attribute to the Stoics the view that the pickpocket might just as well have murdered his father.

If guilt has nothing to do with consequences, and is not proportional to punishment, we are forced into further enquiry as to what it could be. Since it does not admit of degrees, it is clearly not affected by circumstances. If seduction is wrong and the seducer is guilty, he is neither more nor less guilty in different circumstances. It makes no difference whether the girl is a respectable married woman, a servant-girl or an adulteress

[1] Stob., *Ecl.* 2, p. 113, 18 W. (*SVF* iii 529).
[2] Sen., *De Ben.* 4.27 (*SVF* iii 659).

already.[1] Clearly some seductions are more socially damaging, but we have already seen that consequences are irrelevant to guilt. But the Stoics must also have held that it makes no difference to guilt whether the girl is already 'fallen' or not. Justification on these grounds is irrelevant; it is obvious that the wise man would never find himself in the position of having to offer extenuating circumstances as an excuse for his behaviour. The only possible explanation, therefore, of the Stoic position is that something of great importance happens in a similar way whenever any kind of guilty act is committed. In order to understand what this is, we shall have to turn to problems of the physiological or rather psychosomatic structure of man.

We have already seen that, when a sin is committed, the Stoics say that the ἡγεμονικόν is disposed in a particular way. This means that the ἡγεμονικόν in the individual man is disposed in a particular way, for it is clear from the texts that the ἡγεμονικόν is generally identified by the Stoics with πνεῦμα.[2] Πνεῦμα is the basic physical component of the Stoic universe, and its principal function, as Sambursky puts it, 'is the generation of the cohesion of matter and generally of the contact between all parts of the cosmos'.[3] Πνεῦμα, which the Stoics viewed as a kind of fire, has a physical property peculiar to itself; this property is called tension (τόνος).[4] Hence πνεῦμα is said to allow 'tensional movement' (τονικὴ κίνησις).[5] As Sambursky remarks, the verb most commonly used of the movement of πνεῦμα is 'pervade' (διήκω), and there is little doubt what kind of movement the Stoics had in mind. They were thinking of vibration, such as is produced by the twanging of a taut string. Philo specifically distinguishes 'tensional movement' from movement from one place to another,[6] and a number of sources refer to it as 'simultaneous movement in opposite directions',[7]

---

[1] Porph. on Hor., *Serm.* 1.2.62 (*SVF* III 533).
[2] Sext. Emp., *Hyp. Pyr.* 2.82, 3.188. *Hyp. Pyr.* 2.70 (*SVF* I 484) says πνεῦμα or something finer than πνεῦμα.   [3] Sambursky, *Physics* I.
[4] Cf. Sambursky, *op. cit.* 5 with references cited.
[5] Nem., *De Nat. Hom.* 2, p. 42 M. (*SVF* II 451).
[6] Philo, *De Sacr. Abel et Cain* 68 (*SVF* II 453). For this see Sambursky, *op. cit.* 29–31.
[7] Alex. Aphr., *De Mixt.*, p. 224, 24 Bruns (*SVF* II 442).

or as neither inwards alone nor outwards alone, but as a continual variation between the two,[1] or as continually backwards and forwards.[2]

We know that Chrysippus held that the ἡγεμονικόν is disposed in a certain way when a man walks.[3] What this means is that the limbs are connected with the ἡγεμονικόν in a tensional relationship. When physical movements take place, the πνεῦμα vibrates in a certain way, thus keeping the centre of consciousness in touch with the limbs. In a passage attributed to Chrysippus by Chalcidius, we read that the ἡγεμονικόν is like a spider in the centre of its web. It holds the ends of all the threads and perceives from close proximity (*de proximo*) if anything touches any of them.[4] The simile of the web is very appropriate; the best modern equivalent is perhaps a piece of elastic.

It seems that the Stoics thought that air is a continuum, and that, if struck by breath, it produces 'waves' flowing outwards. The comparison they drew was with water in a pool. Ripples flow out if a stone is thrown into the water.[5] The behaviour of the πνεῦμα, acting as a cohesive force both in man and in the universe as a whole, must, in their view, be similar. Indeed πνεῦμα is sometimes identified with air.[6]

In the *De Finibus* Cicero says that it is the view of the Stoics that every sin is a mark of weakness (*imbecillitas*) and instability (*inconstantia*).[7] The word *imbecillitas* is informative; it is the Latin equivalent of ἀσθένεια, and there is a passage of Galen which links ἀσθένεια with the doctrine of tension.[8] According to Galen Chrysippus was in the habit of speaking very frequently of the 'weakness' and ἀτονία of the soul. Since the opposite of ἀτονία is given as εὐτονία, it is almost certain that the word means not absence of tension, but wrong, perhaps insufficient tension. Εὐτονία is right or proper tension. Galen mentions the

---

[1] Gal., *De Tremore* 6 (*SVF* II 446).
[2] Stob., *Ecl.* I, p. 153, 24 ff. (*SVF* II 471).
[3] Sen., *Ep.* 113.23 (*SVF* II 836).
[4] Chal., *in Tim.* 220 (*SVF* II 879).
[5] Aët., *Plac.* 4.19.4 (*SVF* II 425). Cf. Sambursky, *op. cit.* 23.
[6] Cf. Plut., *SR* 1053F (*SVF* II 449).
[7] Cic., *De Fin.* 4.77 (*SVF* II 531).
[8] Galen, *De Hipp. et Plat.* 4.403, p. 377, 3 Mü. (*SVF* III 473).

same doctrine elsewhere in a passage where he is referring to the well known Stoic view, here attributed personally to Chrysippus, that there is health and sickness of the soul as well as of the body. Again health is equated with strength and right tension, sickness with weakness and wrong tension.[1] Clearly the Stoic view was that, when a man acts properly, he has a proper 'tension' in his soul; when he sins, his tension is wrong.

The doctrine of tension certainly makes the proposition that all sins are equal easier to understand. We are to imagine that the πνεῦμα in every man vibrates according to a rational pattern so long as the man behaves rationally. Thus the inward and outward movements which are continually mentioned as features of tensional movement are steady throbbings, without erratic variations of intensity. Perhaps this sheds a little light on the doctrine of the smooth flow of life.[2] We recall the ripples sent out by the stone thrown into water. In the life of the sage the tensional movement flows backwards and forwards with equal calmness. Be that as it may, it is certainly clear that, however slight the variations in the rate of vibration, they will be equally irrational. If we imagine that a striking crime like parricide, which will involve an offence against a large number of 'aspects of appropriateness', will be physically represented in the criminal's soul by violently erratic tensional movements, it will be obvious that the tensional movements caused by the unnecessary killing of a cockerel, though less vehement, will be equally erratic, and, the Stoic would say, equally irrational and therefore inexplicable. The word πτοία, which the Stoics use to describe the πάθη, would give this sense.[3] After all, when the Epicureans introduced their 'swerve' of atoms, for which they offer no physical explanation, the distance of the swerve was always held to be negligible, but the Stoics and other critics of Epicurus thought the irrationality of the doctrine stupendous.

It seems, therefore, that the Stoics held that all sins are equal and that there are no degrees of guilt, because the vibrations in the human πνεῦμα are either orderly or disorderly. If guilt is measured in this way, we can easily see why their doctrine did

[1] Galen, *ibid.* 5.438, p. 414, 8–9 Mü. (*SVF* III 471).
[2] Cf. *SVF* I 184.   [3] See above, pp. 25–6.

not concern itself with the consequences of immoral action or with the occasions for it, but only with the fact that it is criminal and therefore irrational. It is striking that the polemical opponents of the doctrine of the equality of sins want to approach it purely as a moral problem, whereas the Stoics themselves certainly thought that all moral behaviour, because it is human behaviour, must be related to physical facts, to what they call the facts of nature. Much of the argument that went on over this question seems to have reached the level of futility very quickly; and the reason for this is that the two sides were apparently talking past one another. Later Stoics did their school a disservice by their neglect of the physics which their predecessors had worked out. They seemed to think it unnecessary. At best it had all been done by Chrysippus. But Chrysippus did not do it for its own sake. What the later Stoics apparently failed to understand is that it is necessary to understand the physical structure of man in order to grasp the nature of moral problems. For morality is, in the Stoic view, in our power. We are able to choose good or evil; and the older Stoics were prepared to explain how this possibility is a simple physical fact.

There is at this point place for some justifiable speculation. We have argued that the Stoics believed that guilt is marked by irrational movements of the human πνεῦμα and virtue by rational ones. We have considered the physics of this in Stoic terms. It is, however, worth asking ourselves whether there are any phenomena of the moral life as such which might have supported the Stoics in the view they took. There is no clear evidence to go on; but a rational guess is perhaps not out of place. It is certainly the case that the most obvious and striking vices are not necessarily the most difficult to cure. Very often it is the peccadillos, which easily become bad habits, which are the most difficult to eradicate. The temptation not to bother about being unnecessarily rude is often much harder to resist than the temptation to be unnecessarily brutal. But rudeness can be as irrational and senseless as brutality. Hence Chrysippus could say that, since the little sins are often harder to control, they may be as dangerous to the moral character. But, whether they are a danger to the moral character or not, they are certainly irrational, that is, they struggle, as it were, against rational control. And if a man finds them harder to control, they may plausibly be said to put him even farther than his neighbour from being a sage. This sort of argument is certainly repugnant to contemporary evaluations of guilt, but it would have made far more sense to an age in which sheep-stealing was a capital offence. And lest the presentation of the Stoic view in this context seems tendentious, we should recall that Chrysippus does not hold that all punishments should be equal—that idea is specifically rejected—but that moral guilt is equal.

All ordinary men, therefore, are equally guilty. They are not, however, equally far from wisdom. Just as the man immediately below the surface, though in danger of drowning, is in fact nearer to safety than the wretch lying on the bottom, so the προκόπτων is nearer to virtue, in the sense that, if he continues along his present path, he will eventually become virtuous, even though he is still utterly vicious. But he is guilty until he actually achieves wisdom. The Stoics hold that the wise man will do everything from fully moral intentions, and his conduct will be entirely consistent. As the προκόπτων advances, therefore, in the direction of the moral life, his actions will also become more and more consistent, until a stage is reached at which everything he does will be identical with what he would do if he were a wise man. Apparently the Stoics thought that when this stage of total consistency is reached, the προκόπτων, as it were, surfaces.

The change is so sudden that it is not immediately noticed. It is as though everything has 'clicked' into place; hence the strange-sounding view that the wise man will not notice that he has actually become wise.[1] The parallel between the προκόπτων and the drowning man or the blind puppy breaks down here, for clearly the drowing man will instantly be aware of getting his head above water. But it is easy to see why the Stoics nevertheless had to hold that the instantaneous appearance of virtue must take a man unawares. He is already performing the actions which, if done from the right intentions, are all virtuous and moral actions. When he is virtuous, his external behaviour will

[1] *SVF* III 539-42.

be identical, but his intention will be moral. To use a Platonic metaphor, we can say that the last speck of impurity, so small as to be virtually indiscernible, has been removed. Once again the physical explanation makes the Stoic position clearer. When the προκόπτων is almost at the stage of wisdom, the guilty acts, which he will still perform, will not be notorious crimes, but what would normally (unstoically) be called trivial faults. The irrational movements of his πνεῦμα will, though utterly irrational, be very slight indeed. Of course in terms of irrationality and guilt they will, for the Stoic, be the same as ever. Recurring 99.9, though very close to 100, never becomes identical with it. It is, in Stoic language, a different kind of number.

It is clear, therefore, that for the Stoic the question about what guilt is has nothing to do with the problem of becoming a wise man. It was frequently an objection to Stoic theory that, according to that theory, there is no difference between, say, Plato and the tyrant Dionysius.[1] That is not so, replies the Stoic. Both men are guilty (assuming Plato is not a sage), but it makes sense for Plato to be hopeful. As for Dionysius, he might as well despair of wisdom; perhaps death is the best thing that could befall him. This reply seems strange, but the strangeness arises from the fact that we find it difficult to think of guilt in the physical way the Stoics demand. Yet there are more modern parallels which convey something of what the Stoics are trying to say. It is often noticed that those men who are morally the noblest do not have a high opinion of their own moral excellence. In ecclesiastical language this comes out as the view, often held by 'saints', that they are the greatest of sinners. This does not mean that they think they are committing what are commonly thought of as heinous crimes. It means that they have a very strong sense of what it means to be guilty. They recognize guilt where the ordinary man would be insensitive. Chrysippus would doubtless hold that they provide evidence for the Stoic view. It is the consciousness of what it means to do right or wrong which provides the proper measure of guilt. And the man who has progressed the furthest in the direction of virtue will have the strongest sense that he is not actually virtuous.

---

[1] Plut., *Quomodo quis in virt. sentiat prof.*; Cic., *De Fin.* 4.56.

When engaged with classical Greek texts, both philosophical and non-philosophical, we find that words like ἁμάρτημα and ἁμαρτάνω provide considerable problems of interpretation. We are never sure whether they refer to crime, to guilt, or to sin. Scholars often try to give them an exact English equivalent and make them correspond to a specific concept which we use ourselves. Very often this attempt is misguided. The conceptual distinctions which we regularly employ were not always made in fifth-century Athens. We have argued in another chapter that even the concept of moral behaviour as such was only clearly recognized for what it is by the Stoics.[1] The Stoics were often accused by their rivals in antiquity of pedantry, because of their intense interest in distinguishing shades of meaning. It seems that their doctrine that all ἁμαρτήματα are equal provides another instance of their search for linguistic precision. For the Stoics a ἁμάρτημα seems to be a sin rather than a crime. It is basically a matter of the disposition, not the external behaviour, of the guilty man. We have seen that the problem of ἁμαρτήματα is not closely associated with the problem of punishment. Crimes, offences against the *numeri offici*, are punished; they are offences against society. The more such offences one commits, the heavier the punishments one deserves. Sin, however, is not essentially a social matter, though it can obviously have social repercussions. It is something which is 'in our power' and thus a matter of personal responsibility. Throughout our investigations of Stoicism we find a concern with the individual case, and in ethics with the individual act *per se*. This suggests that the Stoics were beginning to use concepts much more in line with our views of personality and of the value of the individual as an independent being than was customary in earlier Greek philosophy.

There is a curious and apparently unresolved paradox in all this. We have found the Stoics comparing the sinner with a man under water, who, until he actually surfaces, is equally short of breath whatever the depth of the water may be. Now the swimmer, when he surfaces, makes physical movements, which may or may not be deliberate, but which nevertheless enable him to emerge safely. In the case of virtue and vice, we

---

[1] See above, pp. 1–21.

are to imagine that quite suddenly, indeed unexpectedly, the bad man becomes good. For a while he does not realize his own change of state. We have seen the explanation of this in physical terms. The irregular vibrations imperceptibly die away and the tranquillity of the movement of the πνεῦμα is restored. But the dependence of Stoic ethics on physics makes it easy to explain what has happened in physical terms only at the cost of great metaphysical perplexities. What has happened to the ἡγεμονικόν in the strictly psychological sense is that it now provides moral motivation for actions which it would previously have performed from mixed motives. How can it be that mere repetition of correct behaviour leads to what we should describe (ethically) as the acquisition of perfectly correct motives? Chrysippus could (and perhaps would) reply that the question is unreal. Such a change can only be explained in terms of physics. But his opponent might come back with the query about whether this does not detract from the concept of a strictly ethical area in which terms like 'good' and 'bad' are properly used. Chrysippus seems to want to emphasize at the same time the psychosomatic nature of man and the strict autonomy of ethical concepts—and this may not be possible.

Understanding the relation of the physical vibration of the πνεῦμα to the moral status of the soul may help to explain a rather curious dispute which went on within the ranks of the Stoics themselves. According to Diogenes Laertius, Cleanthes thought that all human souls survive until the destruction of the world by fire at the end of each particular world-cycle, while Chrysippus held that only the souls of the wise survive so long; the others presumably outlive the body but do not last until the ἐκπύρωσις.[1] The view of Chrysippus became the standard doctrine, and various other authorities describe the different types of soul in a way which bears on our present enquiry. The souls of the moral are 'stronger' and those of the others are 'weaker'.[2] We have noticed references to weakness of soul already. A weak soul seems to be one whose vibrations are irrational. Apparently Chrysippus' view was that the character of the soul at death affects its afterlife. If the vibrations of the πνεῦμα are irregular,

[1] D.L. 7.157 (*SVF* II 811).   [2] Cf. *SVF* II 810, 813.

93

its destruction as an individual entity is hastened. This may become a little clearer if we consider the Stoic definitions of death. They were apparently prepared to describe it, in the manner of Socrates in the *Phaedo*, as a separation of the soul from the body,[1] but this was explained not as the separation of an immaterial element from a material, but as the total slackening of the πνεῦμα of perception (ἄνεσις παντελὴς τοῦ αἰσθητικοῦ πνεύματος).[2] This meant that of the physical parts of the human person, only the ἡγεμονικόν, which is also material, can avoid fairly rapid transmutation after death. It seems, then, that the state of this isolated ἡγεμονικόν was of great importance to Chrysippus and after him to the orthodox Stoics. The view of Cleanthes, that all souls (= ἡγεμονικά) survive until the universal conflagration, might seem the natural one to take, for after bodily death what should prevent any ἡγεμονικόν from continuing? Chrysippus must have thought, however, that the irrationality, the erratic vibrations (which are called 'weakness') of the souls of ordinary men, could not hold the soul together long after bodily death. Irrational souls, souls without the correct tension, will then disintegrate. Perhaps it may be added that the world in general, and the soul of the world, moves through an ordered and rational cycle of events. Naturally the movements of an individual good soul would be in harmony with that movement. Irrational movements, however, would not be, and Chrysippus may have thought that they are gradually swallowed up in the movement of the whole, so that the evil soul loses its identity long before the end of the cycle.

One might wonder why Chrysippus thought that the disposition of the ἡγεμονικόν at death determines all its future dispositions, for it is clear that his view of the afterlife entails that no moral improvement is then possible. The various surviving texts in which death is described in similar language to that used of sleep make the position clearer. Whereas sleep is a 'slackening' of the tension of the senses, death is a total slackening.[3] Therefore, just as the ἡγεμονικόν goes on functioning during sleep, but no progress towards virtue is possible at that time,

---

[1] Plut., *CN* 1077B (*SVF* II 618). [2] Aët., *Plac.* 5.24.4 (*SVF* II 767).
[3] D.L. 7.158 (*SVF* II 766); Aët., *Plac.* 5.24.4 (*SVF* II 767).

a fortiori no progress is possible after death. The personality goes on functioning, but there is no awareness since no more information is being fed in by the senses. Hence there is no material for moral action, and the disposition of the soul will remain unchanged.

It is clear that the thesis that all sins are equal is intimately bound up with the doctrine of tensional movement and with the monistic psychology of the Old Stoa in general. When, at the hands of Panaetius and Posidonius, that psychology was discarded, the thesis that all sins are equal must have looked even more strange than when it was first propounded. According to the psychology of Posidonius, immoral behaviour is to be explained as a failure of the reasoning faculty in man to control his desires. On the all-sins-are-equal theory, the Stoics would then be saying that it makes no difference how much control is exercised. Only perfect control is good; all else is bad. But although this looks adequate on the surface, even in the perfectly controlled man there exists a totally irrational factor, presumably causing totally irrational vibrations of the πνεῦμα. So it would seem that in physical terms the good man and the bad would only differ in the degree of the irrationality of their pneumatic vibrations. And for Chrysippus that would make them both guilty men.

In view of this it is easy to understand why Panaetius and Posidonius wished to play down the importance of the wise man. 'We shall see about the wise man (later)', replies Panaetius when asked whether the wise man will love; he then proceeds to give advice to 'you and me', that is, to ordinary people.[1] Panaetius and Posidonius seem to have abandoned the psychology of the Old Stoics because they thought that it did not enable them to account for moral conflict. They should have abandoned the physics as well—and to some extent they did so[2] —for the two are very closely linked. At any rate the doctrine of tensional movement seems alien to the doctrine of the tripartition of the soul. And it is the theory of tensional movement

---

[1] Sen., *Ep.* 116.5.
[2] Cf. Edelstein, 'The Philosophical System of Posidonius', 290–305, and pp. 175–86, 202–14 below.

which enables the doctrine that all sins are equal to make a certain amount of sense. That is a doctrine of uncompromising Stoicism. It fits well within the picture of a world in which the call to be wise is a predominant motif. We should expect that with the decline of that motif, as in Panaetius and Posidonius, the doctrine that all sins are equal would seem stranger than when it was first formulated. Cicero's portrait of Cato in the *Pro Murena* as a man who still holds the Old Stoic views is a caricature of antique virtue. It was drawn by a man who had been taught a Stoicism in which the reality of the wise man had been lost. What in the minds of Zeno and his immediate followers had been a striking moral theory, backed up by an unusual theory of the physical world, had by the time of Cicero become a merely pedantic, not to say perverse, piece of rigorism.

6

APPROPRIATE ACTS

The Stoics held that there is only one good, virtue, and only one evil, vice; everything else is morally indifferent. Doubtless basing himself on this doctrine, Cicero found it fatally tempting to suggest that there are also, according to the Stoics, three kinds of actions, virtuous actions, vicious actions, and intermediates. These intermediates are appropriate and inappropriate actions (*officia servata praetermissaque*).[1] This suggestion is clearly a false version of what the Stoics taught, for it would imply that no *officium* (= καθῆκον) could be a moral act (κατόρθωμα), whereas the Stoics regularly called κατορθώματα complete and appropriate acts (τέλεια καθήκοντα = *perfecta officia*).[2] Nevertheless, a similarly curious rendering of what the Stoics had to say on this subject occurs in the third book of the *De Finibus*, a work which is often regarded as providing a more accurate version of Stoic theory, since it is probably not an *ad hoc* composition of Cicero's but the Latin version of an originally Greek handbook. But here too we find that *officia* are said to be neither good nor evil but intermediate (*officium medium quiddam esse, quod neque in bonis ponatur neque in contrariis*).[3] This time, it is true, Cicero has avoided the most egregious of his mistakes in the *Academica*. He does not say this time that both appropriate and inappropriate acts are intermediate between good and evil, but only that appropriate acts are intermediate. Obviously inappropriate acts are bad, for not only are they not virtuous, that is, they are bad in terms of intention, but they are also wrong in content by being inappropriate. Every inappropriate act is a vice both in terms of intention and in terms of content; it is therefore particularly absurd to call it 'intermediate'—and this is what Cicero avoids in the *De Finibus*.

According to the *De Finibus*, therefore, it is Stoic doctrine

---

[1] Cic., *Acad. Post.* 1.37 (*SVF* I 231).
[2] Cf. Stob., *Ecl.* 2, p. 86, 11 W. (*SVF* III 499); 2.93.14 (*SVF* III 500).
[3] Cic., *De Fin.* 3.58 (*SVF* III 498).

that there are three kinds of action, virtuous action, vicious action, and action which is neither virtuous nor vicious. Is it possible to understand how Cicero could have made such a statement, and to see what utterances of the Stoics in Greek could have justified it?

Before considering this, however, we should clear the ground by giving a brief exposition of how in fact the Stoics related the concepts of virtue, vice, appropriate action and inappropriate action. First of all, as we have seen, when a virtuous action is performed, that action itself is appropriate (τέλειον καθῆκον). But not only virtuous actions can be so described; besides 'perfect and appropriate actions' (virtuous actions) there are also 'intermediate' appropriate actions (μέσα καθήκοντα),[1] or, as Cicero accurately describes them, incomplete and appropriate actions (*inchoata officia*).[2] We can say, therefore, that in terms of appropriateness the Stoics recognize three classes of act: what is completely appropriate, what is incompletely appropriate, and what is inappropriate (παρὰ τὸ καθῆκον).[3] Both imperfectly appropriate and inappropriate actions are vicious. Since, according to a man's motives, what looks like the same action can be either perfectly appropriate or imperfectly appropriate or inappropriate, we can schematize the position as follows in the case of talking:

1. Talking can be done morally and appropriately. In this case it is a τέλειον καθῆκον or κατόρθωμα.

2. Talking can be done non-morally and appropriately. In this case it is a μέσον καθῆκον and a ἁμάρτημα.

3. Talking can be done non-morally and inappropriately. In this case it is a παρὰ τὸ καθῆκον and a ἁμάρτημα.

There is no fourth possibility. No action can be both moral and inappropriate, for the wise man, all of whose acts are moral, can do nothing inappropriate. That is what the Stoics mean when they say that the wise man does everything well.[4]

When we look at this schematization, we get a better idea of

---

[1] Stob., *Ecl.* 2, p. 86, 3 W. (*SVF* III 494); cf. *SVF* III 499.
[2] *De Fin.* 3.58 (*SVF* III 498).
[3] It might be thought that there is a fourth class (neither appropriate nor inappropriate). We shall consider this later. See D.L. 7.108 (*SVF* III 495).
[4] D.L. 7.125 (*SVF* III 561).

what the Stoics mean in speaking of a μέσον καθῆκον. Such an act is not intermediate between virtuous and vicious behaviour. In terms of morality it is vice, but in terms of content it looks like what is virtuous. Thus if we call a κατόρθωμα *AA* and an act both vicious and inappropriate *BB*, then a μέσον καθῆκον will be *AB*. The significant aspect of a μέσον καθῆκον is not that it is virtuous, for it is in fact vicious. Yet its viciousness is not its most significant aspect either, for then it could not be clearly distinguished from what is inappropriate. The significant aspect of a μέσον καθῆκον is that it is an act which accomplishes neither good nor bad, but natural ends—and these natural ends are indifferent as to virtue and vice. As Stobaeus puts it, a μέσον καθῆκον is measured in relation to certain kinds of indifferents, things called natural and unnatural.[1] This is probably the doctrine which Cicero muddled in the *Academica* when he said that *officia* and *contra officia* are between what is good and what is bad. In terms of virtue and vice, of course, what makes a μέσον καθῆκον vicious is that the disposition of the doer is not fixed. It is possible to perform all the appropriate acts, but these acts remain incomplete (μέσαι πράξεις) until they stem from a fixed disposition.[2]

Let us now return to Cicero. We recall that in the *De Finibus* we found him saying that all actions are either (*a*) virtuous, or (*b*) vicious, or (*c*) neither virtuous nor vicious. The Greek original of this is suggested by a passage of Stobaeus, where we find that according to the Stoics all actions are of three kinds, either virtuous actions (κατορθώματα), or vicious actions (ἁμαρτήματα), or a third class which Stobaeus describes with the words τὰ δ' οὐδέτερα.[3] These οὐδέτερα are later explained by Stobaeus as neither virtuous acts nor vicious (οὔτε κατορθώματα οὔτε ἁμαρτήματα), and examples of them are given: speaking, questioning, answering, walking, going away from

---

[1] Stob., *Ecl.* 2, p. 86, 10 W. (*SVF* III 499).

[2] Stob., *Flor.* 103.22, vol. 3, p. 907, 3 H. (*SVF* III 510). The genuine Stoic view is presented well by Clement (*Strom.* 6.14.111 (*SVF* III 515)). Later Stoics seem to have distinguished perfect from imperfect καθήκοντα in terms of the categories of substance and quality. Cf. Epict., *Disc.* 3.7.25 and Fronto, *Ep. De Eloq. ad M. Anton.* p. 140 Naber (*SVF* III 514).

[3] Stob., *Ecl.* 2, p. 96, 19 W.

home. When considering this list we are immediately struck by a curious fact. Although the actions named are clearly for the Stoics neither virtuous nor vicious in themselves, they can be virtuous or vicious according to the disposition of the individual doing them. In other words, although in themselves these actions are neither virtuous nor vicious, in every particular case of their occurrence they will be either virtuous or vicious. Walking sensibly (φρονίμως) is in fact mentioned by Stobaeus in the very same passage as a κατόρθωμα. Now since the Stoics do not admit the existence of 'things in themselves', that is, they think that 'walking' is merely a name we give to an act in so far as it is actually performed, it is strange that they think in terms of 'things in themselves' when analysing classes of action. And what in fact we wish to suggest is that they meant no such thing, however they may have expressed their intention, or however the doxographers may represent their intention. In other words our proposal is that when the Stoics said that all acts are either virtuous or vicious or οὐδέτερα, they intended οὐδέτερα to suggest that acts which *by definition* are neither virtuous nor vicious are thus in particular cases *either* virtuous or vicious. We should note that the examples of κατορθώματα we are given by Stobaeus present a 'circular' appearance. We ask what is good (moral) action, and we are given examples like doing justly, being wise, walking sensibly.[1] Similarly, examples of vice are activities which are by definition irrational or unjust. It is like saying that murder (unjust killing) is an example of a vicious act. It is true, but not entirely helpful. As for the οὐδέτερα, however, the whole doctrine makes much better sense if we hold that in any individual case every such act will in fact be either virtuous or vicious. Perhaps Cicero's source thought in terms of 'things in themselves', and hence called such actions neither virtues nor vices, but, if Chrysippus said that, he was speaking in contradiction to his generally nominalist doctrines.

Our view is that, if he said οὐδέτερα, he meant that such actions could not on *a priori* grounds be called virtuous or vicious. If someone asks whether walking is virtuous or vicious, all he can be told is that, until we look at a particular example,

---

[1] Cf. *SVF* III 494, 501.

there is no reason why it should be the one rather than the other. Every act of walking is not neither virtuous nor vicious, but either virtuous or vicious. It may be that this explanation of actions that are 'neither virtuous nor vicious' can help us to resolve further problems about things which are called ἀδιάφορα, intermediate between virtue and vice. Before moving further, however, we should briefly consider a passage of Diogenes Laertius.[1] The subject is appropriate acts. Of all impulsive actions, says Diogenes, some are appropriate, others are inappropriate, and others still are 'neither appropriate nor inappropriate'. If our previous suggestion is correct, this passage must be read as saying that the third class is not to be bracketed in general as either appropriate or inappropriate. Actions falling within it may sometimes be appropriate and sometimes not, and there is no significant reason why they are on *a priori* grounds likely to be the one rather than the other. Obviously some actions, like neglecting one's parents—this example is one of those given—are more likely to be inappropriate than appropriate. Hence in general they can be called παρὰ τὸ καθῆκον. Actions 'neither appropriate nor inappropriate' have no general likelihood of this kind. Whether one performs them or not hardly matters; nor does it matter much whether one performs them when they are inappropriate or not.

Let us, therefore, set up interpretations of τὰ οὐδέτερα in two columns, on the left the Stoic doctrine as intended, on the right the version which has reached Cicero's *Academica*.

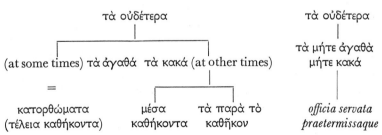

Our interpretation of the sense of τὰ οὐδέτερα will command more support if we can find the phrase occurring elsewhere in

[1] D.L. 7.108 (*SVF* III 495).

contexts where the present explanation helps to solve long-standing puzzles. Such contexts can be found if we consider the Stoic doctrine of value (ἀξία) and of what is preferred (προηγμένα). Bonhoeffer has observed that, although in Stoic texts we find frequent references to a theory that things preferred have much worth (πολλὴ ἀξία), there are no examples given of things of little worth;[1] and he adduces from this that the distinction among things of worth between those preferred and the rest does not belong to the original teaching of Zeno. Suggestions of this kind deserve to be treated with great care. There is no doubt that orthodox Stoicism in its developed form distinguished 'things preferred' as a sub-class of things with value. The doctrine is attested by Stobaeus, Sextus Empiricus and Cicero; and Stobaeus (excerpting Arius Didymus) and Cicero attribute it to Zeno himself.[2] The attribution may be wrong, but can hardly be held to be so without good reason. In fact, the evidence for any other doctrine than that προηγμένα are a sub-class of things with value derives only from Diogenes Laertius,[3] who tells us that everything that is indifferent (neither good nor bad) is of three kinds: it is either preferred or rejected or neither (τὰ οὐδετέρως ἔχοντα). He also suggests in two places that everything which has value is called προηγμένον, everything which has ἀπαξία is called ἀποπροηγμένον. Hence 'things that have neither value nor disvalue' are neither preferred nor rejected. We look to be on familiar ground here; the Stoics are found to be talking, as before about acts which are neither appropriate nor inappropriate, so now about things which are 'neither preferred nor rejected'.

However, one might ask why, as Bonhoeffer seems to have thought, Zeno did not posit three classes of indifferents: things

[1] Bonhoeffer, *Die Ethik* 173.
[2] Stob., *Ecl.* 2, p. 84, 21 W. (*SVF* I 192); 2.80.144 (*SVF* III 133); Sext. Emp., *Adv. Math.* 11.59 (*SVF* III 122), where προηγμένα have ἱκανὴν ἀξίαν; Cic., *Acad. Post.* 1.37 (*SVF* I 193). Although the last part of the passage quoted by von Arnim is a grotesque misreading of Stoicism, the doctrine of προηγμένα as having more worth is attested. Cf. Cic., *De Fin.* 3.53 (*SVF* III 130), where a *praepositum* (προηγμένον) has *aestimatio mediocris*. This *mediocris* may be connected with the μέσον of μέσον καθῆκον etc. The latter suggestion has been made by Professor Sandbach.
[3] D.L. 7.105–6 (*SVF* III 126, 127).

preferred (which have value), things totally indifferent, and things rejected (which have disvalue). The difficulty is that, according to later theory at any rate, all natural things have value, and all unnatural things have disvalue.[1] Hence if this theory was also known to the Stoic whose views are represented by Diogenes Laertius, he must have posited a class of things which are neither natural nor unnatural, but non-natural. But given the Stoic concept of nature, such a class looks rather odd, though that does not mean that the Stoics did not (irrationally) posit its existence. Indeed there are two passages which suggest that some at least of the school took this course. According to Sextus Empiricus it was the view of Cleanthes, diverging here from orthodox Stoicism, that pleasure is not natural, and has no value;[2] the orthodox view was that it is indifferent and not preferred. Since Cleanthes' position is clearly being contrasted with the orthodox view, it looks as though the orthodox view was that pleasure has some value, but not enough to make it preferred. If this is right, then we have an example of what Bonhoeffer tries vainly to find, that is, something of little worth.

Be that as it may, it certainly looks as though the point of Cleanthes' position was to posit something with no value at all and with no standing in nature at all; though there is no evidence that he held pleasure to be unnatural or possessed of disvalue. We must conclude for the present that, when in a second passage about things that are 'neither natural nor unnatural' we ask how Cleanthes would have interpreted this phrase,[3] the answer must be that he thought of things non-natural as comprising a third class; in other words, for Cleanthes there are three classes of indifferents: natural, non-natural, unnatural. We shall consider later why Cleanthes may have adopted such a position; for the moment, however, we should notice that by the time of Archedemus this seems to have been regarded as an impossible position. What could a non-natural class be in the Stoic world? Archedemus was clearly attracted by Cleanthes' account of pleasure. Like him he wishes to deny it any value.

[1] Stob., *Ecl.* 2, p. 83, 10 W. (*SVF* III 124).
[2] Sext. Emp., *Adv. Math.* 11.73 (*SVF* III 155).
[3] Stob., *Ecl.* 2, p. 79, 19 W. (*SVF* III 140).

But he does not now say it is non-natural. He has to argue both that it is natural and that it has no value.[1] Needless to say, this contradicts the orthodox position that natural things all have value;[2] and Archedemus could have been drawn to say it only by admitting that Cleanthes was wrong to talk about a class of the non-natural in addition to the natural and the unnatural.

Forgetting for the moment the problem raised by Bonhoeffer of whether for Zeno all natural things are preferred, let us turn now to the matter of the third class, that group of things which according to Stobaeus are 'neither natural nor unnatural'.[3] In the light of our previous discussion about appropriate acts, we should wish to interpret this phrase to mean that each individual thing that is indifferent will in fact be either natural or unnatural, but that no general norm about the naturalness of such things in particular circumstances can be laid down which is even approximately accurate. We can assume that things οὔτε κατὰ φύσιν οὔτε παρὰ φύσιν are aptly described as οὐδέτερα or οὐδετέρως ἔχοντα in relation to nature. Let us see if any further light can be shed on the problem from this angle.

Another passage of Stobaeus takes us a little further. Here we have the three classes, natural things, unnatural things, and μηδετέρως ἔχοντα, said to arouse ὁρμή, ἀφορμή, and neither the one nor the other, respectively.[4] The point about the third class which is important here is that it does not, on our interpretation, provide clear impulses to action. What this means is clarified in its turn by a further passage of Diogenes Laertius.[5] The class of things which do not provide any obvious impulse is made up of what are 'disposed equally to choice and rejection' (ἐπίσης ἐχόντων). In other words, things which according to Stobaeus arouse impulses neither to accept nor to reject are described by Diogenes more positively. For 'neither...nor' we may again substitute 'either...or'.

In three other passages the same class of objects is referred to, and in these passages the discussion is not about whether they

---

[1] Sext. Emp., *Adv. Math.* 11.73 (*SVF* III 22 Archedemus).
[2] Stob., *Ecl.* 2, p. 83, 10 W. (*SVF* III 124).
[3] Stob., *Ecl.* 2, p. 79, 19 W. (*SVF* III 140).
[4] Stob., *Ecl.* 2, p. 82, 5 W. (*SVF* III 121).
[5] D.L. 7.104 (*SVF* III 119).

are natural or whether they provide impulses to action, but whether they are to be preferred or rejected. One of these passages is Diogenes Laertius 7.106, a section in which we noted the odd identification of things preferred with things of value; the others are from Sextus and Stobaeus.[1] Stobaeus is the most interesting when he writes as follows: 'Things preferred are those indifferents which have much value...things rejected are similarly those which have much disvalue; things neither preferred nor rejected are those which have neither much value nor much disvalue.' This text is the key to the situation. Clearly the orthodox Stoic view was that phrases like 'neither preferred nor rejected' and, we would suggest, 'neither natural nor unnatural' (or τὰ οὐδέτερα with relation to naturalness or preferredness) are to be interpreted not, as Cleanthes wished, as equivalent to 'without value or disvalue', but as 'possessing little value or disvalue'. How this would come about can be understood if we revert to our three classes and interpret them along the lines laid down in this chapter. The classes are natural (with value, causing ὁρμή), unnatural (with disvalue, causing ἀφορμή), and τὰ οὐδέτερα or τὰ οὐδετέρως ἔχοντα. This third class is not neither natural nor unnatural, but (according to circumstances) either natural or unnatural, and therefore possessing value or disvalue in small quantities. It should be noticed that, if we look at members of the third class in the case of things and in the case of actions, the class will be much larger when we are dealing with actions. The reasons for this are clear enough. The appropriateness of a particular action in a particular set of circumstances is obviously less easy to forecast. It is much easier to generalize about the value of things than about the appropriateness of actions.

Let us now return to the passages of Diogenes Laertius with which we began the enquiry into things preferred.[2] Diogenes distinguishes three classes: the preferred, which have value; the rejected, which have disvalue; τὰ οὐδετέρως ἔχοντα, which are neither preferred nor rejected. If our interpretation thus far is

---

[1] Sext. Emp., *Adv. Math.* 11.59 (*SVF* III 122); Stob., *Ecl.* 2, p. 80, 14 ff. W. (*SVF* III 133). The emended text of Wachsmuth is certainly correct.
[2] D.L. 7.105–6 (*SVF* III 126–7).

correct, we can now suggest that this third class is composed of things without significant value (their value is not even *mediocris*). Indeed they are things which cannot be the subject of even rough generalizations as to whether they have value or not. Thus, when Diogenes says that things preferred have value, we must take him to mean that they have significant value, value worthy of the name. If this is the case, there are no passages left in which προηγμένα are to be defined as other than possessing a reasonable amount of value. For the Stoics, therefore, from the beginning, we can argue that according to the available evidence things preferred are always a sub-class of things with value, things rejected a sub-class of things without value. Thus Bonhoeffer's view that this doctrine was not part of the original teaching of Zeno collapses, since it appears to have no properly interpreted evidence in its favour.

The only evidence indeed which might seem remotely helpful to Bonhoeffer is that provided by Sextus Empiricus when he describes first the orthodox view of pleasure, then the heterodoxies of Cleanthes and Archedemus.[1] Apparently, when Cleanthes interpreted the view that pleasure is indifferent and not preferred, he claimed that it is not natural and has no value; not that it has no significant value, but that it has no value at all. That this is what he meant seems clear from the fact that he would not admit it to be natural. But we have already observed the oddity of this position, and how Archedemus felt constrained to give up non-natural things at whatever cost. We can only speculate as to Cleanthes' reasons for his position, but perhaps his difficulties arose from his being unwilling to grant pleasure any value. Things without value would, to an orthodox Stoic, be contrary to nature. Yet how could pleasure, which even Cleanthes must have recognized as a permanent feature of human life, thus provide an unnatural motivation for rational beings? Perhaps the strangeness of this could be reduced if pleasure could be non-natural, not unnatural. Be that as it may, Cleanthes' proposal did not win acceptance, and Bonhoeffer can hardly adduce this passage to show anything about things preferred. Although Cleanthes might have posited three

[1] Sext. Emp., *Adv. Math.* 11.73 (*SVF* III 155).

classes, things preferred, things non-natural, things rejected, it is more likely that he maintained the normal view that things preferred have much value, while claiming that between things of no significant value and those of no significant disvalue there are actually some which have no value whatsoever.

We have reached the point at which we can say that for orthodox Stoicism every actual thing will in particular circumstances be either preferred or rejected, and every particular act will be either appropriate or inappropriate. Apparently the Stoics held that some types of action, such as pursuing virtue, are always appropriate,[1] but in the case of the rest, though many other acts may be normally appropriate, their appropriateness cannot be assumed on every individual occasion; rather each individual occasion must be taken on its merits. This brings us to the question of what a particular appropriate act is. How in fact do we tell whether an act is appropriate?

The standard answer given by the Stoics is that an appropriate act is an act which, when it has been done, admits of a εὔλογον ἀπολογίαν.[2] What this means has been disputed. Hirzel, Grumach and Nebel hold that it means that the action can be defended in terms of probabilities:[3] the act is reasonable rather than unreasonable but not *necessarily* correct, in the sense that it may not necessarily achieve what its author intended. Bonhoeffer and Pohlenz want the word to suggest that the action actually is the correct action:[4] it is reasonable in the sense that true reason would declare it to be so. Clearly the word εὔλογος can have both these senses.[5]

The possibility is therefore open that, when describing an appropriate act and defending it as εὔλογος, the Stoics played on the ambiguity of the word; but there is little justification for proposing this type of interpretation if their language can be shown to make sense unambiguously. We need to determine,

---

[1] D.L. 7.109 (*SVF* III 496).
[2] Stob., *Ecl.* 2, p. 85, 14 W. (*SVF* III 494); cf. D.L. 7.107 (*SVF* III 493), εὔλογον ἀπολογισμόν.
[3] Hirzel, *Untersuchungen* 2.55; Grumach, *Physis und Agathon* 40; Nebel, 'Der Begriff...', 446–9.
[4] Bonhoeffer, *Ethik* 193–8; Pohlenz, *Die Stoa* 2.74.
[5] Cf. *SVF* III 88 (correct) and II 201 (probable).

therefore, whether either of the senses of εὔλογος is suited to all appropriate acts. And first of all, in enquiring into this, we must remind ourselves that we are talking about appropriate acts, that is, that according to the Stoics every καθῆκον, whether it is a moral act (κατόρθωμα) or not, is supposed to be justified by a εὔλογος ἀπολογία. According to Bonhoeffer it is an argument against the view that εὔλογος means 'probable' that some appropriate acts are virtuous acts. These, he thinks, cannot be justified by probability. This argument, however, misses the point altogether. It is the appropriateness that is being justified, not the morality. And, we must remember, an appropriate act does not have to achieve what its performer hopes it will achieve. When we set sail in suitable weather, we cannot know that a storm will not arise before we return to the safety of the harbour.[1] Nevertheless, our actions are appropriate when we set out. As Seneca puts it, we follow where reason (*ratio*), not truth (*veritas*), draws us.[2] Bonhoeffer seems to be aware of this approach to the problem when he points out that for the Stoics external success has nothing to do with the sense of the moral καθῆκον. But this objection is ill founded. Apart from the oddity of saying that the possibility of an action's being successful has nothing to do with its being καθῆκον, we must remember that what is defended by a εὔλογος ἀπολογία is not the morality or virtue of the act at all. Since the εὔλογος ἀπολογία is supposed to defend all καθήκοντα, both those which are virtuous and those which are not, it is of no interest to point out that the success of an action is irrelevant to its goodness.

Although according to the Stoics there are certain preferred things which are preferred for their own sake, and others preferred for the sake of other things,[3] the same distinction does not appear in the case of appropriate actions—and it is logical that it should not. For when we perform actions, we do not perform them for their own sake. We may seek the *ends* of the actions, for example, of προκοπή, for their own sake, but we act in order to achieve the end. Hence it would seem reasonable to suppose that the appropriateness of an action has something to do with

---

[1] Cf. Epict., *Disc.* 2.10.6.　　[2] Seneca, *De Ben.* 4.33.2.
[3] Stob., *Ecl.* 2, p. 82, 21 W. (*SVF* iii 142); D.L. 7.107 (*SVF* iii 135).

the likelihood of its being a successful action; and this will be true in every case when the action is performed. This being so, there seems to be no reason why the word εὔλογος should not relate to the probable effectiveness of the act, and that a εὔλογος ἀπολογία should not be a claim that there is every human reason for supposing that the particular actions will work. Let us see, therefore, how this turns out in the case of those appropriate actions which are virtuous and those which are not.

1. Every καθῆκον has a εὔλογος defence; i.e. it is probably effective.

Repaying A is καθῆκον (even if done unwillingly and therefore without virtue); therefore repaying A will probably achieve its end of satisfying A's just demands.

2. Every καθῆκον has a εὔλογος defence; i.e. it is probably effective.

Repaying A justly is καθῆκον (and also a κατόρθωμα); therefore repaying A will probably achieve its end of satisfying A's just demands.

It should be noticed that in neither case can we be sure that A will in fact be satisfied and not demand interest. Whether he is paid back virtuously or without virtue is irrelevant to this aspect of the question. It seems, therefore, that translating εὔλογος as 'probable' is satisfactory in every case where the word is used in connection with καθήκοντα. The alternative translation would clearly not work in all cases, for neither are all καθήκοντα morally right nor are all κατορθώματα materially successful.

We may notice at this point that Cicero translates the phrase εὔλογος ἀπολογία as *probabilis ratio*.[1] Here the Latin is ambiguous. *Probabilis* could stand for εὔλογος (probable) or πιθανός (convincing). The latter is preferred by Pohlenz,[2] and although it seems unlikely to be correct, since it introduces the flavour of Carneades into a definition of appropriate acts which was current long before Carneades' time, it does not help Pohlenz' case under any circumstances. For if *probabilis* means 'convincing', it is still not the same thing to say that a defence

---

[1] Cic., *De Fin.* 3.58 (*SVF* III 498).
[2] Pohlenz, *Die Stoa* 2.74.

is convincing as to say that it accurately describes reality in the way that right reason would describe it.

There are two final points to be considered. First of all, if a εὔλογος defence is concerned with the effectiveness of the action, might one not say that a well-planned murder is appropriate simply because it succeeds? The answer to this would be that, since all appropriate acts are by definition natural (κατὰ φύσιν), whereas murder is by definition παρὰ φύσιν, the view that a well-planned murder could be defended if it is effective would imply that an inappropriate act (an unnatural act) is at the same time appropriate because it is effective. We must remember that it is only *appropriate* acts which can be defended if effective, and no unnatural act is appropriate.

The second objection is of a different kind. It might be argued that difficulties about whether κατορθώματα (καθήκοντα τέλεια), as well as other kinds of καθήκοντα, can be said to have a εὔλογος ἀπολογία, did not originally arise because in the thought of Zeno only what later came to be called καθήκοντα were to be defended in terms of the probable (εὔλογον). The suggestion would be that the extension of the εὔλογος ἀπολογία to κατορθώματα only came about because Arcesilaus defined not the καθῆκον but specifically the κατόρθωμα as an act ὅπερ πραχθὲν εὔλογον ἔχει τὴν ἀπολογίαν.[1] To investigate this we shall need to consider briefly what Arcesilaus thinks a moral act (κατόρθωμα) is. For Arcesilaus certainty is impossible. No one, not even the wise man, can know that his action is morally right. To use the phrase 'morally right' in the proposition 'The wise man knows he is morally right' is a misuse of language. The wise man is behaving morally when he thinks that he is behaving morally. The moral course is what seems reasonable in the circumstances to the wise man, who can be *certain* of nothing.

It is clear that what Arcesilaus calls a κατόρθωμα is not a κατόρθωμα to the Stoics at all. The Stoic wise man does not and cannot make mistakes about morality. He does not merely try to be moral (as does Arcesilaus' wise man); he always *is* moral. His moral behaviour *qua* moral is not susceptible of error, even theoretically. Thus it would follow that what Arcesilaus

---

[1] Sext. Emp., *Adv. Math.* 7.158.

calls a κατόρθωμα is not a Stoic κατόρθωμα. However, since Arcesilaus describes his κατόρθωμα in terms which the Stoics use for the καθῆκον, we must consider two possibilities. Either Arcesilaus looked at the description of a καθῆκον and said, in effect, 'What you have described is in fact a moral act'; or, the second alternative, the Stoics, who had not originally described κατορθώματα as admitting a 'probable defence', were induced to do so by the application of the εὔλογος ἀπολογία to κατορθώματα by Arcesilaus. In fact the second alternative seems most improbable. For if the term εὔλογον was not in the Stoic view concerned with the morality of the act, nothing that Arcesilaus says about moral acts would have induced them to revise their opinion, since they would find Arcesilaus' concept of a moral act inadequate. On the other hand if εὔλογον was originally relevant to the morality of the καθῆκον—which in our view it was not—then it would have been applied by the Stoics to κατορθώματα from the beginning. Finally, if εὔλογον originally means that the καθῆκον is *in fact* appropriate (and therefore effective), again the Stoics would be unimpressed by the remarks of Arcesilaus about it, for in his view no one could know whether an act is appropriate, not even the sage. It seems best to conclude, therefore, that the most likely sequence of events is that the Stoics from the beginning defined καθήκοντα *qua* καθήκοντα as admitting a probable defence, but that Arcesilaus claimed that such a defence, if properly conducted, would be the defence of a genuinely moral act. We should notice that Arcesilaus' period of philosophical activity begins well within Zeno's own lifetime. As Cicero tells us, Arcesilaus began the feud between Sceptics and Stoics by his opposition to Zeno himself.[1] There seems little reason to deny that it was Zeno's original teaching about all appropriate acts which Arcesilaus applied to specifically moral acts.

[1] Cic., *De Orat.* 3.67.

7

FATE AND NECESSITY

'. . . so that he can both escape necessity and retain fate.'
(Cicero, *De Fato* 41)

The extremely complicated problem of whether the Stoics were determinists, and if so, in what sense, has been clarified by a number of recent studies. However, it seems that misconceptions still remain widely current, and a satisfactory overall picture of the scene has not yet been produced. It is the intention of this chapter to present such an overall picture of the final doctrine of the Old Stoa, as elaborated by Chrysippus.[1] To do this, however, it will be necessary to retread some fairly familiar ground, so that we can be clear what the situation was which confronted Chrysippus when he started to think about fate— or at least what he thought the situation to be! This means that we shall have to begin with the relevant passages of Aristotle, particularly those about future contingents in chapter nine of the *De Interpretatione*.

The brief exposition of this famous passage that will follow *may* not be what Aristotle intended, though I believe it to be basically correct. Our business here, however, is not with what Aristotle intended to say, but with what various other schools of antiquity, the Megarian, Stoic and Epicurean, supposed him to have said. It will be argued that our first knowledge of the arguments which can be briefly summarized as being 'about fate' comes from this passage of Aristotle (with related passages in other Aristotelian works); and it should be added that, if our interpretation of the history of the dispute is correct, that is, if the views of Diodorus, Philo of Megara, Chrysippus, Epicurus, Carneades and the rest take their starting-point from discussions represented for us by the ninth chapter of the *De Interpre-*

[1] Frequent reference will be made in this chapter to the following important studies relevant to the problem of fate: M. E. Reesor, 'Fate and Possibility in Early Stoic Philosophy', P. M. Schuhl, *Le Dominateur*, and W. Theiler, 'Tacitus und die antike Schicksalslehre'.

tatione, then their common opinion as to what Aristotle meant has no small bearing on the problem of what he intended to mean.

The starting-point of Aristotle's discussion is the proposition that every affirmation and every negation is either true or false (18 a 28 ff.). In the *Categories* Aristotle speaks as though this is always a true proposition,[1] but now he hesitates about future contingents. For if propositions about the future, such as 'There will be a sea-battle tomorrow', are either true or false, he argues, then everything is 'necessary', that is to say, determined. A particularly ludicrous conclusion from this, he continues, is that there would be no point in deliberating (βουλεύεσθαι) or troubling oneself about anything, because what is going to happen is going to happen necessarily. This argument is what later became known as the Lazy Argument (ἀργὸς λόγος), and was refuted by Chrysippus, as we shall see. Aristotle, however, seems to suppose that it will hold if propositions about the future are agreed to be either true or false. Clearly we can only understand what Aristotle is saying here if we grasp what he means by 'true' and 'false'. Truth for Aristotle has nothing to do with whether propositions are affirmed or denied. That makes no difference to how things are (δῆλον γὰρ ὅτι οὕτως ἔχει τὰ πράγματα, κἂν μὴ ὁ μὲν καταφήσῃ, ὁ δὲ ἀποφήσῃ, 18 b 37). Statements are true according to how the actual things are (19 a 33), so that, as Ackrill remarks, Aristotle 'seems to hold a rather crude realistic correspondence theory of truth'.[2] This being so, it would follow that, since future events have not yet occurred, statements about them cannot be referred to the events themselves and hence cannot be said to be true. Neither, of course, can they be said to be false, since 'false' would have to mean 'proved false'. Hence we are prepared for the conclusion that while of any pair of contradictories referring to the future, one or the other will be true or false, yet of any particular statement it cannot be said that it is yet true or false. Aristotle then adds that one such statement may be truer than

---

[1] *Cat.* 2 a 7. For details of some current discussion of the sea-battle, see Taylor, 'The Problem of Future Contingencies', 1 note 2.

[2] Ackrill, *Aristotle's Categories and De Interpretatione* 140.

another, that is, more likely to occur, as far as can be forecast. But truer does not imply true.

Now it is apparent that if propositions about future contingents cannot be said to be true, this must be because there is always the possibility that what will in fact occur in a particular situation might not occur. In other words 'possible' must mean 'what may or may not happen'. Thus Aristotle argues that, although it is the case that a particular cloak will wear out before it is cut up, it is always possible for it to be cut up regardless of whether in fact it wears out first (19 a 12 ff.). From this it also follows that nothing can be said to be necessary until it has actually happened.[1] Hence, as the *De Interpretatione* puts it, 'what is, necessarily is, when it is... but not everything that is, necessarily is' (19 a 23 ff.).[2]

Since our present concern is primarily with the Stoics, we do not need to spend much time on the controversies over this theory in Aristotle's own day. Suffice it to say that Aristotle himself tells us that his theories about the meaning of the term 'possible' were questioned by the Megarians.[3] According to the Megarians, what is possible is only possible when it is happening, or, to use the example which Aristotle gives us, a man is only able to build a house when he is actually building it. This, as Aristotle observes, is a very strange theory indeed, and would not have worried the ancient logicians long. But a later Megarian, Diodorus Cronus, constructed a much more interesting and sophisticated version. According to Diodorus the possible is not simply what is happening, but either what is true or what will in fact be true.[4] It can be readily appreciated that the effect of

[1] *Rhet.* 1418 a 5.

[2] For further discussion of this see Schuhl, *op. cit.* 14–18. Schuhl mentions other relevant passages of Aristotle on 'possible' (*N.E.* 1139 b 7–9, *Anal. Pr.* 32 a 18 ff., *Met.*, 1047 a 8, 24 ff., 1047 b 3.

[3] *Met.* 1046 b 29 ff. Cf. Schuhl, *op. cit.* 34.

[4] For this famous thesis of Diodorus see (e.g.) Plut., *SR* 1055 D (*SVF* II 202); Cic., *De Fato* 13 and 17, and, for its role in the Master Argument, Epict., *Disc.* 2.19, Alex. Aphr., *In An. Pr.* p. 184 Wallies. The argument has been discussed endlessly. See especially Zeller, 'Ueber den κυριεύων...', Virieux-Reymond, *La Logique* 198–202, Mates, *Stoic Logic* 38–41, Schuhl, *op. cit.* M. Kneale (*The Development of Logic* 133) thinks that Diodorus constructed his argument with the sea-battle in mind.

this is to close the gap through which Aristotle thought that he had managed to escape the apparently fatal conclusion that, since it is possible to formulate true propositions about the future, the future is therefore rigidly determined. Presumably Diodorus held that all propositions, whether about future contingents or not, are either true or false. For Diodorus a proposition which suggests something impossible about the future is false.[1]

Whatever Diodorus himself may have thought about the implications of his doctrine of the possible in the moral sphere, there is no doubt that others believed, as presumably Aristotle would have done, that, if it were true, it would fix the future in rigid causal chains and leave no room for actions 'within our power' or for anything approaching what we should call moral responsibility. Reactions to it were strong, even among the Megarians themselves, for Diodorus' pupil Philo apparently rejected it and returned to a position more like that of Aristotle. Philo's thesis, in its turn, became a forerunner of the more developed theories of Chrysippus. According to Philo a proposition is possible if there is a 'fitness' (ἐπιτηδειότης) in what it describes; for example, he argued that even if a piece of wood is in the depths of the sea it is still combustible, meaning that it is fit and proper for wood to burn. It is obvious that there is a connection here with Aristotle's example in the *De Interpretatione* that a cloak may possibly be cut up, even if it is not going to be cut up in fact, but simply to be worn out. According to Alexander of Aphrodisias the view of Philo was only different from that of Aristotle in that, whereas Philo held that something is possible if it has a 'fitness' to occur even though prevented by external necessity, Aristotle thought that the possible is 'that which is capable of coming into being and *is not prevented*, even if it does not come into being'.[2] But this looks like an attempt to impose a distinction which the *De Interpretatione* at least does not sanction.

Naturally not only the Megarians objected to what Diodorus

[1] Cic., *De Fato* 12.
[2] Alex. Aphr., *In An. Pr.* p. 184 Wallies. For other evidence on Philo's view cf. Boethius, *In De Int.* p. 234 Meiser; Simp., *In Cat.* pp. 195–6 Kalbfleisch. Cf. Mates, *op. cit.* 40; Reesor, *op. cit.* 291 note 14.

had done. There were two ways out of the situation for those philosophers interested. One solution was to go back to the position of Aristotle, and we have seen that Philo more or less did this in his treatment of possibility. Whether he also did it on the question of whether propositions about future contingents cannot yet be said to be true or false, we do not know. It seems unlikely, however, that he took this step, for it was taken by Epicurus and was regarded by Cicero as betraying a childish ignorance of logic! Cicero does not realize that Epicurus is returning to the view of Aristotle when he writes as follows in the *De Fato*: 'Unless perhaps we wish to follow the opinion of the Epicureans, who say that propositions of this kind are neither true nor false, or, when they are ashamed of that, when they say what is even more shameless, namely that disjunctions consisting of contrary propositions are true, but the statements contained in these propositions are neither of them true. What marvellous effrontery and wretched ignorance of logic!'[1]

But to return to Aristotle with Epicurus, or even with Philo, was not always satisfactory, particularly because following Epicurus means that determinism is avoided at the cost of admitting that because of the case of future contingents all propositions cannot be either true or false. For the argument of Aristotle and Epicurus is: If true, then necessary; if necessary, then determined. Clearly the only way out of this for anyone who wishes both to avoid determinism in the strict sense and at the same time to hold that every proposition is either true or false, is to re-examine the whole concept of necessity and its relation to the concept of truth. If it could be shown that Aristotle's account of the sea-battle contains obvious confusions of thought, progress might be made. But the first step towards such progress would have to be a reconsideration of the position of Diodorus.

According to Diodorus' famous Master Argument the following three propositions are incompatible:[2]

1. Everything true about the past is necessary.

---

[1] Cic., *De Fato* 37; cf. 19 and 21, and *De Nat. Deorum* 1.25. That Epicurus here returned to the view of Aristotle is observed by Schuhl, *op. cit.* 20. On the Stoic view that propositions are either true or false see D.L. 7.65, Cic., *Tus. Disp.* I 14, Gellius, *N.A.* 16.8.8 etc.

[2] See p. 114 note 4.

2. The impossible does not follow from the possible.

3. That which neither is true nor will be true is possible.

Yet although these propositions are, in Diodorus' view, incompatible, they were all accepted by Aristotle.[1] Something must be done, and, as we have seen already, Diodorus rejects proposition 3 with his new account of possibility. The first known Stoic reaction, that of Cleanthes, was, as Epictetus tells us,[2] to reject proposition 1. Unfortunately we have no evidence about his reasons for doing this. A passage of Alexander of Aphrodisias in which a proper distinction between true and necessary propositions is made has been attributed to Cleanthes by Schuhl.[3] In this passage the Stoic is arguing that the Aristotelian proposition 'There will be a sea-battle tomorrow' may be true, but even if true is not necessary, since the necessary is what is always true (τὸ ἀεὶ ἀληθές), and this proposition will be false when the sea-battle takes place. Yet it is hard to see why Schuhl thinks this should be related to the view of Cleanthes on whether true propositions about the *past* are necessary. Since the *De Interpretatione* it had been customary to consider the truth-value and the necessity-value of past and future propositions separately, and arguments about sea-battles tomorrow would presumably not have been acceptable as aids to solving questions about the necessity of past events. It seems more likely, though this is pure speculation, that Cleanthes applied arguments about *possibility* to the past as well as to the future. It is tempting to suppose that he argued that, just as what will not in fact be true is possible (proposition 3 of the Master Argument), so what is not in fact true in the past was possible and hence is non-necessary; in other words, that propositions about the past are not always necessary because some things could have turned out otherwise.

If this was Cleanthes' position, and it seems a reasonable way

---

[1] Cf. Schuhl, *op. cit.* 40, and our earlier discussion. Zeller's view of the reason why Diodorus thought that the propositions are incompatible ('Ueber den...', 151–9) is rejected by Mates (*op. cit.* 39), who, however, confesses inability to solve the problem himself.

[2] Cf. Cic., *De Fato* 14 (*SVF* II 954).

[3] Alex. Aphr., *De Fato*, p. 177, 7 Bruns (*SVF* II 961). Schuhl, *op. cit.* 24–5. Reesor (*op. cit.* 291) is doubtful about the attribution to Cleanthes.

to explain his rejection of the Aristotelian doctrine that everything true about the past is necessary, we are probably safe in
saying that Cleanthes has avoided the kind of determinism
which worried Aristotle. We are at least certain that his account
of necessity must have been different from that of Aristotle,
since the two have different attitudes towards true propositions
about the past. And having rejected Aristotle's account of
necessity in the form 'If true, then necessary', Cleanthes presumably would have felt it unnecessary to retain the Aristotelian
view that contradictory propositions about future contingents (or any other propositions) can be said to be individually
neither true nor false. Certainly there is no evidence from antiquity that any Stoic ever took the Aristotelian line on this
matter. It must be said at this point, however, that if our re-
construction of the position of Cleanthes is correct, we have no
evidence about how he related his statements about necessary
and non-necessary events in the past to his physical theories.[1]

When we turn to Chrysippus, we are on much firmer ground,
and having now briefly considered the background to his
theories, we can evaluate them better and attempt to understand how his attitude towards what is possible is relevant to
his attempt to reconcile the laws of nature with moral responsibility. Since the ancients generally put the work of Chrysippus
on the possible in relation first of all to the positions of Diodorus,
we should consider it in this context, before looking further
afield to the question of how he tried to solve some of the problems about determinism which go back to the work of Aristotle.

Chrysippus breaks with his predecessor Cleanthes in agreeing
with Diodorus and Aristotle that all true propositions about the
past are also necessary (proposition 1 of the Master Argument).
He also agrees with Diodorus against Aristotle that all propositions are either true or false.[2] If we put these two together, it will
follow that Chrysippus must have held a different theory from

---

[1] The importance of the relation between logic and physics in the case of
Chrysippus is well brought out by Reesor. But clearly Chrysippus' account
of the necessary is different from that of Cleanthes, and Chrysippus' explanation of necessity in terms of his own physics would not fit the necessity of Cleanthes.

[2] Cic., *De Fato* 20–1, 37–8.

that of Cleanthes about the non-necessary, and a different theory from that of Aristotle about necessity, for Aristotle held that, if a proposition is true, it is also necessary. What this amounts to primarily is that Chrysippus denied the Diodoran definition of the possible as that which either is or will be true, a definition which equates the possible with the necessary, and substituted for it a view like that of Aristotle and Philo, namely that there are things which will not happen but which are nevertheless still possible. It is possible, argues Chrysippus, for a jewel to be broken even if it never will be,[1] and although an oracle forecast the reign of Cypselus at Corinth a thousand years before it took place, yet it was still 'possible' for it not to take place. Diogenes Laertius[2] and Boethius[3] mention definitions of the possible which, though not attributed to any particular Stoic by name, certainly fit in with the examples of possibility given by Cicero. The possible, according to Diogenes, is that which admits of being true if external circumstances do not prevent it from being true, as, for example, 'Diocles lives'.[4] It should be observed, furthermore, that since Chrysippus held a different opinion from Cleanthes about the non-necessary, his view of the possible must have been to some extent different also. If Cleanthes thought that, because propositions in the past, if true, could also be non-necessary because they were possible, while Chrysippus held that, though once possible, they are later necessary, there would be a difference of attitude between them about the general relationship of the possible and the non-necessary in the case of propositions about the past. If Cicero's evidence is to be believed, Chrysippus argued against Cleanthes that 'all things true in the past are necessary...' because they no longer admit of change and because what is past cannot change from being the case to not being the case (*in falsum e vero*).[5] In other words Chrysippus seems to have argued (rightly or wrongly) that it is no longer *possible* for what has become the case to cease to be so.

[1] Cic., *De Fato* 13 (*SVF* II 954). [2] D.L. 7.75 (*SVF* II 201).
[3] Boethius, *In De Int.* 3.9, p. 234, 27–9 Meiser (*SVF* II 201).
[4] For detailed discussion of Stoic definitions of possible, non-necessary, necessary and impossible see Reesor, *op. cit.* 291–3.
[5] Cic., *De Fato* 14.

However, the argument between Chrysippus and Cleanthes about events in the past is not our immediate concern. What we are concerned with is Chrysippus' attitude to events in the future, for it was in this area that, in Aristotle's mind at least, the problem of determinism appears. We recall that one of the reasons why Aristotle found it necessary to deny that propositions about future contingents are either true or false was that he held that if true, then necessary, and therefore that, if we know that propositions about the future are true, we know what the future has in store. In Aristotle's view this would lead to a kind of paralysis, for what is going to happen will happen necessarily. This thesis, we recall, became known later as the Lazy Argument, and Chrysippus found it necessary to demolish it. The best evidence about Chrysippus' view is given by Cicero.[1] He argued that propositions can be divided into two classes, the simple and the complex. An example of a simple proposition is 'Socrates will die on that particular day'. This proposition may be true or false, but it is intelligible, and it is certainly the case that he will die when he will die (i.e. at that time). An example of a complex proposition is 'Laius will have a son Oedipus, whether he has intercourse with a woman or not'. This complex proposition is, for Chrysippus, unintelligible, because it is impossible to separate having a son and having intercourse with a woman. The two events are, he said, 'condestinate' (*confatalia*). Hence if complex propositions are to be intelligible, the different parts of the proposition must describe compatible situations. To use another of Chrysippus' examples, 'Milo will wrestle at Olympia if he has an opponent' makes sense, while 'Milo will wrestle at Olympia if he does not have an opponent' does not. It seems that the favourite example of the Lazy Argument current was the following: If you are ill, there is no point in calling a doctor, for, whether you call in a doctor or not, you will recover if you are fated to do so, and you will die if you are fated to die. The same argument could be applied, as Aristotle had already realized, to all moral questions. What is the point of deliberating about anything?

[1] Cic., *De Fato* 28–30 (cf. *SVF* II 956). Other accounts are given by Origen, *Contra Celsum* 2.20 (*SVF* II 957) and Servius, *Ad Aen.* 4.696 (*SVF* II 958).

According to Cicero's account, therefore, Chrysippus argued that, if a man is fated to recover through the help of a doctor, he is fated to call the doctor, and his calling the doctor is a deliberate action. But this has not got us very far, and there is reason to believe that Cicero, who apparently did not approve of the doctrine of 'condestinate events', is seeing Chrysippus' way out through the eyes of the sceptical critic of Chrysippus, the Academic Carneades. For Cicero seems to hold that Chrysippus' way out involves him in a rigid causal sequence in which nothing is 'in our power'.[1] It will be argued, however, that what Chrysippus meant was not that if the patient survives he will necessarily call the doctor, but that if he is going to survive, he is going to survive, and if he is going to call a doctor he is going to call a doctor. No one can dispute that what will in fact take place will take place. The name Chrysippus gives to the sequence of events which will in fact take place is fate.[2]

In the rest of this chapter, it will be essential to bear in mind Chrysippus' definition of the possible. The possible is what could happen, whether it actually happens or not. The possible is not to be identified with the necessary, although they had been so identified by Diodorus. To use Chrysippus' most famous example, a cylinder admits of being rolled down a hill whether it is rolled down a hill or not, whereas, since the earth is not equipped to fly, 'The earth is flying' is an impossible proposition.[3] Chrysippus calls the 'rollability' of the cylinder a basic cause of the cylinder's movement when it actually moves. The man who pushes the cylinder is said to supply the 'proximate' cause.[4] We can now begin to see what the importance of the distinction between these causes is. Basic causes are connected with the particular qualities which make any object *qua* object what it is and not another thing.[5] They describe the 'fate' of a

---

[1] Cic., *De Fato* 31.
[2] Cf. A. Gellius, *N.A.* 7.2 (*SVF* II 1000), Cic., *De Fato* 42 (*SVF* II 974) etc.
[3] D.L. 7.75 (*SVF* II 201).
[4] Basic cause = αὐτοτελὴς αἰτία (Plut., *SR* 1056B) = *causa perfecta, causa principalis* (Cic., *De Fato* 41 (*SVF* II 974)). Proximate cause = προκαταρκτικὴ αἰτία = *causa adiuvans, causa proxima.* Cf. Rieth, *Grundbegriffe* 135 ff.; Pohlenz, 'Grundfragen', 104 ff.
[5] Cf. Reesor, *op. cit.* 286.

given object. Thus it is man's fate to have two legs and not four. Fate is a word for describing (quite neutrally) the state of affairs that was, is, and will be. There is therefore no reason why Chrysippus should not speak of the future as 'fated'. This would mean that what will be will be. Necessity in the determinist sense has nothing to do with fate. When we say that something is fated, we are looking at it *sub specie aeternitatis*; when we say, as Stoics, that something is necessarily the case, we must be speaking of the past or of the present, in so far as what is now existentially so cannot be blotted out.

If we use the term 'fate' when we view the world *sub specie aeternitatis*, and if we describe what is and will be as fated, we are obviously describing the effects not only of basic causes but also of proximate causes. Thus if a being outside space and time could say, 'Chrysippus will roll that stone tomorrow', and if this statement were to be true, then Chrysippus could be said to be fated to roll the stone tomorrow. In future time, therefore, as well as in past or present time, a proper account of what is fated will have to take account of both basic and proximate causes. Nevertheless, Chrysippus will allow us to speak of such a future event as fated because 'fate' describes neutrally what will in fact be the case, while he will not allow us to describe his action as necessary, since whatever he will in fact do (by fate), he has the possibility of not doing until he actually does it, thereby making his situation irreversible. For all that is past is necessary. The correct use of the term 'fate' has been admirably summed up by Miss Reesor as follows: 'The word "fate" is used to describe both the relationship of the principal (basic) cause to its substratum (rollability to the cylinder), and the chain or series of initiating (proximate) causes which might cause the predicate derived from the principal (basic) cause to be realized or which might prevent it from being realized.'[1] Presumably because it is a series of events which take place by the action of ever different proximate causes, Chrysippus often defines fate as the series of causes itself. This is perhaps a little misleading, but could have been clearer to both ancient and modern commentators if more attention had been paid to Chrysippus' in-

---

[1] Reesor, *op. cit.* 296.

tentions and less to polemic. Cicero, for example, though aware both of Chrysippus' definition of fate as a 'continued series of causes'[1] and of his desire to separate fate from necessity by an examination of the nature of causes,[2] seems to find the separation trivial, though without explaining why; regrettably this attitude persists.[3]

It must be granted, however, that there are two aspects of the position of Chrysippus which make it more difficult than he seems to have supposed to understand him; these are his use of phrases like *necessitates fati*, if Cicero's evidence is to be trusted, and his strange understanding of what it means for something to be 'in our power' (ἐφ' ἡμῖν). The first of these difficulties is in fact terminological only; the second has much more philosophical significance, but here it should be noticed that, although many of the ancients wanted to fault Chrysippus on the grounds that he left insufficient room for the freedom of the will and for things to be 'in our power', many of these critics themselves operated with very similar concepts of what is 'in our power'. His fault in this matter was that he was clear-headed enough to face the difficulties openly, even though they made his position appear somewhat paradoxical.

In three passages of the *De Fato*, where the reference is either explicitly or implicitly to Chrysippus, Cicero accuses the Stoic of talking about the 'necessity of fate'. In section twenty he says that Chrysippus brings in his everlasting chain of causes and by doing so deprives man of his free will (*voluntas libera*) and binds it in the necessity of fate; in section thirty-eight he affirms his own view that Chrysippus was right to hold that some things are true from all eternity, but wrong to be seduced into believing that this entails a linked chain of causes and hence the 'necessity of fate'; finally in section thirty-nine it is said that, although Chrysippus wants to avoid the 'force of necessity' (*vim necessitatis*), which enjoyed the support of Democritus,

---

[1] Cic., *De Fato* 20 (*SVF* ii 954); Gellius, *N.A.* 7.2 (*SVF* ii 1000); Aët., *Plac.* 1.28.4 (*DG* p. 324); Alex. Aphr., *De Fato*, p. 195, 3 Bruns; Cic., *De Div.* 1.125, 127, *De Nat. Deorum* 1.55; Aug., *Civ. Dei* 5.8 etc. For these and other references and discussion see Theiler, *op. cit.* 43.

[2] Cic., *De Fato* 41–5.

[3] Cf., for example, Schuhl, *op. cit.* 62.

Heraclitus, Empedocles and Aristotle, he was led to lend his support also by certain peculiarities in his own position, so that against his own will he is found confirming the 'necessity of fate'.

Before considering this language and its implications in general, we must clear away a subsidiary point. Cicero insists in section thirty-eight of the *De Fato* that reason will uphold the view that certain things are true from all eternity. Are there any future events which are in fact necessary, despite Chrysippus' formal theory that 'If true, then necessary' does not hold for future contingents? Most interpreters rightly hold that there are not.[1] But one special case comes to mind which, though not an exception to the rule, sheds a little light on Chrysippus' general position. Let it be agreed that Socrates is a sage. Would it have been a necessary proposition if in the year 410 B.C. someone had said, 'If he lives, Socrates will be happy tomorrow'? It would of course be necessary that the wise man will be happy. Our enquiry, however, is not concerned with propositions of this kind, but with particular future contingents. It boils itself down to the question, Is 'If he lives, Socrates, who is a wise man, will be happy tomorrow' a necessary proposition? We have discussed this subject elsewhere, for what we are concerned with here is whether virtue can be lost.[2] The answer to this puzzle, according to Chrysippus, arguing against Cleanthes, is that there are certain circumstances which can arise and produce an effect on the sage—which he cannot avert—of such a kind that virtue is lost. Perhaps Cleanthes, who thought that virtue cannot be lost, ought to have held that 'If he lives, Socrates, the wise man, will be happy tomorrow' is a necessary proposition. But this would be in contradiction to his own view of possibility, which for future contingents was the same as that of Chrysippus. Hence perhaps we have another reason for Chrysippus' arguing that virtue can be lost: he is clearing up a logical confusion which Cleanthes has overlooked.

Having digressed a little to see whether the unusual proposition 'Socrates, the wise man, will be happy' is an exception to

---

[1] Cf. Reesor, *op. cit.* 296: 'A true proposition in the future could not be necessary.'   [2] See above, pp. 16–19.

Chrysippus' rules about future contingents, thus affording slight ground for the Ciceronian jibes about the necessity of fate, let us return to the *De Fato*. It might be supposed that Cicero's habit of using the phrase 'necessity of fate' and consequent suggestion that fated events are necessary and therefore determined in such a way as to leave nothing 'in our power' is a piece of deliberate or careless confusion of the doctrine of Chrysippus about the need to distinguish 'fate' from 'necessity'. But perhaps Chrysippus was not as clear in his terminology as he might have been; we have seen elsewhere that he is prepared to make terminological concessions, if he thinks that they do not affect matters of substance.[1] Perhaps his readiness to compromise with the usages of everyday speech was so great that he could hardly blame his opponents if misconceptions arose.

There appear to be no references extant of the use by Chrysippus of the phrase ἀνάγκη εἰμαρμένης. However, according to a report preserved by Eusebius, the phrase πάνθ' ὑπὸ τῆς ἀνάγκης καὶ τῆς εἰμαρμένης κατειλῆφθαι occurred in the first book of Chrysippus' treatise *On Fate*.[2] We do not know the context of this phrase in sufficient detail to be able to understand how Chrysippus used it, but since even Cicero, a hostile witness, explains that Chrysippus wanted to *distinguish* fate and necessity, we have no reason to believe that by 'necessity and fate' he meant merely 'necessity of fate'. As we have seen, the distinction between necessity and fate arises in the philosophy of Chrysippus in the context of an inherited problem, the problem of the nature of possibility. This problem was largely dead after the time of Carneades (mid-second century B.C.), at least to the extent that new logical theories were not forthcoming. As the reasons for distinguishing fate and necessity faded into history, the demand that the terms be kept rigidly separate would doubtless have also weakened, so that by the time of Marcus Aurelius, when we find the Greek version of the phrase used by Cicero, that is, ἀνάγκη εἰμαρμένης,[3] it is very probable that the original context of the discussion about fate and necessity has been almost entirely lost. What the origin of the phrase is, either in this

---

[1] See above, pp. 11–12. [2] Eus., *P.E.* 6.8.1 (*SVF* II 925).
[3] *Med.* 12.14.1.

Greek version, or in the Latin as given by Cicero, is not clear, though Cicero's account certainly suggests that it may owe something to Carneades. Carneades' discussions of the subject were of course polemical, and, if he thought that Chrysippus had not made out an adequate case for distinguishing fate and necessity, he may have deliberately emphasized this by using the phrase 'necessity of fate'. Certainly the doxographical tradition, represented for us by Aëtius and Stobaeus, states it as a fact that Chrysippus did not distinguish what is necessary from what is fated.[1] And it appears that long before Marcus Aurelius the Stoics themselves had lost touch with the reasons for the distinction: we find Seneca actually defining fate as the necessity of things.[2]

Are there any other reasons, apart from the polemic of Carneades and the possible lack of clarity in the presentation of his theses about fate and necessity by Chrysippus himself, why so much confusion should have arisen? A further source of confusion seems to be revealed by a passage of Chalcidius,[3] which gives evidence of new disagreements between Chrysippus and Cleanthes. This time the dispute was about the relationship between fate and divine Providence. According to Chrysippus everything fated is providential, and *vice versa*; Cleanthes, however, did not believe that everything fated is providential; perhaps he was thinking of some of the side-effects of chains of causation. In general the Stoics think of fate as identifiable with Zeus or the mind of Zeus;[4] one might suppose that they would hold that the mind of Zeus knows what will be and knows the truth. The word 'providence' is to be taken seriously in a Stoic context; it means foreseeing and foreseeing correctly. Hence it is strange that Cleanthes thought that what is fated could not al-

---

[1] Stob., *Ecl.* 1, p. 78, 4 W. (*SVF* II 916). Theiler (*op. cit.* 65) seems to put too much weight on this and similar passages, thus following the view of Carneades. The words of Tacitus (*Ann.* 6.22), '*fatone res mortalium et necessitate immutabili an forte volvantur*' seem to represent the fate and necessity of Chrysippus rather than the 'necessity of fate' of Carneades (?), Cicero, Marcus Aurelius and the doxographers.

[2] Seneca, *N.Q.* 2.36, *Quid enim intellegis fatum? Existimo necessitatem rerum omnium actionumque, quae nulla vis rumpat.*

[3] Chal., *In Tim.* 144 (*SVF* II 933).   [4] *SVF* II 928–33.

ways be foreseen, but it is even stranger that Chrysippus, while believing that everything fated is providential, holds that God does not know everything.[1] There seems to be an unresolved contradiction here. And as for Cleanthes, his view seems to be in opposition to the thesis which he himself held about Reason, Destiny and Zeus as the guiding principle of the world. We recall his famous line, quoted by Epictetus and translated by Seneca: Lead me, Zeus and Destiny.[2] What is fated (πεπρωμένη) is the working out of the divine in the world; and how can this not be excellent, if the Stoic is to be logical? Nevertheless, if Cleanthes was tempted to separate fate from Providence, it is easy to see how a view could arise that the good, which men aim at in the world, can be trampled underfoot by an inexorable fate, which in this context would take on the colours of necessity. From this some justification for the unfortunate phrase 'necessity of fate' could arise.

There is then a difference between necessity and fate, but fate will look like necessity if man does not accept the situation into which he is born. Obviously all men will die; that is fated for them. What will be will be. It is no good in the long run refusing to die; the refusal is hopeless. As Zeno and Chrysippus put it, man is like a dog tied to a cart; if he does not walk along, he will be pulled along;[3] but if he is pulled along, he is a bad man. As Cleanthes himself put it: 'If I do not want to go along the fated path, having become a bad man, I will go along it nevertheless.' But we have to remember that the fated path is simply the path of what will be. Death is the obvious example of something fated, but for the Stoics it is merely the clearest example, an example where we *know* what will be. There are a host of other things that will be which we cannot know. But the *Reason* of the world knows what is fated; that is why, as Chrysippus had to insist, everything fated is providential. It is therefore wrong to suggest, as Miss Reesor does,[4] that the Stoic is portrayed as a man 'struggling against or unwillingly following

---

[1] *SVF* II 1183. Cf. p. 48 note 5, above.
[2] Epict., *Ench.* 53 (*SVF* I 527).
[3] Hipp., *Phil.* 21 (*SVF* II 975).
[4] Reesor, *op. cit.* 289. Cf. Epict., *Disc.* 2.6.9 (*SVF* III 191).

the fate which may involve his own suffering or sorrow, but which will form part of the total good', for, in so far as we struggle against, for example, the fate of death, we are bad Stoics, and, for the Stoics, bad men. The Stoic does not struggle; he follows. As Seneca puts it, summing up Cleanthes' poem: The fates lead the willing man and drag the unwilling.[1]

We have now dealt with the terminological problems which arise from Chrysippus' account of fate and necessity, but, as we have already indicated, the real question is not one of terminology, but of philosophy; it is the question of whether Chrysippus managed to reconcile his theory of causal chains with his other theory that, nevertheless, certain important courses of action are 'in our power', and that we are therefore morally responsible. It is certainly the view of Cicero, who doubtless echoes Carneades, that Chrysippus had failed to prevent human free will (*voluntas libera*) from being submerged in a rigidly determinist system.[2] Now the problem that is touched on here and elsewhere is not merely an argument between Chrysippus and Carneades; Epicurus was also involved, and in Cicero's view had to introduce his absurd theory of the atomic swerve to avoid the necessity of fate. As we have noticed earlier in this chapter, however, in the case of whether propositions must be either true or false, Epicurus' views frequently depend on those of Aristotle, a fact of which Cicero is generally unaware. In the case of theories about the freedom of the will, and of what is 'in our power', this dependence has been startlingly demonstrated by Furley.[3] Furley has shown that like Aristotle Epicurus regards a free action as an action performed by the individual as the result of his character, not of his 'destiny' at birth or before birth. What matters, therefore, is the process of character formation. Aristotle emphasized the training of children and held that only at a particular age does a child grow into a man and become responsible for his own acts. The Epicurean view, as Furley indicates, is similar. Human character is not formed by 'destiny', but by training; hence, runs the argument, man is responsible for his own acts. No account is taken either by the

[1] Sen., *Ep.* 107.11. [2] Cic., *De Fato* 20 (*SVF* II 954)
[3] Furley, *Two Studies* 161–237.

Epicureans or by Aristotle of the fact that the process by which character is formed, even in the best available circumstances, seems to involve something more than rational appeals. Punishments and 'encouragements' are meted out, and these, one would suppose, preclude the character formation itself from being a voluntary process in any significant sense.

Nevertheless, a very similar view seems to have been held by Chrysippus, who was much exercised on educational matters and clearly thought that the education of children is vital if they are to have the possibility of wisdom.[1] There are natural tendencies in the human character which have to be developed, and, if they are properly developed, a sage will appear. The point that concerns us, however, is that dependent on the education received are the moral judgments made by the mature man; and these judgments are moral in the sense that they can merit praise or blame. In other words, at a certain stage in his life a man's character is formed and he becomes responsible for his actions.[2] From that time his reactions to 'possible' situations are in his power. By this Chrysippus does not mean that they are uncaused. What he means is that the cause is not external to the doer; it is the man's character. Epicurus seems to have supposed that the only way rigid causal chains can be broken is by the introduction of the random swerve of atoms, which at least ensures that no man's career is inalienably fixed at any time.[3] Chrysippus held this to be an irrational and unjustified way out of the dilemma. What is needed instead is a more serious investigation of the nature of causes; and as a beginning of this comes his analysis of basic and proximate causes. Phenomena governed by basic causes are fixed; hence every man will die. Nevertheless, how we die is in our own power, as to some extent is when we die. Obviously we shall die when we die; that is fate. But there is no necessity (in Chrysippus' sense) for us to die at any other time than the time we choose. The fact that death is unavoidable for men, and, as all the Hellenistic

[1] Cf. *SVF* III 732–8.
[2] Gellius, *N.A.* 12.5.7 (*SVF* III 181); Cic., *De Fin.* 3.20 (*SVF* III 188).
[3] Cf. Plut., *Sollert. An.* 964 C, ὅπως τὸ ἐφ' ἡμῖν μὴ ἀπόληται, *SR* 1050 C; Cic., *De Nat. Deorum* 1.69, *De Fato* 22. Cf. Theiler, *op. cit.* 55.

philosophers regularly point out, a perpetual source of un-
happiness and disquiet, perhaps has something to do with the
way in which the Stoics think of taking one's own life as in some
circumstances a perfectly reasonable course of action. From the
very beginnings of Stoicism suicide was held to be permissible
for the wise man,[1] but although we know something of Stoic
views of what makes it permissible, we have not much evidence
of how they relate these views to their theories of freedom and
necessity. It is true that the writings of Seneca provide a good
deal of information on this subject, but Seneca is a man of another age from Chrysippus. He lives in a social situation where
political pressures made a justification of suicide seem essential,
and there is no reason to think his attitude more than one possible development of views current at an earlier date.

Briefly, it is Seneca's opinion that suicide is an ultimate expression of what is in one's power, and of the freedom of the
human will. As he puts it in a striking phrase, 'Contempt for
one's body is a sure sign of freedom:[2] You can open the road to
freedom with a lancet, and give tranquillity at the price of a
pinprick.'[3] It must be observed that this kind of attitude reveals
a quasi-Platonic contempt for the body which Seneca has
learned from masters other than Chrysippus. Nevertheless, for
Seneca the body is not despised as a body, but because it can
damage the tranquillity of the personality. In a sense it marks
us out as governed by Chrysippus' basic causes, for the body
will decay while the soul will return to the soul of the cosmos
and be re-assimilated to it. Hence the ability to be a co-worker
with fate and to choose the manner of one's own death is the
highest kind of freedom.[4] The wise man, for all Stoics, is master
of himself. Hence freedom will be the ability to look after oneself fully; and this kind of freedom is best exemplified for Seneca
in the right to choose whether to live or to die. 'Only the wise
man is free' was one of the Stoic paradoxes.[5] Diogenes Laertius,
one of those who record it, goes on to give a Stoic (presumably

---

[1] *SVF* III 757–68. See the discussion of suicide on pages 233–55 below.
[2] Seneca, *Ep.* 65.21.   [3] Seneca, *Ep.* 70.16.
[4] For further discussion and references to Seneca see Sevenster, *Paul and
Seneca* 52–7.   [5] Cf. D.L. 7.121 (*SVF* III 355).

Chrysippean) definition of freedom as the opportunity of acting for oneself (ἐξουσία αὐτοπραγίας); elsewhere acting for oneself is replaced by managing one's own affairs (τὰ αὐτοῦ πράττειν).[1] Since one's life or death is *par excellence* one's own business, choice of dying affords a superb example of the use of human liberty. Such is Seneca's adaptation of the Stoic doctrine of what is in our power.

What we think of actions 'in our power' and whether we regard them as free actions are not our present concerns. What we are concerned with in this chapter is how Chrysippus reconciled fate, necessity and actions 'in our power'. It has been our intention to argue that his concept of what is in our power, if unsatisfactory to us, is in line with the normally accepted view of his own time. In the context of this view his distinction between basic and proximate causes is of considerable importance, as is his related account of possibility; for if possibility were to be equated with necessity, as Diodorus had wished, nothing would be in our power. Hence we could not adopt a moral attitude towards what will befall us. Fate for Chrysippus is what will be, not what must be. If fate were what must be, then in Chrysippus' terms all causes would be basic causes and nothing would be in our power. It might be replied that we could still assent or not assent to what will befall us and hence be moral or non-moral. But under a Diodoran scheme all assent or non-assent would be necessary, and hence one could be no more moral after the so-called moral character had developed than before it.

Here we are back at the question of character formation. In favour of the position of Diodorus, it might be argued that Chrysippus leaves little room for morality if he thinks that a moral act is one performed as a kind of reflex of the moral character, a character, that is, which has been preconditioned to be moral. Perhaps it could be argued that Diodorus' theory of the possible allows us to go deeper into the question of character formation, since it would seem that the Stoic sage's acts are virtually fixed by his character. But Chrysippus has at least something to reply to this: first of all that in his view virtue can

---

[1] Plut., *SR* 1043A (*SVF* III 703).

be lost, which means that, for whatever reason, moral acts may not always be reflexes of character; and secondly that Diodorus' theory makes nonsense of many of the ordinary concepts which seem to enable us to understand the world. If something which is breakable cannot possibly be broken unless it is going to be broken, how can we properly distinguish the seemingly real difference between objects which are breakable and those which are not?

In brief, then, however much Chrysippus' theory of things 'in our power' seems inadequate, a good part of its inadequacy must be traced back to its ancestry in the Aristotelian and Platonic concepts of morality and moral training. In his attempts to break out of the difficulties these concepts introduced, Chrysippus drew the important distinction between what will be (fate) and what must be (necessity) which we have attempted to elucidate.

8

THE CRITERION OF TRUTH

One of the permanent bones of contention in post-Aristotelian philosophy was what they called 'the criterion'. The sense of this word with which we are concerned is explained by Sextus Empiricus as follows:[1] It means the thing in view of which we assert that these things exist and those do not exist, and that these are the case (literally, 'are true') and those are not (literally, 'are false'). Hence the problem is usually referred to as the problem of the criterion of truth. At first sight of the evidence the Stoics were in some confusion on the matter. Diogenes Laertius' account runs as follows:[2]

They say that the recognizable presentation (τὴν καταληπτικὴν φαντασίαν) is the criterion of truth, that is, the presentation which comes from an existent, as Chrysippus says in the fourth book of his *Physics* and as is also said by Antipater and Apollodorus. However, Boethus admits a plurality of criteria, intelligence, perception, appetite and knowledge. And Chrysippus is inconsistent in book one of his work *On Reason*, where he says that perception and preconception are criteria...And some others of the older Stoics made right reason the criterion, as Posidonius says in his book *On the Criterion*.

Allowing for the possibility that there is some wilful or ignorant misconception at work either in Diogenes or in his sources, we can assume that some of the criteria named (such as perception) were not normally spoken of by the Stoics as criteria of truth, and that some variations represent different ways of referring to the same phenomenon. In this context 'right reason' and 'intelligence' are probably attempts at more or less precise variants on the more usual 'recognition' (κατάληψις), understood as 'recognition by the intelligence'. In fact the overwhelming body of evidence that we shall consider suggests that the normal Stoic answers to the question What is the criterion of truth? are either Recognition, or Recognizable Presentation. The latter was mentioned more often, however, and

[1] Sext. Emp., *Adv. Math.* 7.29. [2] D.L. 7.54 (*SVF* II 105).

this fact has led certain scholars, notably Pohlenz, to suppose that the Stoic view of the problem changed, and that Chrysippus reformed the original theory of Zeno.

In order to understand the problem about the criterion we need to put it into the context of the Stoic theory of knowledge in general; and a brief look at that theory is therefore desirable. According to the Stoics all our knowledge is ultimately derived from the senses. When we are born, our souls are like sheets of paper which are suitable for writing (ὥσπερ χάρτην εὔεργον εἰς ἀπογραφήν).[1] This suitability involves the possession of various potentialities for receiving information which begin to be activated immediately after birth, thus giving the individual first of all some kind of primitive consciousness of self and self-interest.[2] Our potentiality to think should not be viewed as the possession of innate ideas of any kind, nor of any 'necessary assumptions' or pre-natal 'anticipations'.[3] It is simply that we possess the power of reason, as yet wholly undeveloped and un-exercised. Misconceptions about this have arisen as the result of a single passage of Plutarch where Chrysippus speaks of ἔμφυται προλήψεις. Sandbach has pointed out that ἔμφυτος does not always mean 'inborn' but sometimes 'ingrained' or 'implanted', and unless Chrysippus was having a temporary aberration when he used the phrase, he meant 'ingrained'. The 'preconceptions' about good and evil, he is saying, begin to take root as soon as we are born. There is no other 'evidence' in the Old Stoic writers for a theory of any kind of 'inborn' belief; their philosophy needs no such beliefs and should not be saddled with them.[4]

When a man is born, therefore, his potentialities for receiving information start to develop. Hence the Stoics are able to say

[1] Aëtius, *Plac.* 4.11 (*SVF* II 83).
[2] Cic., *De Fin.* 3.16.
[3] These phrases have recently been used by Watson, *The Stoic Theory of Knowledge* 24, in an ambiguous account of πρόληψις. For the correct interpretation of this language see the masterly article of Sandbach, '"Εννοια and Πρόληψις'.
[4] It should be pointed out that Sandbach (*op. cit.* 48) inclines towards the 'temporary aberration' theory about ἔμφυτος. His article is particularly important in that it refutes the attempt of Bonhoeffer (*Epictet und die Stoa*) to read the innate ideas of Epictetus back to the Old Stoa.

that all our knowledge ultimately derives from the senses (αἰσθήσεις).[1] This statement must be taken as literally correct, despite certain other apparently contradictory texts. Diogenes Laertius reports that according to the Stoics some of the presentations to our minds are sensible (αἰσθητικαί), while others are not; and he then proceeds to explain various mental processes which can produce presentations which are not sensible.[2] However, as has commonly been observed, this does not mean that the material on which these presentations are based does not derive ultimately from the senses, but rather that, since it was first offered to the 'receiving' subject, it has been analysed by the mind in various ways, and as a result new 'mental' presentations have arisen.[3]

At this point in the theory we are up against a terminological difficulty. On the one hand there are texts which say that all αἰσθήσεις are true;[4] on the other hand we have texts which say that every αἴσθησις is an assent and an act of recognition.[5] If every αἴσθησις is true, it would follow that, if αἴσθησις means 'perception', every assent and recognition in the sphere of perception must also be 'true'—which would go far towards making everyone incapable of being mistaken about perceptions. That is obviously un-Stoic. The only possible way to resolve this is to assume that αἴσθησις is used in two senses: that of bare sensation, and that of perception. Only on the basis of the first meaning of αἴσθησις will it be proper to say 'All αἰσθήσεις are true'; that means little more than 'All sensations are in fact sensations of what they are sensations'. The Stoics must have expunged all connection with any kind of mental activity from this meaning of the word. If seeing is an αἴσθησις in this sense, αἴσθησις means merely seeing as an animal would see, with no awareness of the fact that it sees. That a distinction between bare sensation and perception was current among the Stoics is borne out by a passage of Galen, who quotes a Stoic view that 'it is possible to see and touch and hear without recognition (μὴ καταληπτικῶς), but it is not possible

---

[1] Aët., *Plac.* 4.11 (*SVF* II 83).   [2] D.L. 7.51–2 (*SVF* II 61, 87).
[3] See Watson, *op. cit.* 25.   [4] E.g. Aët., *Plac.* 4.9.4 (*SVF* II 78).
[5] E.g. Aët., *Plac.* 4.8.12 (*SVF* II 72).

to perceive without recognition'.[1] Thus seeing *qua* seeing does not involve recognition (or, presumably, assent in any human way), but seeing *qua* perceiving does. The distinction is similar to that drawn in the *De Anima* between the function of the individual sense and that of the 'common' sense. It is, then, only in this rather innocuous way that the Stoics can say that all sensations (but not perceptions) are true.

All potential knowledge is presented to the mind after the sense organs have performed their particular acts of sensation. This presentation (φαντασία) is defined by the Stoics as an experience that arises in the soul,[2] and is explained further by Zeno as an impression. According to Cleanthes the impression is like that of a seal on wax, while Chrysippus, finding it grotesque that, if the mind thinks simultaneously of three- and four-sided objects it becomes at the same time triangular and quadrangular, holds that by 'impression' Zeno meant 'alteration'. The same body is able to admit of many alterations at the same time, just as, when many people are speaking, the air receives many different impacts and immediately undergoes many alterations.[3] Only by dropping the comparison with wax can memory be explained. If it is retained, every new thought would drive out its predecessor, and we should remember nothing.

It is at this stage that the process envisaged by the Stoics becomes more difficult to follow. We know that all sensations are received by the mind as presentations. But these presentations are of different kinds. Only those which the Stoics call 'recognizable' (καταληπτικαί) are relevant to the acquisition of knowledge. Fortunately our evidence about their definition of a 'recognizable presentation' is fairly clear. It is a presentation caused by an existing object and imaged and stored in the perceiver in accordance with that existing object itself, and of such

---

[1] Galen, *In Hipp. De Medic. Off.* vol. 18B, p. 654 K. (*SVF* II 75).

[2] Nemesius, *De Nat. Hom.* p. 171 Matthaei (*SVF* II 54).

[3] Sext. Emp., *Adv. Math.* 7.228–31 (*SVF* II 56); cf. 7.372; 8.400; D.L. 7.46 (*SVF* II 53). The reasons why Chrysippus changed the explanation of τύπωσις are given in the passages of Sextus. No deeper significance is to be attached to them than Sextus himself attaches (*pace* Pohlenz, 'Zenon und Chrysipp', 181–2).

a kind as could not come from what is not that existing object.[1] As Pohlenz has recognized from the fact that this definition was already under attack by Arcesilaus, it must derive from Zeno himself, as Cicero tells us.[2] Our translation of the last part of the passage as 'of such a kind as could not come from what is not that existing object' (ὁποία οὐκ ἂν γένοιτο ἀπὸ μὴ ὑπάρχοντος) needs further comment. It has commonly been translated as 'such as could not be derived from a non-existent object', and this is certainly a possible translation. Indeed it is a translation which gets part of the meaning of the Greek. That it does not exhaust the meaning of the Greek, however, is shown by a further passage of Sextus, paralleled in other writers, in which Carneades' attitude to the definition is outlined.[3] According to Carneades two kinds of argument can be brought against the last part of the definition (ὁποία οὐκ ἂν γένοιτο ἀπὸ μὴ ὑπάρχοντος). The first of these is that the same presentation can appear both from an existent and from a non-existent object, for example, in waking life a thirsty man can get pleasure from drinking, while in sleep the pleasure is produced by a dream of drinking; thus the same presentation arises from existent and non-existent drink. This kind of objection fits the standard translation of μὴ ὑπάρχοντος as 'non-existent'. The second objection brought by Carneades, however, is that in the case of two identical eggs, the presentation of the one (existent egg) will be indistinguishable from the presentation of the other (also existent egg). Hence the Stoics must have argued—and there is evidence for this—that no two things are alike.[4] Therefore, if a presentation is recognizable, it is not only recognizable as coming from an existent rather than a non-existent object. In Carneades' view, and he certainly knew what the Stoics intended,

[1] Sext. Emp., *Adv. Math.* 7.248; cf. 402–11 etc., 426; *Hyp. Pyr.* 2.4, 3.242; D.L. 7.46; Cic., *Acad. Pr.* 2.18, 40–2, 57, 77 etc.

[2] Pohlenz, 'Zenon und Chrysipp', 177; Cic., *Acad. Pr.* 2.18 (*SVF* I 59).

[3] Sext. Emp., *Adv. Math.* 7.402 ff.

[4] Sextus Empiricus (*Adv. Math.* 7.410) tells us that this view of the Stoics led to the formulation of the so-called Veiled Argument (ἐγκεκαλυμμένος λόγος). On the Stoic view that each particular is unique see Cic., *Acad. Pr.* 2, 50, 54, 56, 85 etc. Further references to the Veiled Argument are to be found in D.L. 7.82 (*SVF* II 274), and Lucian, *Vit. Auct.* 22 (*SVF* II 287).

a presentation of such a kind as could not arise ἀπὸ μὴ ὑπ-άρχοντος must have been one which could not arise from any other existent object than the existent from which it did in fact arise.

Such then are 'recognizable presentations'. There are other presentations, but they are not recognizable. That does not mean that they are necessarily untrue, though some of them will be untrue.[1] Others, however, will be true but beyond human comprehension. One of the reasons for formulating the theory of 'recognizable presentations' seems to have been to explain the fact that some things are unknowable. At any rate Cicero, probably following Antiochus of Ascalon, seems to think that one of the weaknesses in the position of Philo of Larisa, who, while accepting that there is a criterion of truth, would not accept the theory of recognizable presentations, is that, if this theory is dropped, it becomes impossible to distinguish what is knowable from what is not.[2] But we can return to this at a later stage.

A good deal of confusion has been injected into the problem of the criterion by Pohlenz. His thesis, expounded in 'Zenon und Chrysipp',[3] and repeated more briefly in *Die Stoa*, is that, whereas Zeno thought that the criterion of truth is a combination of 'presentation' and 'assent', Chrysippus substituted for this the 'recognizable presentation'. In Pohlenz' view this is a significant change; Chrysippus preferred to think of the criterion as present in the object of knowledge, and much less in the mind of the knower. We must, therefore, look at the evidence to see whether there appears to be such a change of emphasis and whether it is significant. While doing this, we may also be able to clarify certain aspects of the theory of recognition itself, for there is some reason to believe that the rather contemptuous view we have of it depends too much on the readings of critics like Arcesilaus and Carneades to do full justice to the Stoic arguments.

The best starting-point for this discussion is the account of

[1] Sext. Emp., *Adv. Math.* 7.244 (*SVF* II 65).
[2] Cic., *Acad. Pr.* 2.18.
[3] Pohlenz, 'Zenon und Chrysipp', 181, *Die Stoa* 1.62–3.

what Zeno held to be the process of acquiring knowledge which is outlined by Cicero in his *Academica*.[1] According to this account Zeno believed that the acquisition of knowledge from the evidence of the senses depends upon a conjunction of the 'presentation' (arising from an external object) and an act of 'assent' (*adsensio*) which is a free mental act and in our power. This mental act clearly results in a κατάληψις. The process of events, as given by Cicero, is as follows: first there is a presentation; and let us assume the particular presentation is recognizable, though, as we have seen, and as Cicero repeats in this passage, some are not. There are two stages further, both of which are kinds of 'grasp'. First of all the object is grasped weakly: Cicero says that it is sensed (*sensum*). Let us call this stage the grasp of perception. As we should expect from our brief sketch of the general Stoic theory above, a degree of assent is involved at this stage. After this, by a further act of assent, the presentation is grasped so firmly that it cannot be removed by reasoning. This stage is the grasp of knowledge. It is clear, then, that the word *comprehensio* (κατάληψις) has two senses: the grasp of perception and the grasp of knowledge. Zeno hammered this in by giving a homely demonstration of a type of which the Stoics were somewhat over-fond. He used to stretch out his fingers to represent a visual appearance (*visum*). He then closed his fingers slightly and said that that was an act of assent. (This seems to be the perception distinguished from the bare sensation.) He then pressed his fingers and formed a fist. This represented recognition (κατάληψις), a term which he himself first used in this sense. Finally he put his left hand over his right fist and pressed hard; this represented knowledge.[2] Here there are four stages, whereas in the earlier account Cicero only speaks of three. Although the four-stage picture was useful in teaching the theory, it is clear that, strictly speaking, stages two and three should be telescoped.

One or two points about the theory can now be clarified further. It is obvious that the word κατάληψις is ambiguous and could be misunderstood. Arcesilaus was anxious to exploit the

[1] Cic., *Acad. Post.* 1.40–2 (*SVF* I 55, 60, 61).
[2] Cic., *Acad. Pr.* 2.145.

ambiguity. Apparently Zeno was in the habit of saying that recognition is assent to a recognizable presentation, that is, that it is achieved both by the wise and by the foolish, and that it is the criterion of truth.[1] Arcesilaus objected that, if this assent can occur in both the wise and the foolish, in the wise being knowledge and in the foolish opinion, then 'knowledge' and 'opinion' must be two different names for one single thing. If Arcesilaus is reporting Zeno correctly here, and he probably is, then Zeno's account is misleading in that it does not distinguish verbally between what Cicero calls 'recognition of perception' and 'recognition of knowledge'. Both of these are in fact acts of assent, but the same terms 'recognition' (κατάληψις) and 'assent' (συγκατάθεσις) are used in both cases. Nevertheless, even if Zeno's account is open to misreadings, what he intended to say can easily be recovered; and the accounts of Cicero and Sextus Empiricus tally. The process can be tabulated as follows:

(a) reception of bare sensations,

(b) perception by acceptation of sensations (Cicero uses the word *acceptum* in *Acad.* 1.41), leading to

(c) recognition of perception by completed act of assent,

(d) recognition of knowledge by the assent of the wise.

It is possible that, when Cicero uses the words *acceptio* and *approbatio* and their cognates, he is trying to distinguish the degrees of assent for which Zeno had rather confusingly used the word συγκατάθεσις alone.

There remains one further preliminary point before we consider how Zeno supposed the assent of the wise can be distinguished from the assent of the foolish, and it is a point which will help us in that enquiry. In Cicero's account Zeno is made to believe that recognizable presentations have a certain obviousness (*declaratio*) about them which, as it were, leads the mind to recognize that they are genuine representations of their particular source-objects. The word *declaratio* is presumably a translation of the Greek ἐνάργεια—and that might make it look as though Cicero is giving us a paraphrase of Zeno's view rather than the actual words he used. Paraphrases are not always very accurate. Later and un-Zenonian varieties of Stoicism

[1] Sext. Emp., *Adv. Math.* 7.152–3; cf. 397 (*SVF* II 91).

may have intruded. The problem is that, as Sandbach has pointed out, ἐνάργεια is apparently a word not used by Zeno, or even by Chrysippus. It is Epicurean in origin and first appears in the extant Stoic fragments in the work of Antipater.[1] But, although the word may be inappropriate to Zeno, the thought is not. As Sandbach says, 'By ἐνάργεια Epicurus meant to denote just that quality of a φαντασία which Zeno denoted by the word καταληπτική, that quality which makes a man feel certain of its truth'.

So much then for Zeno's general account of knowledge. We must now look closer at particular points. First of all, as Pohlenz insists, Zeno is most emphatic about the voluntary act of assent; it is an act within our power, as the Stoics understand this phrase. No knowledge can exist without the assent of the wise man. Secondly, the recognizable presentations are trustworthy (*adiungebat fidem*), and ought to be believed (*credendum*). However, although they ought to be believed, they are not always believed. Only the wise man will have the sense to believe them in all cases. It would, then, be incorrect to call these presentations 'irresistible' (as the English version of Zeller has it). Although they ought to be believed, there is no reason for saying that they must be believed, let alone that they will be believed.

It seems, however, that Zeno's doctrine was very easy to misunderstand or misrepresent. There is a story current in two slightly different versions about Sphaerus, one of Zeno's pupils.[2] On one occasion in Alexandria king Ptolemy Philopator and Sphaerus were debating the problem of whether the wise man can hold opinions. The Stoic view is that opinion is akin to error, arises from weak acts of assent, and is therefore alien to the wise.[3] Ptolemy had some wax pomegranates served to the philosopher, and the philosopher was deceived; whereupon the king in triumph observed that Sphaerus had assented to a false proposition. Sphaerus, however, came back with the reply that he had assented not to the proposition that they were pomegranates, but to the proposition that it was reasonable to think

---

[1] Sandbach, *op. cit.* 50–1.
[2] D.L. 7.177 (*SVF* i 625); cf. Athen. 8.354ε (*SVF* i 624).
[3] Cf. (e.g.) Cic., *Acad. Post.* 1.41 (*SVF* i 60).

that they were pomegranates. Presumably, however, the more precise reply would have been that only the wise always make proper judgments and that he himself did not claim to be a wise man. If Sphaerus' comment is taken literally, he might seem to claim that the recognizable presentation should be regarded as irresistible.

There is no doubt that Pohlenz is right to emphasize that most of our evidence indicates that, when Stoics were asked what is the criterion of truth, they usually gave the answer that it is the recognizable presentation.[1] This leaves us with two problems. Did Chrysippus and later Stoics regard these presentations as irresistible? Does their account of an irresistible presentation differ from that given by Zeno? In a way these two problems turn on one fundamental problem. Does the 'voluntary' aspect of the assent, which we have seen Zeno emphasize in the version of his views transmitted by Cicero, and which Pohlenz acknowledges to be genuinely Zenonian, become watered down?

Before looking in particular at some passages of Sextus Empiricus, we should notice one more section of Cicero's account. Cicero explains at one point why Zeno held that the recognizable presentations are trustworthy.[2] One reason for this, he says, is that nature has given a rule for knowledge (*norma scientiae*). It is not clear at first what this rule is, but what follows makes it apparent that it is the recognizable presentation itself. For 'from this rule concepts are impressed on our minds'. At this point in his account, therefore, Zeno seems to be emphasizing the *presentation* as the criterion, whereas previously he had equally or more emphatically supported the recognition itself.

If we look at Sextus Empiricus' account of these matters, the same ambiguity appears. Sextus begins to discuss the objections brought against the Stoics, obviously therefore against Zeno, by Arcesilaus.[3] The discussion starts on the assumption that the basic criterion of truth is recognition (κατάληψις, 152). How-

---

[1] E.g. D.L. 7.46 (*SVF* ΙΙ 53), 7.54 (*SVF* ΙΙ 105).
[2] Cic., *Acad. Post.* 1.42 (*SVF* Ι 60).
[3] Sext. Emp., *Adv. Math.* 7.150 ff.

ever, the existence of recognition is held to depend on the existence of recognizable presentations (155), and there are, according to Arcesilaus, no clearly recognizable presentations. This non-existence of a recognizable presentation is then described as the non-existence of the Stoic criterion (156). So Sextus is agreeing with Cicero that Zeno's language about recognitions and recognizable presentations enables us to speak of either or both of these as criteria.

After discussing Arcesilaus, Sextus proceeds to the views of Carneades. These, he says, were directed not only against the Stoics, but against all previous thinkers.[1] But when dealing with obviously Stoic views, his attack is very close to that of Arcesilaus, though the terminology differs slightly. We should remember that Carneades knew not only the view of Zeno, but also that of Chrysippus, so that if the two Stoics held different views, we might expect a different attack to be launched against each of them. There is no trace of such a difference. Carneades first argues that false presentations can always be mistaken in some circumstances for true; hence the concept of a recognizable presentation makes no sense. Since there is no recognizable presentation, there is no judgeable presentation (φαντασία κριτική). And since nothing is judgeable, reason will not be a criterion. Hence an argument that begins by rejecting the concept of recognizable presentations ends by rejecting reason as a criterion. And if reason is rejected, κατάληψις must be rejected also *a fortiori*. What can be more obvious than that Carneades thought the view, which we have already found to be that of Zeno, to have also been that of Chrysippus?

What then has caused the confusion? If Sextus Empiricus and Carneades make no distinction between Zeno and Chrysippus, why do modern scholars attempt to do so? Perhaps the principal reason is a well known passage in Sextus.[2] Sextus begins by distinguishing the older Stoics, presumably including both Zeno and Chrysippus, from the younger. According to the older Stoics recognizable presentations are the criterion of truth; the younger Stoics add 'provided that the recognizable presentation has no obstacle'. In the latter case, according to

---

[1] Sext. Emp., *Adv. Math.* 7.159 ff.   [2] Sext. Emp., *Adv. Math.* 7.253-7.

the younger Stoics, the presentation *practically* (μόνον οὐχί) catches hold of us by the hair and drags us off to assent. Examples given of obstacles in the way of such presentations include the story of Alcestis and Admetus. When Admetus saw Alcestis (that is, received a recognizable presentation), he did not assent to it because he held that those who are dead do not rise again from the dead.

It is not, however, quite clear what the passage means. Is Sextus saying that according to the younger Stoics the presentation practically catches hold of us by the hair and *practically* drags us to assent, or that it practically catches us by the hair and *actually* drags us to assent? If the latter interpretation is correct, then the younger Stoics, though not necessarily Chrysippus, really did believe that the recognizable is in some circumstances absolutely irresistible, that we have no choice but to assent to it. We suggested above that evidence that this view was current at some stage of Stoicism is afforded by the tale of Sphaerus and Ptolemy. Here it is certainly implied that truly recognizable presentations are absolutely irresistible. If this view was ever held—and certainly Chrysippus did not hold it— it should have been accompanied by the elimination of the doctrine of free assent which Zeno had emphasized. In Zeno's picture of the process of grasping facts, only the wise man will assent to every particular recognizable presentation in so far as it is recognizable; on the new view anybody, fool or wise, will accept of necessity the obviously recognizable presentations which actually drag us to assent.

Sandbach seems to think that some such view was current among the later Stoics.[1] But the orthodox tradition of Stoicism persisted in the Zenonian approach, emphasizing the role of the will. It should perhaps be added, as a corollary to the discussion, that the *caveat* about 'obstacles' impeding the 'recognizable presentation' is unnecessary, if the original doctrine of Zeno and Chrysippus is properly understood. We recall that, for a presentation to be recognizable, it has to be of such a kind as could come from no other particular existing object. That is, it must be unique. And if it is unique, it cannot be misunderstood

[1] Sandbach, *op. cit.* 51 note 1.

—though it may not be understood—by the wise man, whatever obstacle is put in his way. In other words the presentation is either recognizable or it is not, though it does not follow that the fool will actually recognize a recognizable presentation. The addition by the younger Stoics is otiose; perhaps it was only meant to remind us that the reason of the fool is encumbered by 'obstacles' which limit its effectiveness.

We must now return to the orthodox doctrine and see whether we have been right in asserting that for Chrysippus and his followers the doctrine of assent as an act within our power is maintained. This thesis seems to underlie the use of the word 'induce' (ἐπάγομαι) in another passage of Sextus Empiricus.[1] Recognizable presentations induce us to assent to them. That does not mean that they compel us to assent, for possible and indeed likely actions in the future are not necessary actions in the Stoic sense of the word 'necessary'.[2] Clearer evidence still is afforded by Cicero in the *De Fato*, where Chrysippus is made to talk about presentations virtually imparting themselves to the mind while assent is still in our power, and by Plutarch, who tells us that Chrysippus did not regard presentation as the complete (αὐτοτελής) cause of the act of assent.[3]

We can see, therefore, that Zeno and Chrysippus maintained similar theses about the relation of recognizable presentations to the act of assent, which was always held to be in our power. The belief that their doctrines were identical on this matter can be supported further if we approach the problem from another angle. Both Zeno and Chrysippus agreed that the recognizable presentation of any object is unique, that it is different from that of any other object. In order to disprove this thesis Arcesilaus and Carneades were continually trying to find instances of presentations which could not be distinguished. It was argued that if there are many snakes in a hole, and one puts up its head, it is impossible to tell, after the head is withdrawn, whether the next head to appear is the same one. The reaction of the wise man to this problem and to others of a similar kind, and in particular to variants of the Sorites, is mentioned both

---

[1] Sext. Emp., *Adv. Math.* 7.405 (*SVF* II 67); cf. ἀπάγομαι (7.165).
[2] See above, pp. 128–32.　　　　[3] Plut., *SR* 1055F (*SVF* II 994).

by Sextus Empiricus and by Cicero. Sextus, expounding Stoic doctrine, remarks that 'in the case of the Sorites, when the last recognizable presentation lies beside the first non-recognizable presentation and is practically impossible to distinguish from it, Chrysippus and his followers say that, where the difference is so small, the wise man will pause and keep silent'.[1] Cicero attributes exactly the same attitude to Chrysippus in the *Academica*.[2] It clearly annoyed the Sceptics, because, although the Stoics held the argumentation of the Sorites to be fallacious,[3] they nevertheless allowed the wise man to suspend judgment in a particular case. However, the objections of the Sceptics are not well taken, since the Stoics did not claim that the wise man knows everything, or even everything knowable, but only that he knows everything necessary for virtue.

At this point we should enter a word of caution. For although the Stoics, including both Zeno and Chrysippus, hold that the wise man will suspend judgment in those (presumably very few) cases where it becomes impossible to tell whether a presentation is recognizable or not, this in no way detracts from the fixed points in the system. It is still the case that every presentation is unique, and this uniqueness of the presentation is due to the fact that every individual is distinct. 'No two hairs or grains of sand are entirely alike' is the Stoic thesis.[4] It proved almost beyond the comprehension of many of their critics.[5]

We are now in a position to estimate the view of Pohlenz that there was a change of some importance made by Chrysippus in the doctrine of the criterion; that whereas Zeno talked about two factors, assent and recognizable presentation, Chrysippus emphasized the latter exclusively. This view is wrong. That Chrysippus changed the Stoic account of the physiological

---

[1] Sext. Emp., *Adv. Math.* 7.416 (*SVF* II 276); cf. *Hyp. Pyr.* 2.253 (*SVF* II 275).
[2] Cic., *Acad. Pr.* 2.93 (*SVF* II 277), cf. 2.49.
[3] Cic., *Acad. Pr.* 2, 49. For the statement that Chrysippus invented but could not solve the 'hair' paradox see *Acad. Pr.* 2.96 (*SVF* II 282). Elsewhere this and other paradoxes are credited to Eubulides of Megara (D.L. 2.108). Cf. Kneale and Kneale, *The Development of Logic* 113–14, Watson, *op. cit.* 67.
[4] Cic., *Acad. Pr.* 2.85 (*SVF* II 113); cf. 2.56–8.
[5] See the discussion on individuals in relation to the categories, pp. 160–4.

mechanism of learning is correct enough. As we have seen, he preferred to explain Zeno's doctrine of τύπωσις not in the literal sense—as did Cleanthes when he talked about impressions on wax—but more metaphorically. Zeno, he held, was talking about alteration. But this has nothing to do with the criterion, and Pohlenz' attempt to link the two must be pronounced a baseless hypothesis. The reasons for the change on τύπωσις are given by Sextus; and they have nothing to do with the criterion.

Before leaving the matter, however, there is a further rather tantalizing point which at least deserves mention, though, because of the thinness of the evidence available to us, we cannot come to any very definite conclusions. Watson has written that 'the Stoics were particularly insistent that all our statements were interpretations of reality, meanings imposed on reality rather than reality itself'.[1] In a sense this is true, for philosophers, according to the Stoics, deal in propositions (ἀξιώματα), and propositions are *lekta*, one of the four groups of incorporeal entity which the Stoics recognized. But it is perhaps not certain how far most of the Stoics recognized the kind of distinction between reality and meaning that Watson attributes to them. Meaning is a function of propositions, and it is generally agreed that according to the Stoics, although the predicates 'true' and 'false' can be applied to propositions, presentations and arguments, the application to propositions is basic.[2] Nevertheless, as Mrs Kneale points out, when the Stoics say that the true is what is real (τὸ ὑπάρχον), there is a problem.[3] It is not certain how far the Stoics would have wished to distinguish between what exists and what is true. The same word (ἀληθής) can carry both senses, and we have already found it difficult to translate a passage of Sextus about the criterion.[4] Using phraseology which there is no reason to deny would have been acceptable to the Stoics, Sextus says that the criterion is 'that by which we assert that these things exist and those do not, and that these

[1] Watson, *op. cit.* 70.
[2] Sext. Emp., *Adv. Math.* 8.11 (*SVF* II 166). Cf. Mates, *Stoic Logic* 34; Watson, *op. cit.* 54; Kneale and Kneale, *op. cit.* 156.
[3] Sext. Emp., *Adv. Math.* 8.10 (*SVF* II 195); Kneale and Kneale, *op. cit.* 151.
[4] Sext. Emp., *Adv. Math.* 7.29.

10-2

are true [or "are the case"] and those are false [or "are not the case"]'.

Now we know that Chrysippus refused to accept the account of conditionals proposed by Philo of Megara, who wished to explain their truth-value in terms of what is now called material implication.[1] The evidence for various views on the nature of conditionals is mostly drawn from Sextus Empiricus and has been much discussed.[2] There is no need to go into details here. At least four types of implication were known, of which the third mentioned by Sextus, and called the 'connection' theory, is probably the one recognized by Chrysippus. The example Sextus gives is 'If it is day, then it is day'. On this view, according to Mates, 'implication is that which holds between the members of a conditional which is logically true, that is, true of all possible worlds'.[3] The version given by Diogenes Laertius is 'If it is day, it is light'. Diogenes' comment is that this conditional, which is a true conditional, is one in which the contradictory of the consequent is incompatible with the antecedent.[4] Diogenes does not specifically attribute this view of conditionals to Chrysippus, though on *a priori* grounds it would be reasonable to assume that he has Chrysippus in mind. However, Chrysippus is specifically credited by Cicero with the view that it is better to express the (assumedly true) conditional 'If some one was born at the rising of the dog-star, he will not die at sea' as 'It is not the case both that someone was born at the rising of the dog-star and that he will die at sea'.[5] This example is not incompatible with the account of implication mentioned by Diogenes as Stoic, and can be understood in terms of the third type of implication (after those of Philo and Diodorus) described by Sextus Empiricus. When we compare the evidence of Cicero with that of Sextus and Diogenes, however, it becomes clear that for Chrysippus conditionals must express natural laws, and that Mates can only be right that 'implication is that

---

[1] Cf. Mates, *Stoic Logic* 43–4, 63. Chrysippus' debt to Philo was considerable; cf. the attitudes to possibility, pp. 115, 119 above.

[2] Sext. Emp., *Hyp. Pyr.* 2.110–12; cf. *Adv. Math.* 8.112 ff., 265, 332 etc. See also Mates, *op. cit.* 43–9, Kneale and Kneale, *op. cit.* 128–38.

[3] Mates, *op. cit.* 49.   [4] D.L. 7.73 (*SVF* II 215).

[5] Cic., *De Fato* 15 (*SVF* II 954).

which holds between the members of a conditional which is logically true' if Chrysippus did not distinguish logical impossibility from empirical impossibility.[1]

However, if, according to Chrysippus, the words 'true' and 'false' can be used of propositions not only about the world but about all possible worlds, that is, if their sphere of reference is logical, it might be argued that he distinguished between meaning and reality (in the sense of existent reality) in the way in which Watson suggests. Perhaps he tried to make such a distinction. Nevertheless, the evidence about the general use of 'true' and 'false' by the Stoics would suggest that, if Chrysippus was always clear on this matter, many other Stoics were not.

This then brings us to the point at which we were aiming when we introduced the question of truth and falsehood. If we are right in thinking that Chrysippus at least was aware that our statements, whether true or false, are interpretations of reality, does that mean that he despaired of reaching reality itself? This does not seem to be the case, because it is clear that he would allow presentations as well as propositions to be true or false. Now it might be objected that in so doing he was only talking about presentations and not about the world itself. Hence presentations might be true or false according to whether one can or cannot make true or false affirmations about them,[2] but these affirmations will still only be about the presentations. The ambiguity about whether truth is a function of propositions or whether it is the equivalent of existence obscures this problem; for it seems that in Stoicism we normally have to assume that true presentations are somehow related to true (that is, existent) things. Needless to say, this would not be the case if Chrysippus' account of implication as relevant also to possible worlds is taken seriously. But whether Chrysippus attempted to deal with this problem, we do not know. We are confronted with a lack of evidence.

At least one later philosopher, much influenced by Stoicism, seems to have faced up to the difficulty. This was Philo of Larisa, who propounded what is described in Cicero as a

---

[1] Cf. Gould, 'Chrysippus', esp. 158–61.
[2] Sext. Emp., *Adv. Math.* 7.244.

revolutionary (*nova quaedam*) doctrine, summarized by Sextus as follows:[1] 'Things (τὰ πράγματα) are unrecognizable (ἀκατά-ληπτα) by the Stoic criterion, that is, by recognizable presentations, but recognizable so far as concerns the nature of the things themselves.' What this means is not quite clear. Perhaps Philo wanted to argue that 'presentations' only give superficial understanding but that some kind of Aristotelian essence can be grasped by other means. In any case, what seems to have worried him is that the Stoics left a gap between the presentation and the object itself. His problem was how grasp of a presentation could tell us anything about the object itself. It is the modern problem of sense-data. Philo was worried about the 'things-in-themselves'.

Why Philo moved in this direction is not known to us: Cicero's unilluminating comment is that he was unable to withstand the criticism of the Academy. He does not tell us which specific arguments hit home. It only remains for us to wonder whether Carneades had uncovered any of the problems underlying the various uses of the word 'true'. Perhaps he had not done so. Perhaps Philo himself, while struggling with the traditional arguments for and against the concept of a recognizable presentation, had come to wonder whether there is, after all, a problem about sense-data, about the relation of presentations to things. At least we can be fairly sure that this had not worried earlier Stoics, including Chrysippus. For when Cicero mentions it, he observes that the position of Philo led to a paradoxical situation, namely that, if the recognizable presentation is rejected, it becomes impossible to explain why some things are knowable and others are not. As we have seen, to explain this was one of the original reasons for the doctrine of recognizable presentations, and the quick abandonment of Philo's position by his pupil Antiochus of Ascalon may allow us to assume that no other explanation of the problem was known. And that means that before Philo, whatever may be the logical implications of Stoic theories about the relation of propositions to things, no one had clearly realized that a problem about sense-data is involved.

[1] Cic., *Acad. Pr.* 2.18; Sext. Emp., *Hyp. Pyr.* 1.235.

Philo was nominally a member of the Academy, brought up on the Sceptical tradition of Carneades. His Stoicism is in a sense a para-Stoicism. His attitude towards the criterion was not accepted by the orthodox Stoics; and indeed we hardly know what it is. We may conclude, therefore, that there was no change of any significance in the orthodox Stoic attitudes to the criterion. Zeno's two factors, assent and recognizable presentation, are there from the beginning of the school to the end. They may be emphasized in slightly different ways, but the differences are trivial. It is only when a fellow-traveller with Stoicism looks at the presentation that a new theory appears—and perhaps a new set of philosophical problems. It seems to be a matter for great regret that we know so little of Philo of Larisa.

9

CATEGORIES AND THEIR USES

In his book *Stoic Logic*, first published in 1953, Benson Mates devotes something less than a page to the Stoic categories. His hesitation about saying more is explained as due to the fact that our best sources for Stoic logic, namely Sextus Empiricus, Diogenes Laertius and Galen, have little to tell us about categories, and that what information we have comes very largely from the Aristotelian commentators, who are both late and 'relatively unreliable'.[1] Since Mates' book appeared, Miss Reesor has made two attempts to clarify the situation,[2] but despite her useful work much still remains unclear. In particular, the category of quality, with its two subdivisions, specific and particular quality, provides considerable problems. Nor, despite the work of De Lacy,[3] is it at all clear what the categories were used for. Nor, again, do we yet fully understand how the categories fit into the materialist world-picture which the Stoics normally offer us.[4]

Zeno seems to have founded his physics on the thesis that everything that exists must be either active or passive, and that it can either act or be acted upon.[5] This necessitates that anything which can neither act nor be acted upon—if there is such a thing—is both 'non-existent' and, in the Stoic view, incorporeal. Hence the theory arose, subscribed to by most members of the school, that there are four kinds of immaterial 'things' which cannot properly be said to exist, but which can be thought of as 'subsistent'.[6] These are void, place, time, and what they called *lekta* or 'things meant'. A thing meant is de-

[1] Mates, *Stoic Logic* 18.
[2] Reesor, 'The Stoic Concept of Quality', and 'The Stoic Categories'.
[3] De Lacy, 'The Stoic Categories as Methodological Principles'.
[4] Earlier work of importance on the categories is to be found in Rieth, *Grundbegriffe*, esp. 22–9, 55–84, and Pohlenz, 'Die Begründung' and 'Zenon und Chrysipp'.
[5] D.L. 7.134 etc. (*SVF* I 85).
[6] Sext. Emp., *Adv. Math.* 10.218 (*SVF* II 331).

scribed as 'the thing itself revealed by sound which we grasp as subsisting together with our thought'.[1] There were some Stoics who were worried about the status of *lekta*, but the evidence which we have about them—and they included a prominent but mysterious figure named Basileides—does not show with any kind of certainty what they actually said. Often the orthodox Stoics seems to have stated that the 'incorporeals' subsist,[2] but the word 'subsist' (ὑφίστασθαι) does not appear in the report of Basileides,[3] although the other word sometimes used by the orthodox, namely ὑπάρχειν, does. We must conclude that we do not know how the argument ran in detail; we only know that there was an argument.[4]

Let us forget about the unorthodox. The normal Stoic view, formulated in detail by Chrysippus, is that there are four kinds of immaterial 'thing'.[5] How is this to be squared with the doctrine, for which there is a great deal of evidence, that according to the Stoics 'bodies alone are real'?[6] The phrase in Plutarch gives the position away. Plutarch writes: ὄντα γὰρ μόνα τὰ σώματα; they call bodies alone existents (ὄντα). This means that incorporeal things would be called something other than ὄντα, namely subsistent things. Thus 'existence' (οὐσία) would not be the most general term the Stoics would be willing to predicate. First of all they speak of 'things'; then they divide these into two classes, (a) existent things and (b) subsistent things like time as well as non-existent (i.e. fictional) things like Centaurs. Our best evidence is a passage of Seneca, where it is pointed out that 'what is' (*quod est* = τὸ ὄν) is not the highest class; in the view of 'certain Stoics' there are 'in the nature of things' certain things which do not exist. Seneca gives examples of these:

---

[1] Sext. Emp., *Adv. Math.* 8.12.
[2] Cf. Sext. Emp., *Adv. Math.* 8.70 (*SVF* II 187), D.L. 7.63.
[3] *Adv. Math.* 8.258 (*SVF* II Bas. 1).
[4] For other evidence about the status of incorporeals in the view of orthodox Stoics cf. *SVF* II 331, 521, 541.
[5] The word πρᾶγμα is used of λεκτά by Sextus (*Adv. Math.* 8.12). I do not think it is necessary to follow Mates (*op. cit.* 11) and translate this as 'entity', so long as we understand that 'things' for the Stoics are not to be identified with 'existents'. See below.
[6] Plut., *CN* 1073E. Cf. Zeller 3¹.119 for further references if needed.

Centaurs and Giants and whatever else can be constructed by the mind but which has no reality (*substantia* = οὐσία).[1] The name given by Seneca to this highest grouping of all, which embraces both what exists and what does not, is 'something' (*quid*); other authorities give us the Greek name (τὸ τί).[2] Confusion about this concept, wilful or otherwise, began early. Alexander of Aphrodisias tries to argue that whatever can be called 'something' (τί) must be an existent (ὄν);[3] this is precisely what the orthodox Stoics were concerned to deny. It is noteworthy that Alexander does not mention the Centaurs and Giants which Seneca had used in his example. If he had, it might have been more obvious than he liked to admit, that there is a category distinction between horses which exist and Centaurs which do not. But in this Alexander is only typical of many Greek thinkers in ignoring problems, partly grasped by the Stoics, about fictional or otherwise non-existent nameables.

We have seen that incorporeal things include *lekta*. And the categories themselves are examples of one type of *lekton*; they are incomplete *lekta*.[4] By this is meant that they need to be combined with subjects to form propositions; they are in fact predicates.[5] In other words, if we put something into a category, we expect to be told something about it; we will understand that x is so and so. Now the Stoics posited four categories only. Passages listing the names of these four together are very late, but there is no reason to believe them to be inaccurate.[6] The usual names are 'substance' (ὑποκείμενον), quality (ποιόν), disposition (πῶς ἔχον) and relative disposition (πρός τί πως ἔχον). Our first problem, therefore, is to determine what is meant by the term 'substance'. The answer to this has been hit upon, though perhaps inadvertently, by De Lacy, though, since in his article it is embedded in a good deal of argument which is not

---

[1] Sen., *Ep.* 58.15. (*SVF* II 332). For Centaurs as examples of non-existent things see the learned note of A. S. Pease in his edition of Cicero's *De Natura Deorum* (Harvard 1955), 483.

[2] *SVF* II 329–30, 333–5. Cf. Goldschmidt, *Le Système stoïcien* 25.

[3] Alex. Aphr., *In Top.* p. 301, 19 Wallies (*SVF* II 329).

[4] D.L. 7.63 (*SVF* II 183).   [5] Cf. Mates, 16–17.

[6] Simp., *In Cat.* p. 67, 1f. Kalbfleisch (*SVF* II 369); Plot., *Enn.* 6.1.25 (*SVF* II 371).

necessarily acceptable, it may not be apparent.[1] De Lacy writes as follows: 'The first category is enlarged somewhat to include not only the inquiry *what* a thing is, but also *that* it is.' As an example of this De Lacy cites Epictetus on the problem of learning 'that God exists', and a little later on 'what the universe is and who arranges it'.[2] But it might be argued that the questions 'What is God' and 'Does God exist?' are not as dissimilar to the Stoic as might at first be supposed. For the Stoics, as we have seen, if God exists, he would be material (and of course he is material). Hence the question 'Does God exist?' could (logically) appear as 'Is God an existent?' (ἔστιν ὁ θεὸς ἐν τοῖς οὖσιν;). Similarly the question 'What is God?' would basically appear as 'Is God an existent or not?' If we now view this in terms of our previous discussion about 'things' and 'existent things', we should be able to conclude that, if God (or anything else) exists, that is, is a material object, he will fall within the scope of the categories. We shall be able to say more of him than simply that he is a 'thing' (τὶ); he will be an existent thing. He will be substantial (*substantia*) and, of course, material.

Our proposition is, therefore, that the test for membership in the first category is simply whether the object exists, that is, is material, or not. We observed that the name of the first category is usually 'substrate' (ὑποκείμενον), but there is good evidence that the word 'being' (οὐσία), which must, as we have argued, have carried the sense of existing as opposed to not-existing, was used, among others, both by Chrysippus and by Posidonius. That Posidonius may not have understood Chrysippus' full meaning is not immediately relevant. The important point for our present purposes is that they both used the word to name the first category.[3]

At this point a slight objection must be considered. According to Zeller the earliest Stoics failed to draw the necessary distinctions; thus there is some justification for the confusion in the

---

[1] De Lacy, *op. cit.*, esp. 255.

[2] *Disc.* 2.14.11; 2.14.25.

[3] For Chrysippus, Philo, *De Aet. Mundi* 48–51 (*SVF* II 397); for Posidonius (*ap.* Ar. Did.) Stob., *Ecl.* I, p. 178 W. A possible Aristotelian background for the Stoic category one (existence) may be provided by *Acad. Post.* 2, 89 b 31–5.

minds of their rivals as to the name of the highest possible grouping of things.[1] Zeller suggests that what we have called 'things' (τινά) were sometimes called ὄντα by the Stoics; thus, by implication, he provides a certain justification for those in antiquity who argued that every 'thing' must be an existent thing (ὄν τι). According to Zeller the word 'thing' (τὶ) was probably introduced only by Chrysippus as the best term to describe not only existing things (ὄντα, οὐσίαι) but non-existing things like Centaurs.

There is a firm tradition, which our authorities refer to Zeno himself, that Platonic Forms have no independent existence, but are ἐννοήματα, false concepts which arise in the mind; they are in themselves neither existing things nor qualified existing things, but likenesses of them (οὔτε τὶ ὂν οὔτε ποιόν, ὡσανεὶ δέ τι ὂν καὶ ὡσανεὶ ποιόν).[2] This evidence would suggest that there are some 'things' which are not existing things but likenesses of existing things. We should think of fictional characters as bearing obviously striking resemblances to existing characters. The evidence thus suggests that the Stoics would not like to call their most general class 'existents' (ὄντα), because such a class could not include likenesses of existents. But even if we reject the *attribution* of the doctrine of likenesses of existents to Zeno, we have only proved that Chrysippus distinguished imitation existents from existents, not that Zeno did not distinguish them. What Zeller needs are passages to prove that some of the earlier Stoics did not make the distinction, or at least that they did not relate it to the categories. He offers two such passages, neither of which serves his turn.

The first passage is from Diogenes Laertius. The Stoics are made to say that the widest γένος is that which, while being a γένος, cannot be put into a γένος, for instance τὸ ὄν (7.61); but all that this proves is that the Stoics held that τὸ ὄν is unique. What would they have said of τὸ μὴ ὄν? It seems that Chrysippus (?) must have held that 'being' and 'non-being' cannot be said to have enough in common to warrant being put

[1] Cf. Zeller, *op. cit.* 94 note 2.
[2] *SVF* I 65. Cf. D.L. 7.50 (*SVF* II. 55) for the distinction between φαντασία and φάντασμα.

into the same γένος. 'Being', therefore, would be the only member of its γένος; it is unique. In the next sentence of Diogenes the Stoics are said to have held that Socrates is εἰδικώτατον because, being an example of a most specific εἶδος, he cannot be subdivided into εἴδη. Like 'being', though for different reasons, Socrates is unique. But the fact that the Stoics said that τὸ ὄν cannot be put into a γένος only means that there is no superior γένος to τὸ ὄν (= ὑποκείμενον); and γένος and category are frequently synonymous in Greek. We know that the Stoics never called 'things' (τινά) a category. Only existing things have to do with categories directly. In the case of non-existents predication and classification can only be by analogy. So all the passage from Diogenes proves is that ὄν is the widest category, that is, that it is a term equivalent to ὑποκείμενον.

Zeller's second (and only other) passage is from a letter of Seneca which we have already examined.[1] We read as follows: 'There is something higher than body, for we say that some things are corporeal, others are incorporeal. What will this be...? That to which we just gave the rather inappropriate name "that which is" (quod est)...That which is is either corporeal or incorporeal.' From the context, however, it appears that this view is not attributed to the Stoics but to Plato! The view of 'certain Stoics', as we outlined it above, is that 'things' form a more general class than 'existents'. But if this is the view of 'certain Stoics', what did the others hold? Did they hold that existents (quod est) form the highest class? That is not the most obvious interpretation of what Seneca says. His argument is: (1) quod est is the highest class for the Platonists; (2) the Stoics offer a higher class; (3) some Stoics say this highest class is 'things' (quid). It is hard to know how to interpret this evidence, but at least Seneca does not mean what Zeller makes him mean, namely that the earliest Stoics began their classification with quod est and that the wider grouping (quid) was added by Chrysippus. Perhaps the ambiguity in Seneca arises from the later controversy within the Stoic school, which we mentioned at the beginning of this chapter, about whether incorporeals should properly be designated 'things'. Perhaps some of

[1] Sen., *Ep.* 58.11.

the Stoics thought that 'things' must mean 'existent things' (τὶ must mean ὄν τι), and were unwilling to accept any kind of classification broader than category one (ὑποκείμενον, οὐσία). These thinkers would find it impossible to classify anything other than material existents. Hence, perhaps, there could be no grouping more general than category one. But if this is the controversy to which Seneca alludes, he does not make his position very plain. Nevertheless, we may conclude that one thing we can be sure of is that there is no evidence for Zeller's claim that the earliest Stoics called their highest class ὄν, and that they neglected what was later called τὶ. Zeller's attempt to solve the problem by alluding to the view of Ritter that the older Stoics 'must' have called their most general class 'being', is a desperate move, unsupported by the evidence. We may conclude that the distinction between 'things' and 'existents' goes back to Zeno and that Zeno regarded 'being' not as the most general class but as the most general category.

If a 'thing', therefore, is to be admitted into category one, it must be an existing thing. If it is in category one, it is an existing material object; it is a substance (οὐσία, ὑποκείμενον). A definition of substance (οὐσία) ascribed to Zeno himself should be mentioned here: 'Substance is the prime matter (πρώτη ὕλη) of all existing things.'[1] The sum total of substance is everlasting and neither grows nor diminishes. There are, of course, particulars, which are 'bits' of substance (ἡ τῶν ἐπὶ μέρους). These particulars, which the Stoics often call οὐσίαι, admit of division and blending. The qualitative change of a particular is explained as a re-configuration of the substance; the 'first' configurations are said to be colours.[2] It is incorrect to say, as Miss Reesor does, that there is no evidence that Zeno distinguished between the substance and the quality of a particular in his treatment of growth and change.[3] According to Galen the thesis that both 'substances' and 'qualities' are capable of total mixture (δι' ὅλων κεράννυσθαι) was that of Zeno himself.[4] And

---

[1] Stob., *Ecl.* 1, p. 132, 26 W. (*SVF* 1 87).
[2] Aëtius, *Plac.* 1.15.6 (*SVF* 1 91).
[3] Reesor, 'The Stoic Concept of Quality', 41 note 5.
[4] Galen, *In Hipp. De Hum.* 1 (16, 32 K.) (*SVF* 1 92).

if qualities are thus susceptible of this kind of material mixing, and are specifically separated in Zeno's sentence from substances, it is hard to think that Zeno did not distinguish between them. Miss Reesor argues that Zeno thought that the substance of the particular is subject to qualitative change, but there is no evidence for that. Two particulars can be compounded into a new unit by total mixture, but their οὐσία does not change its quality as such. Strictly speaking, all οὐσία is one in any case; it is one existing whole. It was only the view of Posidonius, who, as so frequently, misunderstood the original Stoic doctrine, that οὐσία could undergo qualitative change (ἀλλοίωσις).[1] This mistake presumably arose because Posidonius failed to grasp the implications of the fact that having an οὐσία merely means being a material object. *Qua* matter, matter *cannot* change; it *exists* as it is and no other mode of existence is possible.

We have argued that, although Zeno spoke of colours as configurations of substance, he must have regarded them, like other qualities, as material causes capable of the physical act of total mixture.[2] This doctrine was clearly formalized by Chrysippus, as extant fragments make abundantly clear.[3] For Chrysippus qualities are currents of air, and as such are capable of total mixture both with one another and with 'substance'.[4] This means that in any particular existing thing (οὐσία) there are at least two kinds of material totally mixed together, the 'prime matter' and the quality. These can never exist apart; a piece of iron, for example, cannot exist without being hard.[5] Hardness is a quality and is therefore material.

In the world of the Stoics metaphysics concerns itself primarily with two things, the whole (οὐσία in general) and the particular objects. Analysis of the world will therefore be an analysis of particular objects. Each particular object will consist of at least two material components, neither of which can exist

---

[1] Stob., *Ecl.* I, p. 178 W.
[2] Other evidence that qualities were already material for Zeno is provided by Reesor, *op. cit.* 41–2 and 'The Stoic Categories', 63–5, though her conclusion is offered with unnecessary hesitation.
[3] *SVF* II 449, 463 etc.   [4] Cf. *SVF* I 85.
[5] Cf. *SVF* II 449.

in isolation. We can thus understand a passage of Plutarch where it is said that each of us is double and has two substrates. As we should expect, the first substratum is called substance (οὐσία); there is a lacuna in the text where the second substratum should be named, but the gap has been correctly filled by von Arnim, who reads 'quality' (ποιότης).[1]

Our argument is that for the Stoics metaphysics is concerned with particulars. We should expect, therefore, that when we are dealing with existing things (category one), we should be told more about them, such as that they belong to a certain species and genus. But we should also expect the Stoics to emphasize those aspects of the particular which make it a particular, rather than those which make it a member of a class. Hence it is important that the word ποιός means in a Stoic context a qualified object (that is, a blend of two inseparable substances).[2] The Stoics talked about the general and the particular qualities of their qualified objects, but the emphasis on the particular qualities is so great that it has proved very difficult for students of Stoicism to understand what a general quality is. The term 'common quality' occurs first in Diogenes of Babylon, but this is probably due to the fragmentary nature of our sources.[3] There is no reason to suppose that Chrysippus at least did not use it. Certainly he used the phrase 'individually qualified' in passages quoted by Plutarch and Philo which will require detailed consideration.[4] The distinction between particularly and generally qualified objects is mentioned also by Simplicius[5] and Syrianus.[6] Syrianus makes the curious and questionable remark that according to the Stoics οἱ κοινῶς ποιοί are prior. It seems to be easier to understand what an 'individually qualified' entity is than a 'generally qualified' one, so we will start our further enquiries into quality there.

The most important text is provided by Philo in his treatise

---

[1] Von Arnim's reading is printed by Pohlenz in the new Teubner (*CN* 1083 D = *SVF* II 762). Zeller read ποιόν but, as Reesor has observed ('Categories', 81), ποιός denotes not 'quality' but 'a particular qualified entity'. [2] See previous note.

[3] D.L. 7.58 (*SVF* II 22 Diogenes). [4] *SVF* II 396, 397.

[5] *In De Anima*, p. 217, 36 Hayduck (*SVF* II 395).

[6] *In Met.* p. 28, 18 Kroll (*SVF* II 398).

On the Eternity of the World (48–9). It has been discussed at length by Miss Reesor and Colson and compared with a passage of Plutarch on the same theme.[1] Colson professes himself baffled by the problem of reconciling the passages, and Miss Reesor's solution, if I understand it, is not entirely satisfactory. Since the passage in Philo presents a paradox, it is not susceptible of clear and brief summary; it must, therefore, be quoted in full. Philo's text, as translated by Colson with a few modifications, runs as follows:

Chrysippus, in his treatise on 'increase', makes the following marvellous statement. Starting from the premiss that 'two individually qualified entities (δύο ἰδίως ποιά) cannot possibly exist in the same substance (ἐπὶ τῆς αὐτῆς οὐσίας)', he continues, 'As an illustration, suppose that one person has all his members and that another has only one foot, and let us call the first Dion and the defective one Theon, and then suppose that Dion has one of his feet cut off.' Now if we ask which of the two has suffered destruction, he says that Theon is the more correct answer. This seems more of paradox than of truth. For how can one say that Theon the unmutilated is not destroyed (οὐχὶ διέφθαρται)? 'Quite rightly,' he replies, 'for Dion who has had his foot amputated has passed over into the defective substance (οὐσία) of Theon. Two individually qualified entities (δύο ἰδίως ποιά) cannot exist in the same substrate (ὑποκείμενον), and so Dion must remain and Theon has been destroyed.

Miss Reesor argues that the point of this is that when Chrysippus said that δύο ἰδίως ποιά cannot exist in the same substrate, he understood 'substrate' as quality. We recall that Plutarch tells us that each of us is double and has two substrates.

But although it seems possible that in the passage of Philo the word 'substrate' refers to quality, that is, to the air current, it cannot in fact do so, since according to Philo Chrysippus used the word 'substance' (οὐσία) to represent the substrate in which two qualified entities cannot exist.[2] What Chrysippus is

---

[1] For Colson, see appendix to Loeb Philo IX, pp. 528–9, and for Reesor, 'Quality', 46–7.

[2] It is true that Plutarch calls qualities οὐσίαι at *CN* 1085 E (*SVF* II 380); but this is Plutarch's argument against Chrysippus, not Chrysippus himself. I have been unable to find any passages where the Stoics themselves call qualities οὐσίαι. Usually, on the contrary, the two are distinguished, as at *SVF* I 92.

saying is that in the case of every particular existing object, such as Theon, there is only one 'individually qualified entity'; in other words Theon is unique. The paradox arises, and is obviously regarded by Chrysippus as intolerable, because the uniqueness of Theon is being explained in terms of his only having one leg. If being one-legged is Theon's only claim to existence as Theon, then as soon as Dion becomes one-legged he takes on Theon's characteristic, that which makes Theon Theon; and therefore (obviously!) Theon ceases to exist. Presumably the absurd situation was concocted because Chrysippus found it difficult to explain the importance of individual qualities to a philosophical world used to talking only about universals.

There is a passage of Plutarch which seems to contradict the view of Chrysippus reported by Philo, but which does not in fact do so. What it does is make a single exception to the rule that 'two individually qualified entities' cannot be present in a single substance.[1] The context of the passage is an argument between the Stoics and the Academy. According to the Academy, says Plutarch, two doves are two substances (οὐσίαι) with one quality, while the Stoics, he implies, hold that they are one substance (οὐσία) and two qualified entities (ποιοί). Plutarch would seem from the lines which follow to be speaking of 'individually qualified entities'. He regards the Stoic view as paradoxical.

In this passage Plutarch unwittingly brings out the weakness of the Academic position which Chrysippus had obviously grasped. He seems to think that the only difference between two doves is numerical. They are two objects, qualified in the same way by the single quality, doveness. As the passage from Philo makes clear, Chrysippus would have found this intolerable. He said that the two doves are both existents. *Qua* existents they are both one; they both exist and are material (category one). Hence they have one 'substance'. Nevertheless they are individually differentiated and not substitutable; hence they are 'two qualified entities'. There is, of course, a problem here. The problem is why we call them both doves. Have they nothing in

[1] Plut., *CN* 1077 CD (*SVF* II 396 and 1064).

common beyond the fact that they are existent material objects? We shall return to this, the question of 'common qualities', later.

What puzzles Plutarch about the Stoic position is how to square the thesis that two doves are two ποιά with the thesis which, he says, they are continually putting together, that there can be two individually qualified entities (δύο ἰδίως ποιούς) in *one* substance (ἐπὶ μιᾶς οὐσίας). And this is a statement which has puzzled modern scholars also, for it contradicts the dictum attributed to Chrysippus by Philo that two individually qualified entities can *not* exist in the same substrate. And we have argued that by substrate Chrysippus means substance (οὐσία). We must look at what Plutarch attributes to Chrysippus in more detail. Quoting Chrysippus, then, he tells us that, when the universe is destroyed by fire, Zeus, who alone of the gods cannot be destroyed, retires (ἀναχωρεῖν) into Providence (πρόνοια),[1] and that Zeus and Providence, which are presumably qualified entities, will both continue to exist in the single substance aether (ἐπὶ μιᾶς τῆς τοῦ αἰθέρος οὐσίας). It is very unfortunate that we do not know the context of this passage, but something useful can be reconstructed. Clearly Chrysippus wanted to emphasize that Zeus *alone* of the gods survives. And yet he says that Providence also survives in aether. The obvious conclusion is that Zeus and Providence are identical; they are simply names for the same power in different aspects of its activity. This is in any case a well-known part of Old Stoic teaching.

But if Zeus and Providence are different aspects of the same divine power, why are they called 'individually qualified entities', both of which are present in a single substance? The answer to this must depend on what the single substance is. It is, in fact, matter in general, the basic material reality of the world. Clearly every individually qualified entity is present in one substance in this sense of substance, where substance is the prime matter of all things.[2] All things can 'retire' into this substance. What distinguishes Zeus and Providence from ordinary

---

[1] Cf. ἀναδεδράμηκε in Philo (49).
[2] Cf. *SVF* i 87 discussed above.

particulars is that at the conflagration ordinary particulars lose their individuality as they pass into one another; Zeus, on the other hand, who seems to stand for the organizing principle and seed of the world, does not disappear. It is true that he does no organizing during the conflagration; he only 'foresees' what is to be—he has retired into Providence—but he will return to action with the next cycle of world events as the active force in the world. As all the Stoics held, the two basic principles of the world are god (Zeus) and matter.[1]

This seems to be the line on which the passage in Plutarch should be approached. It was almost certainly a misunderstanding on Plutarch's part to suggest that the relations of Zeus, Providence and the substance of the world as a whole can be applied usefully to the relations of particular qualified entities and particular substances. It is impossible to know precisely what Chrysippus wrote from Plutarch's paraphrase, but when Plutarch says that Zeus and Providence come together and continue to exist in the single substance of aether (ἐπὶ μιᾶς τῆς τοῦ αἰθέρος οὐσίας), could Chrysippus have meant that in aether alone two qualified entities can co-exist?

So much for the present for ἰδίως ποιά. We must now turn our attention to the more elusive problem of common qualities. If we think again of the passage of Plutarch, we shall recall that the difficulty of an analysis of two doves as one substance and two particularly qualified entities is that it seems to suggest that there is nothing more in common between them than that they are both existent material objects and that they cannot be substituted one for the other. The problem is: Why do we call them both doves? In other words, what do the Stoics make of species and genera? There is no doubt that it is this problem which they are trying to solve when they talk about common qualities. What we want to understand is the relationship between common qualities and substances (category one), and also between common qualities and individual qualities (category two).

We might expect that the answer to this is that common qualities also fall within category two, simply because they are qualities. The difficulty is that there is no doubt that common qualities are incorporeal, as we shall see. How then can they be classed with individually qualified entities? It would follow from their incorporeal nature that, according to the Stoics, common qualities cannot *exist* (that is, have an οὐσία—category one). This conclusion can be deduced from the Stoic attitude to Platonic Forms and to universals. According to the Stoics 'from Zeno on', what Plato calls Forms are simply our concepts; and concepts are images (φαντάσματα) arising in the mind, which are neither existents nor qualified entities,[1] but mere likenesses of these real material objects. A similar view is specifically attributed to Cleanthes,[2] and there is no reason to believe that it was not held by the whole school from the beginning. Chrysippus was prepared to distinguish genus from species by the argument that it is possible to recognize what is generically pleasant by the mind and what is specifically pleasant through the senses. An example would be that, although it makes sense to say that eating fruit is pleasant, strictly speaking one does not eat fruit but a type of fruit, such as an apple. When we eat a particular apple we obviously taste and enjoy the particular apple, and after eating an apple we say that we enjoy eating apples. It is the apple flavour that we enjoy with our sense of taste, not, Chrysippus would say, the fruit flavour. It is not possible to taste fruit flavour and enjoy it, but only the flavour of kinds of fruit. There are obviously difficulties about this suggestion. What, for example, would Chrysippus reply to a man who said that he had eaten many, or even all, kinds of fruit, and could in fact taste fruitiness whenever he ate an apple?

At any rate we know that the Stoics recognized common qualities, and that these common qualities, as φαντάσματα or ἔννοιαι, are incorporeal. Further evidence that they are incorporeal has been assembled elsewhere and need not be reconsidered here.[3] Our problem is why the Stoics put these common qualities into the category of quality, into the category, that is, of material objects (the air currents) rather than with other incorporeals like time, void, place and the *lekta*. The

[1] *SVF* i 65. [2] *SVF* i 494.
[3] Reesor, 'Quality', 50–2; Zeller, 102 etc.

answer to this is not easy to find. Part of the explanation may be that, whereas common qualities are classes of particular qualities, such things as time are not. Perhaps the Stoics supposed that it is methodologically helpful to bracket sets of qualities with the individual qualities of which they are composed.

It has recently been argued, at first sight very paradoxically, that 'the Stoics must have used the term substance to designate the common factor present in all members of the genus',[1] and that 'the two categories substratum (ὑποκείμενον) and qualified (ποιός) may go back to Chrysippus' distinction between the common and particular quality'.[2] We have suggested earlier, however, that the term substance (οὐσία) was not used by the Stoics to refer to anything other than category one. If this is correct, it must be wrong to associate it with the genus, which clearly is to be discussed in connection with category two. Nevertheless, we must still face the suggestion that what later Stoics call substrate (category one), Chrysippus thought of as common quality. There are two points against this. First, there is no evidence that the Stoic view of common qualities changed after the time of Chrysippus. Secondly, if 'the common quality was the unqualified substratum, which was usually the genus or species',[3] how could it be incorporeal, since the unqualified substratum is corporeal? And if the substratum is genus and species, how is it in fact unqualified? It cannot be unqualified since one genus must differ from another.

The whole attempt to think of common qualities as any kind of substrate must be dropped. Substrata for the Stoics are either substances (category one), elsewhere called prime matter, or individual qualities, which are air currents. Individual existents are material objects qualified in particular ways. The phrase 'common quality' is used to denote the common factor that groups of air currents share. It is only a name and has no ontological importance. That does not mean that it has no importance whatever. It explains, however, why it has been difficult for students of Stoicism to understand common quali-

[1] Reesor, 'Quality', 46. This view has been accepted by Watson, *The Stoic Theory of Knowledge* 49.
[2] Reesor, 'Categories', 81.   [3] *Ibid.*

ties. They have often wanted to make common qualities prior in some sense to particular qualities. Syrianus, doubtless for metaphysical reasons of his own, did the same in antiquity.[1] But precisely the opposite is the case. A passage of Simplicius makes the matter clear. According to the Stoics, says Simplicius,[2] 'the common aspect of quality is a differentiation of substance, not separable by itself, but ceasing in concept and character'.[3] This decisively refutes in advance the view that common quality is the unqualified substrate. Whatever the word 'substance' means in the passages of Simplicius, common quality is a differentiation (διαφορά) of it.

When we turn to the last two categories, disposition (πὼς ἔχον) and relative disposition (πρός τί πως ἔχον), we are faced with a different kind of problem from those we have so far considered, for despite the amount that has been written by Zeller, Rieth, Pohlenz, Miss Reesor and others, it is not easy to conceal the fact that we have very little evidence indeed; in particular we lack good information about what the two categories contain. Dealing with disposition first, we find that we rely on Simplicius, Dexippus and Plotinus to give us examples of what falls within this category.[4] Apparently dispositions included times ('yesterday'), places ('in the Academy'), actions, lengths ('three cubits'), colours ('white'), and others. The category seems to include conditions or states of particulars. If this is so, it is evident that it is dependent on the category of quality. Particular qualified entities, therefore, can be further described by a statement of their various dispositions. Furthermore, we recall that quality itself is a material substrate of a particular 'totally mixed with the substance (οὐσία) which is present in all actually existing things'. It seems from Stoic usage that the category of disposition was used to describe conditions of the qualitative substrate, not of the existential (category one)

---

[1] *SVF* II 598.

[2] *In Cat.* p. 222, 30 Kalbfleisch (*SVF* II 378). Cf. Rieth, *Grundbegriffe* 64–9, 79.

[3] I read (with Kalbfleisch) ἐννόημα for ἐν νόημα. The emendation is Peterson's and is wrongly rejected by Zeller.

[4] Simp., *In Cat.* p. 66, 32 ff. Kalbfleisch (*SVF* II 369); Dexippus, *In Cat.* p. 34, 19 ff. Busse (*SVF* II 399); Plot., *Enn.* 6.1.30 (*SVF* II 400).

substrate of the particular. According to Porphyry, whose accuracy we have no reason to doubt, the soul was described by the Stoics as an air current in a certain disposition (πνεῦμα πὼς ἔχον),[1] while in Sextus we read that virtue is the ἡγεμονικόν (the ruling part of the soul) in a certain disposition.[2] To introduce the category of disposition is to tell the enquirer more about the quality, the air current, which marks the particular individualization of each existing thing. From this it would follow that every qualified entity (ποιός) is also πὼς ἔχων; everything must be in some kind of disposition at any particular time.

It has sometimes been held, for example by Zeller, that the category of disposition provides us with 'accidental' qualities but not essential ones, and that these latter would appear under the category of quality itself. This view involves a misunderstanding of the relationship between 'qualities' and 'dispositions', and represents an attempt to view Stoicism through Aristotelian eyes. Let us go through the process of placing a particular object, say a man walking, in the categories. We first decide whether he exists. If he does, he is a substance (category one). But we need to know more than whether he is an existent material object; and in any case all substances are qualified. He is, then, a particular blend of prime matter with a series of air currents which form the material of his qualities. The man walking is a particular qualified entity. But to say so much is to speak of the man—let us call him Dion—in an abstract way. If we wish to consider Dion as an object of thought unrelated to any actual position in space and time, it might be enough to employ only the categories of substance and quality. But when we wish to talk about Dion's activities as an existent human being, that is, when we make him the subject of propositions referring to actual events in the world, we have to consider Dion's 'disposition'. What happens when we wish to say 'Dion is walking'? What we have to say, according to Chrysippus,[3] is that Dion, or his ἡγεμονικόν, is disposed in a certain way. In other words, if we wish to describe particular events or situations in the world, and not limit ourselves to generalizations,

---

[1] Cf. Eus., *P.E.* 15.11.4 (*SVF* II 806).　　[2] *Adv. Math.* 11.23.

[3] Sen., *Ep.* 113.18 (*SVF* I 525). See above, pp. 33-4.

we have to introduce the category of disposition. Since every particular at every time is in fact (necessarily) in some disposition or other, it is absurd to suggest that dispositions are only 'accidental qualities'. In brief, then, to introduce the category of disposition is to place the existing object (category one), which is an individual entity (category two), in a particular spatio-temporal situation (category three, disposition).[1]

It was argued by Rieth that the phrase πῶς ἔχον refers to something which produces a certain disposition in its substratum.[2] This is a possible, though less natural, way of translating the Greek words, but Rieth's interpretation cannot be correct. For, if dispositions were active powers, they would have to be material objects, that is, in Stoic terms, substrates. Yet there is not a scrap of evidence that they were so regarded. The easier translation of πῶς ἔχον as 'being in a certain state' is also the obvious philosophical sense required. Dispositions do not act on the substrate that is a qualified entity; they are states of that entity. To list in the category disposition is to describe the actual condition of an individual thing.

Our evidence about the fourth category, that of relative disposition, is a little easier to interpret. Examples of relative dispositions are rightness and leftness, fatherhood and sonship.[3] Simplicius, who is our principal source of information, devotes a great deal of time to the fact that the Stoics were concerned to point out that relative dispositions are not simply relations (τὰ πρός τι). Relation is not a Stoic category, and many relatives in the Aristotelian sense of the term would not fall under the head of relative dispositions. Presumably confusion occurred over this matter in antiquity and the Stoics tried to clarify it.

---

[1] The importance of the metaphysics of the individual in Stoicism is illuminated by Edelstein, *The Meaning of Stoicism* 19–28.

[2] Rieth, *Grundbegriffe* 77–84.

[3] Cf. Simp., *In Cat.* p. 165, 32–166, 29 Kalbfleisch (*SVF* II 403). Cf. Chrysippus as quoted by Varro, *De Lingua Latina* 10.59 (*SVF* II 155), though the phrase 'relative disposition' does not occur here. Father, son, right and left are given as examples of πρός τι ἔχοντα by Dionysius Thrax (p. 35, 3 Uhlig). Cf. Pohlenz, 'Die Begründung', 185–8. Chrysippus apparently also regarded 'part' as denoting a relative disposition, since it has no meaning apart from 'whole' (Plut., *SR* 1054E ff. = *SVF* II 550).

Apparently 'sweet' and 'bitter' were regarded as relative terms, and the Stoics wanted to explain how they differed from, for example, 'right' and 'left'. The gist of the very difficult passage of Simplicius where this is explained is that sweet and bitter have a 'power in them' (ἡ περὶ αὐτὰ δύναμις) and that they are 'according to differentials' (κατὰ διαφοράν).[1] In the view of the Stoics this means that they are qualities. Apart from substances (οὐσίαι) only qualities can be said to have power, power, that is, to act or be acted upon. They must, therefore, be material objects existing relatively to substance. Knowledge of an object's relative dispositions does not inform us about the object's existence as an object. Relative dispositions are the relations of an individual thing to other individual things which are associated with it in the world, but on which its continuing existence as an entity does not depend. For the Stoics such relationships are in some sense constructs of the mind, though they are not 'accidentals' in an Aristotelian sense. Relative dispositions, say the Stoics, are observed in accordance with bare disposition towards something else (κατὰ ψιλὴν δὲ τὴν πρὸς ἕτερον σχίσιν). We can recognize a man's existence without knowing that he is a father. If his children die, he ceases to be a father (fatherhood being a relative disposition). He does not cease to exist, but, instead of being a father, he is an ex-father.

We can now determine the similarities and differences between the categories of disposition and relative disposition. Disposition, we found, gives us information about the particular spatio-temporal situation of individuals whose role in the cosmos we may wish to describe. Relative dispositions give us further information about that situation. However, in the case of relative dispositions we acquire information which can only be regarded as true if we have particular knowledge of other material objects besides the one we set out to describe. If walking is to be predicated of Dion, we can discuss Dion's walking activities without reference, according to the Stoics, to other material objects. Since fatherhood is a relative disposition, we cannot properly describe Socrates as a father without at least

[1] For detailed but faulty discussion of this long passage cf. Rieth, *Grundbegriffe* 70–84.

implicit reference to his son. Zeno, though not Chrysippus, seems to have approached the question of the virtues by way of the category of relative disposition, though possibly he did not use the term. Virtue is one—that is, presumably, a disposition of the personality—but it seems to be a plurality because it is operative in different areas of human life.[1]

In his article on the Stoic categories De Lacy claimed to have found the categories in use as methodological principles in the writings of men like Epictetus and Marcus Aurelius.[2] This claim has been received with some scepticism, and I must number myself among the sceptics. Nevertheless, it has been the purpose of this chapter to argue that they are in fact methodological principles of some kind. They are meant to guide the enquirer into the status of particular things.[3] They give us the proper series of philosophical questions. The first question is: Does x exist? If the answer is Yes, x is in category one. Now all substances (category one) are qualified entities (category two). Therefore the next questions must be: What are the differentiating features of x? What are its generic, specific, and above all individual characteristics? Now all individual existing things exist in space and time. Therefore the next question is: What is the spatio-temporal situation of x? This question has two answers. The spatio-temporal situation of x in so far as that situation does not depend on y gives us category three. The spatio-temporal situation of x in so far as that situation does depend on y gives us category four.

Benson Mates has written that 'we are told that these four categories are so related to one another that every preceding category is contained in and more accurately determined by the next succeeding one', and cites Zeller as his authority.[4] A

---

[1] Plut., *SR* 1034 C (*SVF* I 200). Cleanthes seems to have held a similar view to Zeno (*SR* 1034 D = *SVF* I 563), as also did Ariston (*SVF* I 351, 374, 375; III 259). The view of Chrysippus seems to be that relative disposition should not be invoked to account for the plurality of virtue (cf. Reesor, 'Quality', 41–3).

[2] De Lacy, *op. cit.* 18.

[3] Cf. Christensen (*An Essay* 51) for an interpretation of the categories which has certain similarities with the one offered here.

[4] *Stoic Logic* 18.

slightly disbelieving note can be detected, and the statement as it stands is, as we hope to have shown, incorrect. Nevertheless the view of writers like Plotinus that the Stoic categories follow upon one another in a fixed order is correct.[1] Category two cannot be understood without reference to category one, nor category three without reference to category two. Category four does not depend on category three, but it is natural to consider the non-relative dispositions of a qualified entity before its relative dispositions.

[1] *Enn.* 6.1.30 (*SVF* ii 400).

10

THE INNOVATIONS OF PANAETIUS

Schmekel described Panaetius as the founder of the Middle Stoa.[1] Pohlenz, with more respect for the fact that, although in antiquity the term Middle Academy was well known, 'Middle Stoa' was not, preferred to speak of the middle period of the Stoa;[2] Edelstein most recently has spoken of Stoic self-criticism at the hands first of Panaetius, then of Posidonius.[3] It has been argued by most interpreters of Stoicism that the work of Panaetius marks important changes in Stoicism; the problem has been to know what these changes were. Difficulties arise largely from the fact that Panaetius shares with the Old Stoics the misfortune of surviving only in the writings of other people. In his case, however, there are peculiar problems which we do not find in treating of Chrysippus. Although Panaetius was very influential in his day, and influenced many others, notably Cicero, his period of great influence was short. The Stoics of the Imperial Age, though usually familiar with his work, tend to prefer older authorities. Hence we find ourselves in the position of having only a quite small number of texts where the actual name of Panaetius occurs. Yet, apart from a few special cases, it is only these texts which can be used to reconstruct his work. This rather unpalatable, and still by no means accepted, fact was recognized by van Straaten,[4] who limited himself almost entirely in his collection of the fragments of Panaetius to passages where Panaetius' name occurs, and to selections from the first two books of Cicero's *De Officiis*, a work in which Cicero is avowedly following Panaetius very closely indeed.[5]

---

[1] Schmekel, *Die Philosophie der mittleren Stoa.*   [2] Pohlenz, *Die Stoa* 1.191.
[3] Edelstein, *The Meaning of Stoicism* 45–70.
[4] Van Straaten, *Panétius.* The section of this work containing the fragments has run to three editions. References to the collection of fragments are to the third edition.
[5] Cicero, *Ad Att.* 16.4 (fr. 34); *De Off.* 3.7–10 (fr. 35). Cf. van Straaten, *Panétius* 276–83. For further treatment of the *De Officiis* as a source see Pohlenz, *Antikes Führertum*; Ibscher, *Der Begriff*; Labowsky, *Die Ethik.*

In view of the considerable dispute surrounding the source-material for Panaetius, and the no less extensive area of disagreement about the sense of many of the texts admitted to be of Panaetian origin, it may seem rash to attempt within a single chapter any sort of conspectus of Panaetius' work. Although there will be no discussion here of any of Panaetius' activities which are not of strictly philosophical interest, the task still remains a formidable one. However, it seems that van Straaten's collection of fragments, taken in conjunction with much excellent work done on Panaetius in fairly recent times, affords an opportunity for a synthesis. This chapter, therefore, will attempt to describe the impact Panaetius made on Stoicism and to discuss the significance of some of his more important proposals. In the course of the discussion, however, we shall not list every divergent opinion modern scholars have presented. Only major contributions will be mentioned—and sometimes only in the version of one of their supporters. The intention of this procedure, which I hope will not in practice appear too arbitrary, is to allow Panaetius to emerge from his scholarly entourage.

The early Stoics spoke of three divisions of philosophy, logic, physics and ethics. Their course of studies began with logic. Panaetius changed the order. For him physics came first;[1] and logic almost dropped out of sight. By this we should probably understand that he had no interest in logic. There is no evidence that he drove it out of the curriculum, but it is significant that practically nothing is known of his work in this area and that Cicero tells us that he did not approve the *spinae disserendi*.[2] That must at least eliminate most of the branch of logic which the early Stoics called dialectic, and which included investigation of modes of argument and the evaluation of logical fallacies. In other words Panaetius did not approve of logic as we understand the term; he maintained the other branches of Stoic logic, that is, grammar and rhetoric. As for logic properly so called, the only possible evidence we have is provided by

---

[1] D.L. 7.41 (fr. 63). Our sources disagree on the order of ethics and physics in the curriculum of the Old Stoa. Sextus (*Adv. Math.* 7.22 = *SVF* II 44) and Plutarch (*SR* 1035A = *SVF* II 42) say ethics preceded physics, while Diogenes says the opposite (D.L. 7.140 = *SVF* II 43).

[2] Cic., *De Fin.* 4.79 (fr. 55).

Sextus Empiricus—and the passage may have nothing to do with Panaetius.[1] According to Sextus, while the older Stoics held that the criterion of truth is provided by recognizable presentations, the younger members of the school added 'if there is no obstacle to assent'. When considering the criterion of truth, we argued that the addition is unnecessary if the doctrine of Zeno and Chrysippus is properly understood; it may have been introduced to clarify that doctrine because some Stoics misunderstood it, thus making it appear that a large number of impressions are irresistible to sage and fool alike. The younger Stoics mentioned here may be Panaetius and his followers; the doctrine adds nothing to the original Stoic theory.[2] To all intents and purposes we can conclude that Panaetius adds nothing to Stoic logic; and from the lack of evidence of his teaching on this subject, we can reasonably assume his lack of interest.

When we move from logic to physics, Panaetius' activities seem more original, though his treating physics as the branch of philosophy to be studied first probably marks a downgrading of its importance. Ancient testimony repeats that he was prepared to adopt doctrines from outside the Stoic school if they suited his purposes. Plato and Aristotle are often mentioned as influences upon him, and it is rightly said that he gave up some of the basic Stoic tenets as a result of these influences.[3]

It was probably because of the influence of Carneades, however, that Panaetius gave up the Stoic theory that the world will be destroyed by fire. According to Philo, he was not the only Stoic to do so. Boethus had abandoned the theory and Diogenes of Babylon had had his doubts.[4] In place of an eternal

---

[1] Sext. Emp., *Adv. Math.* 7.253–7 (fr. 91).

[2] Van Straaten (*Panétius* 272) is certainly correct in holding that we cannot be sure who the first of the younger Stoics was. See above, pp. 144–5. It would appear that van Straaten's view that in theory of knowledge Panaetius diverged significantly from Zeno and Chrysippus is exaggerated (*Panétius* 133–5). The more elaborate account of Tatakis (*Panétius* 147–52) is *a fortiori* unacceptable.   [3] Frs. 55–9.

[4] Philo, *De Aet. Mundi* 76 (partially fr. 65). Frs. 64–9 deal with ἐκπύρωσις. Although 64 and 69 say only that Panaetius doubted the doctrine, the evidence that he actually rejected it is strong (see van Straaten, *Panétius* 64–9).

sequence of cosmic fires and cosmic renewals, Panaetius held that the world is eternal and imperishable. He probably followed the thesis of Heraclitus that 'measures' of fire are evolved into the other elements in turn;[1] but this is only a guess. However, that it was a possible theory for a Stoic to hold is clear from its being regarded as a possible explanation of the development of the cosmos by Marcus Aurelius. It should be added that our fragments of Panaetius do not tell us that he thought of the cosmos as having existed from eternity, that is, as not beginning in time, but that was almost certainly the view he held.[2] The cosmos is eternal for him as for his Stoic predecessors, but the internal events in that eternity are seen differently. If he had denied more than merely the conflagration, we should probably have heard of it, particularly from Philo, who would have been delighted to find a Stoic arguing that the world had a beginning. Finally we may ask whether denial of a conflagration entailed denial of the void, for the two were associated in the minds of the older Stoics. According to the early Stoics there is a difference between the whole (the cosmos = τὸ ὅλον) and 'everything' (the cosmos plus the void).[3] It was held that empty space is needed to afford place for the expanding and contracting πῦρ τεχνικόν. Such expansions take place at times of conflagration, and contractions come at the remakings of the world. If such events were eliminated by Panaetius, did he eliminate empty space also?[4] It seems quite probable that he did; but we are very far from proof.

Another basic plank of the physics of the Old Stoa was the belief that the cosmos is a living organism whose parts are responsive to one another by 'sympathy'. As a result of this sympathy divination can be justified; future events can be foretold, because *sub specie aeternitatis* every event reacts upon every other. Hence a wise scrutiny of certain events enables us to forecast others. Panaetius' view is not easy to determine with preci-

---

[1] Heraclitus, fr. B 30 (DK); Clem. Alex., *Strom.* 5.14.104. Cf. Schmekel, *op. cit.* 188.
[2] Van Straaten, *Panétius* 70.   [3] D.L. 7.143 (*SVF* III 9 Apollodorus).
[4] This is the view of Schmekel (*op. cit.* 188 note 2), and Tatakis, *Panétius* 106. It is based on Cleomedes, *Cycl. Theor.* 1.1. Van Straaten (*Panétius* 73) regards it as a possible hypothesis.

sion. It is certain that he rejected astrology completely on the striking grounds that events at so great a distance from the earth cannot affect what happens in our world, and that, since at any time the same star is in a different position in relation to different parts of the earth, it cannot be said to cause the same effects everywhere.[1] Van Straaten is probably right in holding that Panaetius rejected astrology because of its claims that the stars *causally* affect the affairs of man.

But astrology is one thing, divination another. If Panaetius denied divination, the theory of the sympathy of the parts of the world, and even perhaps that of the world as a living organism, would be endangered. Van Straaten has pointed out that, in Cicero's account of Panaetius,[2] the Stoic is said to have doubted divination,[3] while in the accounts of Diogenes and Epiphanius he rejected it.[4] It is likely enough that Cicero is reporting Panaetius' utterances more exactly. He probably expressed himself (under the influence of Carneades) as doubting. Cicero specifically says that he did not dare to deny. But we may wonder how far the matter is one of words only. If someone says, 'Is divination valid?', and I reply, 'I doubt it', I am not formally denying the validity of divination, but the effect I deliberately produce is equivalent to a denial. Certainly in the matter of divination Panaetius was an agnostic, not an atheist; but usually neither atheists nor agnostics believe in God.

If astrology is rejected and divination 'doubted', what has become of cosmic sympathy? Clearly Panaetius does not believe that all events have repercussions everywhere. We have seen him say that the stars are too far away to affect us. It is not clear how far this should be pressed. There is no good reason to assume, as some have done,[5] that it follows that *all* sympathy must be abolished. It is likely that such a conclusion would have led to the abolition of providence also—and one clear fact about Panaetius is that he wrote a work *On Providence*.[6] Probably the effect of Panaetius' teaching was to moderate the extreme

[1] Cic., *De Div.* 2.87–97 (fr. 74).   [2] Van Straaten, *Panétius* 79.
[3] Frs. 70–1.   [4] Frs. 68, 73.
[5] Schmekel, *op. cit.* 191; Kaussen, *Physik und Ethik* 20–1; and tentatively Edelstein, *The Meaning of Stoicism* 53.
[6] Cic., *Ad Att.* 13.8 (fr. 33).

interpretations of sympathy. Some acts are so distant, so remote, so irrelevant to others, that they have no effect. The thick-skinned rhinoceros would not notice the ant on his back!

There is a passage of Epiphanius which, if taken at its face value, might be read as attributing to Panaetius the view that what is said about the gods is nugatory. Nothing can be usefully said on this subject. The strangeness of this comment has led some interpreters to reject it out of hand.[1] Others, like van Straaten, have been more sympathetic, and van Straaten goes so far as to follow Tatakis tentatively in regarding Panaetius as an atheist[2]—a suggestion which his maintenance of providence renders immediately impossible. Tatakis bases his views on the fact that Panaetius, in the extant fragments, does not identify the active principle with God. This seems to be the worst kind of argument *ex silentio*; and Tatakis' views rest, apart from Epiphanius, only on a passage of Cicero where we read, not '*I* posit two kinds of reasonable beings, gods and men', but '*They* posit'. Even van Straaten hesitates to put too much weight on this text, thus leaving himself with Epiphanius alone.

The sense of the text of Epiphanius cannot be expounded definitively; it might mean that Panaetius regarded popular accounts of the gods as false, or Stoic allegorizing as false, not that he thought that every theory about the gods or god is false. That the early Stoics attempted to fit all the legendary activities of the gods into their physical theory by means of contorted and, as was often held, obscure allegories is well attested.[3] Quite probably Panaetius took a Platonic line and dismissed the popular religion completely; from the mere fact that he was a Stoic, we can disregard any suggestion that he thought that nothing at all can be said about god or gods.

Most scholars believe that a passage from Augustine throws light on the problem.[4] Augustine describes a theory attributed

---

[1] Epiphanius, *De Fide* 9.45 (fr. 68); Diels, *Doxographi Graeci* 179; Schmekel, *op. cit.* 190 note 3.

[2] Tatakis, *op. cit.* 142; van Straaten, *Panétius* 90.   [3] *SVF* II 1067–1100.

[4] *Civ. Dei* 4.27. Van Straaten (*Panétius* 259–63) argues against treating the passage as Panaetian, though his arguments are not strong. Cf. Grilli, 'L'Opera di Panezio', 351.

In the third edition of the fragments (p. xiv), replying to a review by J.

to Q. Mucius Scaevola, a prominent Roman hearer of Panaetius. Part of Scaevola's theory about the gods is that one class
of divinities, the gods of poetic mythology, are trifling (*nugatorium*). Without committing ourselves entirely to the traditional
position that Scaevola's views are simply those of Panaetius[1]—
though this is probably the case—we should notice the observation of Grilli and Moreau that the word *nugatorium* corresponds
with a term used by Epiphanius, who writes that according to
Panaetius talk about god is trifling (ἔλεγε γὰρ φλήναφον εἶναι
τὸν περὶ θεοῦ). Hence we must conclude, not that Panaetius
is an atheist, or that he rejected the Old Stoic theory that god is
to be particularly identified with the active element in the
cosmos, but that he rejected either popular religion or allegorization of popular religion, or perhaps both.[2] But whatever
the solution to this problem, it is certainly true that, though
Panaetius believes in god and providence, he treats them as
'givens' in the world, and has little thought to spare for them
in his treatment of the aims of human life.[3]

When we turn from Panaetius' account of the external world
to his theory of the constitution of man, we find a number of
changes from the positions adopted by the early school—and
large areas of disagreement among modern scholars as to their

Moreau (*REA* 55 (1953) 183–4), van Straaten argues that the passage in
Augustine is not parallel to that in Epiphanius, because, according to
Epiphanius, Panaetius regards *all* talk about the gods as pointless, whereas
Augustine only mentions that the mythological gods of the poets are rejected. But, as Moreau says, this is to rely too much on Epiphanius' accuracy as a reporter.

However, van Straaten is certainly right to reject Cic., *De Rep.* 1.56 as
evidence for Panaetius. The discussion here is insufficiently close to that
in the *City of God* to allow us to regard it as necessarily Panaetian *even if*
Augustine's material comes ultimately from Panaetius himself.

[1] If Panaetius is to be regarded as source for the whole passage, he must also
be credited with the view that the gods of the philosophers are unsuitable
for the general public, who are best left in their (false) belief that Hercules,
Asclepius and the rest are gods. This somewhat cynical attitude *may* have
been adopted by Panaetius, who would thus be following Plato in the
Laws. Augustine's comment is, *expedire igitur existimat* (Scaevola) *falli in
religione civitates*. 'Expedit esse deos'!

[2] Zeller (*Phil. der Gr.* 3¹.587) and Tatakis (*Panétius* 140) hold that Panaetius
rejected allegory completely. This is not a matter on which absolute certainty can be achieved.   [3] Cf. Pohlenz, *Ant. Führ.* 94–5.

importance and scope. Although the evidence does not point as definitively to the Old Stoa as one would like, it seems clear that Zeno and Chrysippus thought of φύσις as the principle of unity in plants and ψυχή as the unifying principle of animals and man.[1] Animals and man, however, are not bereft of φύσις. In them φύσις, the principle of nutrition and growth, works together with soul. And according to the Old Stoics soul has eight 'parts', the five senses, the power of speech, sexual potentiality, and the ἡγεμονικόν.[2] The activities of the human being, however, are in reality states of the ἡγεμονικόν.[3] The seven other 'parts' of the soul all function, each through a different organ, in relation to the ἡγεμονικόν, and cannot be dissociated from it. For the Old Stoa, therefore, it is possible to talk about both φύσις and soul in man. Φύσις is, so to speak, the raw material on which soul is developed; or, as van Straaten puts it, at the birth of man φύσις is transformed into soul.[4]

When we look at the views of Panaetius, we find that he only counted six 'parts' of the soul.[5] The simplest way of explaining how he comes to reduce the number from eight to six is offered by Nemesius.[6] According to Nemesius, Panaetius did not regard either voice or sexual power as independent parts of the soul. Sex he thought of as a part of nature (φύσις). He thus regarded φύσις as the equivalent of the Aristotelian faculty of nutrition and reproduction (θρεπτικόν–γεννητικόν). As for speech, he seems to have thought of this as a power which must be subordinated to 'movement in accordance with impulse'. Now it is orthodox Stoicism that all impulses are states of the ἡγεμονικόν. Sometimes they are called 'functions' of the ἡγεμονικόν.[7] We

---

[1] *SVF* II 337, 710–13, 718. [2] *SVF* II 827–32.

[3] *SVF* II 823. See above, pp. 22–36.

[4] Van Straaten, *Panétius* 98; Plut., *SR* 1052 F (*SVF* II 806).

[5] Tert., *De An.* 14 (fr. 85). The correct text, not printed by van Straaten or by Waszink in his edition of the *De Anima*, was established by Philippson ('Zur Psychologie', 152 note 6), who reads: *Dividitur* (anima) *in partes, nunc in duas a Platone, nunc in tres a**, ⟨nunc in quattuor a⟩ Zenone, nunc in quinque ⟨ab Aristotele⟩ et in sex a Panaetio.*

[6] Nem., *De Nat. Hom.* 15, p. 212 Matthaei (fr. 86). The explanation offered here is akin to that of Schmekel, *op. cit.* 200–2.

[7] For δυνάμεις see *SVF* II 826, 831. We cannot follow Schindler in treating δύναμις and μέρος as synonyms in the Old Stoa (*Die stoische Lehre*).

know that Chrysippus thought of walking, and therefore of movement of any kind, as a state of the ἡγεμονικόν,[1] and if Panaetius thought of speech as a kind of movement, we can easily see why he could not regard it as a separate part of the soul. We know that Zeno himself thought of the actual sounds uttered as breath from the ἡγεμονικόν, that is, as states of the ἡγεμονικόν.[2] From this it is only a short step to the view of Panaetius that speaking, which is a kind of movement, is another example of the ἡγεμονικόν in action. Thus we can see why he argued that the soul has not eight, but only six, parts.[3]

Thus we have in the theory of Panaetius two parts of the human person, soul and 'nature'. How far is this a change? Van Straaten argues that the innovation of Panaetius was to subtract τὸ σπερματικόν from 'soul' and add it to 'nature'. That means that earlier Stoics would have been prepared to make the antithesis between soul and nature as strongly as Panaetius, but would have understood the composition of each part of the person differently. Van Straaten's evidence for this is that the Old Stoics were prepared to talk about 'soul' and 'nature' in man. But the significant difference between Panaetius and his predecessors is that, whereas Panaetius seems to contrast the two 'parts' of man, his predecessors assimilated them, and spoke of them working together. No member of the early school says that nature is different in man from soul. Rather, soul is transformed nature. The theory of the Old Stoa is strictly Aristotelian in the sense that the higher reality (soul) embraces within itself the activity of nature, just as for Aristotle the power of sensation in man is embraced by, and works with, his power

---

[1] Sen., *Ep.* 113.18 (*SVF* 1 525).

[2] Aët., *Plac.* 4.21.4 (*SVF* 1 150).

[3] Van Straaten (*Panétius* 267–8), cautiously following Schindler (*Die stoische Lehre* 32–9) and Verbeke (*L'Evolution* 95), introduces a further fragment from Nemesius (fr. 86a) into his discussion of the Panaetian soul. This fragment, however, has nothing to do with Panaetius, and only confuses the problem of the parts of the soul. See Pohlenz, *Gnomon* 21 (1949), 117. Grilli ('Studi Paneziani', 73) draws attention to the fact that Mnesarchus, the pupil of Panaetius, also eliminates the φωνητικόν and σπερματικόν as separate parts. His explanation of them, however, differs. For Mnesarchus they are elements of τὸ αἰσθητικόν (the five senses). Cf. *DG*, p. 615, 6–10.

of reason. As Galen puts it, representing, as van Straaten rightly argues, the position of the Old Stoa: Every animal is directed by nature and soul at the same time.[1] However, although van Straaten is wrong to hold that there is any good evidence that Stoics earlier than Panaetius emphasized a real distinction in man between soul and nature, he is right to argue that for Panaetius nature is not an irrational part of the soul. Rather, man is a basically divided being; he is a compound of soul and nature. That would have been far from satisfactory to Chrysippus.

What does Panaetius think of the soul itself? That also is divided in some way into two. As Cicero puts it, 'The natural power of souls is double: one part is situated in impulse (*appetitus*), which the Greeks call ὁρμή..., the other in reason.'[2] And again: 'There are two motions of souls, one of reason, the other of impulse. Reason is primarily concerned with investigating what is true, impulse urges to action.'[3] This looks very like Aristotle's rough division of the soul in the *Nicomachean Ethics*[4] into a rational and an irrational part; and, as we shall see, Panaetius follows Aristotle in talking about a separate virtue for each part. According to van Straaten these passages of Cicero could have been written by someone who subscribed to the Old Stoic theory of the passions.[5] Chrysippus could have written, as Cicero did (fr. 88), that we must take care to render impulse obedient to reason. It is true, of course, that the Old Stoics talk about the passions (πάθη) as impulses that are disobedient to reason,[6] but their view is not that impulses must be

---

[1] Galen, *Adv. Iul.* 5, vol. 18 A, p. 266 K. (*SVF* II 718); van Straaten, *Panétius* 110.

[2] Cic., *De Off.* 1.101 (fr. 87). I read *natura* for the *naturae* of Atzert (and van Straaten) with older editors. The passage is usually paralleled in the commentators by *Tusc. Disp.* 2.47: *est enim animus in partis tributus duas, quarum altera rationis est particeps, altera expers.* The Tusculans are not good evidence for Panaetius (despite e.g. Pohlenz, 'Das zweite Buch'). This particular passage may indeed be Panaetian, but its source is sufficiently obscure to prevent us from using it to determine what Panaetius' views are. In fact there is no need of it; Panaetius' position can be sufficiently elucidated without it.

[3] Cic., *De Off.* 1.132 (fr. 88).   [3] *N.E.* 1102 a 28.

[5] Van Straaten, *Panétius* 106.   [6] E.g. *SVF* II 377–8.

rendered obedient to reason, but that disobedient impulses must be eradicated and replaced by obedient. It is not for Chrysippus a matter of imposing reason on an unruly passion. Unruly passions, which are evil reasonings,[1] must be destroyed; good reasonings, with proper states of emotion, must replace them. In another passage of the De Officiis Cicero reports the view of Panaetius that the πάθη must be restrained (cohibere) and that the impulses (ὁρμαί) must be made obedient to reason.[2] But for Chrysippus a ὁρμή is either already obedient to reason, as a proper state of the ἡγεμονικόν, or it is not, in which case it must be eliminated. It is true that Cicero (representing Panaetius) speaks of being free of all 'passions' (vacandum autem omni est animi perturbatione:[3] ab omni animi perturbatione liber sis[4]), but the contexts make it clear that the soul is to be rid and free of 'passions' by restraining them. As we read in section 67, we must not give way to passion or fortune (neque perturbationi animi nec fortunae succumbere). Just as we cannot eliminate fortune, although we can master it, so, we may reasonably argue, we do not eliminate the disobedient impulses, but master them. In that sense we are free from them. In an ethical context it is easy to see how Chrysippus and Panaetius appear to be talking the same language; but they are nevertheless assuming different psychological theses.[5]

We shall return to this problem when discussing the ethical doctrines of Panaetius; we can safely conclude here that, in analysing the human person, Panaetius recognized three distinct aspects: nature, the impulsive or motivating power, and reason. The division between the first of these and the other two is apparently sharper than that between impulse and reason. After all, the latter are in some sense subdivisions of the soul. In what sense this is the case is not entirely clear. Cicero talks of a 'double power', a 'double nature', a 'double movement',

---

[1] λόγος πονηρός, Plut., De Virt. Mor. 441 c (SVF ii. 459).
[2] Cic., De Off. 2.18 (fr. 89).   [2] De Off. 1.69.
[4] De Off. 1.67.
[5] Contrary to most scholars van Straaten holds—wrongly in our opinion—that the views of Panaetius on πάθη are contradictory and not always in opposition to those of the Old Stoa. See van Straaten, Panétius 105–16, 181–5.

and again of 'parts'.[1] Pohlenz is probably right to contrast Cicero's *Duplex vis animorum* with a passage of Alexander of Aphrodisias in which, according to the Stoics, the soul (more strictly the ἡγεμονικόν) is said to have only one δύναμις and to be the same thing in different states, when thinking, being angry and desiring.[2] Whatever the precise answer to the question whether Cicero was right to attribute to Panaetius a doctrine of *parts* of the soul (and not merely 'powers' or 'motions'), there can be no doubt that Panaetius' tendency to divide the unity of soul further is pronounced. We may, therefore, speak of Panaetius' doctrine of a triple division of the person: reason, impulse, nature. By the last are understood, as we say, the powers of reproduction, nourishment and growth.

Two further points on Panaetius' psychology remain. The first is straightforward. In contradiction to the orthodox Stoic view Panaetius held that the soul does not survive the death of the body.[3] His reasons for this are perhaps not entirely clear, though two of them are mentioned by Cicero.[4] All things born must die; the soul is born, since it receives not only physical but mental characteristics from its parents; therefore the soul must die. And again: all things that grieve grieve because they are sick; all that is sick will die; the soul grieves, therefore the soul will die. The reasoning is probably that of Carneades, whose arguments would be particularly strong against those who held that the soul is material.[5] Schmekel, however, has made a further suggestion which may represent Panaetius' opinion.[6] Since for Panaetius the world is no longer to be consumed by fire, the limit which the Old Stoics fixed for the survival of some or all material souls is removed. Panaetius would have to teach either that the soul perishes with the body, or that it perishes at some other time—a time which could in no way be forecast—or that it is immortal. The last he would rule out as impossible for a particular material object. He may have preferred to say that the soul perishes with the body, rather than at some indeter-

---

[1] Frs. 87, 88.
[2] Pohlenz, *Gnomon* 21 (1949), 117; Alex. Aphr., *De An. Mant.* p. 118, 6 Bruns (*SVF* II 823).
[3] Frs. 83, 84.   [4] Cic., *Tusc. Disp.* 1.79 (fr. 83).
[5] Cic., *De Nat. Deorum* 3.32.   [6] Schmekel, *op. cit.* 308.

minate time after the body, because of a genuinely Stoic insight that the two elements of the person ought to be inseparable; but that is speculation.

The last point we must examine is the problem of the material substance of the soul itself. From a passage in Cicero it is clear that, although the older Stoics thought of the soul as unitary and composed of fire, Panaetius held that it consists of a blend of fire and air.[1] His contemporary Boethus was of the same opinion;[2] they were probably influenced by Carneades' critique of the older opinion.[3] The change could be highly significant. As a scrutiny of the relevant passages from the Old Stoa makes clear, the original view was that the soul is not composed of the element fire, but of the creative fire which is prior to the four elements.[4] Panaetius presumably rejected this. Since for him soul is dual, at least one and possibly both elements are not the basic creative matter of the universe. It is tempting to continue further and, by adding that there is no evidence that Panaetius believed in the existence of a material πῦρ τεχνικόν apart from elemental fire, to suggest that he had rejected this altogether. Our evidence, however, will not allow that, and it is probably a wrong approach. It is possible that in Panaetius' view the soul is a composite of πῦρ τεχνικόν and air. It must be admitted, however, that this solution is unsatisfying; that is underlined by the fact that Boethus, who, like Panaetius, held that the soul is a composite,[5] and that it perishes at death,[6] also denied the Old Stoic doctrine that the world is a living organism.[7] Instead he isolated god in the aether, the sphere of the fixed stars.[8] It would seem to follow that for Boethus the human soul cannot be composed of divine material, that is, that, since it has fire in it, that fire must be elemental fire; it is not therefore the

---

[1] For the Old Stoa, *SVF* II 773-5 etc.; for Panaetius, Cic., *Tusc. Disp.* 1.42 (fr. 82).

[2] *SVF* III 10 Boethus.

[3] Cic., *De Nat. Deorum* 3.36. The view of, for example, van Straaten (*Panétius* 103-4) that *SVF* II 786-7 (where soul is a composite of fire and air) should not be regarded as Old Stoic is certainly correct, as will appear from the following discussion. Contrary Verbeke, *L'Evolution* 93.

[4] This is especially clear from D.L. 7.156 (*SVF* II 774).

[5] *SVF* III 10 Boethus.   [6] *SVF* III 11 Boethus.

[7] *SVF* III 6 Boethus.   [8] *SVF* III 2-3 Boethus.

divine and etherial πῦρ τεχνικόν. But to the question whether Panaetius also made the soul a composite of material fire and air we can answer no more than that it is likely.

It is, however, at least clear that for Panaetius the soul is a composite of some kind of fire and air. Whether the fire is the rational component and the air the irrational, as is usually believed, cannot be proved, but must at least be held to be highly likely. If the fire is πῦρ τεχνικόν, then the chances that Panaetius recognized it as the rational component are obviously increased; but even if it is ordinary fire, it seems likely that this element would have a greater resemblance to πῦρ τεχνικόν than any of the others. It is possible, however, that Panaetius did not talk about the relationship between the physical composition of the soul and its psychological operations.

In studies of ancient philosophy psychology always enables a transition to be made from physics to ethics, and when we come to Panaetius' ethical theories we are much better informed. Though the De Officiis cannot be taken as if it were straight from Panaetius' own lips, there is no doubt that much of it can be used confidently. And we shall see as we proceed that passages in it which are not specifically tied to Panaetius harmonize well with evidence from other authors who mention him by name. This becomes particularly clear when we consider the problem of the end of life or τέλος. According to Chrysippus happiness is achieved by living according to nature; according to Panaetius we must live in accordance with the means of achievement, the starting-points, given to us by nature (3ῆν κατὰ τὰς δεδομένας ἡμῖν ἐκ φύσεως ἀφορμάς).[1] Whereas Chrysippus had in mind a life in which we harmonize the reason-principle in ourselves with the Reason that governs the whole of the universe, so that a life which is consistent (as Zeno put it) will be consistent with itself, because it is consistent with Reason as such, Panaetius meant something very different. Although it would be wrong to think that Chrysippus underestimated the differences of individual human character—he held that living in agreement with nature implies living after the pattern both of human nature and of our nature as indi-

---

[1] Clem. Alex., *Strom.* 2.21.129 (fr. 96).

vidual men[1]—he supposed that somehow this human and individual life would be and must be in harmony with a wider life
that is cosmic. Panaetius, however, seems to have abandoned
the attempt to reconcile the human and cosmic orders, or at
least to have thought that the cosmic order is too remote to
require emphasis. His version of the τέλος formula, as quoted
by Clement, seems to emphasize that we should live in accordance with what is given *to us*. How the formula is to be understood is made clear by a number of passages in the *De Officiis*
and in Stobaeus. We must not strive against 'universal nature'
and at the same time we must follow our individual nature
(*propriam naturam*).[2] There is a slight problem with the phrase
'universal nature'. Van Straaten takes it to mean 'la φύσις
générale et cosmique',[3] but the context of the *De Officiis* rules
this out. It is clear that the 'universal nature' of chapter 110
is the *communis persona* of chapter 107, which is shared by all
men, and which marks them off from beasts. Similarly the *propria natura* will be the *persona* which is distributed severally to
each individual man (*quae proprie singulis est tributa*). Thus we
see that the ἀφορμαί, the starting-points and means of virtue
which are given to us, are our specifically human and individual characteristics. Hence Stobaeus can quote Panaetius as
saying that each individual virtue attains the goal of a life consistent with nature in a different way.[4]

We should pause a moment on the *propria natura*, the *persona*
or set of features which is individual to each man. This is not
the human personality. Panaetius seems to think of human
beings as presenting two natural 'faces', one the face of humanity
and the second the face of individuality, *before* (metaphysically)
they have been affected by the circumstances of life, the passing
of time and the taking of moral decisions.[5] There is a kind of
natural self which provides the ἀφορμαί on which life is built.
A much closer approximation to a modern concept of personality, or at least of character, is provided by a combination

[1] D.L. 7.89 (*SVF* III 4). [2] Cic., *De Off.* 1.110 (fr. 97).
[3] Van Straaten, *Panétius* 140. [4] Stob., *Ecl.* 2, p. 64 W. (fr. 109).
[5] Cic., *De Off.* 1.115. For the influence of climate on character see frs. 74 and
76; for the need of helpers if anything is to be achieved, fr. 117.

of the two further *personae* which are superimposed on our natural, but presumably hypothetical, selves. Circumstances and the passage of time affect us, thus helping to produce a real as opposed to a hypothetical character (this is the third *persona*); above all we can make ourselves into the *persona* we wish by our own decisions (this is the fourth *persona*). The decisions we take, however, will, if we are wise, be relevant to the kind of people we naturally are. There is no point in pursuing what we cannot acquire. The implication, not so much in logic as in practice, for the Old Stoic theory that our goal is the life of the sage should not be missed. The effect of this doctrine must have been, and was probably intended to be, a banishing of the sage still further into the realm of the hypothetical; for who would think seriously that it was in his own power to achieve, not merely to try to achieve, so much? As Panaetius put it to the youth who asked him whether the wise man would love, *de sapiente videbimus*, but as for you and me, we must not commit ourselves to such a thing.[1]

If we ask ourselves what the ἀφορμαί are, we must bear in mind that they vary in strength in individual cases; but as human beings all of us will possess a number of drives. First is the drive to self-preservation, which eventually leads men out beyond themselves to seek the good of their families and ultimately the good of society at large and the maintenance of justice; then there is the desire for truth, and associated with the desire for truth is a social urge, for no well-trained man would wish to obey those who neither instruct nor teach nor give just and legitimate orders for good reasons; hence the third ἀφορμή is a sense of independence, an urge to what we shall call manliness (*magnitudo animi, humanarumque rerum contemptio*); finally there is a sense of order, fitness and beauty in speech and action.[2] Grilli has suggested that the use of the term ἀφορμή for these drives is a novelty introduced by Panaetius;[3] accordingly he tries to explain various passages in von Arnim's collection where the word occurs in this sense, which is of course not its usual

---

[1] Sen., *Ep.* 116.5 (fr. 114).
[2] Cic., *De Off.* 1.13–19 (frs. 98, 103, 104).
[3] Grilli, 'Studi Paneziani', 33; cf. *Il Problema* 116 note 1.

sense in the Old Stoa, as improperly attributed to the early period. The point is not important, and Grilli's case, though possible, is not very convincing. It may, however, be observed that Panaetius' apparent emphasis on these drives could help to explain the undoubted fact that later Stoics, who take over Panaetius' terminology about ἀφορμαί,[1] subscribe to the originally un-Stoic concept of innate ideas. Whether Panaetius introduced that concept is beyond our knowledge; but there is no evidence that he did. Finally we should observe that the theory of Grilli that the ἀφορμαί are essentially rational, in contrast to the ὁρμαί which, as we have seen, are irrational, is somewhat misleading.[2] There is no need to regard the ἀφορμαί as essentially rational or irrational. They are rather to be thought of as instincts, though they are admittedly directed by nature to rational ends, and thus potentially rational. They will only become rational when they are recognized for what they are by reason and 'rationalized'. The ἀφορμαί point towards the way a man 'works' naturally, with both his reason and his impulses performing their primary functions. A man living a life of ἀφορμαί alone would be a purely hypothetical being, displaying only his human and individual *personae*, unaffected by events, the passage of time and, above all, moral decisions. Hence when Panaetius says that the end is living 'according to the ἀφορμαί given to us', he means that we should base our choices on our natural propensities. To live 'according to one's propensities' means to develop one's potentialities to the full.

It is clear that Panaetius' formulation of the end for man is this-worldly. It is our natural capacities which are to be developed, and Panaetius seems to have little interest in the relationship between the nature of man and Reason in the universe at large. That is why his views are frequently said to be humanist. It may be that the shift of emphasis which we are observing is also to be connected with his notorious proposition, mentioned by Diogenes Laertius, that virtue is not self-sufficient, but that in addition we need health, property and strength.[3] We have argued elsewhere that this statement is to be accepted as a true

---

[1] E.g. Epict., *Disc.* 4.1.51; cf. Grilli, 'Studi Paneziani', 45.
[2] Grilli, 'Studi Paneziani', 31–67.   [3] D.L. 7.128 (fr. 110).

account of Panaetius' position, and there is no need to repeat the arguments here.[1] Panaetius is clearly much more concerned than his predecessors in the Stoic school with the question of the natural achievement of virtue, and with the content of moral action, though, as we have suggested above, this was not as totally neglected in the Old Stoa as has sometimes been believed. It seems that, whereas the early Stoics held that the wise man makes use of such things as health, Panaetius said that he needs them; he emphasized that virtue cannot be achieved without them. There is an obvious weakness in Panaetius' position, however, which we cannot know whether he recognized. If health and strength and property, or even health or strength or property, are necessary for happiness, does this mean that the sick, the poor and the weak cannot be happy? If Panaetius meant that, Chrysippus would have condemned him—and he certainly may have meant that at least extremes of these stand in the way of happiness. It should be observed, however, that even if Panaetius did mean that, he could still hold, and did in fact hold, that virtue is the only good in the sense of the only moral good.[2] What he is saying is that moral goodness alone is insufficient to make a man happy. We should not, however, overestimate the scope of the change. Van Straaten is wrong to argue that for the achievement of happiness we need not only property, health and strength, but everything else that is natural. Van Straaten thinks that property, health and strength are meant to be classes under which all else that is natural can be subsumed. That is incorrect; beauty, for example, cannot be subsumed in this way.[3] What Panaetius does think, however, is that all natural things are useful. Nothing, he holds, that is useful is in conflict with moral goodness; but since by 'useful' he means 'really useful', his views do not seem to diverge from traditional Stoicism at this point.[4]

According to Panaetius moral goodness is not only the true good; it is also fitting (πρέπον, decorum).[5] The background to this

[1] See pp. 7–10.   [2] De Off. 3.12 (fr. 101).
[3] Van Straaten, Panétius 154–5. The objection is due to Professor Sandbach in an unpublished paper.
[4] Cic., De Off. 3.34–5 (fr. 102); cf. De Off. 3.12 (fr. 101).
[5] Cf. De Off. 1.93–101 (fr. 107).

idea seems to be Peripatetic, but that is not our concern here.[1] What Panaetius is trying to say is that moral action is not only good but that it is recognized as fitting and appropriate action by mankind—he presumably means men of good will. This fittingness has two aspects: Panaetius speaks of a *generale quid-dam decorum*, which is present in every moral action in so far as it is moral and in so far as it is a specifically *human* action; and again of an *aliud huic subiectum* which 'pertains to the individual parts' of moral action. The second kind of fittingness is treated somewhat obscurely by Cicero, but since he relates it to 'individual parts' of morality (*pertinet ad singulas partes honestatis*, 1.96) and to 'each individual kind of virtue' (1.97), and then proceeds to say that, just as the body's beauty makes its effects because of the appropriate arrangement of the limbs, so the consistency of words and deeds in a particular life (*in vita*) produces what is fitting, it must be that by his second kind of *decorum* Panaetius meant a well-ordered and harmonious arrangement of the various individual virtues within a single life. Bravery, for example, would not be allowed to clash with temperance in an inappropriate way.[2] The problem is an old one; it is mentioned by Plato in the *Statesman* (cf. 308 B). It remains only to point out that Cicero does not say that the second type of appropriateness belongs primarily to the virtue of moderation (σωφροσύνη, *verecundia*), and only secondarily to other virtues,[3] but that its action can be seen principally in the use of moderation. But the virtue of moderation itself must have an appropriate relationship to the other virtues; it is not simply the relationship between the other virtues.

Turning next to the question of the nature of the virtues themselves, we can be in no doubt that the attitude of Panaetius differs from that of the Old Stoa. The early Stoics defined the virtues as kinds of knowledge and insisted that virtue is therefore ultimately one. This does not mean, as has often been alleged, that their view was intellectualist. Chrysippus, as we have argued, does not believe in purely intellectual acts; all

[1] Cf. Philippson, 'Das Sittlichschöne', 357–413.
[2] Cf. van Straaten, *Panétius* 161–3; Labowsky, *Die Ethik* 112.
[3] As is the view of, for example, Pohlenz, *Ant. Führ.* 62, τὸ πρέπον 73–4.

intellectual acts are at the same time emotional, all emotions are intellectual acts. The Stoics probably emphasized the notion of knowledge in their definition of virtue because Socrates had done so; but Socratic knowledge is not purely intellectual either. For both Socrates and the early Stoics knowing implies trying to do. Hence when Posidonius defines the end of life as contemplating truth and order and trying to bring them about,[1] he may not be as far from the early Stoics as has sometimes been suggested, though it would be rash to think that the early Stoics would have accepted his definition. But whatever Posidonius' position may have been, Panaetius seems to have spoken of virtue as dual: virtue as knowing (θεωρητική), and virtue as doing (πρακτική).[2] This division (*pace* van Straaten) corresponds to Panaetius' division of the soul.

But virtue can also be seen, and was apparently so seen by Panaetius, as having four aspects, the θεωρητικὴ ἀρετή and three others of a more practical nature. These four 'virtues' correspond with the four basic ἀφορμαί or impulses of the human being: his desire for knowledge (the distinction between acquiring knowledge and contemplating it seems to be disregarded), his urge for the preservation of himself and the community, his feeling of independence and self-respect, his sense of moderation. Hence the four virtues are wisdom (φρόνησις), justice (concern for the *communitas*), manliness in the fullest sense, including courage and greatness of soul, and temperance.[3] We must consider each of these briefly, but before doing so it is important to notice their connection with the ἀφορμαί. Virtue is not considered by Panaetius in relation to the universal Reason, but in relation to the basic potentialities of man considered simply as man. The proper balance of emphasis in each individual's quest for excellence will, as we shall see, depend on his individual proclivities.

In the case of the first virtue, φρόνησις, we are already in a position to see the direction in which Panaetius has moved. Wisdom can be conceived as purely theoretical, and the pas-

---

[1] Clem. Alex., *Strom.* 2.21.129.

[2] D.L. 7.92 (fr. 108); cf. Cic., *De Off.* 1.16–17 (fr. 103).

[3] Frs. 98, 103, 104; cf. also widely in the *De Officiis*, especially 1.152.

sages at the end of book one of the *De Officiis* indicate some of
the problems which this causes, and which Cicero says on two
occasions were *not* treated by Panaetius.[1] Purely theoretical
learning and study is a virtue. But what, Cicero asks, is its value
in relation to the active life? Which life is superior? Panaetius,
we must repeat, did not ask this question. He may have thought
it misguided. At any rate, he apparently contented himself with
asserting, against the Old Stoa, that learning is virtuous for its
own sake. And the reason is obvious. If one has a natural impulse to learn, Panaetius will argue, it is right to develop it.
Panaetius himself took an interest in philological, geographical
and historical studies.[2] It should be noticed, however, that,
while Panaetius did not evaluate the respective merits of the
active and the contemplative life, Cicero did; and he pronounced the active superior, thus dogmatizing and perhaps inadvertently contradicting Panaetius' view. For, presumably, in
the opinion of Panaetius the active life would be superior only
for the man who has the gifts for it and lacks more academic
skills. The man who has both will be required to develop both.

When we turn from wisdom to justice, we find that Panaetius
has developed the Old Stoic concept of the urge to self-
preservation, leading to a sense of solidarity and support for one's
family and circle, into a drive for the well-being of humanity at
large. This is the sphere of justice, and there is no trace remaining of the older Cynic side of Stoicism, according to which the
wise man is the fellow citizen only of other wise men. It is true
that Panaetius wrote his work περὶ τοῦ καθήκοντος for aspirants
to wisdom,[3] but he seems to believe that not only the aspirant
but all men, including the wise, are fundamentally motivated
by an urge to solidarity with all of mankind. There are, of
course, precursors of this in older Stoicism, but the uncompromising commitment to it is new. Again Panaetius' thinking

---

[1] *De Off.* 1.152–61.
[2] Frs. 123–36. For the role of Panaetius in developing the ideal of the life of
scholarly leisure see Grilli, *Il Problema*. Grilli's idea that almost all later
instances of this theme 'derive' from Panaetius, an idea which entails misreading Antiochus of Ascalon and Posidonius, must be rejected. See the
review of Grilli by Festugière in *Paideia* 9 (1954), 180–7.
[3] *De Off.* 1.46.

should be related to his tendency to regard each man as a member of the human race rather than as one of the fragments of the divine Reason that permeates the cosmos as a whole. Panaetius' down-to-earthness makes him more human and more humane. As Cicero says: *tristitiam atque asperitatem fugiens Panaetius nec acerbitatem...probavit fuitque in altero genere mitior.*[1]

On the other hand, as has often been pointed out, Panaetius' outlook is aristocratic and paternalist. He associates the virtue of liberality or generosity very closely with justice.[2] It is good to despise riches if we are poor or to be liberal with them if we are rich.[3] But, although the first part of this disjunction maintains the traditional Stoic austerity, the latter emphasizes once again the connection of happiness with external goods. It is impossible not to think that the display of benevolence—which is just for the rich—has many of the characteristics of the Aristotelian μεγαλοψυχία. Happiness needs a certain χορηγία. Happiness is virtue, and justice is one of the virtues.

When we turn to the third Panaetian virtue, the virtue of manliness (ἀνδρεία), we are in an even more Aristotelian world.[4] For the Old Stoics ἀνδρεία is concerned primarily with knowing what should be endured and enduring it. For Panaetius this aspect of the virtue is maintained; the wise man will admire nothing but the morally good and will not give way contrary to the right to any man, to his own emotions, or to the blows of fortune. But there is also an Aristotelian and active side, as there is in the case of justice. The man of ἀνδρεία will not only despise what is irrelevant to the moral end (*rerum externarum despicientia*, 1.106; *humanarum rerum contemptio*, 1.13), he will also have the drive to perform great and useful deeds at great personal risk.[5] It is not the case, however, as some have suggested,[6] that this virtue as a whole would be better called

---

[1] Cic., *De Fin.* 4.79 (fr. 55). It is true that Panaetius seems to have thought that excessive study of 'obscure and unnecessary' matters (*De Off.* 1.19 = fr. 104) is a vice; that is an Old Stoic position. Panaetius' reasons for maintaining it were probably that excessive study would upset the balance of the personality. See below.

[2] *De Off.* 1.20 (fr. 105).   [3] *De Off.* 1.68.
[4] *De Off.* 1.66 (fr. 106).   [5] *De Off.* 1.66 (fr. 106); cf. 1.17 (fr. 103).
[6] Ibscher, *op. cit.* 75.

'greatness of soul', or that it was so called by Panaetius. Perhaps the nearest our evidence comes to that is at *De Officiis* 1.20, where Cicero speaks of *fortis animus et magnus*. The word ἀνδρεία can in fact carry the sense that Panaetius required; it means not merely bravery but manliness. Does not Marcus Aurelius appeal to this when he so often challenges himself to be a man?

The final virtue, σωφροσύνη, need not detain us long.[1] We have already considered its relationship to the concept of *decorum*; and it only remains to be repeated that it is not to be identified with *decorum*. Cicero clearly states that *decorum* (τὸ πρέπον) is a part of this larger virtue; the general features of the virtue are temperance, modesty and a calmness of the emotions. As Cicero remarks, it is the part of justice that men be not injured; it is the part of respect (*verecundia*) that they be not offended. In this virtue the efficacy of what is appropriate is most obvious. We need only say that this is certainly not the old Stoic view of σωφροσύνη, which is defined, rather oddly, as a knowledge of what should be chosen and what not.[2]

Such, then, are the cardinal virtues according to Panaetius. Three of them are practical virtues while one is speculative and academic. They are, as we have seen, virtues of two different parts of the human soul. We have also seen that it is Panaetius' moral ideal that one of these powers, the reason, should keep the other under control. This last fact perhaps helps us to understand an otherwise rather puzzling passage of Aulus Gellius,[3] in which Panaetius is said to have rejected ἀναλγησία and ἀπάθεια. This is probably to be interpreted as meaning that Panaetius rejected even the word ἀπάθεια. We have already seen that the early Stoics understood ἀπάθεια to mean a suppression of irrational emotions.[4] Ἀπάθεια means not absence of emotion but absence of bad and irrational emotions; in other words for the Old Stoa ἀπάθεια means εὐπάθεια. But the terminology is confusing and Panaetius apparently did away with the term ἀπάθεια altogether. He would have been encouraged to take this step by the fact that for him virtue consists not in the suppression of irrational emotions but in the restraining of

[1] Fr. 107. [2] *SVF* III 262, 266.
[3] Gellius, 12.5 (fr. 111). [4] See pp. 25–7.

a non-rational part of the soul. The word ἀπάθεια may have suggested too much the concept of suppression rather than restraint. Better and clearer to be rid of it altogether. In any case it had undesirable Cynic overtones.

Associated with doctrines of πάθη in traditional Stoicism are doctrines of pleasure. There is little new in Panaetius' views on this subject. Corporeal pleasures are rejected.[1] There are two kinds of pleasure, those that are natural and those that are unnatural. Panaetius is prepared to use the word ἡδονή for natural pleasures. Probably the Old Stoics would have preferred χαρά, but not always. Archedemus, for one, postulated natural pleasures and called them ἡδοναί.[2]

Strictly speaking, we should consider Panaetius' political views within the framework of his ethics, but, since they have caused so much disagreement, it will be convenient to summarize certain of his ethical principles before moving on to politics. We have seen that Panaetius rejected the word ἀπάθεια as a description of the goal for man. It is highly likely that the word he substituted for it was εὐθυμία—we know he wrote a treatise περὶ εὐθυμίας[3]—and that by this he meant a proper harmony in the natural development of each man, a proper relationship between each of his impulses (ἀφορμαί). The term εὐθυμία, in its Latin version tranquillitas animi, occurs twice in the De Officiis,[4] and van Straaten's suggestion that it is only an effect of ἀνδρεία has not much force. It seems very probable that in both passages Cicero (or Panaetius) has veered from the 'great-souled' aspect of ἀνδρεία to speak of the disposition of the good man in general; and it is noteworthy that in 1.69 tranquillitas animi is closely connected with constantia. Constantia, we recall, is the Stoic εὐπάθεια, the proper state of the emotions.[5]

---

[1] De Off. 1.65.   [2] Sext. Emp., Adv. Math. 11.73. See p. 48 above.
[3] D.L. 9.20 (fr. 45).   [4] De Off. 1.69, 72.
[5] It has often been held that more information about Panaetian εὐθυμία can be recovered from Plutarch's treatise of the same name. Cf. especially Siefert, Plutarchs Schrift περὶ εὐθυμίας, and Broecker, Animadversiones. As a result of these enquiries the influence of Democritus on Panaetius has been argued, and this is probably right. However, there is no good evidence that Panaetius was the sole source for Plutarch. And lack of such evidence is still fatal to using the treatise for detailed reconstructions of Panaetius' views.

The aim of Panaetian man is to attain a properly harmonious relationship between the instincts and powers of the individual. In this aim we can detect no trace of the Old Stoic distinction between the wise man and the fool. Panaetius, who addressed his work περὶ τοῦ καθήκοντος to aspirants to virtue,[1] and who concerned himself in ethics with the ordinary man,[2] is clearly prepared to allow those who are not sages to possess virtue. For virtue is measured in Panaetius' eyes as much by what a man does as by his motives in doing it. We recall that the word καθῆκον, in orthodox Stoicism, denotes an action. It tells us nothing about motive. If the action is done by a wise man, it is moral (κατόρθωμα); if not, it is a sin (ἁμάρτημα). But since the act itself may be the same act in the two cases, the Stoics indicated the difference in the morality of those who perform them by calling the wise man's act a τέλειον καθῆκον, the fool's a μέσον καθῆκον.[3] Of all this we have no trace in Panaetius. If scholars are right, as seems to be the case, that *De Officiis* 1.8 does not stem from Panaetius, we find no reference to the doctrine of κατορθώματα in the Panaetian work περὶ τοῦ καθήκοντος as we know it.[4]

Indeed a concentration on what we do rather than why we do it would seem to spring naturally from Panaetius' account of the end for man. We must develop our capabilities, and that means all our capabilities, to become well-rounded men. Our success will be apparent in what we do (our *iustitia* and μεγαλοψυχία); our actions will be visibly *decorum*. This does not mean that Panaetius has abolished the sage; he probably only agrees with Chrysippus that he is as rare as a phoenix. But the sage has become irrelevant for Panaetius. While the only good is still the moral good, trying to reach it is the mark of the good man; not, as Chrysippus would have it, complete purity of motive. Panaetius tends to test our trying pragmatically. What has been achieved?, he asks. What have you done with your

---

[1] *De Off.* 1.46.   [2] Sen., *Ep.* 116.5 (fr. 114).

[3] See pp. 97–9 above.

[4] Schmekel, *op. cit.* 24; Ibscher, *op. cit.* 114; van Straaten, *Panétius* 197. That the actual achievement of results had already been emphasized by Antipater of Tarsus as the σκοπός of moral action, though not its τέλος, is discussed by Long, 'Carneades...', 78–83.

talents? It may be that in some sense this is *more* 'Stoic' than Chrysippus; Panaetius recognizes intention as the test of moral goodness and forgets about a purity of motive which is only a dream and hardly existent in the world. At its best Panaetius' ethic can be seen as an inspiring humanism which urges man to fulfil himself and to develop his skills to the utmost; at its worst, however, it may be read as little more than the trite imperative 'Do your best', with the implication 'I know that best is not much of an achievement'. At least this much can be said of Panaetius, that he is not an idealist; no one is asked to do more than develop his ἀφορμαί. But, says the objector, Chrysippus could be imagined as agreeing. After all, he wants us to live in accordance with nature, and we ourselves are rational beings in a rational universe. But the introduction of the rational universe makes all the difference. Compared with Panaetius, the admirer of Plato, Chrysippus is in this respect far more of a Platonist.

Panaetius had something to say about what we should call political questions in his work *On Duty*; he also wrote a treatise on politics (περὶ πολιτείας). This treatise apparently differed from works of the same title written by early members of the Stoa in that it dealt not only with theoretical questions about the ideal kind of public life, but went into details on such matters as the number of magistrates and their various functions.[1] But Panaetius did not entirely give up the attitudes of the early Stoa; like his predecessors he had no time for elaborate public buildings—an attitude which embarrassed Cicero.[2]

Yet in many other areas Panaetius clearly advanced from Cynic positions. He was not only concerned with the πολιτεία

---

[1] Cic., *De Leg.* 3.13–14 (fr. 61); cf. *De Off.* 1.124 (fr. 121). I take *ad hunc usum popularem atque civilem* (fr. 61) in its context to refer to the details of a constitution, such as Plato gives in the *Laws*. Van Straaten (*Panétius* 58) thinks that the contrast between *verbo tenus* and *ad hunc usum popularem atque civilem* is a contrast between 'théoriquement scientifique' and 'pratiquement populaire'. 'Populaire' does not seem to be justified by the Latin *popularis*. Grilli (*Il Problema* 91 note 2 and 'Studi Paneziani', 67) wants to translate *ad hunc usum* etc. as 'secondo la tradizione praticamente politica' (propria dei Romani). But this translation is not justified by the context of the passage, though plausible on other grounds.

[2] *De Off.* 2.60 (fr. 122). For the views of Zeno and Chrysippus see p. 68.

of the wise or with citizenship of the world in the negative Cynic sense of citizenship in no particular city. He seems to have regarded individual states as justified by some kind of extension of the principle of οἰκείωσις.[1] Cities arise through our desires and hopes, which are justified, of keeping possession of our own property. Each man looks after his own, and the state is the product of this concern. As to which kind of state is to be preferred, Panaetius is to be numbered among those who supported the Roman constitution as ideal, because it contained both monarchical and popular elements;[2] but he is not an innovator in adopting such a position.

The early Stoics did not reject politics as an activity of the wise man, but on the other hand they did not emphasize it.[3] Panaetius certainly increased the emphasis, but political life did not become all-important. For Panaetius the impulses which drive men to politics are the impulses to the maintenance of justice in society and to manliness. Manliness, we recall, involves the doing of noble deeds and an unwillingness to obey illegal commands. The man of ἀνδρεία will have a certain impulse to what Cicero calls *principatus*—a most difficult word to translate. Certainly independence is part of its meaning; the ἀνδρεῖος is a free agent who will choose to obey the right. But *principatus* cannot be wholly separated from the sense of superiority. The ἀνδρεῖος is in fact the natural ruler; as Cicero says, there are many people he will not be willing to obey. There is probably a Platonic strain here. In the *Republic* the good man rules for fear of an inferior doing so in his stead.

It is clear that the virtue of manliness, thus understood, is not far from the virtue of justice, which, as we saw, is for Panaetius an extension of the natural desire of all men to look after their

---

[1] *De Off.* 2.73 (fr. 118), 2.41–2 (fr. 120). It is true that in fr. 118 general associations of men (*duce natura*) are contrasted with the formation of individual states (*spe custodiae rerum suarum*), but this does not mean (*pace* van Straaten, *Panétius* 209) that separate states are not natural. They arise as nature's answer to the fact that men are not wholly governed by reasons and hence despoil one another unless concrete political structures are formed.

[2] *De Rep.* 1.34 (fr. 119); cf. *SVF* III 700.

[3] Cf. *SVF* III 611. This does not mean that the wise man will enter politic, only in ideal or near-ideal societies.

own. Their own now includes the whole human race, and just as the parent looks after his children in a paternal way, so there will be something of the paternal attitude in the just man's looking after the community of mankind and dispensing his liberality to all. In view of this it is easy to see how Pohlenz was tempted to say that for Panaetius the ideal is not 'unpolitische Humanität' but 'Führertum'.[1] Pohlenz' theories about the general nature of Panaetius' thought, that it marks a 'hellenizing' of the Stoa,[2] and that Panaetius himself had 'den klaren nüchternen Sinn des Doriers'[3] can be left for analysis by experts on racialism, but his view that Panaetius' ideal is one of leadership is sufficiently well founded to demand examination. In fact Pohlenz has been misled. We must never forget that the political side of man's character is only a part. At most it involves two of the ἀφορμαί which lead to practical virtue. But Panaetius does not hold that practical virtue is superior to θεωρία; as we have seen, it is Cicero who holds that view. And Cicero specifically states that Panaetius did not discuss whether the 'theoretical' or the practical life is the higher form. If our interpretation is correct, Panaetius' view would be that the ideal for each man is that he should develop *all* his capacities. Some men will have stronger practical capabilities than others, and in a sense leadership is the ideal for them. But their ideal is not superior in general to what is ideal for the more theoretical minds; it is only superior for them. The general ideal of Panaetius is that all one's capacities should be developed to the full, and that at the same time the greatest possible internal harmony should be maintained.[4]

[1] Pohlenz, *Ant. Führ.* 140–3.
[2] Pohlenz, *Ant. Führ.* 142; cf. *RE* 18³, col. 426, 'seinem hellenischen Herzen'.
[3] Pohlenz, *Ant. Führ.* 138.
[4] Since Pohlenz' thesis about the ideal of *Führertum* must be discarded, it becomes irrelevant to consider what kind of Führer is to be preferred. Pohlenz, of course, has his views on this: 'Sein [*scil.* Panaetius'] Führer ist kein jugendlicher Stürmer, kein Revolutionär, der einen Wunschstaat gründen oder sein Volk von innen heraus erneuern will...er spricht aus und zu einem Kreise, der aus Überzeugung konservative Politik treibt...' Not the S.A. but the Conservatives are to be the guiding spirits of the new Reich.

11

THE IMPRINT OF POSIDONIUS

For nearly a hundred years Posidonius has baffled students of Stoicism. While it is agreed on virtually all hands that his thought differs in many essentials from that of the Old Stoa, there has been little agreement on what these essentials are. While it is generally recognized that his psychological theories are to be contrasted with those of Chrysippus, and differ from those of his unorthodox teacher Panaetius, the extent of Posidonius' heresy even in this area is disputed. And about other branches of his thought the confusion is almost total. The problems arise in part, though by no means entirely, from disagreement about our evidence for Posidonius, but even when dealing with passages of ancient authors attributed to Posidonius by name, scholars are still in very large measure unable to reach a consensus. There is as yet no adequate collection of fragments attributed to Posidonius by name,[1] though the existence of such a collection is a first essential for the study of his work. Nevertheless, after the fantasy pictures of this philosopher drawn by such writers as Jaeger[2] and Reinhardt,[3] there now exist studies by Edelstein of Posidonius as a philosopher,[4] and by Nock of Posidonius primarily as a man of science;[5] and recently Mlle Laffranque has produced at great length a portrait of all sides of Posidonius' activity, which marks a major advance in our understanding.[6] Mlle Laffranque has in general approached the problem of Posidonius through texts in which Posidonius is mentioned by name, and the sane estimate she draws of the man

[1] The collection made by J. Bake (Lugduni Batavorum, 1830) is out of date. I. G. Kidd is preparing a collection (compiled by Edelstein) for publication in the near future.
[2] Jaeger, *Nemesios von Emesa.*
[3] Reinhardt, *Poseidonios, Kosmos und Sympathie,* 'Poseidonios'.
[4] Edelstein, 'The Philosophical System of Posidonius'.
[5] Nock, 'Posidonius'.
[6] Laffranque, *Poseidonios d'Apamée.* On pp. 1–44 Laffranque gives an admirable and well-documented account of the history of Posidonian studies.

and his work bears marks of truth where truth seemed to be impossible to attain. Nevertheless, even after Mlle Laffranque's work, one is still left with what seems to be the basic question about Posidonius largely unsolved: Do his philosophical divergencies from orthodox Stoicism stem from a philosophically coherent view of the world, or are they *ad hoc* resolutions of particular problems left behind by Chrysippus, which Posidonius tried to solve in isolation from one another? In other words is there a particular brand of Stoicism, in the form of a largely coherent and interrelated body of doctrine, which can be described as Posidonian?

At first sight it might appear that Posidonius' philosophical role in the Stoic school was to put the clock back, to reject some of the untraditional teachings of his master Panaetius. Certainly this is the case in some areas. Posidonius restored divination and astrology to their traditional places in Stoic physics, and, though his account of world-periods and destructions may have been unorthodox, he almost certainly did not follow Panaetius in rejecting them altogether.[1] But a very puzzling doctrine which Posidonius undoubtedly professed must be considered as indicative of a most unorthodox view of the physical world. According to Posidonius, God, nature and fate are not identical; on the contrary they form a sequence of realities in terms of which the physical world must be understood. Fate, says Posidonius, is third from Zeus.[2] The orthodox view makes all three identical,[3] though Cleanthes had kept fate distinct,[4] but Posidonius seems to have been prepared to think of them as different in some physical and corporeal way, so that he can derive divination from each of them differently.[5] From our point of view it is the distinction between God and nature which is primarily rele-

---

[1] One reading of Philo, *De Aet. Mundi* 76, makes Posidonius reject the destruction of the world by fire, thus apparently contradicting our other evidence (*DG* p. 338a 18, b19; D.L. 7.142). Perhaps the best explanation of this—if in the text of Philo we are to read Βόηθος καὶ Ποσειδώνιος rather than Βόηθος ὁ Σιδώνιος—is that Posidonius' explanation of the nature of ἐκπύρωσις is unorthodox, as, in the doxographical tradition, was his concept of empty space. According to Posidonius empty space is not ἄπειρον but 'adequate for a dissolution'.

[2] *DG* 324a 4, b11, 620.20.

[3] D.L. 7.135 (*SVF* II 580).

[4] Chal., *In Tim.* 144 (*SVF* II 933).

[5] Cic., *De Div.* 1.125.

vant; and this distinction had not even been made by Cleanthes; it is a novelty of Posidonius. Its significance must be determined.

The distinction made by Posidonius between God and nature has been emphasized by Edelstein,[1] but the construction put upon it does not stand up. Nevertheless, Edelstein's thesis about Stoic physics, though unacceptable as it stands, is an essential stage in the further elucidation of the problem. According to Edelstein, Posidonius, like all his Stoic predecessors, posited two basic principles, an active and a passive. The active principle, sometimes called God, is an intelligent πνεῦμα which extends throughout the cosmos;[2] the passive is the substance and matter of all things. It is qualityless and without shape (ἄμορφον) in itself, but although *per se* devoid of form (σχῆμα) or particular quality, it always exists in a specific form and quality. But, continues Posidonius, the existing substance differs from matter only in our thought.[3] Edelstein interprets all this to mean that Posidonius completely separated the active and passive elements, and added that the passive element only exists in the form of the four elements, that is, as qualified substances. For Edelstein's Posidonius 'the elements exist always as the material principle'.[4] In Edelstein's interpretation Posidonius is made to hold that qualified matter is distinguishable from the unqualified in thought alone, and that the active principle is separate from both of them; but this is certainly a misreading of the evidence.

There is no reason to believe that Posidonius wished to separate the active and the passive in such a radical fashion. All matter is shaped and formed, and the active principle is the shaper. Hence, wherever there is matter, the active principle will be present. Active and passive principles are, as in orthodox Stoicism, means of looking at the basic material substance, which, for the orthodox, exists in varying degrees of tension (τόνος). Posidonius seems to be quite orthodox in holding that there is a single basic substance (πῦρ τεχνικόν), which can be

[1] Edelstein, *op. cit.* 292–3.
[2] *Commenta Lucani*, p. 305 Usener; *DG* 302 b22.
[3] *DG* 458, 8–11; cf. D.L. 7.134 for the general Stoic position.
[4] Edelstein, *op. cit.* 291.

viewed as active or passive. All existent things exhibit this single substance in various conditions. Qualityless matter, the so-called passive element, is only a mental construct; what exists is matter qualified, that is, matter exhibiting the features of the so-called active *and* passive elements. What exists is simply the cosmos, which is material; but it is in fact matter qualified in such a way as to be a cosmos.

But although the active and passive 'principles' of the universe cannot be dissociated in the Posidonian world in the way proposed by Edelstein, and Edelstein is wrong to hold it a novelty of Posidonius that uninformed matter can only be distinguished conceptually—this seems to have been the doctrine from the beginning—yet we still have the dichotomy between God and nature with which we began, and there is in fact a difference in the way Posidonius relates the active and passive aspects of the cosmos from that in which they are related in the systems of earlier members of the school.

We have already noticed that Posidonius speaks of the 'material principle' as devoid of shape. Elsewhere he says that the active principle or God has no shape 'but changes into whatever it wishes and becomes likened to everything'.[1] The function of God, therefore, is not to have shape but to give shape (μορφή) and form (σχῆμα). This affords at least part of the explanation of why Posidonius thought that the circumference of the cosmos, the ἐσχάτη περιφέρεια, is the most divine, and why he located the ἡγεμονικόν of the cosmos there, agreeing on this point with Chrysippus and rejecting the view of Cleanthes, which gave the predominance to the sun.[2] Posidonius in fact thinks of the active element or God as working in the world in two ways; on the one hand it binds matter together like glue, permeating each part of the universe[3]—we shall return to this later—while on the other it has its principal seat around the borders of the cosmos.

At this stage we can make progress by considering Posi-

---

[1] *DG* 302 b22.

[2] D.L. 7.138–9. For a rejection of the 'solar theology' of Posidonius see Jones, 'Posidonius and Solar Eschatology'. Reinhardt's reply ('Poseidonios', col. 691 ff.) is unconvincing.

[3] Achilles Tatius, *Comm. on Aratus*, p. 41.

donius' view of the limits of physical bodies, a subject on which there is fairly good evidence. According to Diogenes Laertius, Posidonius differed from the Stoic school in that he held that geometrical surfaces exist both in our thoughts and in reality.[1] This would imply dissent from the orthodox Stoic view of the infinite divisibility of matter. Thus the external surface of the cosmos will not be merely a conceptual reality, the end of the material of which the cosmos is composed. Rather it will be a physical reality, as it must be if it is to possess the distinction of being especially divine with which Posidonius credits it. It seems, therefore, that one way in which Posidonius viewed the 'active element' in the world, the πνεῦμα which is divine, is as a physical body ringing the outside of the world and giving it a spherical form. Diogenes tells us that in the fifth book of his *Physics* Posidonius argued for the spherical shape of the cosmos on the grounds that it would then be in a most suitable condition for movement.[2]

Our suggestion is that Posidonius thought of the active element in the world as being associated with making the world spherical, and further with actually being a kind of band round the outside of the world which holds the world in its spherical form. This interpretation appears to be supported by evidence in Plutarch about Posidonius' comments on the *Timaeus*. Plutarch writes as follows:[3] 'The followers of Posidonius did not remove the soul far from matter, but took the phrase "divided about the bodies" to mean the substance within the limits, and by confusing these limits with the intelligible claimed the soul to be the form (ἰδέαν) of what is extended in every way, a form which exists according to a number which comprises harmony.' This extraordinarily difficult passage has been best explicated by Merlan,[4] and must be viewed in its context. The context is an equation by Posidonius and his followers of the world-soul

---

[1] D.L. 7.135. For the orthodox view of limits see Proclus, *In Eucl.* 1, p. 89 Friedlein (*SVF* II 488). Cf. *SVF* II 485.

[2] D.L. 7.140.

[3] Plut., *De An. Proc. in Tim.* 1023 B.

[4] Merlan, *From Platonism to Neoplatonism* 33–40. The translation of τὴν τῶν περάτων οὐσίαν as 'the substance within the limits' is defended by Merlan. My explanation of ταῦτα τῷ νοητῷ μίξαντες differs from Merlan's.

with τὰ μαθηματικά. These objects of mathematics are a third class of entity between the πρῶτα νοητά—Forms for Plato, concepts for Posidonius—and ordinary sensibles. They are, as the earlier passage of Diogenes Laertius showed, both concepts (κατ' ἐπίνοιαν) and existentially real (καθ' ὑπόστασιν). We can see why Plutarch objects to Posidonius' materialism. According to Posidonius the world-soul, which is the ἰδέα of the world, that is, the shape of the world,[1] is both a geometrical and a physical and material entity. It exists 'according to the number which comprises harmony'.

It seems, therefore, that, when Posidonius formulated his exegesis of *Timaeus* 35A, he did so with his own system in mind. It is now generally agreed that Posidonius did not write a commentary on the *Timaeus*, but explained parts of it.[2] Since he was not writing a commentary, there is no reason to suppose he was particularly concerned with what Plato meant, but rather with 'interpreting' him to suit his own purposes. That he was quite capable of neglecting Plato's obvious meaning is demonstrated by his claim that in Plato's view only the world-soul is immortal.[3] Since, therefore, it seems that Posidonius' interpretation of the *Timaeus* squares admirably with his generally attested views about the relation of the soul of the world and the οὐρανός, we need not distinguish in this case, as many have done,[4] between Posidonius the historian of philosophy and Posidonius the philosopher. The concept of Posidonius the historian of philosophy is certainly over-inflated.

Before leaving this problem, we should notice a further point briefly. We have argued that according to Posidonius, both in his exposition of the *Timaeus* and in his own philosophical scheme, the world-soul, which is God, is to be identified primarily with the physical limits of the cosmos, for a limit is not only a conceptual entity; it also exists in physical space. This perhaps is the context in which we should comment on what has happened to the Platonic Forms, the πρῶτα νοητά, as

---

[1] Proclus, *In Eucl.* p. 143, 8–21 Friedlein.
[2] See Reinhardt, 'Poseidonios', cols. 569–70.
[3] Hermias, *Comm. in Plat. Phaedrum*, p. 102 Couvreur.
[4] E.g. Reinhardt, 'Poseidonios', col. 791; Pohlenz, *Die Stoa* 2.215.

Plutarch calls them; for Posidonius has been found to argue that the soul of the world lies 'between' these intelligibles and sensibles. What this must mean for Posidonius is that, while the sensibles are obviously recognized by sense, and the mathematicals (= world-soul) by sense and by the formation of concepts, the 'forms' are purely concepts. And it is reasonable to speculate that, since the whole discussion of this passage of the *Timaeus* by Posidonius is concerned not with human souls but with the soul of the world, this was the place in which a Stoic said for the first time that the Platonic Forms are not merely human concepts, but God's concepts.[1]

It must be admitted that Posidonius' comments on the Platonic Forms have to be reconstructed; but his views on the world-soul are clearly attested, and may be regarded as certain. But, an objection may run, Posidonius was not the only Stoic to associate the ἡγεμονικόν of the world, the active principle or God, with the οὐρανός. Indeed that was the general view, and those who dissented from it, like Cleanthes, were unorthodox. It is true that to regard the οὐρανός as especially divine is the normal Stoic position, and this was certainly expounded by Chrysippus,[2] but the 'realist' concept of mathematical limit is, as we have seen, a novelty in Stoicism, and Posidonius' interpretation of the relation of the soul and body of the world seems to have implications for soul–body relationships of other kinds which we shall have to consider later. In particular we shall have to consider how far Posidonius' interpretation affects his view of the possibility that the individual soul is able to survive the destruction of the body.

The fact is that, if our interpretation of Posidonian limits is correct, the identification of the active material principle with the οὐρανός is much more important for Posidonius than it was for Chrysippus, or indeed for any of the earlier Stoics. For the early Stoics, although the divine may be seen in fuller strength in some particular place, the fact of its being at the circumference

---

[1] Cf. Rist, *Eros and Psyche* 65, with the bibliographical information given there on the much discussed question of who first claimed that the Forms are God's thoughts.

[2] D.L. 7.139 (*SVF* II 644).

of the world was not closely associated with its role of holding the world together. But for Posidonius the concept of a limit as a kind of container, composed, in the case of the world-soul, of a more divine substance than what is contained, must be related to a theory of why the world is shaped as it is. And in general, although the concept of shape and shaping is discussed by the Stoics from the beginning, it may have been more important for Posidonius than for his predecessors in view of his doctrine that the limits of body are actual material exist-ents.[1]

There might seem to be a contradiction in the views, who-ever held them, that the active principle is present both at some particular place in the world, such as the circumference, and also in every natural object, such as a man, where it plays the part of holding the particular together. But there is in fact no contradiction in the function of the active element; in both cases its task is to unify. Where the difference comes is in its method of unifying. If the active element is viewed primarily as a limit, it would necessarily have to lie round the outside of the objects it holds together; if it is viewed as binding everything together like glue, it would seem to be, in Stoic phraseology, totally mixed with what it binds. And we have already found Posidonius comparing the soul to glue which binds the body together. The comparison with glue appears to be more in the spirit of early Stoicism, for the early Stoics would certainly have regarded the active element as wholly interpenetrating the passive wherever the two are found in combination. That being so, there would seem no good reason, in the early Stoa, for associating the ἡγεμονικόν with any particular part of the physical cosmos. Indeed their theory would be much more con-sistent if they had not connected it with any particular place. Nevertheless, they undoubtedly did so associate it, and the probable reason is that they thought of the cosmos as analogous to the individual living thing, such as an individual man. In the case of the individual they believed that the soul is localized in a particular place. Indeed, what else could they have done but regard some parts as more ensouled than others, for they were

[1] For the concept of shaping see *SVF* II 310, 311, 314 etc.

aware that, if a man loses his leg he can still live, whereas if he loses his head he cannot?

Thus the Old Stoics were left with the position that the ἡγεμονικόν is present both at the circumference of the world and throughout the world; but in their cosmology the latter was by far the more important. On it the whole theory of tension depends. Individuals like Cleanthes and Chrysippus would dispute where the precise seat of the ἡγεμονικόν is without diverging in their account of the constitution of particular physical objects. But if we are right in supposing that Posidonius held that the world-soul is properly defined as the 'idea' (= shape) of the physical universe, and if this is emphatically tied to a specific view of the nature of the physical universe, it is clear that the problem of the relation between the unifying (shaping) factor in the world as a whole and the unifying (shaping?) factor in particular parts of the world is intensified. For Posidonius it is *important* that the ἡγεμονικόν of the world is the οὐρανός; for the Old Stoics it does not matter very much. For Posidonius, in other words, there is a much stronger tendency to emphasize the specific localization of the world-soul rather than its spread throughout the cosmos. And if we call the cosmos the body of the world, and its limits the soul, we can see that Posidonius has in fact emphasized a distinction between body and soul, or, if you like, between the passive element in the world and the active element or God. Thus, although Edelstein was wrong in his explanation of the relation between these two principles in Posidonius' physics, he was right to detect a tendency to separate them. They are not, however, separated completely. Like the Old Stoics Posidonius still talks of the soul as glue; nevertheless, the localization of soul has become noticeably more marked and the tendency to a dualism of body and soul thereby strengthened.

We have suggested that in the system of Posidonius the traditionally Stoic relationship between the world-soul and the individual soul must have been developed or altered. The emphasis on the world-soul as limit would make this inevitable if Posidonius were not to regard the human skin as the most divine part of man, one absurdity at least which we can be sure he did not perpetrate. Before considering this problem, and indeed the whole problem of the individual soul in the thought of Posidonius, we must return to the question of the distinction between Zeus and nature with which our enquiry began. The early Stoics, who identified nature and Zeus, thought of nature as the governing principle in the world. Thus, although they might distinguish between the powers of soul and the powers of nature (φύσις), the distinction was only one of convenience, for soul is simply one kind of nature, nature endowed with powers of sensation.[1] It appears that for Posidonius the distinction must have been much more important, as it already was for Panaetius.[2] And it is easy to speculate what Posidonius' position might have been, though difficult to demonstrate exactly what it was. It is quite wrong to suggest, as Edelstein does, that a distinction between ἕξις, φύσις and ψυχή has anything to do with the unity of the objects these binding factors respectively control. It seems to have been a Stoic view that stones are unified by ἕξις, plants by φύσις and animals by ψυχή, but Sextus Empiricus, who is one of our sources for this information, regards all these things as unified objects (ἡνωμένα).[3] Edelstein misreads the passage when he says that stones and wood are not unified bodies; and in any case there is no good reason to attribute the passage to Posidonius in particular, even though its origins are later than Chrysippus. However, in our search for the distinction between Zeus and nature, it is not nature as the binding principle of plants with which we are concerned, but nature in some much wider sense. Clearly it is nature regarded as a basic element. And if it is natural and certainly Stoic to identify Zeus with the active principle of the cosmos, then nature must either be the passive principle, matter unqualified, or rather the 'prime matter' present and conceptually distinguishable in all things or, if not that, then the existing world itself, viewed as the product of the two basic forces, God and matter. Nature, then, in the sense we require, is either the passive principle of the world, or the existent world itself, or the body of that world.

---

[1] D.L. 7.156. [2] See pp. 180–2 above.

[3] Sext. Emp., *Adv. Math.* 9.81; Edelstein, *op. cit.* 299. Cf. Leeman, 'Seneca and Poseidonios', 65, Reinhardt, *Kosmos* 34, Seneca, *Ep.* 102.6–7.

Which of the three it is has no bearing on our basic problem, for in each case Posidonius' tendency to separate the active principle, Zeus, from everything else is obvious. It is at least worthy of consideration, however, that Posidonius meant by nature the body of the physical world. That would be a treatment along the lines laid down by Plato in the *Timaeus*. Nature is the world's body and Zeus is its soul. As for Fate, Posidonius' third source of divination, that would correspond with the Platonic errant cause or necessity (ἀνάγκη).

We have argued that there is a strongly dualistic strain in Posidonius' theory of the physical world, and a tendency to separate the 'body' and 'soul' of the world along quasi-Platonic lines. Posidonius seems to have used the term 'God' to denote the controlling force of the world, and 'substance' to denote what is controlled, that is, the world's body. We have already noticed the phrase 'the οὐσία within the limits'; this may be paralleled by a text from Diogenes Laertius in which we read of the whole cosmos being the οὐσία of God.[1] In Posidonius himself this probably meant the οὐσία physically within God, that is, within the limits of the divine οὐρανός. It goes without saying that, although this sort of theory may have been 'found' by Posidonius in Plato's *Timaeus*, it bears no relation to Plato's genuine thought, or, for that matter, to the thought of the Neoplatonists later. Posidonius' thought is entirely dominated by Stoic materialism. The effect of the *Timaeus* on that materialism would be to differentiate between two kinds of matter, one of which is called God.

Posidonius says that God directs all;[2] any of the Stoics might have said it. But Edelstein may be right, for the wrong reasons,[3] in holding that, when Posidonius says it, he means something different from Chrysippus. Both Chrysippus and Posidonius might say both that God is the all and that God directs the all, but while the first would represent Chrysippus' position less misleadingly than the second—for the second implies a dualism of God and matter—the second is perhaps the better indicator of the tendencies of Posidonius.

For the Old Stoics problems of man are essentially the

---

[1] D.L. 7.148.   [2] Lydus, *De Mens.* 4.48.   [3] Edelstein, *op. cit.* 291.

problems of the cosmos. The microcosm parallels the macrocosm. Hence the view that man can become a creature who lives a rational life accompanied by proper states of emotion, and that vicious passions can and should be eliminated. Man's personality can resemble the personality of God, and that is wholly good. This parallelism between man and the world-soul has begun to break down in Panaetius, and does not exist in Posidonius. It is now generally recognized that Posidonius' psychology is fundamentally different from that of Chrysippus and the Old Stoa. There is no need to discuss this problem in detail here. We know from many sources, but in particular from Galen, that Posidonius, presumably to give an account of moral conflict, rejected the psychological theories of Chrysippus and based his own views on the Platonic tripartition of the soul. Posidonius held that, since children and animals can display anger and desire without reason, the rational faculty must be distinct.[1] This illustration also shows that for Posidonius, as for Plato, although there is a tripartition between reason, spirit, and passion, yet the basic distinction is between reason and the other two together, between the rational and the non-rational. Some scholars have tried to moderate the extent of Posidonius' break with orthodox Stoic psychology by pointing to a passage in Galen where it is said that Posidonius, like Aristotle, did not talk about kinds of soul or parts of soul, but about faculties of a single soul with its seat in the heart.[2] It is quite possible that Posidonius used the word δύναμις rather than εἶδος or μέρος; this would have sounded more in the spirit of orthodox Stoicism. But although perhaps he did not speak of parts, there is little doubt that he meant to distinguish the faculties in a very similar way to that in which Plato distinguishes parts. For Posidonius each faculty has its own οἰκείωσις, and in a famous passage he argues that we have two *daimones* within us, a good and a bad, one of which is akin to the ruling principle of the world, while the other is bestial.[3] This is a degree of dualistic psychology

---

[1] Galen, *De Hipp. et Plat.* 5.459–61, pp. 437–40 Mü.

[2] Galen, *De Hipp. et Plat.* 5.515, p. 501, 10 Mü.; cf. Laffranque, *op. cit.* 399.

[3] Galen, *De Hipp. et Plat.* 5.469, p. 448, 15–449, 4 Mü. It should be noticed that it is not absolutely certain that Posidonius always avoided the word 'part'. Galen attributes it to him at *De Hipp. et Plat.* 5.470, p. 449, 14 Mü.

rivalling Plato at his most extreme, and one of its sources may be the baffling passage of the *Laws* about the soul which is capable of achieving the opposite of goodness.[1] Be that as it may, there can be no doubt that whether or not Posidonius used the word 'part', Clement of Alexandria was perfectly justified in attributing it to him.[2] According to Galen Posidonius said that we should not be led by what is irrational, evil (κακοδαίμονος) and godless (ἀθέου) in the soul.[3] Clement repeats a similar formula, but adds the word 'part' (κατὰ μηδὲν ἀγόμενον ὑπὸ τοῦ ἀλόγου μέρους τῆς ψυχῆς). Perhaps Pohlenz, who follows Wilamowitz, is right to hold that these are the words of Clement and not of Posidonius himself;[4] that would seem to be a necessary conclusion if we believe Galen when he says that Posidonius rejected μέρος in favour of δύναμις. But words apart, Clement understands Posidonius' meaning aright. If the irrational faculty is a *daimon*, it is at the very least a Platonic part. We must accept that Posidonius maintained the Platonic tripartition of the soul in a strict sense, differing only in making the heart the seat of all three of the δυνάμεις.

One of the important results of this acceptance is that Posidonius believes that moral evil arises in man by nature,[5] that is, by the domination of one of the inferior parts of the soul. Since this is a part of the soul itself, it is not eliminated, but controlled. Posidonius himself recognized the importance of his new psychological theories for the student of ethics. Consideration of goods and evils, of the end for man, and of the virtues depends in his opinion on correct investigation of the emotions.[6] There is no need, however, at this stage to go through his detailed application of the theory of tripartition. All we need to know is that Posidonius' psychology emphasizes a duality within the soul itself. There is a rational and an irrational force. Now it may be said that the dualism in man between rational and irrational soul is not the same as the dualism in the cosmos

---

[1] *Laws* 896 E.   [2] Clem. Alex., *Strom.* 2.129.4.
[3] Galen, *De Hipp. et Plat.* 5.470, p. 449, 6–7 Mü.
[4] Pohlenz, *Die Stoa* 2.121: Wilamowitz, *Die Glaube* 2.407 note 2.
[5] Cf. Galen, *Quod animi mores corporis temperamenta sequantur* (*Scr. min.* 2, p. 78, 8ff. Mü.).
[6] Galen, *De Hipp. et Plat.* 5.469, p. 448, 9–11 Mü.

between world-soul or God, and matter. We shall return to this. For the moment let us conclude that in physics Posidonius tends to separate the governing principle of the world from all else, while in psychology he clearly distinguishes a governing and rational principle in man.

What is more, in his discussion of the end for man, he brings the governing principles of the world and of man into a close relationship. According to Galen, Posidonius held that the principal cause of an unhappy life is a man's refusal to follow the *daimon* within him (the reason), which is of the same nature as that which rules the world (τῷ τὸν ὅλον κόσμον διοικοῦντι). This sounds orthodox in a way, but in our present context we can see how it leads Posidonius to a rather different picture of man's role in the universe. As we have seen, Posidonius' tendency to dualism in physics pushes him in the direction of treating God not so much as the world itself but as the governor of the world. The man who leads the right kind of life, therefore, and who lives in accordance with the *daimon* within him which is similar to the governing principle of the cosmos, will himself take a share in the ordering of the physical world. Hence, in the definition of the end for man, as reported by Clement, Posidonius says that we must live investigating (θεωροῦντα) the truth of the world and its order, and striving to bring about truth and order as far as possible.[1] Posidonius' life-long preoccupation with the sciences, and with historical and geographical enquiries, is evidence of the seriousness with which he took the call to co-operate in the ordering of the world, and he handed the habit of enquiry on to others in succeeding generations. Posidonius' ethics calls for an active co-operation of the rational in man with the rational in the cosmos. Once again we may detect a return to Plato and to Aristotle, and a drastic modification of the attitudes of the Old Stoa. Where the Old Stoa urged us to follow nature, Posidonius wants us to join in the organization of nature.[2] Mlle Laffranque is probably right to explain a puzzling passage of Diogenes Laertius in this context.

---

[1] Clem. Alex., *Strom.* 2.21.129. I read συγκατασκευάζοντα αὐτήν, rejecting Sylburg's αὐτόν; cf. Pohlenz, *Die Stoa* 2.121.

[2] Cf. Laffranque, *op. cit.* 477–9.

Although other evidence makes it clear that Posidonius did not abandon the Old Stoic insistence that virtue is the only good,[1] Diogenes claims that he said that wealth and health are goods.[2] It is very probable that, if Posidonius said this, he was speaking loosely, as even Chrysippus was willing to do in an unambiguous context. What Posidonius would have meant is that, although virtue is the only good, the possession of health and wealth enables us to co-operate with the governing principle more effectively. The problem would not have arisen for the Old Stoa, because, although, contrary to much modern comment, Chrysippus was not necessarily opposed to scientific enquiry, he did not regard it as a co-operation with God in the way suggested by Posidonius. And Posidonius only came to regard it in this light because of the dualism in his physics and in his psychology.

We must return briefly to a problem we mentioned earlier, but of which discussion was postponed. We have seen that there is a definite tendency to dualism in Posidonius' physics, but it is, or looks to be, a dualism of soul and body. In Posidonius' psychology, however, the dualism is, as in Panaetius, between rational and irrational aspects of the soul. However the difference between the dualisms is not as sharp as might appear at first sight, because, although we began our discussion of Posidonian physics with the distinction between God (world-soul) and matter, when he talks about God at the limits of the cosmos, or the οὐρανός being the most divine part of the cosmos, it is the ἡγεμονικόν (equivalent to νοῦς) which Posidonius names. There is little doubt that Posidonius, like many other Stoics, tends to talk about soul when strictly he means ἡγεμονικόν, and ἡγεμονικόν when he means soul. The reason for this is clear. For Chrysippus the ἡγεμονικόν is the personality, and the rest of the soul is subordinate. Thus the habit easily arose of speaking of the ἡγεμονικόν when the whole soul was meant, because the ἡγεμονικόν is the most characteristic and prominent

[1] Cic., *Tusc.* 2.25, Sen., *Ep.* 87.35.
[2] D.L. 7.103; cf. 7.128 and Laffranque, *op. cit.* 479. The version of Epiphanius (*Adv. Haer.* 3.2.9 = *DG* p. 593, 9–10), that for Posidonius health and wealth are the *greatest* goods, may be ignored.

aspect of soul. In physics we have seen that, although the ἡγεμονικόν is at the circumference of the cosmos, Posidonius also calls the world-*soul* the form of the all-extended, thus using the word 'soul' (at least in expounding Plato) when technically he may have meant ἡγεμονικόν. In fact his view probably was that the ἡγεμονικόν, located primarily at the circumference, affects all other parts of the cosmos through its various faculties. He would also call these faculties the faculties and powers of the soul. Thus in a limited sense it can be argued that there is a tendency to dualism within the soul even within Posidonius' physics, a dualism between the ἡγεμονικόν and its faculties and effects.

Nevertheless, there must be an important difference between the faculties of the world-soul and the faculties of the individual soul in man. In man's soul tendencies to evil are innate; no such tendencies appear in the world-soul. The nature of the human soul and that of the soul of the world must, therefore, though in many ways similar, also exhibit great differences. There is no evil *daimon* in the soul of the world. The human soul is a composite of good and evil in a manner in which the world-soul is not. It would be reasonable to suppose, therefore, that their ultimate fates might be very different. According to a passage which has received considerable attention, Posidonius claimed that Plato regarded only the world-soul as immortal.[1] This is impossible for Plato and could only be attributed to him by a man who believed it to be the case himself. We have no other direct evidence on the way in which Posidonius regarded the fate of the human soul, but it is quite possible that Hermias has presented his view correctly and that Posidonius followed Panaetius in denying its individual immortality or even its individual survival after death. The fact that its composition is manifestly different from that of the world-soul would make its dissolution with the dissolution of the body a reasonable possibility, but perhaps Posidonius thought it survived, without individuality, wholly assimilated to the soul of the world. It need hardly be said that such passages as De Divinatione 1.64, where, according to Cicero, Posidonius said that the air is full of im-

[1] Hermias, *Comm. in Plat. Phaedr.* p. 102 Couvreur.

mortal spirits, tell us nothing about the fate of the human soul or spirit. Posidonius almost certainly regarded such spirits as parts of the world-soul, just like the sun and the other heavenly gods.[1] Needless to say, with individual survival gone, all the elaborate eschatology invented by such scholars as Cumont[2] and Reinhardt can be forgotten; it has nothing to do with Posidonius.

We have attempted in this brief discussion of Posidonius to indicate the fundamental points on which he disagreed with the early Stoic tradition. His dispute with Chrysippus was basically about philosophical issues, but had ramifications into other areas of study with which we are not immediately concerned. We have argued that the dualist strain in Posidonius' thought does not make him an other-worldly thinker, for his basic materialism precludes another world for man. Indeed in his this-worldliness Posidonius is after all the apt pupil of Panaetius. He extends and enlarges Panaetius' scientific interests. Although his theory of the cosmos itself is generally much more traditional than that of his master, his apparent dissociation of the human soul as a whole from the world-soul as a whole kept him fully engrossed in this world's problems. Indeed his this-worldliness was even emphasized by the transmuted fragment of Old Stoic theory he maintained in his psychology, the kinship of human reason with divine Reason. The effect of this similarity is to stimulate man to join in God's work of ordering the physical world to the best of his ability.

But the psychological dualism could be used very differently from the way in which Posidonius used it. Although the old and happily discredited view that Posidonius was the virtual founder of Neoplatonism can be safely forgotten, his feud with Chrysippus over the human soul and his emphasis on dualistic tendencies in Stoic physics, were in many respects fatal to Stoicism. The old view of man as a unitary person, and of the world as almost a divine person, action being in both cases psychosomatic,

---

[1] Cf. Jones, *op. cit.* Laffranque, *op. cit.* 519–27.

[2] Cumont, *La Théologie*; Reinhardt, *Kosmos*, and 'Poseidonios', cols. 778–91. See Schubert, *Die Eschatologie. Contra*, in addition to the works of Jones, Edelstein and Laffranque, see especially Boyancé, *Etude*.

had been destroyed, never fully to recover in the Stoic school. It is no accident that most Stoicism after Posidonius tends to degenerate into mere moralizing. Posidonius had rejected the most original features of Stoic thought; the only useful path open to metaphysics was a more whole-hearted espousal of Platonism at full strength.

12

KNOWING AND WILLING

It is sometimes said that the philosophers of antiquity had no concept of the will. It is also said that the ancient philosophers did not posit a faculty of the will, separate from the intellect. Many historians of philosophy have held both these generalizations to be true, and some have tended to think of the two propositions as identical, which they manifestly are not. Plato, for example, does not posit a will as a faculty of the soul, yet he believes that the man who really knows what is good will try to act in accordance with his knowledge. He will want to act morally, and hence will be a good man. Thus Plato can be said to have some grasp of the concept of willing, but no idea of a faculty called the will. Aristotle's position, though different in detail, is basically similar. Since he does not make use of Plato's unusual concept of 'really knowing', he is perhaps more conscious that there appears to be a difference between knowing what is right and being a good man. He distinguishes sharply in the first book of the *Nicomachean Ethics*.

It is commonly (and correctly) held that the essential thesis of Stoic ethics is that the wise man's motives are pure. He always does the right thing for the right reasons. We should assume, therefore, that what we shall somewhat un-Stoically call problems about choice would be central in the thought of Zeno and Chrysippus, and for the latter at least our assumption is well supported by evidence. According to Chrysippus God has given us the power to select (ἐκλεκτικόν) what is natural.[1] There is no reason to accept the odd suggestion of Pohlenz that Diogenes of Babylon was the earliest member of the school to emphasize the problem of selecting, even though he brought the matter into the clearest possible light by defining the end for man as a rational selection of what is natural.[2] What we must investigate, therefore, is what the Stoics could have meant by

---

[1] Epict., *Disc.* 2.6.9 (*SVF* III 191); cf. Cic., *De Fin.* 3.31 (*SVF* III 190).
[2] *SVF* III 44–6 Diogenes; cf. Bonhoeffer, 'Die Telosformel'.

'rational selection', and in particular whether they viewed the matter purely in intellectualist terms. If so, they held that the bad man's decision to commit a crime is to be explained as a reasoned decision to do what is wrong. But how can reason by itself make an irrational, and therefore for the Stoic, immoral decision? We have argued already that for Chrysippus and his followers in the Stoic school there is no such thing as a purely intellectual act, and that the ἡγεμονικόν which 'decides' and 'chooses' our courses of action is more than a rational faculty. It is rather something like what we should call character or personality, and is therefore capable of both rational and irrational behaviour, according to the type of people we are.[1] In the ἡγεμονικόν, we learn, exist our impressions, assents, impulses and reason (λόγος).[2] These are the various psychological activities which the individual performs. Now what will happen when we assent to a particular course of action, be it good or bad? Clearly what the Stoic means when he says that a man assents to do *x* is that he has *decided* to do *x* and he *intends* to do it. All assents in the moral sphere will involve the *intention* of pursuing a particular course of action.

Let us think the matter out a little further. The wise man, according to Chrysippus, will live a life in which he will experience natural happenings;[3] his life will be in accordance with nature in so far as is possible in his individual circumstances, and in the moral sphere he will recognize the moral course, intend to pursue it, will to pursue it, and pursue it in fact. Let us suppose the wise man sees someone drowning. He knows he ought to pull him out; he therefore wants to pull him out and actually tries to pull him out. Whether or not he is successful is morally irrelevant. The point is that, if he has assented to the fact that he ought to pull the wretch out of the water, he has assented not merely to the fact that someone ought to pull him out, but that *he* ought to pull him out. But, we might suggest, it is possible to say 'I ought to pull Jones out' without attempting to do so. For the Stoic, however, the moral question poses itself not in the form 'Ought I to pull him out?', but

---

[1] See pp. 22–36. [2] *SVF* iii 831.
[3] D.L. 7.87 (*SVF* iii 4).

'Shall I pull him out or not?' If in such circumstances he does not make the attempt, it is obvious that he does not want to pull Jones out, *or* that he has decided against pulling Jones out, *or* again that he does not intend to pull Jones out. The decision is: I will not pull Jones out. In other words all moral acts involve a recognition of the moral end and an attempt to bring it about. That is why it is in this respect at least good Stoicism for Antipater to define the end of life as 'doing everything possible to obtain what is prior by nature'.[1]

For Antipater happiness will be attained if we know what is appropriate and make every possible effort to achieve what is most natural.[2] The talk of effort is new, but in substance the doctrine does not differ from the views held by Zeno and Chrysippus. It is interesting, however, to notice that, whereas Chrysippus and Diogenes of Babylon speak of *selecting* what is natural, Antipater is prepared to be explicit about expending effort as well as selecting. For, like Diogenes, he too defined the end—perhaps at an early stage of his career—as selecting what is natural, provided, presumably, that it is appropriate in the particular circumstances. It can be argued that he did not think that 'selecting what is natural' is substantially different from 'expending all one's efforts to obtain what is natural'; and this could only be the case if 'selecting' implied not merely making an intellectual decision that x is appropriate but willing and intending to do x. Long believes that Antipater could not have simultaneously held that the end is 'rational behaviour in the selection of τὰ κατὰ φύσιν' and 'doing everything in one's power to obtain τὰ κατὰ φύσιν', for, he says, 'to be rational in the choice of x is quite different from making every effort to obtain x'. It might be, he would argue, that the latter formula implies that what is natural is always and invariably appropriate, a view which is alien to traditional Stoicism.[3] We may admit that perhaps Antipater's remarks about effort are liable to let us lose sight of those rare occasions when the unnatural is nevertheless the appropriate course, but, leaving this

---

[1] *SVF* III 57 Antipater; cf. Long, 'Carneades and the Stoic Telos', 79–86.
[2] See Long, *op. cit.*
[3] Cf. p. 75 note 5 above; Long, *op. cit.* 76.

aside, we may still argue that the Stoics in general and Antipater in particular could have held that 'to be rational in the choice of *x*' means both (1) to make an intellectual choice of a particular course and (2) to try to act in a particular way. Indeed our argument is that they must have held this view, for if they had not, they would have required two 'parts' of the soul, one to decide that *x* is appropriate, and the other to will to carry it out. And this sort of dichotomy is precisely what all the Old Stoics rejected. For them, as for Plato, to know what is appropriate, to decide in favour of a particular course, implies necessarily to try to do what is appropriate, to intend the appropriate, to will the appropriate. This is one of the things Chrysippus means when he treats both impulse (ὁρμή) and reason (λόγος) as functions of the personality, but not as separate faculties.

When Antipater defined the end as expending all one's effort to obtain what is primarily natural, he did not mean that anyone who does this is a sage. Obviously it is possible to strive for the appropriate thing for the wrong reasons; the amount of effort exerted has nothing to do with the goodness or badness of one's motives. Hence Antipater must have held that the good man would expend all his efforts for the appropriate end for the right reason; and there might still be a bad man who would expend similar effort for a similar end for the wrong reason, for example, for the sake of pleasure or pride. Thus none of the early Stoics should be saddled with the doctrine that the expenditure of effort, the use of the will, the making of attempts, is *per se* desirable. Moral intention is not to be explained in terms of effort for 'natural' ends, but in terms of properly motivated effort. The kind of effort we make depends on the kind of people we are.

If Chrysippus were asked 'With what do I know that *x* is right?', he would reply 'With my ἡγεμονικόν'. If asked 'With what do I decide to do *x*?', he would give the same answer. He is, of course, as aware as the rest of us that it is possible to have a correct opinion about what is right without doing it. In such a case, he says, the ἡγεμονικόν, the personality, is sick. The individual is, as it were, not functioning properly. For

in the 'natural' man, knowing the moral course implies trying
and wanting to do it. It is not true to say, therefore, that Chrysippus does not distinguish understanding and will. He recognizes on the contrary that all 'fools', that is, virtually everyone,
are capable of opining correctly—he will not call it knowing—
without willing. This very capability is the essence of being a
fool, a sick and misguided individual. Clearly in this sort of
situation Chrysippus would see no need for a separate faculty
of the will.

The Old Stoic position was less liable to misinterpretation
because of the peculiar sense of some of the 'knowing' words
which they inherited from Plato. Greek words like διάνοια, and
even νοῦς, convey the idea not only of ratiocination but of
something like intention. Pohlenz has indicated how this double
meaning can only be translated into Latin by the use of
periphrases, so that Cicero is prepared to render κατὰ νοῦν as
ex sua mente ac voluntate (*Tim.* 6). Sometimes, however, *voluntas* is
used by itself as a rendering of διάνοια, though the sense is not
merely 'will' but 'intention', and 'reasoning' (*Rep.* 1.47).[1] This
kind of usage is not limited to Cicero, and its appearance seems
to indicate that Latin words like *mens* or *ratio* were too 'intellectualist' to carry naturally the full sense of their apparent equi-
valents in Greek. And once one starts talking about a reason
(*mens*) and a will (*voluntas*) or intention, it might seem an easy
step to move from the fact that there are two words in Latin for
one word in Greek to the proposal that there are two faculties,
an intellect and a will, instead of Chrysippus' ἡγεμονικόν. Be
that as it may—and we shall return to it shortly—the apparent
need to talk of both a *mens* and a *voluntas* bears out our interpretation of the position of the Old Stoa. Although it makes sense
in Greek to say that all the virtues are ἐπιστῆμαι, as the early
Stoics said, for the proposition depends on the peculiar sense of
ἐπιστήμη, it is much odder to say that they are all *rationes*, let
alone *mentes*. It is true that Seneca can write *omnes virtutes
rationes sunt* (*Ep.* 66.32), but the meaning of the Latin almost
depends on our recognition of it as a translation.

[1] Pohlenz, *Philosophie und Erlebnis* 112–13 and *Die Stoa* 2.139–40. Other
references are given by Pohlenz.

According to Pohlenz a distinction between intellect and will was made by Seneca. For Seneca the will is vital, and this is a quite new emphasis in Stoicism. The reason is that Seneca wrote and thought in Latin. Although Cicero had employed the term *voluntas*, his thought was dominated by older ways of looking at the problem. Seneca, however, from the time of the *De Beneficiis*, and perhaps particularly in the letters to Lucilius, has the will in the forefront of his mind. It dominates his work.[1] The matter needs investigation, for, if Pohlenz is right, it is of some importance. It is certainly true that Seneca talks about *voluntas* a great deal. And he understands something like will or intention by it. But let us look at a few of the passages on which Pohlenz places particular emphasis. From *Epistle* 80.4 Pohlenz quotes the words *Quid tibi opus est, ut bonus sis? velle*. What do you need to become good? To want to be. According to Pohlenz this is a voluntarist attitude, with which a passage of Epictetus, of a 'much more strongly intellectualist character', should be contrasted.[2] Epictetus' words are: 'It is not enough to want to be noble or good, you must also learn something.' The things to be learned are the truths about God and providence.

But the passage of Seneca must be viewed in its proper context. If you want to be good, what does Seneca suggest that you want? You want to free yourself from servitude. Free yourself, he says, from the fear of death and poverty. How do you do this? His answer is, By a kind of learning. If you want to know that there is no evil in poverty, compare the faces of the poor and the rich. The poor smile more frequently; the rich are more anxious. In other words, willing to be good depends for Seneca on a knowledge of certain facts about the world. If you want to be good, you must learn how to free yourself from fear. Thus, although Seneca says that wanting to be good is necessary if one is to become good, he does not think that to will to be good is decisive or adequate or in practice separable from knowing what is good. As they stand, the words *Quid tibi opus est ut sis bonus? velle* could represent the view of Chrysippus or of Epictetus. They must not be taken out of context.

[1] Pohlenz, *Philosophie und Erlebnis* 113–17; *Die Stoa* 1.319–20; 2.159.
[2] Pohlenz, *Die Stoa* 1.334; Epict., *Disc.* 2.14.10.

Another passage from the letters which Pohlenz considers significant runs as follows: *Neminem mihi dabis qui sciat quomodo quod vult coeperit velle* (37.5). Pohlenz' slightly tendentious translation is, 'Niemand kann sagen, welches der Ursprung seines Wollens ist'; this sounds as though Seneca is talking about a faculty or power called the will or willing, whereas what he says is that no one can understand how the act of willing comes about. But let that pass. More important is Seneca's next sentence, which says that the man who wants something does so 'not led on by reason but impelled by impulse' (*impetu*). The word *impetus* is clearly the Greek ὁρμή. Seneca is saying that what happens when we want something is that we are led on by an impulse whose origins we do not know. Now this is obviously true, but the fact that we do not know the origins of our impulses does not mean that they have no origin. According to Chrysippus ὁρμαί are themselves 'judgments'. There is no such thing as an 'impulse' in man which is unrelated to man's mind. That does not mean that impulses are rational in the sense of being the products of right reason. In brief, there is nothing in this passage which is out of harmony with the most traditional Stoicism. It is no coincidence that, shortly before the remark about willing which Pohlenz has emphasized, Seneca discusses reason (*ratio*). It almost looks as though he is saying that *ratio* is the origin of our wishes, though we do not recognize its operations on any particular occasion. 'If you wish to subject all things to yourself, subject yourself to reason.'

Epistle 81.13 is another instructive passage. Seneca is expounding the notorious Stoic paradox that only the wise man can thank in the full sense of the word. The wise man possesses the virtues; the ordinary people have only images and likenesses of virtue (*simulacra rerum honestarum et effigies*). Paying thanks affords an example of this. The wise man knows how to do it. As for the fools, let them do as well as they can. And then follow the words: *scientia illi* (the fool) *potius quam voluntas desit: velle non discitur*. This presumably means, 'Let the fool lack knowledge rather than intention (the will): willing (intention) is not learned'. Seneca's point is that *velle* is the 'image and likeness' of virtue, but *scientia* combined with *voluntas* is the virtue. The προκόπτων may want to be virtuous, though not entirely for the right reasons, but only the wise man *knows*. Let the fool do as well as he can. In this sense Seneca's position seems identical with that of Epictetus which we discussed above. Willing is not enough. There may be an impulse to virtue but that is not virtue. That impulses do not originally occur as a result of teaching is part of the earliest deposit of Stoicism. We all have impulses; the effect of teaching is to make our impulses good or bad. And the teacher is in a way in an advantageous position, for, according to the orthodox Stoicism of Chrysippus, human impulses are *per se* directed to the good. They are misdirected to the bad as the result of influences from outside the human self.

Velle non discitur. It is easy to want to be good. But we have other wants as well. What matters for the Stoic is the character of our desire. Why do we want to be good? The orthodox answer, which was probably Seneca's also, is that it is 'natural' to have such impulses. That is why understanding the order of nature helps us to have the right kind of wants. And if we do not want to be better, clearly we never shall be. Seneca says elsewhere that 'a great part of progress to virtue is wanting to progress' (*velle proficere*).[1] Only an imbecile would deny it. Certainly Chrysippus would hold that no one would become a Stoic philosopher unless he *wanted* to be a better man. But, the argument runs, it is Seneca who specifically says this, who brings the matter into the open. It is Seneca who talks about *voluntas* and *velle*. His achievement is, for Pohlenz, a particularly Roman one!

What is the aim of life, asks Seneca?[2] Always to want the same things and not want the same things (*semper idem velle atque idem nolle*). Let us compare this with an Old Stoic (probably Chrysippean) definition of the highest good. It is, says Chrysippus, to be unswerving and constant in judgments (τὸ ἀμετάπτωτον ἐν ταῖς κρίσεσι καὶ βέβαιον).[3] Chrysippus talks of 'judgments', Seneca of 'willing'. But is there any difference in the substance of their thought? Our answer, if we take into account

[1] Sen., *Ep.* 71.36. [2] *Ep.* 20.5.
[3] Plut., *CN* 1061 F (*SVF* III 542).

what Chrysippus means by a judgment and its connection with choosing and intending, must be No. If a modern looks at Seneca and says he is emphasizing the factor of the will, we must conclude that he is overestimating the importance of the *word voluntas* and the *word velle*. What is really important for Seneca is the kind of *voluntas*. As Pohlenz himself has pointed out,[1] Seneca talks about kinds of *voluntas*. The gods are honoured in sacrifices by the 'upright and pious intention' (*voluntas*) of the worshippers.[2] Pleasure is the companion, not the commander, of an upright and good will.[3]

What we are suggesting is that, when Seneca talks about willing and the will, what he is really concerned with is our moral character. The man who has the right kind of moral character will want to do the right things for the right reasons. Our will springs from our habits, as Aristotle and Chrysippus would agree. Nevertheless, Seneca's use of *voluntas* does not always harmonize with this explanation. We noticed that, when in the case of the fool we found Seneca saying, 'Let *scientia* (possessed by the sage) be absent rather than *voluntas*', the προκόπτων is supposed at least to have *voluntas*, and the meaning is obviously more like 'good intention', or 'will to good', rather than moral character, for clearly he will have *some* moral character, be it good or bad. However, in this as in other passages we looked at, the terms for willing seem to convey the sense of, or to be associated with, terms for impulse.[4] The *voluntas* of the προκόπτων is in our passage a 'good' impulse, an impulse towards virtuous action. It is partly the Greek ὁρμή and partly διάνοια. It clearly stands for *bona voluntas*, for some kind of will is certain to be present in a man in every situation. And we have already observed that an impulse towards the natural is for the Stoics something given. *Velle non discitur.* It is easy to see why, if *bona voluntas* is not present, *scientia* cannot be. *Scientia* is the mark of the wise man, but a man can become wise if and only if his will and intention is to do the right thing.

[1] Pohlenz, *Philosophie und Erlebnis* 117 note 2.
[2] Sen., *De Ben.* 1.6.3; cf. *Ep.* 115.5.
[3] *De Vita Beata* 8.1; cf. the contrast of *voluntas nuda* and *optima ac plenissima voluntas* at *De Ben.* 6.10.2.   [4] *Ep.* 37.5.

With the προκόπτων we are concerned with the development of character.

If our conclusions about Seneca are correct, we shall have good reason to compare his views on *voluntas* with those of Epictetus on what he calls προαίρεσις. Pohlenz has pointed out that Epictetus' προαίρεσις is not simply will, but, he continues, it must be also distinguished from Seneca's *voluntas*. Epictetus' ethic, he says, is not voluntarist.[1] Pohlenz' view of Epictetus, however, is clearly not identical with that of Bonhoeffer, who, without mentioning Seneca's *voluntas*, describes προαίρεσις as a term used for the whole spiritual being of man, looked at not from the point of view of thinking but rather of willing.[2] The matter must be considered further.

Again and again Epictetus is concerned to point out that the good for man lies in his προαίρεσις, his moral character.[3] This use of προαίρεσις is found only rarely in the writers of the Old Stoa, as has often been noticed.[4] For Epictetus a man's προαίρεσις may be good or bad.[5] If the man is good, his προαίρεσις will make good use of what is external to his true self: his life, his body, external possessions, and so on. And the προαίρεσις itself is the product, continually undergoing modifications, of judgments (δόγματα) about what is external. Good judgments make our moral character good, bad ones bad. In a sense one's προαίρεσις can itself be called a judgment.[6] As Pohlenz saw, Epictetus' theory is basically akin to Chrysippus', though in our view there is no need to apply the term 'intellectualist' to it, if 'intellectualist' bears the sense it usually bears in this context.

Bonhoeffer has pointed out that, since the term προαίρεσις is used to cover willing as well as other mental activities, specific and unmistakable words denoting the will or its operations or the act of willing are rare in Epictetus.[7] A man's προαίρεσις, his moral character, includes all the mental activities which have to do with moral behaviour. At the beginning of the

---

[1] Pohlenz, *Die Stoa* 1.334.
[2] Bonhoeffer, *Epictet und die Stoa* 118.
[3] Epict., *Disc.* 1.8.16; 1.29.1; 2.10.25; 4.5.12 etc.
[4] Bonhoeffer, *Epictet und die Stoa* 260.
[5] *Disc.* 1.29.1.　　　　　　　　　　　[6] *Disc.* 1.17.26; cf. 3.9.1-2.
[7] Bonhoeffer, *Epictet und die Stoa* 261.

Encheiridion (1.1) Epictetus lists all the things which are in our power, that is, all the powers of our προαίρεσις. The list includes ὁρμή, ὄρεξις, ἔκκλισις and 'in brief' everything that is our own act. Naturally assent, will, intention, are our own acts.

When speaking of the views of Chrysippus and his followers in the Old Stoa, we argued that the ἡγεμονικόν is a man's character, and pointed out in passing that Chrysippus does not have a particular word for one's moral character. This is perhaps because, if pressed, he would say that all acts are in some sense moral acts, or at least acts relevant to morality, and hence there can be no real distinction between character in general and moral character. Perhaps in theory Epictetus would agree with this, and accept that walking, for example, is an act related to the moral character of the individual who walks. But Epictetus tends in practice to limit the sphere of morality to the domain in which the word is conventionally used. That being so, we might expect him to emphasize more than Chrysippus had done the distinction between moral acts and others; and indeed he certainly does this, as does Seneca, in his distinction between acts of the προαίρεσις and, for example, acts of the body, such as feeling pain. Nevertheless, Epictetus is Chrysippean enough at times to treat ἡγεμονικόν and προαίρεσις as synonyms, and to write ἡγεμονικόν where we might more naturally expect to find προαίρεσις. A man must make his ἡγεμονικόν pure, he writes at 3.22.19; and again, 'So long as you occupy yourself with externals, you will have them as no one else does, but you will have your ἡγεμονικόν in the state you want to have it, dirty and neglected'.[1]

For Epictetus, then, the moral character shows itself in our behaviour. We have a moral character of such and such a sort, and this character is moulded by our previous decisions. From it spring our individual acts of will, whether for the good or for the bad. Epictetus would have heartily approved Seneca's language about a *pia* or *recta voluntas*, and both of them would have been reflecting the traditionally Stoic position that in our moral behaviour it is motive and intention which distinguish

---

[1] *Disc.* 4.7.41.

the good man from the bad. In view of the fact that Seneca is the first Stoic to talk at length about *voluntas* and *velle*, and that Epictetus is the first to emphasize the term προαίρεσις, and in view of the fact that they are not too different in time, and that both were associates, if not of one another, almost certainly of one another's acquaintances, such as Musonius Rufus, we may conclude that our discussion justifies us in saying that, whatever slight differences there may be between Seneca's *voluntas* and Epictetus' προαίρεσις, they are both attempts to describe the same phenomenon, the moral personality. There is nothing particularly Latin, as Pohlenz holds, about Seneca's position. When Seneca chose the word *voluntas*, he was doubtless governed principally by the fact that from Cicero's time this word had been treated as a partial or complete translation of Greek words like διάνοια. And the word διάνοια, with its senses of both 'thought' and 'intention', expressed exactly the fundamental belief of Chrysippus that the two concepts cannot be dissociated. If one's intention is wrong, one's judgment has somewhere been wrong.

It is generally recognized that the Stoics of the Imperial period are primarily interested in morality in a narrow sense of the word. Hence their tendency to contrast moral acts with other acts and to talk in a somewhat dualistic way about the contrast between the moral personality and the 'flesh' (σαρκίδιον). This emphasis in the school led to an accentuation of the already strong tendency for the masters to be teachers of righteousness or spiritual directors. And those who need to be taught are very obviously those *seeking* virtue, seeking to make themselves better men, wanting to be better men. We can understand why in such a context it appears to scholars like Pohlenz that Seneca is putting a striking new emphasis on willing and effort. But, as we have seen, it is chiefly the language which is new here; if anything else can be said to be new, it is the tendency to restrict the concept of human personality to moral personality in a limited sense of the word 'moral'.

Why did Epictetus choose the word προαίρεσις to express moral personality? He could, as we have seen, have stuck to ἡγεμονικόν. He did so occasionally, but the wider associations of the word were probably too strong. For Epictetus, as for Seneca, and for that matter for Diogenes of Babylon and Antipater of Tarsus, when we are in the strictly moral sphere, what matter are the choices we make, the things we prefer. And προαίρεσις, as in Aristotle, means choice. If we ask why Epictetus did not make use of the more 'intellectualist' words for choice which the Old Stoa could have provided, we can only guess that since he, like Seneca, was a teacher and spiritual director, he preferred, as Bonhoeffer put it, to look at the matter in more voluntarist terms. But let us make no mistake; to use voluntarist emphases is not to posit a faculty called the will, or, fundamentally, to deviate from the teachings of Chrysippus on the relation of willing and knowing.[1] It is most likely that what voluntarist tendencies there are in Seneca (and in Epictetus) are less accountable to a Roman mentality than to the exigencies of spiritual direction. Nevertheless, the appearance of two words, *mens* and *voluntas*, from the time of Cicero to represent in Latin a single Greek concept certainly affected post-Stoic theories of the human person. Whether the introduction of a faculty of the will was a good thing or not is another matter.

A final sidelight on Seneca's position is afforded by his attitude to suicide, which we shall consider in the next chapter. Here we shall argue that Seneca often thinks of suicide as the free act *par excellence* of which man is capable. But how does he relate this free act to the will? Suicide is not an arbitrary act of the will, but rather a brave and noble act resulting from the recognition that one's moral integrity is in danger. It is undertaken after consideration, and is not only heroic but in accordance with reason; in Seneca's view it is the act by means of which we are masters of our own destiny. Although, as we shall see, Seneca tends to think of suicide as a means by which the fool can obtain instant wisdom, it is at the furthest pole from being an act of the will *rather* than of reason. On the contrary, it is the assertion of reason itself as the controlling factor in human destiny.

We must conclude that neither Seneca nor Epictetus has

---

[1] It should be noticed that Seneca also supports Chrysippus against Posidonius on the doctrine of πάθη; cf. *De Ira* 1.8.2–3.

made any significant variation on the doctrine of the Old Stoa relating to willing and knowing. However, the language of προαίρεσις maintained itself; the word προαίρεσις or προαιρετικόν occurs three times in Marcus Aurelius,[1] one of them being a quotation from Epictetus. The sense Marcus gives to the words is identical with the Senecan and Epictetean sense; they represent the ἡγεμονικόν in its role as the moral personality of man. And this moral personality is to be seen in action when we make choices. The solitary occurrence of the word προαίρεσις in the fragments of Zeno already gives us this sense. Why is the sage great, he asks? It is because he is able to achieve the things that he chooses, and that are available to him (τῶν κατὰ προαίρεσιν ὄντων αὐτῷ καὶ προκειμένων).[2] These προκείμενα are clearly what Epictetus and Seneca would call 'the things in our power', or the things that are 'ours'.[3] When Zeno used the word προαίρεσις, everyone would have thought immediately of Aristotle. It is therefore important to recall a text of the *Nicomachean Ethics* in which Aristotle equates τὸ προαιρούμενον with τὸ ἡγούμενον.[4] For ἡγούμενον understand ἡγεμονικόν, and Zeno's first formulation of the Stoic position on knowing and willing becomes clear.

[1] Marcus Aur., 8.56; 11.36; 12.33.

[2] Stob., *Ecl.* 2, p. 99, 14 W. (*SVF* I 216). There is no good reason to deny these words to Zeno himself, or at the least to the Old Stoa.

[3] On Seneca's concept of what is ours see the perceptive article of Thévenaz, 'L'Intériorité chez Sénèque'.

[4] *N.E.* 1113a.

13

SUICIDE

During the whole of classical antiquity suicide was not only common but acceptable and justified by a variety of circumstances.[1] For a number of reasons, some of them good, justification of the practice has been regarded as an especially Stoic phenomenon. In the Roman period at least, a large number of the more famous suicides were Stoics or would-be Stoics; and in the writings of one Roman Stoic in particular suicide seems to be almost the principal concern of the philosopher. Seneca regards suicide as the ultimate justification of man's freedom, perhaps even as the only genuinely free act.

It has been customary to think of Seneca's attitude as more or less identical with that of the older Stoics. At least it has continually been claimed that from the earliest days of the Stoic school the problem of suicide is, as Benz puts it, a problem of free will.[2] The difficulty about this way of looking at the matter, however, is that in the period of the Old Stoa suicide does not seem to have been a problem; it was assumed that it is permissible for a number of reasons. The problem of free will seems to have become involved with that of suicide in part for purely historical reasons, in part because of the habit, widespread in the time of Cicero and later, but not according to our available evidence earlier, of using Plato's *Phaedo* as a jumping-off point for theoretical discussions of suicide. Plato, oddly at first sight, was used both as a justification for suicide and as a means of moderating what can only be described as a suicide cult. Before considering Stoic approaches to the problem, therefore, it will be worth while examining what precisely Plato says. After that we can briefly notice a few comments of Aristotle before looking at the Cynics, the immediate precursors of much of the ethical thought of Zeno.

[1] For suicide in antiquity see Hirzel, 'Der Selbstmord'.
[2] Benz, *Das Todesproblem in der Stoischen Philosophie* 68. Cf. Hirzel, *op. cit.* 282; Zeller, *Phil. d. Griech.* III 1.314; Bonhoeffer, *Die Ethik des Stoikers Epictet* 38; Dyroff, *Die Ethik* 242 note 3.

Plato discusses suicide in two passages, one in the *Phaedo* (61 B–62 D) and the other in the *Laws* (873 CD). According to the *Phaedo* it is unlawful (οὐ θεμιτόν) to take one's own life, because to do so is to arrogate to oneself what belongs by right to the gods. The gods have arranged our human life and it would be wrong to abandon it. But Socrates leaves one point obscure, and this point was at the centre of discussion of the ethics of suicide throughout classical antiquity and beyond, to appear again in the first book of Augustine's *City of God*. It is not unreasonable, Socrates concludes, to hold that a man, who is one of god's possessions, should not kill himself 'until god sends some compulsion upon him, as he sends compulsion on us at present'.[1]

Socrates seems to refer to his own death as self-inflicted, and we may pause to consider in what sense this might be true. The law at Athens specified that the condemned should administer the death penalty to himself by drinking hemlock. This was to place the condemned in the role more normally taken by the executioner. We do not normally regard the executioner as guilty of the death of his victim, though we might notice in passing the old English custom by which the condemned gave his pardon to the headsman in anticipation. There seems, therefore, to be a good case for regarding the acts of Socrates and of all the others condemned under the same law as instances where the material act of self-killing cannot be termed immoral. Are we then to term it suicide? Or are we to confine the term 'suicide' to cases which we believe to be parallel to murder, so that there will be two kinds of self-killing, one of which is immoral while the other is not? This in turn raises the whole question of our use of the word suicide—which is generally condemnatory. It may therefore be relevant to pay some attention to the various ancient attitudes to the killing of the self.

The *Oxford English Dictionary* defines suicide summarily as the act of taking one's own life and as self-murder. This definition

---

[1] The problems underlying Plato's phraseology are observed by Hirzel, *op. cit.* 245 note 2. Cf. also his *Untersuchungen zu Ciceros philosophischen Schriften* 2.300 note 2.

is based on the assumption that in every case where a man takes his own life he is committing a murder; and murder, it should be noted, is a loaded term, denoting a wrongful act of killing. There are enormous problems involved in the definition. Should one make a distinction between suicide (to be thought of as reprehensible) and a justifiable killing of oneself? Could there possibly be an element of guilt in the behaviour of Socrates in that he of all people did not refuse to be his own executioner and thus force the Athenians to take his blood on their own hands? What is the moral difference between preferring death to the committing of an unlawful act (which Socrates would have committed if he had slipped off to Thebes, and which a prisoner might escape if he killed himself to avoid implicating his friends) and committing suicide because one has been supposedly dishonoured, like Lucretia? Or again, if it is morally acceptable to lay down one's life for a friend, is it not acceptable to do so for a principle? Has one the right to value one's ideology above one's life? And if it is right to die for a principle, how do we determine what principles are important enough to warrant it? Most basic of all, perhaps, what if anything is the difference between letting oneself be killed for a principle, like More, the 'modern Socrates', or Cranmer, and killing oneself for a principle, as did the suffragette Emily Davidson who flung herself under the King's horse and the Buddhist monks who more recently immolated themselves in Vietnam? In sum, as the Stoics would have put it, is it ever reasonable to kill oneself? Is there such a thing as a rational way out (εὔλογος ἐξαγωγή)? It is worth while to raise these questions both because they are perennial and because they provide a framework for our estimate of the theories and ideals of the ancient world.

As we have seen, in the *Phaedo* Plato allows a very small loophole in his condemnation of the frequent Greek practice of suicide. One is allowed to take one's own life when god intervenes by bringing an ἀνάγκη. Apparently Plato thought that such occasions would be simple to recognize—a rash estimate, as perhaps he might have foreseen. When we move to the *Laws* there is some strikingly Stoic phraseology. What ought a man to suffer, asks Plato, if he kills that which is most truly his own (οἰκειότατον),[1] that is, if he takes his own life? And the appropriate penalties are prescribed for the unfortunate corpse. But here again the ban on suicide is not absolute. Apparently suicide is permissible at the command of the state (the case of Socrates), if one is under the oppression (ἀναγκασθείς) of incurable pain, or if one is faced helplessly with intolerable shame. These reasons are, in fact, the ones commonly invoked by most Greeks who speak of suicide, and they are mentioned by historical as well as fictional characters as providing grounds for their acts of self-destruction. What Plato is trying to forbid is suicide from mere indolence or from fear of facing the ordinary hardships of life.

In making suicide a matter for legislation, Plato assumes that man must live a life governed by the concept of civic duty. The state is a natural phenomenon and the gods are associated with it. Hence crimes against the state are crimes against the gods, and *vice versa*. When a man kills himself without good reason, or, as Plato would put it, without god bringing some ἀνάγκη to bear on him, he is committing a crime which it is the state's right to punish. For damage is inflicted on the state by the crime itself. Aristotle, we should observe, takes a similar line in the *Nicomachean Ethics* (1138a 9ff.). The man who kills himself in a fit of rage—which Aristotle regards as an inadequate ground—is guilty of a crime for which the state should properly exact the due penalty. However, like Plato, Aristotle also appears to admit that there are some circumstances in which the taking of one's own life is permissible, and perhaps right. Since he takes the trouble to point out that taking one's own life to avoid poverty or desire or pain is unmanly (*N.E.* 1116a 12ff.), or rather cowardly, it seems that he would have subscribed to the normal Greek view that there are some other circumstances in which suicide is permissible.

It is notable that in their remarks on suicide both Plato and Aristotle think in terms of man's duties, the services for which he is to be held responsible as man. Perhaps Plato's use of the term

---

[1] This may be relevant to the Stoic theory of οἰκείωσις. See also the passages about οἰκεῖον and the good in Plato discussed by Brink, 'Plato on the Natural Character of Goodness'.

οἰκειότατον, when he comments how strange it is to kill what is οἰκειότατον to oneself, is an indication of a different conception, a conception that there is something inherently unnatural or perverted in taking one's own life, and that such an act is in itself the work of a fundamentally distorted personality; but if he had this in his mind—and there is no need to deny that he had—we have insufficient evidence to determine what further developments he might have wanted to propound along these lines. When we move on briefly to look at the attitudes of the early Cynics, however, a very different viewpoint emerges. For the Cynics the tenet that virtue is the only good must be understood in its most literal sense. Everything else is not only not good but, if not bad, then totally indifferent. Death is totally indifferent; and the Cynics are prepared to prescribe it as the remedy for any kind of failure to live a rational life. 'Either Reason or the Rope,' remarks Diogenes;[1] and Crates says that if Eros cannot be checked by hunger or the passing of time, the noose will certainly do the trick.[2] The Cynics regarded themselves as independent beings, superior to those who are committed to a life as citizens of a city-state. In the Cynic view such citizens are deprived of their freedom; and freedom, in the sense of a total release from external compulsions, or from duties imposed by any external power whatever, is the mark of the virtuous man. This is what the Cynics mean when they say that they put nothing before freedom.[3]

If, then, the Cynics were to consider that suicide is in some circumstances unjustifiable, they could not and would not have appealed to the Platonic–Aristotelian concept of man as a social being. In fact, as we have noticed, they were ready to advocate suicide for quite trivial reasons—and, as far as their own teaching is concerned, they have little to interest us at present. But since the Stoics were in many areas pupils of the Cynics, it was inevitable that they would discuss suicide with the Cynic view of the person in mind. Any prohibition on suicide could not necessarily be defended on civic grounds alone; the relation of

[1] Literally 'noose', D.L. 6.24.   [2] D.L. 6.86.
[3] D.L. 6.71. For the relationship between Cynicism and Stoicism see pp. 54–80.

suicide to the character, the moral character, of the wise man would have to be considered. If a man cannot live a fully rational life, says the Cynic, then suicide is the best thing for him. But the problem here is obvious: if a man cannot live a rational life, how will he recognize that suicide is his best policy? Would it not seem to follow that suicide could only be reasonably undertaken by the wise man or by the fool who is willing to take wise advice? And since there are very few wise men, there would be very few justified suicides.

We observed earlier that it has often been held that suicide, viewed as the final vindication of human freedom, is a fundamental problem in Stoicism from the beginning. And with the Cynics we have the emphasis again and again on the freedom of the wise man. Can we find in the attitudes of the Cynics this radical view of the nature of suicide? The answer is No. Although the Cynics advocated, and sometimes practised, suicide for a variety of reasons, they did not attach great importance to it. It is indeed a matter of indifference. Of course the wise man is free to commit suicide, just as he is free to do anything else which is not vicious—and it is hard to tell what the Cynics regarded as vicious—but his freedom to take his own life is of no more importance than his other freedoms. Indeed one of the tales told of Diogenes may indicate that he thought the wise man better off alive.[1] Diogenes, when in considerable pain, was asked why he did not commit suicide. His answer was that it is appropriate for the wise to live—they have something better to do than commit suicide; fools, however, are better dead. It is 'Either Reason or the Rope' again. So far from suicide being the ultimate act of freedom, it is hardly worth wasting a moment's thought on.

It is now time to consider the views of the early Stoics themselves; and having considered the evidence for their views, we can look at the evidence of their lives, for, according to the doxographers, Zeno, Cleanthes and Antipater of Tarsus all committed suicide. First of all we should notice that the concept of suicide as the ultimately free act is lacking. In none of the fragments collected by von Arnim does the word freedom occur

---

[1] Aelian, *V.H.* 10.11.

in this context.[1] The Stoics realized that suicide is a possibility for man; they accepted the convention of Greek society on this point without query. They never speak of any view which would rule out taking one's own life in any circumstances. What they are interested in is when it is reasonable (εὔλογον) to commit suicide. The act itself, like all other acts in the Stoic world, is unimportant; what matters is the intention. The intention must be rational. Hence we find Diogenes Laertius recounting the Stoic doctrine by saying that they consider that a man takes his own life rationally for one of the following reasons: on behalf of his country, or his friends, or if he is afflicted by intolerable pain or an incurable disease.[2] It is obvious that these reasons are of two kinds. Death may be self-inflicted either for the sake of somebody else or, under special circumstances, for the sake of oneself. The different nature of these justifications did not invariably escape the later Stoics, as we shall point out, but the earlier members of the school did not discriminate in detail.

An immediate problem arises with the attempt to explain when and under what circumstances it is justifiable to take one's own life. Does not the possibility of committing suicide because of pain make it likely that many men would feel justified in killing themselves on occasions when the wise man would think it right to survive? Might it not seem that only the wise man could be sure about when it is justifiable to commit suicide, since he alone will invariably recognize what is natural, and what is natural provides the basis for a proper decision to die?[3] This would lead to a position opposite to that ascribed to Diogenes the Cynic by Aelian. According to Diogenes the wise man will not be bothered to kill himself, while, according to the Stoics, if anyone else decides to do so he cannot be sure that his action is natural, let alone moral. Diogenes Laertius, we recall, only speaks of the occasions when the wise man may commit suicide. It is not quite clear how far the Stoics are aware of problems of this kind, but there are indications that

[1] *SVF* III 757–68.
[2] D.L. 7.130 (*SVF* III 757). Similar lists are given elsewhere, e.g. *SVF* II 768.
[3] Cic., *De Fin.* 3.60 (*SVF* III 763), Plut., *SR* 1042 D (*SVF* III 759).

Chrysippus at least gave them attention. According to the testimony of both Cicero and Plutarch,[1] the latter of whom ascribes the view to Chrysippus himself, the Stoics argued that there are occasions when the wise man will commit suicide; indeed it will be an appropriate act (καθῆκον). Conversely there will be occasions when the fool, despite his wretched condition, should remain alive. The idea that the wise man is able on occasion to reason in favour of a self-inflicted death should now be familiar; but the other proposition, that the fool, despite his condition, ought sometimes to remain alive, is of more interest. It is the exact opposite of the Cynic thesis that, if you cannot be reasonable, you might as well be dead. Chrysippus says that it may be appropriate (καθῆκον) for the fool to remain alive. Why should this be so? Could it not be because the fool cannot be sure of formulating a rational justification to take his life? Certainly all the acts of the fool are, in the eyes of the Stoic, morally bad. His character is vicious, and, as Chrysippus puts it, vice has no connection with our having to die.[2]

According to our passage of Diogenes Laertius the wise man may commit suicide under certain circumstances. No passage from the Old Stoa tells us specifically when the fool should do so; we only have Cicero's general statement that suicide is to be undertaken when his life is dominated, or will probably be dominated, by what is unnatural. Although in one passage Plutarch observes that the Stoics restrain many of the foolish from suicide—the implication being that there are some of the foolish whom they do not restrain[3]—he also quotes Chrysippus' own words that the bad ought to remain alive.[4] A number of other passages on this subject present a philological difficulty. It is clear that Chrysippus' words at one point in his discussion of suicide were to the effect that *sometimes* the wise man should kill himself and the fool remain alive.[5] It is not entirely clear whether he meant the word 'sometimes' to apply to the fool as well

---

[1] Cic., *De Fin.* 3.60 (*SVF* III 763); Plut., *SR* 1042 D (*SVF* III 759).

[2] Plut., *SR* 1039 D (*SVF* III 761).

[3] Plut., *CN* 1063 D (*SVF* III 759). Cf. *SR* 1060 CD (*SVF* III 146).

[4] Plut., *SR* 1039 D (*SVF* III 761).

[5] Stob., *Ecl.* 2.110.9 W. (φασὶ δέ ποτε τὴν ἐξαγωγὴν etc.). Cic., *De Fin.* 3.60 (et sapientis esse *aliquando* officium etc.).

as to the wise man. Does he mean, 'Sometimes the wise man should die and sometimes (but not always) the fool should live'? Or does he mean, 'Sometimes the wise man should die, but the fool should always live'? An absolute decision on the point is impossible, but in view of Plutarch's claim to quote Chrysippus directly to the effect that fools should remain alive,[1] it seems not unreasonable to suggest that Chrysippus at least was concerned about whether the fool is able to justify a self-inflicted death. Plutarch again purports to be quoting Chrysippus' own words when he says that it is profitable (λυσιτελεῖ) for the fool to live rather than to die even if he is not going to become wise.[2]

The passage on which scholars have relied to argue what now looks an unlikely thesis, that suicide, viewed as a problem of human freedom, was central and basic to Stoicism from the beginning, is also from Plutarch.[3] The Stoics were in the habit of arguing that the wise man is as happy as the gods because he is virtuous; and happiness is virtue.[4] To the objection that the gods must be happier because they do not suffer illness and mutilations of the body Chrysippus apparently replied that this is irrelevant, because the wise man may take his own life and thus evade these unbearable human troubles. This statement, however, should not be read in isolation. Clearly Chrysippus did not mean that any illness would justify the wise man's self-inflicted death. Only an illness which threatened his virtue in some way would be relevant. It might be objected to this that on Stoic theory there should be no such illnesses; but that is not our present concern. What we are concerned with is whether this passage justifies talking about suicide as the ultimate act of freedom. Clearly Chrysippus is not thinking of it in that kind of context at all. For the wise man suicide is a way out to be taken if necessary; it is a useful right that men have. But its use is in a sense incidental. It is not the centre of the wise man's consciousness. Many wise men would presumably live without making use of their privilege. Far from being at the centre of Old Stoic ethical theory, suicide is, as it were, mentioned in

---

[1] Plut., *SR* 1039D (*SVF* III 761).   [2] Plut., *SR* 1042A (*SVF* III 760).
[3] Plut., *CN* 1076B.   [4] *SVF* III 245–54.

passing. It is not being the arbiter of one's own life and death which makes the wise man the equal of the gods; it is his moral intention.

It is possible that the views of the early Stoics on the rights and wrongs of suicide were not entirely similar. That is something on which any number of guesses can be made, but the evidence is largely lacking. All that we have to support an objection that perhaps Chrysippus did not treat suicide as a basic problem of human freedom, while Zeno and Cleanthes did, is the fact that, according to the doxographers, Zeno and Cleanthes themselves committed suicide while Chrysippus did not. Most of the theory we have considered so far is traceable to Chrysippus; and if it is correct that Chrysippus thought that normally at least only the wise man may take his own life, this may be the reason why he did not take his own. He did not regard himself as a wise man.

Here an interesting query arises. Chrysippus might have accepted the suicides of Zeno and Cleanthes on the ground that they were wise men, but they did not apparently regard themselves as such. Nevertheless, they committed suicide. Does this mean that Zeno and Cleanthes held a view more like that of the Cynics that anybody can commit suicide if he wishes? The interpretation is possible but most unlikely. We should at this point consider the death of Zeno himself—or at least the account of it.[1] At the age of seventy-two Zeno was one day coming out of his school when he tripped over and broke his toe (or perhaps his finger). He struck the ground with his hand, quoted the words of the *Niobe*, 'I am coming; why do you call me?', and killed himself forthwith. The incident may be dismissed as invention, but there is no reason to do so. If we accept it as an account of what happened, is it possible to see why it happened? There is certainly the possibility that Zeno, to use the modern phrase, killed himself while the balance of his mind was disturbed. But there is no reason for thinking that, if he had not tripped and broken his toe, he would have killed himself in any case. One of the authorities says that he was on his way to the Assembly. There is little doubt that Zeno read the acci-

---

[1] *SVF* I 288; for Cleanthes see D.L. 7.176 (*SVF* I 474).

dent as a divine call; hence the quotation from the *Niobe*. He had, he thought, received the signal to depart. Now it may seem to us, as it has seemed to many since antiquity, that Zeno's action was grotesque, but it looks like a grotesque parody of what happened to say, as is often said, that Zeno killed himself *because* he broke his toe. The truth is more probably that he thought he had received a sign that his hour had come. Now was the fated moment for death—and a curious muffled echo of the *Phaedo* comes to our minds.

The suggestion is that Zeno believed himself to be like Socrates in holding that god gives the word for our departure. We can hardly say that god brought an ἀνάγκη on Zeno; but rightly or wrongly Zeno thought he had received his marching orders. The theme that god may send such orders to the individual by *divina auctoritas* recurs even in Augustine at the far end of classical antiquity. To the objection that Zeno seemed to have no particular reason for death at that moment, Zeno himself would probably have thought an allusion to his completed philosophical work an adequate reply.

There is a more puzzling matter which cannot be passed over. We have argued that Chrysippus may have recognized a problem about how to justify the suicide of the foolish. We have no reason to believe that Zeno thought of himself as wise. Does this mean that in his view suicide is more widely justifiable for the foolish? If they are foolish, how can they tell when it is permissible? What can be deduced about Zeno's attitude from his own actions? It seems that Zeno must have held that, while the wise man is himself the judge of when it is right to live or to die, the fool—and that is most of us—may be enlightened as to the proper moment for departure by some direct intervention of providence. Whether Chrysippus allowed this way of escape for the foolish—and we should note that it is a way which makes every man his own priest—is not clear. Perhaps the ambiguities in Plutarch's account indicate that he did, and there is no doubt that later Stoics were in this matter true disciples of Zeno. Yet it is at the least surprising that no direct trace of this theory appears in the ancient evidence for Chrysippus. But whether Chrysippus differed from Zeno at this point or not, there is no evidence that either of them paid much attention to the allegedly fundamental relation between theories of suicide and doctrines about the freedom of the will.

When we enquire into the theories of the so-called Middle Stoa we are up against different kinds of problem about evidence. It is usually impossible to be sure whose doctrines Cicero is presenting unless he mentions his sources by name; but at least we can enquire whether what he says about suicide is in opposition to theories current in the earliest days of the Stoic school. If the views of Ciceronian Stoics differ from those of Zeno and Chrysippus, we may ascribe the difference to the work of Panaetius or Posidonius. But in fact there is nothing substantially new. There are passages from the *Tusculans* and the *De Officiis* which chime in very well with what we have argued the older Stoics taught. It is true that the *Tusculans* are by no means of entirely Stoic inspiration. The influence of Platonism is considerable, but the striking thing from our point of view is that the apparently Platonic ideas used do not conflict with the Stoic view. Cicero seems to have regarded the two as complementary.

There is a passage of the *Tusculans* in which Cicero describes the death of Socrates.[1] It is followed by an account of the end of Cato of Utica, the Stoic 'martyr'. The connection between the two deaths seemed obvious to Cicero, and Cato, if we believe Plutarch, himself thought that Socrates' death was in some sense a model for his own. Before committing suicide he not only discussed the Stoic paradox that only the good man is free while the foolish are slaves; he also read most of the *Phaedo*.[2] Cicero remarks strikingly that Cato's manner of death showed that he was delighted to find a reason to die. For, he continues—and he obviously has the *Phaedo* in mind—the god within us forbids us to depart without his command, and god had now given to Cato, as previously to Socrates, a proper reason to die (*causam iustam*).

In a later section of the *Tusculans* the same idea recurs, though Cato is not mentioned.[3] We can depart from life when a

[1] *Tusc. Disp.* 1.71–5. [2] Plut., *Cato* 67–8.
[3] *Tusc. Disp.* 1.118.

message to do so has been received from god. We should do so joyfully. Death is a haven and refuge prepared for us. We should compare a passage from the *Somnium Scipionis* where the question is again, as in the *Phaedo*, Why not die at once?[1] The answer is also similar. Until god permits, we must continue our terrestrial duties. The passage contains language which will recur. The entrance (to death) cannot be open until the appropriate moment. Now it may be objected that the whole context here is Platonic, or at least Posidonian, but is it far from an interpretation of the theory and practice of the Old Stoa? Certainly Cato found a synthesis of Platonism and Stoicism acceptable, and if we are right in thinking that Zeno held and acted upon the belief that at least the foolish have to await a sign from the gods before they can justifiably take their own lives, then Cato has followed his master's precepts admirably.

We should consider a further passage from the *De Officiis*.[2] Again the subject is Cato, but here we are dealing with Cicero's view of Cato rather than with Cato's view of himself. Cicero's description is so laudatory that it may be said that he is already building the legend of Cato the Sage. On similar occasions, says Cicero, one man ought to kill himself while another ought not. Cato's situation after the triumph of Caesar was different from that of other people. His character was marked by extraordinary dignity (*incredibilem gravitatem*), and he had strengthened that dignity with unceasing consistency. This looks like the description of the Stoic wise man, and, if that is what Cicero intended, he is justifying Cato's death solely on the ground that Cato was wise. For the decision of the wise man to take his own life is *ipso facto* a reasonable decision.

Briefly, then, we say that in Cicero's Stoic treatises and in his comments about the Stoic Cato there is no significant variation on what the early Stoics taught about suicide; and as in the earlier Stoics, so in Cicero, the matter is not in the forefront of the philosophical stage. Indeed in Cicero, as in Chrysippus, it is still so far from being central that no apparent effort is made to examine in any further detail any of the traditional grounds which will justify the suicide of the wise man. When we move

---

[1] *De Rep.* 6.15–16. [2] *De Off.* 1.112.

from Cicero to Seneca, however, at least one difference will be obvious from the outset. For Seneca suicide is certainly important and a matter for continual thought. The circumstances of his time and his own political situation made it inevitable that this should be so. What we must consider, therefore, is whether we are dealing with a new theory of suicide, or whether it is a matter of more continual repetition of traditional doctrine.

In view of Seneca's obsession with the propriety of taking one's own life, it is astounding that the tradition, backed by a spurious correspondence, that he was a Christian sympathizer, could ever have developed.[1] Anyone who views his attitude even in terms of the Stoic tradition will find it startling. If we contrast what Seneca says about the death of Cato with what is said by Cicero, we immediately notice that any direct reference to god's giving a particular sign to indicate the right moment for suicide is excluded. Instead of stressing the Socratic and in our view early Stoic idea that, although the wise man has the authority to take his own life, a sign from heaven will be the required sign for most of us, Seneca stresses the right to suicide in general. Despite the failure of all worldly hopes Cato has the wide road to freedom open to him;[2] he only has to take his own life. His freedom is a part of the providential ordering of the universe. In one of his *Moral Epistles* Seneca mentions Cato again in very similar language.[3] He is the upright man, who by his death keeps virtue before the eyes of mankind. And despite the absence of any suggestion that god provided a particular sign, Seneca still compares Cato with Socrates.

There is no need to suggest that Seneca did not believe that a man might see in particular circumstances god's chosen moment for him to depart; but it is a fact that despite the earlier tradition on this matter he chooses not to stress it. This is particularly striking since he is aware of the importance of the case of Socrates in the tradition, and since in a famous passage he alludes to what must be a distorted version of the Platonic theory about the ἀνάγκη that is a sign indicating death. Quoting Epicurus, he remarks to Lucilius, 'It is hard to live under

[1] Aug., *Ep.* 153.4; Jerome, *De Viris Illustribus* 12.
[2] Seneca, *De Prov.* 2.9–10.   [3] *Ep.* 71.8–16; cf. 13.14; 24.6–8.

constraint, but there is no constraint to live under constraint (*Malum est in necessitate vivere, sed in necessitate vivere necessitas nulla est*).' And the familiar phrases follow. Many gates to liberty lie open everywhere; they are short and easy. Let us thank god that no one can be held in life; we can trample our constraints down.[1] Other passages are similar: above all be aware that nothing holds you against your will; the way out is open; if you do not want to fight, you can fly.[2] If you want to get rid of vice, you must retire from places where there are examples of vice. Cross over to the better people. Live with the Catos, with Laelius and Tubero. If you like to live with Greeks, join Socrates and Zeno. Socrates will teach you to die if necessity arise, Zeno before it arises.[3] We notice here the tradition that Zeno's suicide was an arbitrary act of decision, unconnected with external pressures or signs. That is the Zeno Seneca would like to follow; it is not, we suggest, the Zeno of history.

Think about death, Seneca challenges the long-suffering Lucilius. The man who says this bids you think about freedom.[4] Scipio Aemilianus breathes his last in the embrace of freedom.[5] The seventieth letter, which is virtually a paean to suicide, opens up the topic with the ordinarily heroic statement that the wise man will live as long as he ought, not as long as he can;[6] but Seneca continues by saying that the wise man will calculate the possibility of suicide long before he is under extreme constraint. It is effeminate to say 'While there is life there is hope'. It does not matter how one kills oneself—a German choked himself with a lavatory sponge—as long as one dies well. A self-inflicted death is the assertion of human freedom.

We have argued that Seneca's identification of suicide as a free act, perhaps as the supremely free act, is at the very least a new emphasis in Stoicism, and that his neglect of the requirement of the divine call is a radical departure. Naturally Seneca condemns those who oppose the general right to suicide;[7] that would be to bar the path to freedom, and, it might be correctly

---

[1] *Ep.* 12.10.
[2] *De Prov.* 6.7.
[3] *Ep.* 104.21.
[4] *Ep.* 26.10.
[5] *Ep.* 66.13.
[6] *Ep.* 70.5; cf. 77.15–16.
[7] *Ep.* 70.14–15.

maintained, any Stoic would have agreed with Seneca's conclusions, if not with his methods of reaching them. But to allow suicide in certain circumstances is one thing, to exalt it is quite another. And to exalt it as the act *par excellence* of the free man does not square, despite the commentators, with early Stoic accounts of the nature of freedom. The man who kills himself has committed his last free act, if it is a free act. And we should notice that people often resort to suicide to avoid *ultimae necessitates*.[1] It is not clear how Seneca can be justified in regarding his own suicide, and others of a similar kind at the orders of the Emperor, as entirely free acts. As Tacitus observes of one imperial victim, his freedom consisted only in the free choice of the means of death.[2] It is true that Seneca could say that under the Emperors people committed suicide to avoid the possibility of being forced into vice, but why is killing oneself in such circumstances so much superior, and apparently freer, than allowing oneself to be killed? It is certain that it may be more dignified, but Seneca does not demonstrate adequately why it is more of a free act. Could it be that he assimilates freedom too much to pride, dignity and the traditional greatness of soul? Or is it that he somewhat legalistically thinks of the act of self-destruction as morally superior to the passion of being put to death?

In a traditionally Stoic context, to think of suicide as the free act *par excellence* is rather odd. The early Stoics defined freedom as the opportunity for personal action; slavery is the deprivation of this power.[3] But all the acts of the wise man are free. If he chooses suicide, that is free like the rest; there is nothing special about it. Seneca, on the other hand, comes very close to arguing that suicide itself makes one a free man. Of course it does this in so far as it frees a man from constraint, but this seems to be a means of taking away the possibility of future moral action as well as of saving the present situation. Seneca seems to regard freedom not so much as the opportunity to act as a state in which one cannot be forced to act. His emphasis on suicide is an emphasis on a negative concept of freedom which is almost

[1] *Ep.* 17.9.   [2] Tac., *Ann.* 11.3; cf. Hirzel, *op. cit.* 245–6.
[3] D.L. 7.122.

totally absent among the early Stoics. This negative concept of
freedom is linked with an obsession with the possible means by
which freedom can be attained. A passage like the following
from the *De Ira* overrates the relevance of suicide in a way which
would have been unintelligible to Chrysippus: 'In any kind of
servitude the way lies open to liberty. If the soul is sick and because of its imperfection unhappy, a man may end its sorrows
and at the same time himself...In whatever direction you
may turn your eyes, there lies the means to end your woes. See
you that precipice? Down that is the way to liberty. See you
that sea, that river, that well? There sits liberty at the bottom.
See you that tree, stunted, blighted and barren? Yet from its
branches hangs liberty. See you that throat of yours, your
gullet, your heart? They are ways of escape from servitude. Are
the ways of egress I show you too toilsome, do you require too
much courage and strength? Do you ask what is the highway
to liberty? Any vein in your body' (trans. Sevenster).[1]

It seems that not only is the choice of suicide open to everyone, it is also peculiarly ennobling—a wholly novel concept for
a Stoic. Apparently the fool can be transmuted into a sage by a
well-judged and opportune death. Here indeed is the concept
of an *ambitiosa mors*.[2] In view of this Seneca's occasional reversals
to a more traditional view that suicide should not be lightly
undertaken seem almost in contradiction to his real opinion.
Some people, he complains, take their own lives for cowardly
reasons, such as the avoidance of arrest, others out of mere
boredom.[3] It is wrong to hate life too much.[4] The remark gives
him away; his own view is based on a hatred of life, and the
older theory of suicide, which has nothing to do with such
hatred, only pulls him up short when he begins to wonder about
his own motivation. Fundamentally Seneca's wise man is in
love with death. He is looking out for a tolerable pretext to die.
Seneca has abandoned the old view which made life and death
matters of indifference. In spite of his formal rejection of the
death-wish (*libido moriendi*) in his twenty-fourth letter, we must

---

[1] *De Ira* 3.15.3–4.   [2] Tac., *Agr.* 42.
[3] *Ep.* 4.4; *Tranq. An.* 2.15; *Ep.* 24.22.
[4] *Ep.* 24.24.

still evaluate his very need to reject it.[1] Perhaps at times he recognizes it as un-Stoic, but these times are few.

In many circumstances death is highly desirable, but there are restraining factors. The wise man may remain alive for the sake of his wife and friends.[2] Sometimes it is a proof of nobility to live even when circumstances are harsh. But when talking in this way, when he is finding reasons not to commit suicide, Seneca is in a mood far from that of the older members of his school. It might be said that he is only adapting their teaching to a new world where suicide has become a cult. There would be a measure of truth in this, but, when such passages are placed alongside the many others which glorify suicide as the superb act of freedom, it is not hard to determine where Seneca's deepest loyalties lie. Zeno and Chrysippus would have felt no need to justify their behaviour in not committing suicide. Still less would they think that, if the wise man remained alive when there was an excuse for death, he was 'indulging his honourable emotions'. The act would be either reasonable—and hence justified—or not. In brief, then, we may say of Seneca that the judgment recently passed by Sevenster is basically correct. 'Who is it', asks Sevenster, 'who gives us freedom (freedom to die), that gift for which men may be grateful? A God who in this way, and at a particular time, shows how much he cares for man? Or is this freedom incorporated in the natural order of things, so that man can, whenever he desires, make use of the possibilities embodied in nature? I believe that Seneca intended the latter.'[3] This may be a slight overstatement, doing a little less than justice to Seneca's occasional words of caution, but in essence it corresponds to the texts.

When we leave Seneca for Epictetus, however, we find that the pendulum has more or less swung back again. Epictetus is also considerably concerned with death, but his intention is again and again to emphasize its indifference.[4] Normally he is concerned with death in general rather than with taking one's

---

[1] *Ep.* 24.25. In *Ep.* 117.22–3 Seneca argues that longing for death is disgraceful. If one wants to die, one may die! It is the *longing* that is disgraceful.

[2] *Ep.* 104.3–4.   [3] Sevenster, *Paul and Seneca* 58.

[4] *Disc.* 2.1.17; 2.5.14; 2.6.8; 2.19.13; 3.22.33; 3.26.4.

own life, but the problem of suicide occurs in his writings and his view marks a return to older paths after Seneca's exoticism. One must not give up one's life irrationally or out of lack of endurance, or for some trivial reason. Perhaps Seneca might have said it. But for Epictetus the reason is that god does not wish this. God gives the signal to retreat, just as he gave it to Socrates.[1] If he does not give one enough to eat, obviously that is the signal for death.[2] Here Epictetus is somewhat ambiguous on an important point. It is not clear whether he is saying that in such circumstances the wise man anticipates his coming death or merely accepts it. The matter has some importance for the ethics of suicide, for in such cases the older Stoics would probably have held suicide to be reasonable, while later Marcus Aurelius sometimes had doubts. The underlying issue is whether killing oneself, that is, taking full responsibility for one's own death, is the same kind of act if done in anticipation of external hardship and probable death as it would be if done for one's friends or country or ideals. The early Stoics did not distinguish; yet perhaps distinctions should be made. In general Epictetus compares life to a game where moral principles are the rules. If one is ordered to break a rule, to transgress a moral principle, then one ceases to play, one gives up one's life.[3] Whether death is self-inflicted is immaterial. But the mere imposition of hardship is not normally a justification for death; exile to Gyara is a much overrated misfortune.[4] At the worst it will lead to death, which is a matter of indifference. Threats against one's person are made against the body; if a man worries about them he is the slave of his body. This is the nearest Epictetus comes to Seneca's views about suicide and freedom. The free man, for Epictetus, is not ultimately concerned with his physical fate. The distance from Seneca is immense.

There are a few passages where Epictetus seems to forget his emphasis that suicide must be at god's command, in favour of something like the Cynic view that, if life becomes unbearable,

[1] *Ep.* 1.29.29; cf. 1.9.16. For the relationship between Epictetus and Plato see Jagu, *Epictète et Platon*, and Schweingruber, 'Sokrates und Epiktet'.
[2] *Ep.* 3.26.29.   [3] *Disc.* 4.7.31.
[4] *Disc.* 3.24.101; cf. 1.25.20; 2.6.22.

one simply gives up. If there is too much smoke in the house, he says, then walk out.[1] Death is the harbour for all men—the words echo those of Cicero. But there is no exaltation. Even when Epictetus comes nearest to Seneca in neglecting to mention god's signal to depart—and it is not entirely clear how this is to be read—he is wholly free from the exaggerated cult of suicide, the worship of death as the free act *par excellence* that the letters to Lucilius so repeatedly promote. In general Bonhoeffer was right when he said that for Epictetus suicide becomes permissible in cases of physical suffering only when that suffering is at its most extreme.[2] That is perhaps orthodox Stoicism, but there is a curious passage in the first book of the *Discourses* which finds no parallel in the Old Stoa. Rather it appears as a perversion of the older and commonplace view that a man may die for his principles.[3] There was an athlete suffering from a disease which necessitated the removal of his genitals if he were to recover. He refused the treatment and died. Did he die as an athlete or as a philosopher, someone asks Epictetus? As a man, comes the reply, a man who has won fame and recognition as an Olympic victor. He acted according to his character (κατὰ πρόσωπον). The term πρόσωπον here seems to mean something like a mask of office, which is presented to the public.[4] Part of Epictetus' own mask as a philosopher is his beard. If someone says 'Shave it off or I will kill you', he prefers to die. Doubtless this attitude arises from the view that life and death are matters of indifference; but why should Epictetus imagine that the command to shave off his beard is god's signal that it is time to die? It seems again to be a matter of pride. The Stoic can never be humble; that would be an affront to his dignity as a free man. We have met the phenomenon before. It smacks of the theatricality which was both part of the legacy of Cynicism to Stoicism and, more widely, an unexamined premiss of most ancient conceptions of nobility.

The problem of nobility arises again with Marcus Aurelius,

---

[1] *Disc.* 4.10.27.   [2] Bonhoeffer, *op. cit.* 33.
[3] 1.2.25 ff.
[4] For πρόσωπον cf. Panaetius in Cic., *De Off.* 1.107 ff. The Aristotelian Greatness of Soul (μεγαλοψυχία) was also emphasized by Panaetius. See e.g. Pohlenz, *Die Stoa* 2.101.

the last of the Stoics and the devoted reader of Epictetus. But the views of Marcus are more varied than those of his predecessor; they sum up most of the inconsistencies on the subject of suicide we have traced in the Stoic school. On the one hand Marcus will quote Epictetus: if there is too much smoke, get out of the house; death is the way out of an excess of trouble.[1] On the other hand there are the Epicurean passages where the Emperor argues that, if pain is severe enough, it leads to death and is therefore insignificant, while if it is less severe it can be borne.[2] If the logic of this had been worked out, Marcus would have found himself arguing against the traditional Stoic thesis that death is a permissible way out in certain kinds of illness. Again in one passage Marcus follows the old Cynic view that if a man cannot live reasonably he ought to kill himself; he has been disowned by Reason.[3] This reminds us of Diogenes' tag, Reason or the Rope. Elsewhere, however, Marcus holds that suicide is only permissible after proper consideration of the specific and detailed circumstances of one's life.[4] We should not die like the Christians out of sheer obstinacy (what did Marcus think of Epictetus' willingness to die for his beard?), but after reasoning the thing out in a dignified manner, without display (ἀτραγῴδως). If any general feeling—the word is used advisedly —of Marcus on the problem can be recognized, perhaps ἀτραγῴδως sums it up. Suicide should be undertaken simply and with that due sense of moderation which is the mark of the free man.[5] It is a deed requiring the highest self-respect; we should, as he puts it, depart εὐμενής.[6] Death is the culmination of a gracious life. Clearly in all this there is little consistency, except in so far as suicide is essentially a matter of indifference which, if performed, should be performed properly. Any hope that Marcus' varying comments might indicate a critique or reformulation of Stoic theories of suicide is doomed to disappointment. For Marcus moral behaviour is a kind of dignified deportment. The long-standing association of suicide with pride, almost explicit in

[1] *Med.* 5.29; cf. 8.47; 10.8.
[2] *Med.* 7.33; 7.64. Cf. Epicurus in Plut., *De Poet. Aud.* 36B (fr. 447 Usener). See Farquharson, *The Meditations of Marcus Aurelius* 2.737.
[3] *Med.* 10.32.   [4] *Med.* 11.3.
[5] *Med.* 10.8.   [6] *Med.* 8.47.

Epictetus, is here displayed at its most naked. It is hard not to admire it and pity it at the same time.

There is, we should conclude, no single Stoic theory of suicide, though we can recognize a number of largely unformulated assumptions common to many of the Stoics. If we want even a partial critique of them, we must go outside the school. As in many other areas, it is Augustine who provides some of the most interesting comment on ancient attitudes to suicide. Chapters sixteen to twenty-seven of the first book of the *City of God* are devoted to this problem. The matter was important to Christians of the time. Suicide was in general forbidden on the authority of Holy Writ; but exceptions were made. Jerome thinks that girls can commit suicide to preserve their virginity.[1] Ambrose holds the same view,[2] and it is mentioned by Augustine.

The discussion of suicide in the *City of God* arises from the fact that nuns had been raped during the sack of Rome. Some had killed themselves rather than suffer. In his discussion of the matter Augustine touches upon one of the traditional features of suicide, its association with pride. The suicide of Lucretia is condemned; she was *nimium laudis avara*. So much for one's πρόσωπον or *dignitas* in the Roman or Stoic sense. On the specific issue of fear for one's virginity Augustine evades a final answer. He wants to say—and at times says—that in no circumstances is it right to take one's own life. Why should one kill oneself because someone else might sin? But he knows that such well-meaning suicides are afforded *cultus* as saints. I do not dare to judge anything rashly about them, he comments. Elsewhere he says that it is natural to pardon them; but to be pardoned entails to have sinned.

Augustine discusses cases where ancient practice and Stoic philosophy prescribed suicide as a release from hardship or indignity.[3] He is well aware that willingness to suffer indignities, to be apparently humiliated in public, is the mark of the Christian. It distinguishes him from the Stoic and Platonic wise man. But in his treatment of suicide Augustine does not provide a

[1] Jerome, *Comm. on Jonah* 1; cf. *Adv. Iovin.* 1.41.
[2] *De Virg.* 3.7.32.
[3] Cf. his further discussion in 19.4, where Cato is found wanting again.

complete scrutiny of Stoic practice. Can a man commit suicide for his family or his friends? Augustine's answer is presumably No, but he does not enlarge on this side of the problem. Perhaps one of his comments on those who killed themselves for their Christian virginity would have helped him. Were these people, he wonders, summoned to die by *divina auctoritas*? The echo of the *Phaedo*, of Zeno, of Cato and of Epictetus is plain. The problem of how to recognize that the authority is divine has not been resolved.

14

THE UNITY OF THE PERSON

We have argued in a previous chapter that it was the intention of Chrysippus to explain human acts, feelings and emotions as activities of the total individual, and that with this in view he spoke of walking, or of feeling angry, as different states of the ἡγεμονικόν.[1] But, although the tendency of the Old Stoa can thus be seen as explaining human activity as psychosomatic activity, it did not bring them much nearer to an explanation of the nature of the human person itself, as distinct from its activities. This curious state of affairs, this unresolved paradox at the heart of the system from the beginning, almost certainly helped promote the ultimate collapse of Chrysippus' psychosomatic thesis of activity and its replacement by various Platonisms or quasi-Platonisms. The fact is that Chrysippus did not go far enough for his own purposes in exorcizing the talk of soul and body which he had inherited from earlier philosophers.

The problem is perhaps best approached if we consider the doctrine of the Old Stoa on the subject of death. It was not a controversial doctrine in the school. The Stoics held that at death the material soul is separated from the material body;[2] indeed they were prepared to define death itself, almost in the manner of Plato's *Phaedo*, as the separation of the soul from the body.[3] Furthermore the majority of the school held that the separate material souls continue to exist apart from the body for varying periods of time, though none outlasts the periodic destructions of the world by fire, into which they are subsumed. Only Panaetius, who curiously enough began the abandonment of Chrysippus' monistic psychology, took what might seem to have been an intelligible step for Chrysippus himself, and denied that the soul survives its separation from the body in any mode whatsoever.[4]

[1] See above, pp. 22–36.   [2] *SVF* I 145.
[3] Plut., *SR* 1052 c (*SVF* II 604); cf. Alex. Aphr., *De An. Mant.* p. 117, 21 Bruns (*SVF* II 792).   [4] Cic., *Tusc.* 1.79.

When the early Stoics talk about the soul surviving until the destruction of the world by fire, it is not easy to grasp what they mean. Obviously they do not mean that the soul can carry on all its normal activities, that is, the activities of the living person, in the period between death and the general conflagration. At death, they naturally tell us, there is a 'complete slackening' of our powers of sense perception.[1] In fact, of the eight 'parts' of the soul of which the majority of the orthodox speak,[2] namely the five senses, voice, the reproductive powers and the ἡγεμονικόν, it is clear that only the ἡγεμονικόν, now fixed in a particular condition which depends on the state of the person at death, will survive. In other words, when the Stoics speak of the survival, albeit limited, of the soul, they mean the survival of the ἡγεμονικόν in a certain condition. That on occasions, from the beginning down to the time of Marcus Aurelius, the school was prepared to use the term 'soul' when ἡγεμονικόν was meant, in other words to identify the terms which elsewhere they wished to distinguish, has been clearly demonstrated by Bonhoeffer.[3] It should, however, be noticed at this point that the doxographical evidence which suggests that the Old Stoics sometimes used the term λογιστικόν instead of ἡγεμονικόν for this surviving part is at the least misleading. It seems improbable that the early Stoics spoke of a λογιστικόν. It is true that Diogenes Laertius uses it[4]—he also uses διανοητικόν[5] —where normally ἡγεμονικόν would be found, but Diogenes is writing after the time of Posidonius, who certainly used λογιστικόν in the manner of Plato for the highest human faculty. The original situation about terminology is perhaps given away by Alexander of Aphrodisias,[6] who, after speaking of the rational (λογιστικόν) aspect of the soul, adds that it is properly called the ἡγεμονικόν (ὃ καὶ ἰδίως ἡγεμονικὸν καλεῖται). The reason why it would be misleading to say that the rational aspect of the soul alone survives the separation from the body is that reasoning is not the only activity of the ἡγεμονικόν. At

---

[1] Cf. Aëtius, *Plac.* 5.24 (*SVF* II 767).

[2] D.L. 7.110 (*SVF* II 828); cf. *SVF* II 830, 831 etc.

[3] Bonhoeffer, *Epictet und die Stoa* 105–12.

[4] D.L. 7.110 (*SVF* II 828).   [5] D.L. 7.157 (*SVF* II 828).

[6] Alex. Aphr., *De An.* p. 98, 24 Bruns (*SVF* II 839).

death the ἡγεμονικόν, with all its sins upon it, is what survives. It is a character in a certain state. Clearly if the ἡγεμονικά were all alike, all purely rational faculties, there would have been no point to the dispute between Cleanthes and Chrysippus as to whether all souls (ἡγεμονικά) survive until the conflagration, or whether only the souls of the wise can exist for such an extended period of time.[1]

It can at least be said for Chrysippus' theory that the soul, or ἡγεμονικόν, which survives its separation from the body and apparently maintains an existence in space and time, is a material object. The Stoics are not faced with the problems that must baffle the interpreter of Plato, when he finds the *Phaedo* arguing for a non-corporeal existence in some kind of spatial and probably also temporal setting. The surviving ἡγεμονικόν, now no longer receiving impressions or alterations through the mediation of the senses, must either maintain itself in its actual situation, or be reabsorbed into the basic substance of the world. It is probably because of this reasoning that the Stoics apparently dropped any kind of doctrine of punishments to be meted out after death. Hence, on the rare occasions when we find in the extant remains of the Old Stoa a reference to punishments meted out by the gods, the context is this-worldly. As Cicero has it, if anyone escapes punishments for his crimes by dying, the due punishment will be meted out to his children, or more generally to his descendants.[2] It should of course be noted that a doctrine of divine punishments of any kind is rendered unnecessary by the nature of the Stoic theory itself. The belief seems to have been that, as one dies, so one continues to exist until all identity is lost. Hence, if death overtakes us in a gloomy despair or when overwhelmed by the gnawings of conscience, we shall remain in that state so long as we remain at all. And so an important decision the Stoic has to take is the decision about the right moment to die; but we have considered this problem already.

The difficulty of the relation between soul and body is not only an anthropological problem. It arises in the macrocosm

---

[1] D.L. 7.157 (*SVF* II 811).

[2] Cic., *De Nat. Deorum* 3.86 (*SVF* II 1179).

as well as the microcosm, for at the level of the cosmos as a whole, although the Stoics talk about the unity of the whole and the 'sympathy' of the parts, there is also some sort of soul–body or ἡγεμονικόν–body dichotomy. This dichotomy is at the basis of Stoic physics and is certainly present in the original Zenonian picture of the world. The doxographical evidence is overwhelming that Zeno and all his orthodox followers spoke of two basic aspects of the cosmos, an active principle and a passive, or, as they often put it, god and matter.[1] Yet at the same time they seem to hold that the one never exists without the other, that qualityless substance always in fact exists with qualities; hence the world does not depend on two principles, for these principles can only be distinguished in abstraction. The point puzzled critics of the Stoa in antiquity; Plotinus pushes the Stoic position to its logical conclusion when he says that for the Stoics god is matter in a certain state.[2] The Stoics themselves seem to have avoided using such a startling phrase; and some modern scholars have thought that Plotinus' language is a caricature. Yet, although the phrase itself does not occur in the writings of any individual Stoic, it is easy to see both why it could have done and again why it could not have done. When the Stoics wanted to emphasize the unity of all things, they could have used it, as Plotinus saw; but had they defined god in this way, it might have been difficult for them to argue for a cyclical theory of the universe. For, according to their view of the end of the various world-periods, Zeus, identified with the active principle, alone maintains his individual character.[3] If he did not do so, there would presumably be no reason to suppose that the world-cycles would be similar to one another, or even that they would have any pattern or order at all.

But the Stoics not only talked about the active and passive elements of things, they also identified the ἡγεμονικόν of the cosmos. According to the majority of the school, including Chrysippus and Posidonius, this is to be identified with the heaven itself; Cleanthes, however, preferred to choose the sun.[4]

---

[1] *SVF* I 85–7.   [2] *Enn.* 2.4.1.12 (*SVF* II 320).
[3] Cf. Seneca, *Ep.* 9.16 (*SVF* II 1065); Plut., *CN* 1077E (*SVF* II 1064).
[4] Cf. *SVF* I 499, II 644.

For our present purposes, the actual parts of the universe selected are less important than the fact that some part was selected, but in view of the importance of the sun in various modern reconstructions of the theories of Posidonius, the fact that he did not regard it as the ἡγεμονικόν is, as Jones pointed out, of great historical significance.[1]

The doctrine of the ἡγεμονικόν of the cosmos sheds a certain pallid light on the problem with which we are concerned, namely that of the survival of the ἡγεμονικόν in a certain state after the separation of the soul and the body. In the case of the cosmos as a whole no permanent separation of the ἡγεμονικόν and its body, the rest of the world, occurs. Even at the conflagration there is no question of any of the cosmic material ceasing to be cosmic material, and indeed ceasing to be dominated and controlled by its 'ruling part'. Hence there has always been a cosmos, soul and body, in some condition, and there always will be. In the case of the human person, however, the matter is quite different. Although allowing a limited survival of the ἡγεμονικόν, the Stoics had no time for doctrines of the pre-existence of souls. For a soul to pre-exist it would have to exist outside its particular spatio-temporal context. Hence its ἡγεμονικόν would be in no kind of disposition; it would be quite simply a qualityless substance, and such substances are only the abstract inventions of logical enquirers into the nature of the universe. But although pre-existence is ruled out, once the soul has come into existence along with the body by the ordinary processes of birth, its ἡγεμονικόν begins to take on characteristics. Hence, since it is itself a material object, it becomes analogous to the ἡγεμονικόν of the cosmos as a whole, and although it can take on no further impressions after its separation from the body, there is no reason why at that very moment it should disintegrate. Indeed the odds against its doing so would be fantastic. It should be added here as a corollary, that, if the soul were able to change its character apart from the body, the argument against pre-existence would be considerably weakened. The Stoic might even have to admit innate ideas. And, of course, if pre-existence were granted, then the

[1] Jones, 'Posidonius and Solar Eschatology', 126.

soul would already have a partially fixed character at birth, and there would be no reason why this fixed character should be identical from one world-cycle to the next. And if that were the case, then the world-cycles would not be identical and another plank of the Stoic edifice would have to be removed.

Thus we may conclude our enquiry up to this point by saying that, although Chrysippus and the early Stoics in general keep up the Platonic talk about bodies and souls, they are able to surmount some of the difficulties of this dualistic language by means of their theory of the material nature of the soul, and still others by their careful refusal to allow the independent soul or ἡγεμονικόν to experience change and development after its separation from the body. We must now move on, however, to consider some of the implications of other language used about these separated souls or ἡγεμονικά. Doubtless following an idea current in popular theological opinion and given philosophical respectability by Plato's *Symposium*, and perhaps by the writings of Xenocrates, the Stoics seem to have adopted the habit of associating surviving souls with *daimones*, being more than mortal and less than divine. It seems from a passage of Diogenes Laertius, the precise meaning of which will later require close investigation, that talk about *daimones* was already occurring in Chrysippus,[1] though the absence of books *On Daimones* should be noticed for all the early teachers in the school.

Nevertheless, although Chrysippus mentioned *daimones*, and there is a little other evidence about them which may go back to the Old Stoa, we must be very careful before accepting a view like that of Bonhoeffer,[2] that when the late Stoics, Epictetus and Marcus Aurelius, who have much more to say on this subject, are discussing the nature of *daimones* and their relationship to the human soul, the doctrines put forward in their writings are necessarily the same as those of Chrysippus and the early Stoics in general. The very fact that the late Stoics make so much more of *daimones* than did their predecessors should make us hesitate before pronouncing for a unity of doctrine.

According to Plutarch Chrysippus was one of those who

---

[1] D.L. 7.88 (*SVF* III 4).   [2] Bonhoeffer, *op. cit.* 83.

distinguished *daimones* from both gods and men.[1] However, it appears that the Stoics recognized not only gods, *daimones*, and men, but also a fourth class, which they called the class of heroes, consisting of the souls of the dead now separated from their bodies. According to Aëtius some of these heroes are good and some bad.[2] As we have seen, this would depend on the state of the individual person at the time of his death. The evidence of Aëtius is reinforced by Diogenes Laertius, who also speaks of *daimones* and heroes as separate classes. *Daimones*, he tells us, were held to have a certain 'sympathy' with human beings and to watch over their affairs; heroes are the surviving souls of the wise.[3] A notoriously difficult passage of Sextus Empiricus, of which scholars have been unable to trace the source, at least corroborates that the Stoics at some stage distinguished *daimones* from souls surviving the death of the body. Sextus does not use the term 'heroes'; but he tells us that, if souls survive, they become the same as *daimones* (εἰ οὖν διαμένουσιν αἱ ψυχαί, δαίμοσιν αἱ αὐταὶ γίνονται). We should notice that he does not say that they become *daimones*, but that they become the same as *daimones*. Thus even Sextus seems to have an inkling of what our other evidence suggests was the original Stoic doctrine, namely that surviving souls and *daimones* are not identical. As Aëtius puts it, *daimones* are 'entities' (οὐσίαι ψυχικαί), not simply souls.[4]

We are now better equipped to look at the most controversial passage on this subject, preserved by Diogenes Laertius and attributed to Chrysippus himself.[5] The Greek has often been mistranslated or paraphrased misleadingly. Hence it will be advisable to quote it in full. According to Chrysippus the virtue of the happy man and his smooth flow of life occur ὅταν πάντα πράττηται κατὰ τὴν συμφωνίαν τοῦ παρ' ἑκάστῳ δαίμονος πρὸς τὴν τοῦ τῶν ὅλων διοικητοῦ βούλησιν. Mistranslations or misinterpretations have occurred in two parts of this. It has been

[1] Plut., *De Iside* 360E (*SVF* II 1103).
[2] Aëtius, *Plac.* 1.8.2 (*SVF* II 1101).
[3] D.L. 7.151 (*SVF* II 1102).
[4] Aëtius, *Plac.* 1.8.2 (*SVF* II 1101).
[5] D.L. 7.88; cf. Erbse, 'Die Vorstellung', 134–5.

said that κατὰ τὴν συμφωνίαν means something like 'with a view to promoting the harmony', whereas it clearly means 'in terms of the harmony'. More important, however, is the phrase τοῦ παρ' ἑκάστῳ δαίμονος. Even so able an interpreter of Stoicism as Bonhoeffer[1] has been induced by the apparent similarity of this to late Stoic talk of a *daimon* or god within us[2] to make παρ' ἑκάστῳ simply the equivalent of ἐν ἑκάστῳ and to think that Chrysippus is treating some part of the human person itself as a *daimon*. That would be Platonism indeed; and as such it should arouse our suspicion.

The correct translation of Chrysippus' sentence is that a smooth flow of life occurs 'whenever everything is done in terms of the harmony which exists between the *daimon* that is present with each man and the will of the director of the universe'. The doctrine about *daimones* is thus seen to be similar to what we found mentioned by Aëtius, Plutarch, Sextus Empiricus and Diogenes Laertius in another part of his work. Each man has his own *daimon*; the *daimon* is present with the individual, but not in the individual. It is, we might almost say, not a part of man, but his guardian spirit. We recall our other passage from Diogenes, where it is said that the *daimon*, which has 'sympathy' with man, oversees human affairs.[3]

We have no evidence to give us an explanation of what is certainly puzzling about the whole problem of *daimones* in early Stoicism, namely why they are accepted at all. In the event, it turned out that Chrysippus and his successors had said just enough about them to enable later Stoics to put them to new, unforeseen, and, probably to Chrysippus, undesirable uses. We have no evidence of Zeno's interest in the subject, though like Chrysippus he may have said a little. The reason why *daimones* remain in the Stoic world-picture can only be guessed at, but two approaches may have slight merit. First and more obvious is the fact that the Stoics tended to take over traditional theology and rewrite it, give it new meaning, rather than simply

---

[1] Bonhoeffer, *op. cit.* 83.
[2] Cf. Posidonius in Galen, *De Hipp. et Plat.* 5.469, p. 449, 1 Mü.; Sen., *Ep.* 41.2; Epict., *Disc.* 2.8.1; Marcus Aurelius 3.5; 3.16 etc.
[3] D.L. 7.151 (*SVF* II 1102).

discard it, and *daimones* were by now a fully established part of that theology. Secondly—and the textual evidence is at least not opposed to the suggestion—Chrysippus may have thought that the doctrine of 'sympathy', the harmony between the separate parts of the cosmos, and between the parts and the whole, could not be entirely explained without them. In particular he may have held the view which underlies Plato's discussion of *daimones* in the *Symposium*, that the connection between gods and men can only be maintained through some intermediary which shares in the characteristics of both.

Throughout the whole of the history of the school, the Stoics seem to have maintained the habit of calling some aspect of the human person an ἀπόσπασμα from the divine. In the later Stoics, as we shall see, this was easily explained. The ἀπόσπασμα is identified with νοῦς, or the ἡγεμονικόν, and viewed as some kind of inner man in a Platonic sense. It is the god or *daimon* within. Earlier Stoics apparently did not talk in this way, but they held that man is in some sense of divine origin. 'We are a race deriving from you,' as Cleanthes put it in his hymn to Zeus.[1] And, according to Diogenes Laertius, Chrysippus and Apollodorus, as well as Posidonius, argued that our soul is an ἀπόσπασμα of the cosmos.[2] This passage might be evaded by the suggestion that Diogenes is only using the position of Posidonius, the last-named before the doctrine of the soul as an ἀπόσπασμα is mentioned, but there is no reason to believe the doctrine specifically Posidonian. It seems to square well enough with the language of the hymn of Cleanthes, a fact which sufficiently supports its existence in the earliest days of the school.

In the passage of Diogenes the doctrine is that the soul is an ἀπόσπασμα of the cosmos, not, we should notice, of any particular part of the cosmos: not the sun, which, as we have seen, was regarded as the ἡγεμονικόν by Cleanthes, nor the heavens, which were so regarded by both Chrysippus and Posidonius. The suggestion seems to be that the soul is a small-scale version of the cosmos *as a whole*. In other words, the doctrine that the soul is an ἀπόσπασμα seems to have no connection in the mind of Diogenes' source with the doctrine that some particular part

---

[1] Stob., *Ecl.* i, p. 25, 7 W. (*SVF* i 537).   [2] D.L. 7.143.

of us is an ἀπόσπασμα of some particular part of the cosmos. The suggestion is not that the soul (or any faculty of any soul) is an ἀπόσπασμα even of the active or ruling element in the cosmos, but it is an ἀπόσπασμα of the cosmos as a whole. If we may so phrase it, it is a small-scale version. Hence Diogenes must be referring not merely to the ἡγεμονικόν, but to the whole soul, the whole 'eight-parted' phenomenon.

Slight confirmation that the original concept of the soul as an ἀπόσπασμα is to be so interpreted is afforded by a common use of the word from the time of Zeno. The Stoics were in the habit of calling semen an ἀπόσπασμα of the soul and at the same time a blend produced from all the different physical parts of the soul.[1] This sense would exactly correspond to that in which the soul itself is said to be an ἀπόσπασμα, the sense, in fact, of its being a small-scale version of the cosmos. We may conclude, therefore, that there is no reason to suppose that for Chrysippus, since the soul is an ἀπόσπασμα, this has any connection with the doctrine of *daimones*, or that it tells us anything whatsoever even about the nature of the ἡγεμονικόν.

There is no doubt that the basic change in Stoic doctrine about the relation of the soul to its *daimon* comes with Posidonius. It is connected with the Platonizing psychology he introduced into the Stoa, which we discussed in an earlier chapter. As for the general psychological doctrines, so here too there can be little doubt in the mind of the unbiased reader of the evidence that it was his interest in Plato's *Timaeus* which led to Posidonius' heresies.[2] Posidonius was probably led to the *Timaeus* in the first instance by its scientific material, but later came to find the psychology sympathetic. For our present purposes it is various passages near the end of the dialogue (90 c) which are important. Here Posidonius could find the doctrine that our νοῦς, which he would immediately associate with the ἡγεμονικόν, in his new understanding of the term, is in fact itself a *daimon*. This discovery is probably one of the very few significant facts that lie behind the myth of Posidonius the

---

[1] *SVF* I 128.
[2] On Posidonius' work on the *Timaeus* see p. 206. Cf. Sext. Emp., *Adv. Math.* 7.93, Plut., *De An. Proc. in Tim.* 1032 B, Reinhardt, *RE* 22¹, col. 569.

Neoplatonist. Beside it his use of a Platonic tripartition of the soul seems almost insignificant, for Plotinus at least had little interest in that. He only maintained it because it happens to occur in Plato's writings.[1]

We have only one piece of evidence about Posidonius' treatment of the theory of *daimones*, but it is conclusive. It marks a fundamentally different conception from the earlier Stoic doctrines we have been considering. It is to be found in Galen and tells us that the bad man does not follow the *daimon* in himself (τῷ ἐν αὐτοῖς δαίμονι) which is akin and like in its nature to the ruler of the whole cosmos. Instead of doing that, the bad man follows his lesser and animal side.[2] Now we see that the *daimon* is not overseeing a man, like a guardian angel, but is actually some part of his being. The *daimon* is the individual's true self in the Platonic sense, and could easily have been fitted out with Platonic attributes. Our evidence about Posidonius is insufficient to tell us whether he believed in innate ideas; the theory is alien to the Old Stoa, but with a Platonic *daimon* installed in the human person, Posidonius could have maintained them. At any rate, the door is now open for the introduction of innate ideas into Stoicism—and Epictetus certainly accepted them.[3]

In the writings of members of the Stoic school after Posidonius, we can see the effect of the change he introduced. We shall consider it very briefly in the writings of Seneca, Epictetus and Marcus Aurelius. That Seneca actually read Posidonius seems certain from the number of references to him by name that occur in the course of his writings. That Epictetus and Marcus knew him directly is much more doubtful, though scholars have tried hard to prove it at various times. But whether they read his works or not, his doctrine about the *daimon* became a commonplace. Seneca and Marcus generally follow it; Epictetus generally does not, though a number of rather confused passages in his writings would suggest that he knew

---

[1] On Plotinus' use of tripartition see the unpublished Cambridge dissertation of Dr H. J. Blumenthal on Plotinus' psychology.

[2] Galen, *De Hipp. et Plat.* 5.469, p. 448, 15 Mü.

[3] Cf. Sandbach, '"Εννοια and Πρόληψις', esp. p. 49; Cic., *Tusc.* 1.57, *De Nat. Deorum* 2.12.

the views of Chrysippus and Posidonius so well that he could see no difference between them![1]

We may consider Seneca first and most briefly. His tendencies to dualism have long been recognized, and he cites Posidonius by name. These tendencies are, of course, not only due to Posidonius. The direct and powerful influence of the writings of Plato themselves is well known. Again and again in his letters in particular he speaks of a holy spirit living within our bodily frame. This divine spirit is an immortal part which has entered a mortal body—the language echoes the old 'Orphic' theory of the body as the tomb of the soul. Seneca writes in Latin, so that the word *daimon* does not appear. The Latin equivalent is *spiritus*.[2]

With Epictetus the problem is considerably more complex. The most startling passage is a section of the *Discourses* in which Epictetus seems to talk the language of Chrysippus and Posidonius at the same time (1.14.11–13). He begins by discussing a faculty (δύναμις) within each of us which is equal to Zeus— which sounds dualist enough. Then, however, instead of continuing in the Posidonian manner and saying that this power is our reason, which is divine and a *daimon*, he reverts to the view which we identified as that of Chrysippus, according to which Zeus has set a watchman over each of us, and committed each of us to his care. This watchman is our guardian *daimon*. Epictetus does not identify this *daimon* with the ἡγεμονικόν.

There follows an even stranger section where it is difficult, and perhaps impossible, to be sure whether Epictetus means the *daimon* to be within us or by our side. Perhaps the latter (the Chrysippean view) is the more likely, but it is by no means impossible that the two theories are inextricably blended in

---

[1] Bonhoeffer had already recognized the 'un-Stoic', that is, Posidonian, views of Marcus on the ἡγεμονικόν (*op. cit.* 30–1). His contrast between Epictetus and Marcus is further examined by Erbse (*op. cit.* 136–7). More wide-ranging parallels between Marcus and Posidonius are suggested by Neuenschwander (*Marc Aurels Beziehungen*), but Neuenschwander should be used with caution; he seems to know more than is warranted about Posidonius.

[2] For Seneca's view see *Ep.* 31.11, 41.2, 66.12, 120.14 etc. Cf. *Ep.* 92.10: *Huic committitur inutilis caro et fluida, receptandis tantum cibis habilis, ut ait Posidonius.*

Epictetus' mind. 'When you lock your doors and make darkness within, remember never to say that you are alone. For you are not alone, but god and your *daimon* are within.' It would be a brash and insensitive scholar who would pronounce authoritatively that this passage is one to be taken literally, that Epictetus is only speaking of closing the doors of an actual material building. The suspicion cannot be allayed that he is talking of the doors of the self, and saying that the *daimon* is not only within the building but within the very self.

A second passage of Epictetus which deserves our attention in this context is 2.8.11. Epictetus begins by contrasting man with everything else in the universe. Man is different because he is a fragment (ἀπόσπασμα) of god. The term ἀπόσπασμα should by now be familiar; but we recall that both Chrysippus and Posidonius said that man is an ἀπόσπασμα of the cosmos. Or perhaps Epictetus is thinking of Cleanthes, who in his hymn taught that the race of men is sprung from god? Certainly he asks just below, 'Why do you not know whence you have come?' But Epictetus' meaning is probably brought out most clearly when he says not that we are parts of god but that we have some part of god in us. This looks very like the idea that a specific element in man, presumably νοῦς or the ἡγεμονικόν, is the divine part—the view of Posidonius.

However, as Erbse has observed,[1] Epictetus nowhere says specifically that νοῦς in us is a *daimon*. This particular refinement of Posidonian theory is lacking. As we saw above, whenever he talks about our *daimon*, he manages to avoid an unequivocal identification with νοῦς. Nonetheless, he thinks of it as a part of man, of something which we carry about, as something which has to be kept pure.[2] It all reminds us not so much of the psychology of Chrysippus as of the tenth book of the *Republic*, where the λογιστικόν is compared with the sea-god Glaucus, who in the grime of life becomes encrusted with seaweed and barnacles, which have to be cleared away before he can be seen in his pristine splendour.

When we come to Marcus, the un-Chrysippean aspects of the theory of the ἡγεμονικόν and the *daimon* which we have seen

---

[1] Erbse, *op. cit.* 136. [2] *Disc.* 2.8.13, 21.

are further enlarged. As has often been observed, Marcus divides the human being into spirit (ἡγεμονικόν), soul or *pneuma*, and body. Bonhoeffer noticed that there are even certain passages where he suggests that the ἡγεμονικόν is not composed of any of the same basic elements (earth, air, fire, water) as the rest of the cosmos.[1] Presumably his view would be that it was made up of the special creative fire which is god, the fire which the Stoics called πῦρ τεχνικόν. This seems to be a stage beyond Posidonius. Yet in other areas the Posidonian version of Stoic doctrine on the relation of νοῦς and the *daimon* is quite clear. Again and again νοῦς or the ἡγεμονικόν is identified with the *daimon* within us.[2] Sometimes, as in Seneca, it is called a god. In his commentary on Marcus, Farquharson has suggested that the interpretation of the *daimon* as dwelling within the person rather than as a guardian spirit may be strengthened in Roman writers by the old Roman belief in a man's indwelling *genius*[3]—and perhaps this accounts for the fact that this version of the theory is more strongly represented in Seneca and Marcus Aurelius than it is in Epictetus.

Yet, whatever the reasons, the dualist thesis is promoted by Marcus unequivocally. Perhaps 5.27 is the most striking example: 'Live with the gods. But he is living with the gods who continuously exhibits his soul to them, as satisfied with its dispensation and doing what the *daimon* wishes, the *daimon* which is that fragment (ἀπόσπασμα) of himself which Zeus has given to each man as his guardian and leader. And this *daimon* is each man's mind and reason' (trans. Farquharson, slightly adapted). Here all the elements of Posidonius' theory are present, with something of Chrysippus (the notion that the *daimon* is a guardian) thrown in for good value. The *daimon* is internal; it is a fragment of Zeus. It is identified as a leader (ἡγεμόνα), thus being ἡγεμονικόν. Above all it is clearly and unhesitatingly identified with the highest part of the human being, his νοῦς. And we should recall those passages in which Marcus, by

---

[1] E.g. 4.4. Cf. Bonhoeffer, *op. cit.* 31. There is no need to accept the view of some scholars (e.g. Benz, *Das Todesproblem* 43) that passages like 12.2 suggest that the ἡγεμονικόν is immaterial. Marcus only meant that it is not composed of the four vulgar elements.

[2] 3.3, 12.26 etc.   [3] Farquharson, *The Meditations* 2.529.

separating the νοῦς from the four elements of ordinary matter, is even more of a Platonist than Posidonius. Finally we should notice that language suggesting a tending of our divine part (already employed by Epictetus) is almost a commonplace in Marcus.[1]

A further startling fact should be noticed. In Stoic literature before Marcus, if mention has to be made of the fact that the human being or a faculty of the human being is of divine origin, the words 'fragment' (ἀπόσπασμα) or 'part' (μέρος) are used. Marcus does not avoid this kind of language, as we have seen, but alongside it there is another set of words; and these words sound very Neoplatonic. Everything flows from another world (πάντα ἐκεῖθεν ῥεῖ, 2.3); we are an effluence from the gods (ἀπόρροια, 2.4); God teaches with his own mind only what has flowed from him (ἐρρυηκότων, 12.2); you have forgotten that each man's mind is god and has flowed from another world (ἐκεῖθεν ἐρρύηκεν, 12.26). Parallels for this are found by Farquharson only in the book of *Wisdom* (7.25) and in Clement of Alexandria (*Protrepticus* 6.68). Another passage of Clement perhaps provides a closer parallel: the mind is said here to be an ἀπόρροια of god flowing through the hearts of men.[2] Doubtless other parallels are available, but the language is not Stoic. The notion in 12.2 of our mind, and in 2.3 of everything, flowing from another place (ἐκεῖθεν) has a particularly Neoplatonic ring.[3]

There is no doubt that Marcus is a very selective Stoic. We recall the passages where he considers what would be the case if all is to be explained as atoms and the void, as well as if traditional Stoic accounts of physics are valid. And in the Stoic school itself, there was by his time, as we have seen, an indisputably Platonic strain. Nevertheless, it is worth noticing where he draws the line, and here two related pieces of doctrine are relevant. As Farquharson says, 'He never takes up the position, which is, for example, expressed in Plutarch, that the δαίμων is able to leave the body it inhabits, to give information about events remote in place and time, and to forecast future events'.[4]

---

[1] 2.13, 12.3 etc.   [2] *GCS* 17.202, 21.

[3] ἐκεῖθεν (though without ῥεῖ) occurs once in Epictetus (*Disc.* 1.9.13).

[4] Farquharson, *The Meditations*, 2.529; Plut., *De Genio* 591 D, 592 C, 593 D.

The second point where Marcus is, even in his psychology, still Stoic enough to disagree radically with the Platonists concerns the immortality of the soul. It might be supposed that, with his Platonic-sounding ideas about the composition of the soul as opposed to the composition of the body, he might move towards the Platonists on this question also. But he does not regard the soul as immaterial. It is interesting to see how, in what starts as one of his most Platonic-sounding chapters, Marcus concludes in an ultra-Stoic vein (12.3). The individual, he says, is composed of body, *pneuma* and mind. Only mind is properly one's own. It is necessary to keep the mind clear of all the distractions of sense and all worries about the past or the future. One must live in the eternal present of the mind, like the sphere of Empedocles. This all sounds very Platonic. It is the doctrine of the true self within and the dross without. But the conclusion Marcus draws is in a totally different tradition. If one lives in this way, he says, it will be possible to survive until death untroubled, in a kindly frame of mind and at peace with one's *daimon*. The emphasis is entirely on enduring this life; there are no Platonic notions of purifying the soul for an eternal existence. Even the modified survival of the ἡγεμονικόν, as taught by Chrysippus, is not mentioned; and it is hard not to think here and elsewhere that Marcus is at one with his predecessor Panaetius in denying any kind of survival.[1]

In this chapter we have attempted to follow some of the Stoic concepts about the soul, the ἡγεμονικόν, the body and the *daimon* from the beginning of the school down to its last significant representative. Perhaps we should close by noticing a strange development of the doctrine. We have already observed how at the hands of Marcus Aurelius various Stoic theories come out in a particularly Platonic guise. There are a number of passages in Plotinus where we hear of the inner and the outer man.[2] The thought is Platonic, but the commentators on Plotinus have failed to find parallels for the mode of expression. It is at least worth pointing out that, if Marcus' version of Stoicism

[1] Marcus is usually unwilling to commit himself as to whether there is any kind of survival; cf. 2.11, 3.3 etc.
[2] E.g. *Enn.* 3.2.15.58–9.

is in any way representative of the state of the school at the end of the second century, Plotinus could as well have found the language he uses among Stoics as among Platonists. There is no reason to believe that Plotinus had read Marcus' *Meditations*,[1] but he could easily have been familiar with the views and especially with the language to be found in them. By the time that language came to be regularly employed, the original un-Platonic insights of Chrysippus about soul and body had been forgotten or rejected.

[1] For knowledge of Marcus' work before Themistius (A.D. 364) see Farquharson, *op. cit.* 1.xiii–xvi.

15

THREE STOIC VIEWS OF TIME

A fairly recent book on theories of time in antiquity omitted the theories of the Stoics.[1] Perhaps the author thought that they are unimportant or merely parasitical on the views of Plato and Aristotle, with which they are obviously connected. Plotinus, however, does not think that they should be passed over in silence, and, although his critique does not always do the Stoics justice, its existence at least recognizes their importance.[2] As far as we can see, there are three stages of thought within the Stoic school on the concept of time, represented by the ideas of Zeno, Chrysippus and his followers, and Marcus Aurelius. These stages need not be viewed as the replacement of one thesis by another, though in some respects this is the case, but rather as elaborations based on an original insight. The view of Marcus, however, indicates a considerably different outlook, which is not fully explained by formal differences in philosophical theory. There is not very much in what Marcus says about the nature of time which might not have been said by Chrysippus, but the context in which he situates his theories removes him a considerable distance from any of the early members of his school.

When Zeno began to reflect on the nature of time, he would have had the ideas of Plato and Aristotle in his mind. In the *Timaeus* Plato had considered time as the moving image of eternity,[3] while in the *Physics* Aristotle had defined it as the measure or number of motion.[4] Both these theses were influential for Zeno, and later for Chrysippus, but, although Zeno's own definition, that time is the extension of movement,[5] is

---

[1] Callahan, *Four Views of Time.*   [2] Plot., *Enn.* 3.7.7. and 3.7.10.
[3] *Tim.* 37c.   [4] *Physics* 217b–224a.
[5] The evidence for Zeno, from Arius Didymus and Simplicius, is given in *SVF* i 93. Cf. Sambursky, *Physics of the Stoics* 101. The statement of Aëtius (*Plac.* 1.22.7) that Zeno defined time simply as movement, is, as Bréhier (*La Théorie* 56–7) saw, a mistake.

formally closer to that of Aristotle, its spirit may have been closer to that of Plato. For Zeno himself we cannot be sure of this, since almost all we know about his theory is the definition itself. In its fullest form this seems to have been that time is not just the extension of movement but, more specifically, that it is the extension of any movement. We can, Zeno seems to be saying, recognize the concept of time by reflecting that objects move in space, that the same material object cannot be in Oxford at the same time as we are holding it in Cambridge. In order to travel between Cambridge and Oxford it must pass through a series of intermediate points, and, while this process is going on, other events may be completed. Furthermore, if two men set off from Cambridge to drive to Oxford, one might reach Oxford, turn round and meet the other still on his outward journey. We use terms like 'fast' and 'slow', 'faster' and 'slower' to explain this situation. We say that one man has driven faster than another. The man who has driven from Cambridge to Oxford to Bicester has driven 'faster' than the man who has driven from Cambridge to Bicester. If we want a general word to describe the sequence of events, and to allude to the fact that it is of interest that the driver who has reached Oxford and returned as far as Bicester has travelled faster than his rival, we say that he has covered more ground in the same time. This is what Zeno seems to have meant when he said that time is not only the extension of movement, but the measure and criterion of quickness and slowness.[1]

The Stoics generally spoke of time as an incorporeal.[2] They could not easily say that there is no such thing as time, for they, among others, made use of the concept. They were apparently unwilling to make it purely a mental construct, as they held the Platonic Ideas to be. It is in some sense real. Hence, since it is obviously not material, it has to be given the twilight reality of one of the incorporeals. Presumably Zeno, as well as Chrysippus and later Stoics, gave it this position. Exactly what else Zeno thought about it, however, must be left to speculation. There is no evidence; we can only talk about the tradition of

---

[1] Stob., *Ecl.* 1, p. 104, 7 W. (*SVF* 1 93).
[2] Sext. Emp., *Adv. Math.* 10.218 (*SVF* 11 331).

the Old Stoa in general on this matter. And that probably means that the teachings we have are those of Chrysippus.

It seems clear that Chrysippus altered the deposit of Stoic doctrine on time in at least two ways. First, he explained Zeno's phrase 'extension of movement' (διάστημα) as 'extension accompanying movement' (τὸ παρακολουθοῦν διάστημα),[1] or possibly even as 'accompaniment of movement';[2] secondly, he thought that time is not the extension accompanying any movement, but only the movement of the cosmos.[3] We must try to understand the significance of these changes.

When Zeno said that time is the extension of any movement, he must have been making the (tacit) assumption that the beginnings and ends of movements are in some sense fixed points. This is, of course, a perfectly natural assumption to make. Our drivers from Cambridge to Oxford assume that their starting points and finishing lines do not move about. But they assume more than that; they also assume that time can be measured by a stop-watch. When the driver passes the finishing line, his time of movement can be precisely measured. In other words time is not a continuum. Zeno's theory about time must have depended on similar axioms. For Zeno, even if time is a continuum, it must still be possible to mark it off on a scale, to begin at a point and to end at a point.

We have said 'even if time is a continuum', thus making the assumption that this was Zeno's view. Of that we cannot be certain, but it undoubtedly was the view of Chrysippus and of all later Stoics, and it was also the view of Aristotle, whose thesis that time is the number or measure of movement clearly supplies the basis for Zeno's own position. It is reasonable to

[1] Stob., Ecl. 1, p. 106, 5 W. (SVF 11 509).

[2] Compare Plot., Enn. 3.7.10.1 (τὸ παρακολούθημα τῆς κινήσεως) with παρακολουθοῦν αὐτῇ (movement) in 3.7.7.26. There may also be an allusion to Epicurus here (fr. 294 Usener). Clark ('The Theory of Time') thinks that the definition given by Plotinus is 'broader than Chrysippus's'. He suggests that Plotinus may also have Strato in mind. This seems unlikely.

[3] SVF 11 509–13. Clark's view ('The Theory of Time', 341) that this position of Chrysippus was not generally accepted is unsupported. We do not know whether it was or not. On a priori grounds it is more likely that it was, but perhaps some accepted it while others did not.

assume that in theory Zeno too held that time is a continuum. But the weakness of his position is that, although holding this view, he did not apparently meet its philosophical implications at any level. The theory demands a detailed examination of the concept of a point in time, a 'now', and we do not know that Zeno offered such an examination. If he did in fact look at this problem, Chrysippus must have regarded his solution as unsatisfactory, for the problem of the point of time or the 'now' was almost certainly the jumping-off place for his decision to define time, not as the extension of any movement but as the extension of the movement of the cosmos.

What we wish to argue is that Chrysippus took the Heraclitean (and also Platonic) background of Stoic physics more seriously than Zeno, and realized its philosophical implications at a deeper level. For Heraclitus, in some sense everything is in a state of flux; and Plato followed him in so far as he believed that particulars in the sensible world are always changing. Time too, for Plato, is a *moving* image of eternity. Unless we take the myth of the *Demiourgos* as indicating a beginning of time and the physical world—which is not justifiable—we must believe that for Plato there are no fixed points of time. It is in this respect the antithesis of eternity, of the life of the Forms. The difficulty to which this view of time leads, as Plato was obviously aware, is that it seems to deny any stability to events. Perhaps 'difficulty' is not the right word here. Plato saw this instability as a fact about the world, explicable only in terms of another world of Ideas. But without such another world the Heraclitean nature of the world of particulars becomes a philosophical problem of another kind. How can we talk about things happening at all? How can time words have any meaning? Time words frequently imply that the flux of the world can be stopped and a 'static' description given. If this is false, all those concepts of the world which are based on temporal categories are misleading, if not actually false. Some means has to be found by which we can speak of events in a meaningful way.

Apparently the solution to this dilemma which presented itself to Chrysippus was to treat the beginning and end of each world-cycle as fixed points. Events can be said to happen in time because their position on the continuum can be plotted with reference to these fixed points. The beginning and end of each cosmic cycle can be viewed as analogous to two positions from which searchlights shine out towards one another. As the length of the beam of one searchlight is shortened, the other is lengthened. Where the lights, which are themselves always moving, cross one another's path, there is the particular event we wish to describe. The shortness or length of each beam represents the nearness or remoteness of any particular event from the beginning or end of a particular cosmic period, or, as Chrysippus would say, from the beginning or end of each fixed movement of the cosmos.

It must be admitted that the theory we have sketched out for Chrysippus is not presented in the available evidence as it has been offered here. It has been offered as an hypothesis, which fits our knowledge about Chrysippus' theory of time and accounts for the significance of his divergence from Zeno on the definition of time. Unfortunately, our evidence is largely restricted to what Chrysippus said and leaves out his reasons for saying it. Nevertheless, it is not easy to formulate another theory which accounts more adequately even for the little evidence we have; and in general commentators have left the matter in abeyance.

The Stoic theory of the beginning and end of each cosmic cycle gave Chrysippus an opportunity to explain events in a continuum which was not available to Plato and Aristotle. Plato was not worried about the instability in which this situation left individual events; he had his Ideal theory as an explanation and a salvation of phenomena. Aristotle thought that the uniform circular motion of the heavens is primarily the measure of time,[1] but presumably Chrysippus would have found this unsatisfactory, since it does not provide fixed points in terms of which time can be measured. Zeno seems to have followed Aristotle's theory in general terms, substituting his own phrase 'extension of movement' for Aristotle's number or measure of movement as his definition. But although this change

---

[1] Aristotle, *Physics* 223b 19ff. Cf. Callahan, *op. cit.* 79, Goldschmidt, *Le Système* 34.

is itself substantial, the theories of Zeno and Aristotle seem to present the same difficulty about fixed points of time. Zeno clearly did not see theories of the beginning and end of cosmic cycles as the way out, while Chrysippus' modified definition suggests that he at least thought that this was the area in which a solution might be found.

Perhaps confirmation of our account of Chrysippus will be found in his more detailed comments on the nature of time and their reception in some quarters of antiquity. The standard Stoic theory, presumably deriving from Chrysippus, was that only the present is fully real.[1] The Greek word here translated as 'fully real' is ὑπάρχειν, the literal meaning of which is 'to be present, to be there, to be available'. Clearly, present time is the only time which is there; and yet the Stoic view (taken from Aristotle) that time is a continuum leads Chrysippus to add that this present is itself composed of the past and the future.[2] It cannot be isolated; strictly speaking there is no 'now'. Since there are no minimum parts of time, the present itself must be viewed as a continuum or as an extension (πλάτος).[3]

No time is wholly (ὅλως) present, says Chrysippus. That does not mean that a little bit of it is present; that would imply that time is finitely divisible. It must mean that time in the strict sense is not present. We can only talk of present time by convention. At the same time Chrysippus is maintaining that time is a continuum (with Plato and Aristotle), but refuting or rejecting the Platonic view that this continuum gives present time an unreality. It is fully real (ὑπάρχειν); but it is not present in the strict sense. The recognition of time as a continuum need not imply the unreality of the present, or indeed of events in the present. And, our interpretation runs, Chrysippus is only able to escape from the theory that events in time are unreal, which he clearly wishes to deny, because of his definition of time as the extension of the movement *of the cosmos*. Time ceases to

[1] *SVF* II 509, 518; cf. *SVF* II 331.   [2] *SVF* II 509, 519.

[3] *SVF* II 509; cf. *SVF* III 8 Apollodorus, Goldschmidt, *op. cit.* 37–9. For πλάτος see Posidonius *ap.* Ar. Did. 26 (*DG* 461, 19–21). For the problem of the reality of time see Samburssky, *Physics of the Stoics* 101–2.

be unreal if it can be envisaged as a dependent reality. It is true that Chrysippus holds that, like space, it extends indefinitely in each direction,[1] but this extension is limited and controlled by the recurring cycles of the cosmos. Chrysippus has the advantage of maintaining the eternity of the world (hence nothing is created from nothing and nothing fades into nothing) and at the same time a means of imposing some control, some fixed points, on the endless sequence of time. As we shall see, a later Stoic used different terms for the boundless time (ἄπειρος χρόνος) of the universe and for the time from the beginning to the end of a particular cosmic cycle.

According to Proclus, Chrysippus' theory tends to deny the reality of time.[2] Time, he says, is for the Stoics very near to nonbeing; it is something which exists only in the mind. Proclus points out that time is not an existent in the strict sense (οὐκ ὄντα καὶ ἐν ἐπινοίαις ὑφιστάμενα ψιλαῖς), but he does not mention the precise phraseology which the Stoics used about present time. He does not discuss the word ὑπάρχειν. He does not grasp that Chrysippus and the Stoics want to distinguish between what exists (the various material objects) and what is real (which includes the material objects as well as incorporeals like time). He thinks that Chrysippus ought to be able to tell us more about the essence of time—which is just what Chrysippus refuses to do. In these attitudes Proclus is in the full Platonic tradition. His approach can be found in different degrees of sophistication in both Plutarch and Plotinus. We shall need to look at some of the comments of these thinkers on the Stoic theory of time in order to grasp fully the other thesis of Chrysippus, which we observed to differ from the view of Zeno, namely the explanation of the doctrine that time is an extension of movement by the idea that it is an extension accompanying movement, or, as Plotinus puts it, simply an accompaniment of movement.

Goldschmidt has commented on the fact that already for

---

[1] *SVF* II 509. For 'dependent reality' cf. the use of παρυφίσταμαι of place (*SVF* II 507).

[2] Proc., *In Tim.* 3, p. 95, 8 ff. Diehl (*SVF* II 521). Cf. Goldschmidt, *op. cit.* 39–40, Bréhier, 'La Théorie', 55–9.

Aristotle time is a derived reality.[1] As Plutarch observed, in this respect the Aristotelian and Stoic views are similar. Both of them, objects Plutarch, fail to account for the essence and function of time (τὴν οὐσίαν αὐτοῦ καὶ τὴν δύναμιν).[2] Plotinus offers a critique along similar lines in *Ennead* 3.7.10. It is no good saying that time is an accompaniment, he argues, unless one knows what it is that does the accompanying. In other words Plotinus thinks that Chrysippus should have told us what is the essence of time *qua* time. It is no good saying what time does, before we know what time is.[3]

From Chrysippus' point of view this tradition of Platonic criticism is totally misconceived. It was probably to avoid being asked 'What is the essence of this extension of movement?' that he altered Zeno's definition to read 'extension accompanying movement'. This would suggest that for Chrysippus time cannot be understood in itself; it can only be understood in relation to objects in motion, and is in a sense parasitical on them. No definition of time without reference to motion, and thus by implication to material objects, is possible. The concept of time can only be understood by a grasp of the proper use of temporal words like 'before', 'after', 'quicker', 'slower'. And the ontological justification for the use of these words in a meaningful way is provided by the concept of world-cycles.

When we know how to use temporal words and to justify our usage, we know all that can be known about time. Before considering to what use Marcus Aurelius put the Stoic theory of time, we should examine the philosophical implications of our knowledge a little further. For Chrysippus words like 'before' and 'after' are both precise, in that their point of reference is ultimately the beginning and end of the world, and also relative in that they 'place' events relatively to one another. What does this tell us about the uses of another class of temporal words, namely verbs? Clearly, in both English and Greek, verbs do not necessarily carry an immediate reference to a specific

---

[1] Goldschmidt, *op. cit.* 31.
[2] Plut., *Quaest. Plat.* 1007 A (*SVF* II 515).
[3] Cf. Callahan, *op. cit.* 116–17.

THREE STOIC VIEWS OF TIME

time. The phrase 'I am an opera-goer' does not mean that I am going to an opera at any particular time. But on Chrysippus' theory action-words like 'walk', 'see', 'kick' must all, properly speaking, be descriptive in a continuative sense. As Priscian puts it, clearly quoting Stoic theory, when in the middle of a verse I say 'I am writing a verse', I am using a present imperfective, since some of the verse remains to be written.[1] Similarly 'I see' must mean 'I am seeing', 'I kick' must mean 'I am kicking', 'I walk' must mean 'I am walking'. That Chrysippus intended something of this sort is further borne out by his description of various actions and emotions as states of the ruling principle of mind (ἡγεμονικόν πως ἔχον). States or dispositions are not instantaneous events; they are precisely not immediately completed acts.

Before we leave Chrysippus, there are two further points to be considered. It has been argued that Chrysippus talked about time as an accompaniment of the movement of the cosmos, because he thought that the beginning and end of the world provide fixed points for the measurement of time. Might it not be objected that, although this world begins and ends at particular points in a sense, these points are by no means more fixed than any other points on the cosmic cycle? Thus Chrysippus' theory would be no improvement on that view of Aristotle which we have suggested he rejects, that time is measured with reference to the uniform circular movements of the heavenly bodies. There would seem to be a number of answers Chrysippus could make to this, the principal one being that such an objection seems to rely on the assumption that the conflagration of the world is itself an event which occurs in time and lasts for a particular period. But Chrysippus' view seems to be that time arises with the cosmos, as Plato argued in the *Timaeus*, and will therefore end with the destruction of the cosmos. When there is no cosmos, there is no kind of regular movement; hence time is not even potentially measurable, and thus cannot exist. In other words, Chrysippus' position depends on the fact that it is only

[1] Priscian 8, p. 414, 24. For the concept of the present imperfective (*praesens imperfectum*, ἐνεστὼς παρατατικός) see Stephanus' scholion on Dionysius Thrax, p. 250, 26, and Pohlenz, *Die Begründung* 176–84.

in the context of the physical cosmos and of physical bodies with regular movements that time is even potentially intelligible. Perhaps we have co-operated with Chrysippus a little here, but his ideas seem to lead us along these lines. In none of the fragments is there any attempt to depict the conflagration as lasting for longer or shorter periods of time; it cannot be understood in those terms.

A second and more sophistic objection to Chrysippus' position would be that, since all temporal events must be viewed as continuing processes, there is no particular point which could properly be the beginning or the end of the world-cycle. The answer to this would be that, while events in time in the particular world-cycle are determined solely by relation to the beginning and end of the cycle, the beginnings and ends of the cycles themselves have nothing which could 'place' them in terms of sequence. The comparison would be with human life. The words 'old' and 'young' refer to distance from the fixed point which is considered to be the beginning of life. They have no independent status. But the end of life is a fixed point in the sense that it is at the same time the end of one kind of existence and the beginning of another. We have already shown how Chrysippus holds that the present is *real*, even if it is not strictly speaking a momentary 'now'. The difference between a relative fixed point, like the end of life, and the fundamental fixed points (the beginning and end of the world-cycle), is that, whereas in the case of death we can still speak of 'before death' and 'after death', this is not the case with world-cycles. Strictly speaking, there is no 'before' the cycle began and no 'after' the cycle ends.[1]

In considering the theory of time put forward by Chrysippus, and while trying to fill out the meagre evidence by an attempted explanation of what Chrysippus might have meant, we have

[1] Sambursky (*op. cit.* 106) would seem to deny this explanation. His objection must be based on his view that the 'ekpyrosis originally denoted that period of the cosmic cycle where the preponderance of the fiery element reaches its maximum'. However, the ancient evidence does not describe ekpyrosis as a *period* of the cosmic cycle, but as the *destruction* of the cosmos. See Plut., *CN* 1067 A (*SVF* II 606); cf. *SVF* II 611. The cosmos is 'burnt up' and then 'reconstituted', according to Simplicius (*SVF* II 617).

always found him insisting on the reality of present experience, despite the difficulties of explaining what present time is. We have found him giving no recognition to any sort of quasi-Platonic mood or theory that physical events are unreal because time is a continuum—and that despite his well known acceptance of much of the Heraclitean conception of the physical world. But with the same, or very similar theories about the philosophical nature of time, a man could form a very different psychological outlook on temporal events; and that man, Marcus Aurelius, could still claim to be a Stoic.

When considering the view of Marcus, we must always bear in mind that his distinction between man's life (ψυχή) and his *daimon* (νοῦς) is something he does not share with orthodox Stoics. This distinction enables him to suggest that the life of νοῦς has a reality in the Platonic sense which the ordinary sequence of life has not.[1] But although the distinction, if handled by a more confident follower of Platonizing ideals, might have relieved Marcus' worries about the transitoriness of physical life, the Stoic theories about time, now transposed into a new key, induce in the Emperor a very strong feeling of the actual unreality of events. As Dodds puts it, Marcus has the feeling that 'man's activity is not only unimportant, it is also in some sense not quite real'.[2] If this reading of the Emperor's words is correct, we have an attitude radically different from that of Chrysippus, the express purpose of whose theories about time is to show that the present, though to be understood by the philosopher as a continuum, is nevertheless fully real (ὑπάρχειν).

Marcus' writings about the unimportance of human life are much affected by the notion that length of time indicates importance, briefness unimportance. Every present moment of time is a pinprick in eternity.[3] Doubtless this is true, but would it have mattered to the early Stoics? For them immediate moral action is important, not duration of time. And for Posidonius a single day in the life of the educated man is longer than the longest life of the uneducated.[4] The older idea occurs in Marcus

---

[1] See above, pp. 268–72. [2] Dodds, *Pagan and Christian* 8.
[3] *Med.* 6.36. On the background of the idea see Dodds, *op. cit.* 8.
[4] Sen., *Ep.* 78.28.

himself at times. The life of the rational soul, when it is living well, is complete at any time.[1] But Marcus cannot maintain this attitude. The phrase he uses in 6.36 to devalue present existence is one which he must have known was traditionally used in his school in the course of discussion of time: τὸ ἐνεστώς. It was precisely this present which Chrysippus had attempted to define, and the value of which he clearly meant to maintain. For only the present, for orthodox Stoics, is fully real.

Marcus uses the word *aion* to denote infinite or boundless time, and he is willing to call each world-cycle itself a particular *aion*.[2] Hence he will speak of infinite time as proceeding from age to age.[3] The word *aion* has echoes of the *Timaeus*, and its connection with Marcus' sense of the unreality of physical events has a Platonic ring; but little can be built on this. The word was commonplace in the tradition in Marcus' day, and we cannot know whether his use of it is conscious Platonizing. But Dodds is certainly right to draw our attention to the way Marcus uses the Platonic comparison of the world to a stage, where men are puppets.[4] Plato talks in this way in the *Laws*,[5] a pessimistic work by Platonic standards. When Plato thinks about the world in Heraclitean terms alone, he is inevitably pessimistic. The theory of Forms, his testimony to belief in a stable world of reality, usually leads him to overcome this pessimism, but in the *Laws*, where the Forms, though mentioned, are rather in the background, it is certain that doubts about the possibility of permanency and value reappear more strongly than anywhere else in his writings.[6] And for as Marcus, he has the Heraclitean world-picture, viewed through Platonic eyes as moments of time against a backdrop of eternity. It is not surprising that, without the promise of another and more stable

[1] 11.1; cf. Goldschmidt, *op. cit.* 205–7.
[2] *Med.* 2.12; 4.43; 6.15; 7.19; 9.28; 9.32; 11.2; 12.32.
[3] *Med.* 9.28. [4] *Med.* 7.3; Dodds, *op. cit.* 8–9.
[5] *Laws* 644 DE, 804 B.
[6] There is no need to subscribe to the fashionable view that Plato had to give up the Forms in his latest period of philosophizing. We should rather maintain that, although his acceptance of them was still absolute, his awareness of the philosophical problems they bring with them was very much keener. His knowledge may be said to have given way to faith.

world, he is constantly aware of a feeling of unreality. Our life is the empty pomp of a procession, a play on the stage; we are as futile as ants or panic-stricken mice. We are puppets on strings. Man's life is a perpetually changing reality. So uncertain is it that it can fairly be called a dream.¹ Here again Marcus is on Platonic, and older than Platonic, ground. Dreams appear to be real, but are not; they appear to be long-lasting but are extremely brief. Again we ask ourselves why Marcus, as a Stoic, is concerned with the continuum of time. Is he suggesting that moral action is a dream? In fact he does not come to this, since he is able to separate the true life, the life of the ἡγεμονικόν, in Platonic fashion from the fate of the body and the ψυχή. Marcus is in the curiously unsatisfactory position of being halfway to Platonism. While accepting a Platonic dichotomy between intelligent and physical life, he has no Platonic external world to support his Platonic psychology. In a sense he has gone behind both Plato and the Stoics to Heraclitus; he is left with little more than the flux of physical events and the Reason which guides them providentially. And sometimes even his belief in reason seems hesitant. While steeling himself to act a moral part, on three occasions he tries to convince himself that he must stand upright, whether the world is providentially governed (the Stoic view), or whether it is simply a random assembly of atoms, as taught by Epicurus.²

We cannot be sure why Marcus could not find Chrysippus' explanation of the reality of human acts entirely satisfying, but the Emperor's scepticism, which we have already noticed, seems also to have been at work on the necessary supports of the traditional Stoic position, namely the belief in the beginning and end of the world. Normally Marcus accepts the doctrine of conflagration,³ but sometimes he considers a quasi-Heraclitean view of eternal exchanges among the four elements as equally satisfactory.⁴ But from the point of view of the Stoic theory of time, the latter version would have all the weaknesses of the Aristotelian theory. There would be no reason to count one

---

¹ *Med.* 2.17.   ² *Med.* 4.2; 9.28; 10.6.
³ E.g. *Med.* 5.13.   ⁴ *Med.* 10.7.

point any more than another as the beginning or end of a cosmic cycle.

What a tiny portion of infinite and gaping time has been allotted to each man![1] To this sentiment we must return constantly when trying to understand Marcus' frame of mind. It is clear that his extreme scepticism, his almost total propensity to doubt, at times even cuts into his Stoic belief that moral action is all-important. He is so overwhelmed by man's puny strength on the cosmic scene that none of man's actions appears more than trivial. One's only resource is to subordinate oneself to 'universal nature'. For in this kind of identification, if nature is in fact providential, is to be found the sole value of life. It might be argued that this is the Old Stoic spirit, but it is not. It is not even the spirit of Marcus' spiritual master Epictetus. What is lacking is the confident assertion of the value of right action.

As soon as each thing is seen, it is carried away, Marcus laments.[2] Chrysippus would have agreed with him; the consequence follows from his theory of time. But Marcus seems desperately to need to stop the flow; he is obsessed with what has passed away. How many physicians have died after trying to save their patients! How many philosophers after debating immortality! How many cities like Pompeii and Herculaneum![3] Consider the time of Vespasian and what men did then, marrying, bringing up children, being ill, dying, fighting, feasting, flattering, praying for one another's death. All was repeated in the time of Trajan.[4] All is now over; all will soon be forgotten. When Dodds suggests that Marcus experienced a 'crisis of identity', he was thinking primarily of his incessant self-reproach;[5] but his tendency to total scepticism about the reality of the world, of events in the world, and therefore of his own actions, points in the same direction. The Stoics regarded the philosophical school as a kind of hospital for sick souls, and the souls of all but the wise are sick; but it was the worst kind of hospital for Marcus. Chrysippus' theory of time, with its subtle account of the reality, but also the ever-flowing nature, of the

---

[1] *Med.* 12.32.
[2] *Med.* 4.43.
[3] *Med.* 4.48.
[4] *Med.* 4.32; cf. 8.5.
[5] Dodds, *op. cit.* 29 note 1.

present could only exacerbate the problem of a man who had almost lost faith in his own existence.

In Goldschmidt's excellent book on the Stoic theory of time there is a tendency to present Marcus Aurelius as a follower of Chrysippus, whose variations on the Stoic attitude to time are to be put down to his pessimism.[1] There is a degree of truth in this, and it may be said that this pessimism, associated with Marcus' enormous capacity for doubt, is an un-Stoic accretion. But what Marcus presents is not merely Chrysippus' theory buried under pessimism and hesitancy. For Marcus the problem of time is in a quite different context from that familiar to the early Stoics. For Zeno and Chrysippus time is viewed primarily as a problem in physics. They accept this attitude from Aristotle and offer solutions in an Aristotelian spirit. Even though they make use of ideas of time related to those used by Plato in the *Timaeus* and sharing a common origin in the writings of Heraclitus, the fundamentally scholarly attitude to time persists. Problems about time are, for the Old Stoics, second-level problems. They arise after enquiry into the nature of physical bodies, of physical nature and of moral life. Time does not intrude upon the moral sphere. With Marcus the position is quite different. Time, the ever-changing flux, is itself a moral problem. How is it possible to live a good life at all, so long as one has the sense that all actions are turned by time into triviality? The fact that, despite having to overcome his own anxieties about time and actions, Marcus nevertheless persisted to the end in his struggle to live an upright life according to Stoic theory as he understood it, is an indication of no small importance of the strength of his will and of his sense of duty. At times it seems as though it is a sense of duty, a sense not rationalized philosophically as a categorical imperative, but accepted instinctively, which carries him through.

Nowhere in his *Meditations* does Marcus Aurelius mention the definitions of time offered by Zeno or by Chrysippus, or, for that matter, by any other Stoic. Perhaps the omission is coincidental, but the coincidence is made odder by the fact that the way in which Marcus speaks of time would not square easily

---

[1] Goldschmidt, *op. cit.* 197.

with these definitions. We recall that it was a Platonist objection to the Stoic theory of time that the Stoics refused to treat time as a 'thing', the 'essence' or being of which could be described. They defined it—and defined it consciously—as a kind of accident. Now, whatever Marcus may have claimed about his adherence to traditional Stoic theories of time, he is far from those theories on this point. Marcus again and again almost personifies time. Time seems almost to be the governor of the physical world and the source (or destroyer) of its reality. Time swallows up all actions. In these circumstances one might ask Marcus what the essence of this power is. Clearly an accident, an extension accompanying movement, could not properly be looked on in this way.

As so often, Marcus did not think the matter out. If Plotinus met Stoics who talked about time as Marcus does, he was quite justified in asking about its essence. We are bound to conclude that the intentions and ideas of Chrysippus on the *nature* of time had lost all their original significance. They were almost certainly not understood. It is often said that by the time of Marcus Stoicism had degenerated into an arid moralism, and, although this is in some respects a misleading generalization, it is at least true that Marcus, who knows many of the theories of the early Stoa, has lost all sense of their import. The fundamental interrelationship of ethics and physics has eluded him. Some of the gaps this leaves in his Stoic armour he tries to plug with bits of Platonism. But the bits in isolation from one another are inadequate; and the cosmic pessimism and fearful instability of Marcus' world are the results. It is clear from a consideration of Marcus' treatment of time in what sense he is the last of the Stoics. With much of the meaning of Stoicism lost, the only course open was to adopt more and more of the Platonic alternative.

16

POSTSCRIPT

The old historians of Stoicism were right when they said that Marcus Aurelius was the last of the Stoics; not in the most literal sense, for there were Stoics in the third century and later, but in a more fundamental way. As far as we can tell, there was then no new thought in the School, and the number of Stoics was small. Nor was Stoicism the influence on outsiders that it had been up to about A.D. 200. Clement of Alexandria marks a turning-point in the relations between Stoicism and Christianity. In the first two centuries of our era the influence of the Stoics was strong, and never so strong as on Clement's contemporary Tertullian. But with Clement the struggle between Stoicism and Platonism is finally decided in favour of the latter, and though in later writers Stoic ideas, particularly in ethics, are mingled with the dominant Platonism, they play an inferior role. In the non-Christian world the narrowness of Marcus' Stoicism, combined with the onslaught of Alexander of Aphrodisias on key positions of Stoic thought, contributed to its failure to hold the minds of the intellectuals. As for the ordinary man, Cynicism could provide all the Stoicism he needed.

Historically the movement was dead, and, though in later ages there have been periods in which the thought of the Roman Stoics in particular has been valued, Stoicism has been treated largely as a moralism. It has been our purpose to help to show that at its best it was far more than that. The most interesting positions of Zeno and Chrysippus, particularly in logic and psychology, were forgotten, ignored, or misunderstood in the school itself. Even now we are only beginning to rediscover them.

BIBLIOGRAPHY

Details are given of all books and articles mentioned in the text and a number of other relevant studies of Stoicism.

ACKRILL, J. L. *Aristotle's Categories and De Interpretatione* (Oxford 1963).

ARNIM, J. VON. 'Arius Didymus' Abriss der peripatetischen Ethik', *S.B. der Öst. Akad. d. Wiss. phil.-hist. Kl.* 204.3 (1926).

ARNOLD, E. V. *Roman Stoicism* (Cambridge 1911).

BABUT, D. 'Les Stoïciens et l'Amour', *REG* 76 (1963), 55–63.

BALDRY, H. C. 'Zeno's Ideal State', *JHS* 79 (1959), 3–15.

—— *The Unity of Mankind in Greek Thought* (Cambridge 1965).

BARTH, P. and GOEDECKEMEYER, A. *Die Stoa*[6] (Stuttgart 1929).

BENZ, E. *Das Todesproblem in der Stoischen Philosophie* (*Tübinger Beiträge zur Altertumswissenschaft* 68, Stuttgart 1929).

BONHOEFFER, A. *Epictet und die Stoa* (Stuttgart 1890).

—— *Die Ethik des Stoikers Epictet* (Stuttgart 1894).

—— 'Die Telosformel des Stoikers Diogenes', *Philologus* 67 (1908), 582–605.

BOYANCÉ, P. *Etude sur le songe de Scipion* (Limoges 1936).

—— 'Sur la Théologie de Varron', *REA* 57 (1955), 57–84.

BRÉHIER, E. 'La Théorie des incorporels dans l'ancien stoïcisme', *Archiv für Geschichte der Philosophie* 22 (1909), 114–25.

—— *Chrysippe* (Paris 1910).

—— *Etudes de philosophie antique* (Paris 1955).

BRINK, C. O. 'Οἰκείωσις and Οἰκειότης: Theophrastus and Zeno on Nature and Moral Theory', *Phronesis* 1 (1955), 123–45.

—— 'Plato on the Natural Character of Goodness', *HSCP* 63 (1958), 193–8.

BROCHARD, V. 'Sur la logique des Stoïciens', *Archiv für Geschichte der Philosophie* 5 (1892), 449–68.

BROECKER, H. *Animadversiones ad Plutarchi libellum περὶ εὐθυμίας* (Diss. Bonn 1954).

CALLAHAN, J. F. *Four Views of Time in Ancient Philosophy* (Harvard 1948).

CHRISTENSEN, J. *An Essay on the Unity of Stoic Philosophy* (Copenhagen 1962).

CLARK, G. H. 'The Theory of Time in Plotinus', *PR* 53 (1944), 337–58.

COLOMBO, A. M. 'Un nuovo frammento di Crisippo', *PP* 9 (1954), 376–81.

BIBLIOGRAPHY

COUISSIN, P. 'Le Stoïcisme de la Nouvelle Académie', *Revue d'Histoire de la Phil.* 36 (1929), 241–76.

CRÖNERT, W. *Kolotes und Menedemos (Studien zur Palaeographie und Papyruskunde 6,* ed. C. Wessely, Leipzig 1906).

CUMONT, F. *La Théologie solaire de paganisme romain (Mém. de l'Acad. des Inscriptions et Belles Lettres,* Paris 1909).

DE LACY, P. 'The Logical Structure of the Ethics of Epictetus', *CP* 38 (1943), 112–25.

—— 'The Stoic Categories as Methodological Principles', *TAPA* 76 (1945), 246–63.

—— 'Some Recent Publications on Hellenistic Philosophy', *CW* 52 (1958), 8–15, 25–7, 37–9, 59.

DIELS, H. *Doxographi Graeci* (Berlin 1879).

DIRLMEIER, F. 'Die Oikeiosis-lehre Theophrasts', *Philologus Supp.-band* 30 (1937), 1–100.

DOBSON, J. F. 'The Posidonius Myth', *CQ* 12 (1918), 179–95.

DODDS, E. R. *Pagan and Christian in an Age of Anxiety* (Cambridge 1965).

DOERRIE, H. Ὑπόστασις' (*NAG, Phil.-hist. Kl.* 1955), 35–92.

DUDLEY, D. R. *A History of Cynicism* (London 1937).

DYROFF, A. *Die Ethik der alten Stoa* (Berlin 1897).

EDELSTEIN, L. 'The Philosophical System of Posidonius', *AJP* 57 (1936), 286–325.

—— *The Meaning of Stoicism* (Harvard 1966).

ERBSE, H. 'Die Vorstellung von der Seele bei Marc Aurel', *Festschrift Fritz Zucker* (Berlin 1954), 129–52.

FARQUHARSON, A. S. L. *The Meditations of Marcus Aurelius* (Oxford 1944).

FESTUGIÈRE, A. J. Review of Grilli, *Il Problema, Paideia* 9 (1954), 180–7.

FRITZ, K. VON. *Quellenuntersuchungen zu Leben und Philosophie des Diogenes von Sinope, Phil. Supp.-band* 18² (1926), 1–97.

FURLEY, D. J. 'Lucretius and the Stoics', *BICS* 13 (1966), 13–33.

—— *Two Studies in Greek Atomism* (Princeton 1967).

GAUTHIER, R. A. and JOLIF, J. Y. *L'Ethique à Nicomaque* (Louvain 1959).

GEYTENBEEK, A. C. VAN. *Musonius Rufus and Greek Diatribe* (Assen 1963).

GOLDSCHMIDT, V. *Le Système stoïcien et l'idée de temps* (Paris 1953).

GOULD, J. B. 'Chrysippus: on the criteria for the truth of a conditional proposition', *Phronesis* 12 (1967), 152–61.

GRILLI, A. *Il Problema della Vita Contemplativa nel Mondo greco-romano* (Milan 1953).

BIBLIOGRAPHY

GRILLI, A. 'L'Opera di Panezio', *Paideia* 9 (1954), 337–53.

—— 'Studi Paneziani', *Studi Italiani di Filologia Classica* n.s. 29 (1957), 31–97.

GRUMACH, E. *Physis und Agathon in der alten Stoa (Prob.* 6, Berlin 1932).

HAYNES, R. P. 'The Theory of Pleasure of the Old Stoa', *AJP* 83 (1962), 412–19.

HIJMANS, B. L. '"Ασκησις': *Notes on Epictetus' Educational System* (Assen 1959).

—— 'Posidonius' Ethics', *Acta Classica* 2 (1959), 27–42.

HIRZEL, R. *Untersuchungen zu Ciceros philosophischen Schriften* (Leipzig 1882).

—— 'Der Selbstmord', *Archiv für Religionswissenschaft* 11 (1908), 75–104, 243–84, 417–76.

HURST, M. (Mrs Kneale). 'Implication in the 4th century B.C.', *Mind* 44 (1935), 484–95.

IBSCHER, G. *Der Begriff des Sittlichen in der Pflichtenlehre des Panaitios* (Diss. Munich 1934).

JAEGER, W. *Nemesios von Emesa, Quellenforschung zum Neuplatonismus und seinen Anfängen bei Poseidonios* (Berlin 1914).

—— *Diokles von Karystos* (Berlin 1938).

JAGU, A. *Epictète et Platon: Essai sur les relations du Stoïcisme et du Platonisme à propos de la morale des Entretiens* (Paris 1946).

JONES, J. W. *The Law and Legal Theory of the Greeks* (Oxford 1956).

JONES, R. M. 'Posidonius and the flight of the mind through the universe', *CP* 21 (1926), 97–113.

—— 'Posidonius and Solar Eschatology', *CP* 27 (1932), 113–35.

KAUSSEN, J. *Physik und Ethik des Panätios* (Bonn 1902).

KIDD, I. G. 'The Relationship of Stoic Intermediates to the Summum Bonum with reference to change in the Stoa', *CQ* n.s. 5 (1955), 181–94.

KNEALE, W. and M. *The Development of Logic* (Oxford 1962).

LABOWSKY, L. *Die Ethik des Panaitios* (Leipzig 1934).

LAFFRANQUE, M. *Poseidonios d'Apamée: Essai de Mise au Point* (Paris 1964).

LE HIR, J. 'Les Fondements psychologiques et religieux de la morale d'Epictète', *Bull. Assoc. G. Budé* 4 (1954), 73–93.

LEEMAN, A. D. 'Seneca and Poseidonios: A philosophical commentary on Seneca *ep.* CII 3–19', *Mnemosyne* s. 4.5 (1952), 57–79.

LONG, A. A. 'Carneades and the Stoic *Telos*', *Phronesis* 12 (1967), 59–90.

—— 'Aristotle's Legacy to Stoic Ethics', *BICS* 15 (1968), 72–85.

—— 'The Stoic Concept of Evil', *PQ* 18 (1968), 329–43.

BIBLIOGRAPHY

LUSCHNAT, O. 'Das Problem des ethischen Fortschritts in der alten Stoa', *Philologus* 102 (1958), 178–214.

MATES, B. *Stoic Logic* (Berkeley 1953).

MERLAN, P. 'Beiträge zur Geschichte des antiken Platonismus II. Poseidonios über die Weltseele in Platons Timaios', *Philologus* 89 (1934), 197–214.

—— *Studies in Epicurus and Aristotle* (Wiesbaden 1960).

—— *From Platonism to Neoplatonism*[2] (The Hague 1960).

MOREAU, J. *L'Ame du monde de Platon aux Stoïciens* (Paris 1939).

—— 'Ariston et le Stoïcisme', *REA* 50 (1948), 27–48.

MURRAY, O. Review of Baldry, *The Unity of Mankind*, *CR* 80 (1966), 368–71.

NEBEL, G. 'Der Begriff des ΚΑΘΗΚΟΝ in der alten Stoa', *Hermes* 70 (1935), 439–60.

NEBEL, G. 'Zur Ethik des Poseidonios', *Hermes* 74 (1939), 34–57.

NEUENSCHWANDER, R. *Marc Aurels Beziehungen zu Seneca und Poseidonios* (*Noctes Romanae* 3, Bern 1951).

NOCK, A. D. 'Posidonius', *JRS* 49 (1959), 1–16.

PHILIPPSON, R. 'Panaetiana', *Rh. Mus.* 78 (1929), 337–60.

—— 'Das Sittlichschöne bei Panaitios', *Philologus* 85 (1930), 357–413.

—— 'Das erste Naturgemässe', *Philologus* 87 (1932), 445–66.

—— 'Zur Psychologie der Stoa', *Rh. Mus.* n.F. 86 (1937), 140–79.

POHLENZ, M. 'Das zweite Buch der Tusculaner', *Hermes* 44 (1909), 23–40.

—— 'Poseidonios' Affektenlehre und Psychologie', *NGG* 73 (1922), 163–94.

—— 'Τὸ πρέπον. Ein Beitrag zur Geschichte des griechischen Geistes', *NGG, phil.-hist. Kl.* 1 1.16 (1933), 53–92.

—— *Antikes Führertum: Cicero de Officiis und das Lebensideal des Panaitios* (*Neue Wege zur Antike*, Reihe II 3, Leipzig, Berlin 1934).

—— 'Zenon und Chrysipp', *NAG, phil.-hist. Kl.* 1 2.9 (1938), 173–210.

—— 'Die Begründung der abendländischen Sprachlehre durch die Stoa', *NAG, phil.-hist. Kl.* 1 3.6 (1939), 151–98.

—— 'Grundfragen der stoischen Philosophie', *Abh. Gött. Ges., phil.-hist. Kl.* 3.26 (1940), 1–122.

—— 'Philosophie und Erlebnis in Senecas Dialogen', *NAG, phil.-hist. Kl.* 1 4.3 (1941), 55–108.

—— 'Panaitios', *RE* 18[2] (1949), cols. 418–40.

—— *Stoa und Stoiker* (Zurich 1950).

—— *Die Stoa: Geschichte einer geistigen Bewegung*[3] (Göttingen 1964).

—— *Kleine Schriften* (ed. H. Doerrie, Hildesheim 1965).

BIBLIOGRAPHY

REESOR, M. E. 'The "Indifferents" in the Old and Middle Stoa', *TAPA* 82 (1951), 102–10.

—— 'The Stoic Concept of Quality', *AJP* 75 (1954), 40–58.

—— 'The Stoic Categories', *AJP* 78 (1957), 63–82.

—— 'Fate and Possibility in Early Stoic Philosophy', *Phoenix* 19 (1965), 285–97.

REINHARDT, K. *Poseidonios* (Munich 1921).

—— *Kosmos und Sympathie. Neue Untersuchungen über Poseidonios* (Munich 1926).

—— 'Poseidonios', *RE* 22¹ (1953), cols. 558–826.

RICH, A. N. M. 'The Cynic Conception of ΑΥΤΑΡΚΕΙΑ', *Mnemosyne* s. 4.9 (1956), 23–9.

RIETH, O. *Grundbegriffe der stoischen Ethik* (*Prob.* 9, Berlin 1933).

—— 'Über das Telos der Stoiker', *Hermes* 69 (1934), 13–45.

RIST, J. M. *Eros and Psyche* (Toronto 1964).

—— *Plotinus: The Road to Reality* (Cambridge 1967).

—— 'Integration and the Undescended Soul in Plotinus', *AJP* 88 (1967), 410–22.

RUETHER, T. *Die sittliche Forderung der Apatheia* (Freiburg im Br. 1949).

SAMBURSKY, S. *Physics of the Stoics* (London 1959).

SANDBACH, F. H. '῎Εννοια and Πρόληψις in the Stoic Theory of Knowledge', *CQ* 24 (1930), 44–51.

SCHINDLER, K. *Die stoische Lehre von den Seelenteilen und Seelenvermögen insbesondere bei Panaitios und Poseidonios und ihre Verwendung bei Cicero* (Diss. Munich 1934).

SCHMEKEL, A. *Die Philosophie der mittleren Stoa in ihrem geschichtlichen Zusammenhangen dargestellt* (Berlin 1892).

SCHUBERT, P. *Die Eschatologie des Poseidonios* (Leipzig 1927).

SCHUHL, P. M. *Le Dominateur et les Possibles* (Paris 1960).

SCHWARTZ, E. 'Hekataeos von Teos', *Rh. Mus.* 40 (1885), 223–62.

SCHWEINGRUBER, F. 'Sokrates und Epictet', *Hermes* 78 (1943), 57–79.

SCHWYZER, H. R. 'Bewusst und Unbewusst bei Plotin', *Entretiens Hardt* 5, *Les Sources de Plotin* (Geneva 1960), 341–90.

SEVENSTER, J. N. *Paul and Seneca* (Leiden 1961).

SIEFERT, G. *Plutarchos' Schrift Περὶ Εὐθυμίας* (Progr. Pforta, Naumbach a.-S. 1908).

SOLMSEN, F. 'Greek Philosophy and the Discovery of the Nerves', *Mus. Helv.* 18 (1961), 150–63, 169–97.

—— *Cleanthes or Posidonius? The Basis of Stoic Physics* (Amsterdam 1961).

SPANNEUT, M. *Le Stoïcisme des Pères de l'Eglise de Clément de Rome à Clément d'Alexandrie* (Paris 1957).

BIBLIOGRAPHY

TATAKIS, B. N. *Panétius de Rhodes* (Paris 1931).

TAYLOR, R. 'The Problem of Future Contingencies', *PR* 66 (1957), 1–28.

THEILER, W. 'Tacitus und die antike Schicksalslehre', *Phyllobolia für P. von der Mühll* (Basel 1946), 35–90.

THÉVENAZ, P. *L'Ame du Monde, le devenir, et la matière chez Plutarque* (Paris 1938).

—— 'L'Intériorité chez Sénèque', *Mélanges Niedermann* (Neuchâtel 1944), 189–94.

TOYNBEE, J. M. C. 'Dictators and Philosophers in the First Century A.D.', *GR* 13 (1944), 43–58.

VAN STRAATEN, M. *Panétius, sa vie, ses écrits, et sa doctrine* (Amsterdam 1946). The third edition of the fragments was published in 1962 at Leiden.

VERBEKE, G. *L'Evolution de la Doctrine du Pneuma du Stoïcisme à S. Augustin* (Paris, Louvain 1945).

VIRIEUX-REYMOND, A. *La Logique et l'épistémologie des Stoïciens* (Chambéry 1950).

VOGEL, C. J. DE. *Greek Philosophy III. The Hellenistic-Roman Period* (Leiden 1959).

WATSON, G. *The Stoic Theory of Knowledge* (Belfast 1966).

WIERSMA, W. 'Τέλος und Καθῆκον in der alten Stoa', *Mnemosyne* s. 3.5 (1937), 219–28.

WILAMOWITZ-MOELLENDORFF, U. VON. *Die Glaube der Hellenen* (Berlin 1931).

ZELLER, E. 'Ueber den Κυριεύων des Megarikers Diodorus', *SB. der Kgl. Akad. der Wiss. zu Berlin* (1882), 151–9.

—— *Die Philosophie der Griechen* II. 1⁴ (Leipzig 1889), III. 1⁴ (Leipzig 1909).

INDEX

References to Zeno, Cleanthes and Chrysippus, who occur
passim, are not given